LIVING
ICONS

LIVING ICONS

Persons of Faith in the Eastern Church

MICHAEL PLEKON

Foreword by Lawrence S. Cunningham

UNIVERSITY OF NOTRE DAME PRESS
Notre Dame, Indiana

Manufactured in the United States of America

Paperback edition published in 2004.

Library of Congress Cataloging-in-Publication Data
Plekon, Michael, 1948–
Living icons : persons of faith in the Eastern church /
Michael P. Plekon ; foreword by Lawrence S. Cunningham.
p.   cm.
Includes bibliographical references and index.
ISBN 0-268-03350-1 (cloth : alk. paper)
ISBN 0-268-03351-x (pbk. : alk. paper)
1. Christian biography.   2. Orthodox Eastern Church—Biography.
3. Spirituality—Orthodox Eastern Church.   I. Title.
BX390.P58   2002
281.9'092'2—dc21   2002003617

∞*This book is printed on acid-free paper.*

CONTENTS

Foreword
Lawrence S. Cunningham
vii

Acknowledgments
xi

FOREWORD

Pope John Paul II has tirelessly reminded us that the church must "breathe with two lungs," by which he means that the vitality of the gospel derives from the inherited traditions of the Christian churches in East and West. The pope understands that need better than most since he is the first bishop of Rome to come from Eastern Europe, where Orthodoxy and the church of Rome have touched and interacted with each other—warily to be sure—for nearly two millennia. The influence of these two traditions has been mutual even though the relationship has been a tense one. We can only hope that in our time tensions are beginning to ease. The two traditions hold much in common in the modern era, including the fact that both have experienced waves of persecution and the derivative of persecution: martyrdom.

The modern Catholic Church has had the good fortune to benefit from the rich intellectual and spiritual tradition of Russian thinkers living in the diaspora after the revolution of 1917. Anyone who reads Michael Plekon's comprehensive overview of those thinkers, who, for the most part, have been associated with the St. Sergius Institute in Paris, will recognize crucial figures in the development of the Roman Catholic *la nouvelle theologie* that led up to the Second Vatican Council and whose influence extends to this day. These thinkers mediated the wisdom of Russian Christianity from the heart of the Western church and, in so doing, not only kept alive their tradition but enriched the West in the process.

What do the Orthodox thinkers teach us? They remind us, first of all, that true theology cannot be divorced from the life of prayer in general and liturgy in particular—that theology is doxology. They help us recover the biblical and patristic notion that Christ is Wisdom in the deepest and most fundamental sense of the term. They highlight an anthropology that insists that we can be radically re-formed under grace to become by adoption what Christ is by nature—a true child of God. They enlarge our sense of holiness by recovering for us ancient forms of spiritual practice developed and refined in the great schools of asceticism and monastic observance. By their insistence on the iconic they help us again to privilege the concept of beauty as a vehicle for sanctification. They allow us to understand fully what Father Zossima meant in *The Brothers Karamazov* when he said, in a line that Dorothy Day loved, that "beauty will save the world."

The figures set before us in this book are not merely of historical interest. Their works still have influence. Contemporary currents in Christian spirituality draw deeply from the thinking of Lev Gillet, Paul Evdokimov, and the late Vladimir Lossky. Our present theological thinking on the hotly debated issue of communion ecclesiology, for example, draws inspiration from the writings of Nicolas Afanasiev (the intellectual heir of the brilliant thinker Sergius Bulgakov). This is transparently clear when one reads the influential works of the late Jean-Marie Tillard, O.P., or the writings of Yves Congar, O.P. American theology has been enriched by the passionate work of John Meyendorff and Alexander Schmemann, who not only stood for the living tradition of Orthodoxy but witnessed to that tradition to those who know little about the riches of the thinking of Orthodoxy. Both scholars had deep roots in the school of St. Sergius in Paris, but they came to America to teach at St. Vladimir's Seminary in New York. The present generation of scholars at St. Vladimir's keeps their influence alive. Rightly, Michael Plekon calls Meyendorff, Schmemann, and the other Orthodox figures he presents in this book "icons"—living images that permit us to see through them the limpid piety of the Russian tradition.

Many of the men and women described here were exiles from their native Russia. However, Plekon also includes analyses of the pre-revolutionary Seraphim of Sarov, who was canonized in 1903 in the period of the last tsars, and of Alexander Men, who was murdered during the final collapse of Soviet rule in 1990. The author's account of how these people of faith lived and how they died gives us a historical frame for understanding the modern history of the Russian Orthodox Church.

Thomas Merton, while engaged in an intense study of the work of Nicolas Berdiaev and Sergius Bulgakov in the late 1950s, wrote these words in his journal entry of April 28, 1957 (and rewrote them for publication in his *Conjectures of a Guilty Bystander*): "If I can unite in myself, in my own spiritual life, the thought of the East and the West of the Greek and Latin Fathers, I will create in myself a reunion of the divided church and from that unity in myself can come the exterior and visible unity of the Church. For if we want to bring together East and West we cannot do it by imposing one upon the other. We must contain both in ourselves and transcend both in Christ." Plekon's chapter on Lev Gillet shows that Father Gillet, who frequently used the pseudonym "A Monk of the Eastern Church," actualized in a profound way Merton's insight.

All dialogue (and unity comes only after dialogue) starts with listening, and listening presumes that one is listening to something that makes true exchange possible. These pages provide ample material to convince us that what the great Orthodox tradition has to offer is not only worthy of being listened to but must be heard. Today, the church in the West has shown a renewed interest in the spiritual treasures of the Eastern church. Many people have found their spiritual home within its walls. Many impulses within Orthodoxy have eroded the heavy burden of ethnic separation—always a curse—within Orthodoxy. To the degree that such changes have come about, they are explained by the efforts of generations of serious thinkers and activists like those profiled in this volume.

The lives of these luminous figures and the writings that come from their lives were refined in the awful fires of modernity. They knew persecution, exile, and marginalization. They were centrally concerned with speaking from their ancient tradition to the world, which not only rejected their message but actively sought to suppress it. It takes enormous faith to speak to a seemingly indifferent world, but speak they did. Michael Plekon brilliantly shows how they spoke through their lives and their work, and what they say to us.

Lawrence S. Cunningham
December 14, 2001
Feast of Saint John of the Cross

ACKNOWLEDGMENTS

This book has been years in the making and like all things in the Church has involved the collaboration of many. In particular I want to thank those who share the "little church" of home, my wife, Jeanne, and our children, Paul and Hannah. They knew something would come from all those hours before the computer. I am grateful to my colleague and friend Fr. Alexis Vinogradov. He introduced me to the lives and work of several persons of faith, especially his teacher Fr. Alexander Schmemann. He has translated with me and alone the writings of several of the individuals whose lives I examine, and a good deal of this book has come from our reading and discussion over the past fifteen years. He also welcomed our family into his parish, St. Gregory the Theologian, in Wappingers Falls, New York, and shared with me his ministry there.

Fr. Michel Evdokimov has been a good friend and has shared much about his father, Paul, and others. Tomoko Faerber-Evdokimoff, Paul Evdokimov's widow, and Elisabeth Behr-Sigel, who remains an active theologian and leader in the Church at the age of ninety-five, also shared valuable information with me. Elisabeth Osoline graciously shared her reminiscences of Frs. Gregory Krug and John Meyendorff. Others who shared memories and to whom I express gratitude are Juliana Schmemann, Katherine Berdnikoff, Sophie Koulomzine, Paul Meyendorff, Father Alvian Smirensky, Oleg Wilson, and Hélène Arjakovsky-Klépinine. Nikita Struve generously assisted in obtaining photographs, as did Ted Bazil, director of St. Vladimir's Seminary Press. For assistance in gathering photographs, I also want to thank Fr. Steven Belonick and the St. Vladimir's Seminary archives, Didier Lefebrve, Alan Carmack, Abraham Goodman, Amber Houx, Anna Hulbert, Marie Meyendorff, Fr. Deacon Stephen Platt, and the Fellowship of St. Alban and

St. Sergius, Fr. Yakov Ryklin, Fr. Viktor Sokolov, and the Alexander Men Foundation in Moscow. I thank those who read and offered
suggestions on the manuscript, among others, Jenny Schroedel; Professors Paul Hinlicky, Anthony Gythiel, and Lawrence Cunningham; Fr. Christopher Savage; and Ellen Hinlicky. Fr. John Breck has
been very supportive of this project, as has Fr. John Shimchick, who
put earlier versions of profiles into both the on-line and the hard-
copy versions of *Jacob's Well*. Robert Ellsberg and Jim Forest gave
sound advice. Bishop Seraphim (Sigrist), retired from the diocese of
Sendai, Japan, who ordained me to the priesthood, has been a good
friend and very helpful respondent. Fr. John Tkachuk and those who
participated in the Orthodox Theological Institute Lenten retreat in
Montreal in March 2000 had much of this book presented to them.
So too the Five Day Academy of Spirituality of the United Methodist
Church Rocky Mountain Conference in Sedalia, Colorado, in April
2001. My thanks to both groups for patience and helpful response.

I thank the members of the Department of Sociology and Anthropology at Baruch College of the City University of New York
(CUNY) for their friendship and support, especially Juanita Howard
and Parmatma Saran, the most recent chairs. I also thank the various committees on reassigned time and the deans of the Weissman
School of Liberal Arts and Sciences, for helping me have more time
for research and writing. Several Professional Staff Congress–CUNY
faculty research awards between 1996 and 2001 (nos. 667121, 66813,
669124, 61140, 62176), enabled me to travel and to work in the sum-
mers, not only on this book, but also, with my colleague Alexis
Vinogradov, on three volumes of translation. Joyce Mullen, who
helped this work in many ways, administered the grants through the
Research Foundation of CUNY.

Finally, I want to thank the University of Notre Dame Press director, Barbara Hanrahan, and art director, Marge Gloster, and my
editor Rebecca DeBoer and copy editor, Sheila Berg, for all their
hard work in bringing the present volume to publication.

CHAPTER ONE

Finding "Living Icons"

"Come and see"

Throughout the Gospels, the true epiphanies and moments of revelation are always encounters—between the Son of God and the men and women with whom he lived and among those who met Jesus and were forever marked by it. This book is an invitation to such encounters with several Christians of our time, men and women who encountered Christ and were transformed by him but in the intense swirl of modern life. They lived through the greatest turmoil of the twentieth century: the Russian Revolution, emigration forced and voluntary, the Great Depression, the death and terror of World War II. Their era was also that of the Iron Curtain, the cold war, and the bomb. Closer to the present, they lived through more international conflicts as well as struggles for justice.

The personal path to Christ through others is not insulated from troubles and demands. The way of the gospel always winds through the world's turbulence. The Lord invited those who first encountered him, including his apostles, to "Come and see." They, in turn, extended the same invitation to others (John 1:39, 46). Quite often the initial encounter was not with Jesus but with another who had come face-to-face with him. The Samaritan woman he met at Jacob's well in Sychar, whom the Eastern Church knows by the name Photina, "bearer of light," cannot contain what she has heard and seen in her dialogue with Christ. "Come and see a man who has told me every-thing I have done," she blurts to her neighbors. "Could this be the Christ?" (John 4:29). The women who came to Jesus' tomb "very early in the morning, after the Sabbath," and who received the good news of his resurrection from the angel are called, again in the East-ern Church, "equal-to-the-apostles." Even before the coming down of the Spirit, the gospel is proclaimed, the Risen Christ is present, in a world full of conflict and disbelief, through these women and men who are the Church.

There is a great "cloud of witnesses" to the Lord, honored by the Church down through the ages. I think of them as the procession of martyrs and confessors, the holy men and women approaching Christ along the walls of the basilica of San Apollinare Nuovo in Ravenna and along the nave of the church of the monastery of New Skete in Cambridge, New York, and dancing in the frescoes of St. Gregory of Nyssa Episcopal Church in San Francisco. It is an assembly the end of which one cannot see. It is the people Christ is pulling out of the darkness of the kingdom of death, in icons of the Resurrection also known as the harrowing of hell. Several figures are easily recognizable: Adam and Eve, Abraham and Sarah, David and Solomon, various prophets of the Old Testament, Zechariah and Elisabeth and their son, John the Baptist. Behind them one catches just a glimpse of the nameless, faceless saints. These all the others who have met the Lord and are taken by him to the Kingdom. These women and men are not just monastics and clergy but husbands and wives, teachers and physicians, farmers and workers. None of us are excluded from the way of holiness. In the Last Judgement there is no favorite or special category of people among those called to heaven or those condemned to enter the mouth of hell. Archbishops and priests, monks and nuns, lay men and women of all classes, are de-picted, equal in their nakedness and terror, being pulled by demons into hell or being carried by angels up to the kingdom of heaven, where Christ sits as both judge and compassionate savior, with the Virgin, his mother, and the saints.

There is a point often made about iconography and the viewer. We are not objective spectators but invited to participate in the reality of the icon. The icon calls through its inverse perspective, pulls us into its reality. We find a seat open at the table of the three angels who visit Abraham and Sarah in Andrei Rublev's well-known icon the "Hospitality of Abraham" or the "Old Testament Trinity." We are called to be there in the assembly gathered around Christ, who ascends to bid farewell to the Mother of God at her falling asleep, to follow the Risen Christ as he emerges from the kingdom of death into life. These images bring to life the claim of Tertullian, *Solus christianus, nullus christianus:* There is no such thing as a solitary Christian. The one who thinks he or she can alone be saved is deluded. We are saved together with the rest of our brothers and sisters in the faith, our fellow saints. It is only in our sin and its condemnation that each of us is alone and makes a choice to cut ourselves off from "the One who is the very source of life."

We always are part of a communion, a community of saints. Those of us who grew up in church probably remember saints who looked down at us during services. On stained-glass windows, on frescoes, and in statues and icons we encountered Francis of Assisi, Nicholas of Myra, and Joseph. Perhaps we saw the great apostles Peter and Paul and the evangelists Matthew, Mark, Luke, and John. Through the church year we heard of martyrs like George, Lawrence, and Catherine and often saw depictions of them holding the implements of their torture and execution. We read the writings of wonderful teachers like the two Gregorys, of Nyssa and of Nazianzus, Basil the Great, John Chrysostom, Augustine. We heard the exploits of missionaries such as Cyril and Methodius, Francis Xavier, Olga and Vladimir. Some saints had special ministries: Anthony of Padua, who found things that were lost; and the apostle Jude, who took care of seemingly hopeless cases. We have more recent saints such as the American nuns and educators Elisabeth Seton and Katharine Drexel and the missionary monk Herman of Alaska. There have been calls for the modification of canonization procedures in the case of Mother Teresa, whom many already regard as a saint for the whole world. And in 2000, the Catholic Church declared "venerable" that remarkable mother, writer, activist, and woman of prayer, Dorothy Day, thus initiating her case in the process for canonization.

The case of Dorothy Day reveals that the procession of saints winds its way from the recent past into our own lifetimes. Recently much attention was given to the American Catholic bishops' nomination of the Reverend Martin Luther King Jr. to Pope John Paul II's list of martyrs of the twentieth century. On May 7, 2000, in a special service in the Coliseum in Rome, the pope commemorated these contemporary witnesses to Christ in a special service. He mentioned several by name, including Metropolitan Benjamin of St. Petersburg and the Lutheran pastor Paul Schneider who died, respectively, at the hands of the Bolsheviks and the Nazis. The list of more than twelve thousand martyrs, many relatively unknown, is to be released later.[1] Several churches already commemorate such witnesses in their liturgical calendars, along with others not yet canonized. One may be surprised to hear the names of the UN peacemaker Dag Hammarskjöld, the missionary doctor Albert Schweitzer, Pope John XXIII, and the Lutheran theologian and martyr Dietrich Bonhoeffer.

Very quickly the list lengthens. One could name the Trappist monk and writer Thomas Merton, the martyrs Archbishop Oscar Romero and the monk Charles de Foucauld, the theologian Karl Barth, the philosopher and seeker Simone Weil, the writer Flannery O'Connor. Robert Ellsberg has masterfully gathered a year's worth of short biographies of such persons of faith, together with those we know from previous centuries in his marvelous collection, revealing that if one casts the net farther ecumenically, the catch is even more astounding.[2]

This book is a much smaller enterprise. It is a more intimate meeting with one canonized saint and nine men and women of our time who were, in very different ways, people of faith. All are "living icons"; in their personalities and work, in their struggle and joys, in all of their lives, they are images of the Lord and of his gospel and Kingdom. All were Christians of the Eastern Church and thus are not well known in the West, although most spent all their lives in western Europe and America. They were citizens of the West and at the same time Orthodox Christians of the Eastern Church. The list could have been two, three, even four times as long. Some may argue that only those who have been officially recognized as saints in the Orthodox churches should be included.

Throughout the religious world there has been greater concern for recognizing holy people of our time and our location. Hence American Catholics can celebrate not only the Native American Kateri Tekakwitha and the missionary bishop John Neumann but also perhaps Pierre Toussaint, the Haitian immigrant barber-surgeon who cared for the sick. In addition to early Russian missionaries in the United States, such as the monk Herman, the priest Juvenaly, and Bishop Innocent of Alaska, the Orthodox Church in America (OCA) has more recently recognized the twentieth-century figures Alexander Hotovitsky and John Kotchurov, priests who were later martyred in the Russian Revolution; Tikhon, who served here as archbishop and later as patriarch of Moscow during the revolution; and Raphael Hawaweeny, the Lebanese Arab who was bishop of Brooklyn.[3]

There are many remarkable Christians of the Eastern Church in our time. As soon as some peruse my list they will object, claiming that a figure dear to their hearts and faith is missing. Why not the remarkable bishop Nikolai Velimirovich, now canonized, who worked in Serbian-American parishes for many years, studied and taught at Cambridge, survived Dachau, and spent his last years teaching at St. Tikhon's seminary and monastery in Pennsylvania? Why not the erudite, warm, and humorous Metropolitan Leonty Turkevich, who came here as a young married priest, headed a seminary and parishes, and after his wife's death served as bishop and then archbishop in America? Perhaps other internationally known figures should have been included, such as the mathematician and theologian Pavel Florensky, the patristics specialist Georges Florovsky, the fiery philosopher Nicolas Berdiaev, Ecumenical Patriarch Athenagoras I, who with Pope Paul VI laid aside the condemnations of the great schism in 1966, the gifted Romanian theologian Dimitru Stanliloe, the now canonized monk of Mount Athos, Silouan, and his disciple, recently deceased, Sophrony Sakarov.

Clearly, the list of candidates is long and deserving. It would grow even more quickly, and perhaps will in the future, to include still living figures such as the Romanian monk Roman Braga, of the Dormition monastery in Rives Junction, Michigan, or Archbishop Anthony (Bloom) of London, well known for his books on prayer, or Elisabeth Behr-Sigel. I would hope that the lives, the work, and the witness of these few will be shown to be significant enough to warrant their presence here. There is yet another reason for referring to the persons of faith here as living icons. More than anything else, what has determined the selection of this group is their openness to the world, their creative yet ordinary ways of living out the gospel. They themselves became images of the Kingdom. With the exception of Alexander Men, all lived the better part of their lives in the West and understood themselves as part of the culture in which they lived.

Though deeply committed to their cultural past, all saw the Christian faith as transcending a particular culture, no matter how beautiful and dear these specific embodiments of the gospel were. They were open to other cultures, to the science and technology as well as the music and art and poetry of the modern era. Some had been trained in philosophy, the social sciences, art, and literature. They saw Christ, in Niebuhr's view, as always present in and transforming culture. They did not understand faith to be in opposition to the society and culture around them. One of them, not examined here, once slipped a statement of his conviction under the door of the Russian embassy church in Istanbul: Evgraf Kovalesky wrote, "The revolution was allowed by God for the purification of the Church and for the universal shining forth of Orthodoxy."[4] It is in this spirit of love and openness that I present these profiles of ten persons of faith from the Eastern Church.

Both Paul Evdokimov and Mother Maria Skobtsova shared this perspective, typically with different shades of interpretation. The catastrophe of the revolution was apparent. When all the cultural, political, and financial supports of the Church were removed and her institutional grandeur and power destroyed, once again absolute freedom was given to each Christian. The Church would now have to be renewed and reformed not by external forces but from *within*, in the interior of every believer, "the place of the heart," as Behr-Sigel has written, the place where God meets us in love and works with us.[5] What was seemingly a disaster for the Russian Church was in fact a gift. She was open in a new way to become the very place and vocation of Christ, the Christ she knew so well as "kenotic," as humbled, self-emptying, abused and rejected, our true companion in suffering. The threesome of friends, Fr. Lev Gillet, Paul Evdokimov, and Elisabeth Behr-Sigel, were to highlight this charism of the Russian Church and her spirituality to the world. It is no coincidence that they, along with many other Russian émigrés, cherished as a holy friend and held as an "icon" of holiness Batiushka Seraphim, "little Father," the diminutive monk-priest Seraphim of Sarov, canonized only in 1903.[6]

St. Seraphim was indeed the antithesis of the splendor and power of official, that is, institutional, Russian Orthodoxy.[7] He was a prefigurement of an authentic sanctity open to all in the acquiring of the Holy Spirit. Like St. Francis of Assisi, St. Seraphim was an embodiment of simplicity and freedom, one in whom even the forest animals could recognize the scent of Paradise: Francis had his wolf and Seraphim his bear. In both of their faces the radiance of the kingdom of heaven was visible. The people of faith examined here, despite differences of temperament and vocation, were nevertheless impelled by this impulse of so many of their confreres: to share the treasure of the Eastern Church's spiritual life, liturgy, theology, and iconography with the West.

Excursus: The Eastern Church, Her Troubles and Gifts

Because the Eastern Church is at once so different and mysterious, we should pause to consider some aspects of this churchly "home" of the persons of faith we shall meet. It used to be said that the Eastern Church was the best-kept secret of Christianity. That is both true and false today. Many Western Christians remain confused about the numerous jurisdictions or church bodies, about the ethnicity of the churches, about what these churches believe and how they worship.[8] How long, for example, did many assume that easterners actually worshiped the sacred icons in their churches? For some a dividing line was the often misunderstood, always obscure theological meaning of the West's added phrase in the Nicene Creed about the procession of the Holy Spirit also from the Son, *Filioque.* Perhaps more obvious are the papal claims to universal jurisdiction over all churches that separated West from East.

Others, remembering fragments of the historical record, believe it was primarily language and ethnic differences that divided the East and, in turn, estranged the Eastern churches from the West. Many recall the earlier "iron curtain" that Islamic expansion placed between the churches of the East and those of the West. More recent views have pursued many of these paths and caricatured the East. A favorite, particularly among Protestant theologians, is merely a variation on Adolph von Harnack's critique. The claim is that the Eastern churches remain frozen in a pre-Enlightenment, uncritical perspective with respect to the Bible, liturgy, theological expression, ecclesiastical organization, and relationship to government, culture, and society.

Further, the charge sometimes goes, the Eastern Church remains turned in on herself, lost within the incense-filled, icon-clad walls of her temples, bewitched by her long, repetitious services. These are precisely the images of the Eastern Church that illustrate the covers of CDs of Russian and Byzantine liturgical music that can be found in profusion in any sizable music store these days. There are also the images in news reports: clerics in gold vestments swinging censers, chanting; the faithful crossing themselves, lighting candles, kissing icons, walking in processions.

There is good reason for the fascination. The liturgical rites and devotional practices of the Eastern Church are beautiful, otherworldly, and ancient in a time when so much worship has been modernized. When asked why he attended services at the Orthodox cathedral of a major American city, a scholar of international renown, who happened to be Lutheran, easily explained: "For the transcendence of the worship there."

But accurate images quickly can become stereotypes. The Eastern Church's otherworldly intoxication can turn into and be perceived as an obsession that suffocates concern for the poor, that lacks the impulse for mission work. At the extreme, the Eastern Church is seen as so world-denying that it is estranged from science and art, concerned only with things sacred. That the Eastern Church does not ordain women to the priesthood today starkly distinguishes her from many of the churches of the West. In the Eastern Church monasticism remains very important as a sign of what Evdokimov calls "eschatological maximalism," a strong reminder of the Kingdom's otherness from this world. Many Eastern churches adhere to the "old calendar," the Julian, hence celebrating Christmas and Easter thirteen days later than the West. Rules for fasting have not been modified in the Eastern churches, and fasting from dairy and meat foods takes place not only during Lent but also during several other prefestal seasons and on Wednesdays and Fridays throughout the year. In her ethical outlook, while very free and always personal, the Eastern Church remains unflinchingly biblical and faithful to the historical witness of previous centuries of Christians. These are but a few of the features that have given Eastern Christianity both a good and a bad name among many. A liberal Episcopal clergy colleague of mine once confessed that the only worthwhile contribution the East had made was the portable icon that could be used in one's home as a focus for prayer.[9]

In a serious engagement with the Orthodox Church from an evangelical perspective, Daniel Clendenin finds much to admire but also much to criticize.[10] The centrality of the liturgy and sacraments, the adherence to the all-too-human tradition of the Fathers and the services, and finally the apparent inability of Orthodox theology to adapt to new conditions and problems of the modern world—all this was for him the consequence of not being sufficiently biblical and evangelical. Other commentators are drawn to what Evdokimov characterized as apparent ecclesial "anarchy" that rules the East.[11] They criticize the absence of a centralized head or magisterial body, of any one bishop or group short of an ecumenical council, that can speak for all the Orthodox churches. Some see so much diversity of practice across the various Orthodox churches that it is often hard to recognize unity. *Fr. Josiah's concern*

Yet another angle is that of nationalism merging with Eastern Christianity, even overtaking it, which was condemned as heretical "phyletism." Still today, when you tell someone you are an Eastern Orthodox Christian, the frequent assumption is that you are Greek, Russian, or of some other Slavic background or are married to one who is and therefore a convert. (Many Orthodox Christians in America are converts but not all due to marriage.) Not long ago Samuel Huntington identified Eastern Orthodoxy and Islam as international forces ideologically in conflict with the West.[12] Huntington's thesis is dubious, but this is not the place to directly engage it. Victoria Clark has apparently attempted to field-test Huntington's thesis in the history of the Christian East, finding a few individuals remarkable for their goodness and beauty but far more examples of all the worst cases of the confusion of Christianity with ethnicity and politics.[13](The Christians of the Eastern Church examined here speak to Huntington's thesis and clear up much of the misunderstanding of the Church of the East.)

In this century the Eastern Church has been wounded but also made more open. This has enabled her to contribute her tradition as a gift to the West. After centuries of schism, misunderstanding, and isolation, the East has entered authentic relationships with the churches of the West. I refer here, not only to the almost eighty years of captivity of the Russian and many other Slavic churches by Soviet regimes and their sudden, recent liberation from some forms of containment, but also to a much earlier dialogue between East and West, one that began almost in the days and weeks after the Russian Revolution. Nicolas Zernov described this "Russian religious renaissance,"[14] an astonishing reappropriation of Orthodox Christianity by intellectuals in the last decades of the nineteenth century that continued with the great Church Council in Moscow of 1917–18.

Cultural wonders such as icons and liturgical music in eastern Europe remind us in the West of the beauty and mystery of the Orthodox Church. On the NBC telecast of the 2000 Summer Olympics in Sydney, one could watch scenes of the Romanian women gymnasts' participation in Holy Week services and the Russian swimmer Alexander Popov lighting candles before icons in an Orthodox church not back home but in Australia. The distinctive black monastic headdress of Orthodox bishops, the *klobuk* or *epikamilaukion,* was much in evidence at the funeral liturgy of Cardinal John O'Connor of New York in spring 2000. Bookstores now regularly stock reproductions of icons, pictorial essays on Orthodox monasteries from Mount Athos to Romania and Russia, translations of classic texts on Orthodox spirituality, such as the *Philokalia,* and the writings of many of the persons of faith included in this volume: Alexander Men, Alexander Schmemann, Lev Gillet, and Maria Skobtsova. Reproductions or actual painted icons are present for veneration and as foci for prayer in many Western churches and homes.

With the fall of state socialism in the East, churches and monasteries are being reopened and there is a renewal of all forms of religious expression. Orthodox liturgy is transmitted by recordings and captured by books and exhibitions of iconography. Orthodox clergy and laity have become a presence in international ecumenical bodies and even in efforts at conflict resolution. The ecumenical patriarch, Bartholomew I, has become known for his vigorous, theological defense of the environment. The powerful gestures of reconciliation by Ecumenical Patriarch Athenagoras I and Pope Paul VI in praying together, laying down the anathemas of the great schism, and recognizing each other as bishops remain memorable ecumenical actions of our time.

The presence of Eastern Church representatives became significant in the World Council of Churches (WCC) from the 1950s to the 1980s, despite the minority status they held. In the 1983 document produced by the WCC's Faith and Order Commission, *Baptism, Eucharist, Ministry,* the ecclesiology and liturgical theology of the Eastern Church is unmistakably evident. This shaping of the fundamental vision of the Church and sacraments by Orthodox participation has been explicitly criticized by some Protestant theologians in their "reception" of the document.

The Eastern churches have become part of the culture and religious landscape of the West. Three generations of "cradle" Orthodox—Russians and other Slavic groups, Greeks, Arabs—have assimilated into the West. Christians from Western churches have passed into the churches of the East, not only through marriage, but also through sacramental reception, or "conversion." Father Meyendorff insisted that it was theologically incorrect to speak of the Orthodox in the West as a diaspora, merely transplants of other "mother" churches.

It is now necessary to speak not of "Eastern" Orthodoxy but of Orthodoxy, the Orthodox Church, indeed Orthodox Christian women and men who are Westerners: Americans, Britons, French, Scandinavians, and so on. The all too often used stereotype of Orthodox Christians as essentially "ethnics" is simply not accurate any longer. Yet here lies the complex of problems that make the Orthodox Church still a marginal reality in American life. Both Fathers Schmemann and Meyendorff saw as uncanonical and abnormal the lack of visible unity among the Orthodox churches in America. While it is correctly claimed that most of these churches are in communion, in reality in one city various jurisdictions overlap and compete.

Ethnic identity appears to be the primary reason for the ecclesiastical proliferation, despite greater assimilation. With every successive generation there are more hyphenated Americans and through marriage, more mixed households. Even where clergy and laity are American born and perhaps second generation, there is little real co-operation among jurisdictions' parishes. There are occasional liturgical gatherings for funerals, feasts, and special Lenten services. Yet for all practical purposes, the various Orthodox churches function as competing voluntary organizations or nonprofit corporations. In sociology of religion terminology, they behave like "denominations," even though the entirety of their theology and liturgical life, and the tradition they revere, runs counter to this.

The Standing Conference of Orthodox Bishops in America (SCOBA) has no official, canonical status in the eyes of other Orthodox churches worldwide. It does not function as the synod of bishops here because there is no unified church in this country and no chief bishop. In 1994 SCOBA was aggressively challenged, and the bishops of the Greek archdiocese in one jurisdiction were reprimanded by the ecumenical patriarch for supporting the emergence of a unified Orthodox Church in America without an ethnic identity. Though in principle a symbol and supporter of church unity, Bartholomew I has tragically become its chief enemy. Where there could be cooperation in important areas such as theological education and social ministry, with but few exceptions each church body maintains its own expensive, elaborate corporate organizations: seminaries, presses, offices for governmental and ecumenical affairs, divisions for establishing mission parishes. The exceptions have been in humanitarian aid and mission work abroad. Rather than the vibrant witness of the tradition of the ancient Church, the Orthodox churches remain distant from one another, indifferent, if not hostile, and their presence is muted, their impact on the rest of the culture minimal.

Among the Orthodox there is also a reactionary movement, one that sees the West as corrupt and in particular the Western churches as "heretical" bodies, in which there is no grace, no real sacramental life, no authentic Christianity.[15] This exclusivist tendency has been present among the Orthodox in one form or another for a long time. In the past ethnic hatreds and political tensions were strong factors. Today, they are manifest in outright condemnation of all exchange and interaction passing under the rubric of ecumenical dialogue. While there is deep self-scrutiny under way in ecumenical organizations, the WCC in particular, and while there is much to be challenged or criticized about the content and drift of ecumenical activity, it is quite another matter for all that is "ecumenical" to be defined as "heresy." All contact with the non-Orthodox and in particular any sharing of prayer has been condemned, on the basis of third- and fourth-century canons that forbid prayer with those who explicitly deny the basic dogmas. The use of the Julian calendar as opposed to the "new," or worse, "Papist" and "heretical," Gregorian calendar has become a defining mark of authentic Orthodox Christianity, along with the baptizing again of all non-Orthodox Christians who seek to enter the Orthodox Church.[16]

Further badges of difference or means of isolation include the length of services, terminology, clothing styles, and observance of rules regarding fasting, liturgical posture, and prayer. In short, it is impossible to avoid seeing the creation of a total lifestyle and consciousness that sets the Orthodox apart from the rest of society, like Hasidic Jews and the Amish. While many of these specific lifestyle elements may not be crucial to the faith, their elevation to necessity status for "true" Orthodoxy is another matter entirely. The mind-set behind them contains positions that are not just dubious and debatable but erroneous. Perhaps the most radical is that "nothing can change" in the Tradition, a position denied by the Tradition's having a history in the first place. The historicity of tradition is confirmed by countless sources: many documents, details of the liturgical services in the collection called the *Typicon*, and depiction in paintings, novels, poems, and lyrics of popular songs. The efforts of the so-called Renewal Church in the aftermath of the Russian Revolution to implement real reforms and adaptations contaminated the very idea and possibility of renewal for some.

Likewise, the efforts of many for authentic church renewal in the twentieth century have been condemned. In the liturgical realm Fathers Afanasiev and Schmemann encouraged frequent communion and the audible recitation of the liturgical prayers. Lowering the icon screen, or iconostasis, and opening the royal doors that allow passage to the altar have also been suggested, so that the faithful might be able to see as well as hear and participate in the celebration of the liturgy. Bulgakov, Lev Gillet, Men, and Evdokimov recognized the active presence of the Holy Spirit among the divided churches and possessed the fervent hope that the schisms would be healed. Many had profound regard for the saints and heritage of the Western churches. However, such openness and their truly healing spirit have resulted in book burnings, ridicule, and slander.[17]

I have chosen to focus primarily on Orthodox Christians originally of the Russian Church who found their way to the West. Since the Russian Revolution and other upheavals of the early twentieth century, many Orthodox Christians have come to live and work in the West, among them poets, musicians, philosophers, historians, theologians, and great spiritual teachers. Not since Nicolas Zernov's study, more than three decades ago, has there been any effort to examine their presence in the West, and in that time additional important figures have appeared.[18] While I believe their own lives and voices will express this vividly, I base this study on the conviction that the Eastern Church, with her preservation of Christianity's ancient tradition of faith and worship, shaped them distinctively.

Quite unlike the stereotype of the Eastern Church as completely otherworldly and unchanging, the living icons discussed in this volume embody the openness of the gospel to all times and peoples. The Eastern Church recognizes the immense love of God for the world, so deep that he became part of it, in flesh-and-blood humanity, in space and in time. Evdokimov, echoing a much earlier theologian, calls this "God's absurd love" for mankind. The Eastern Church's reverence for the Incarnation and the presence of the Holy Spirit in each human being is dramatically witnessed in her love for the icon, that sacred image in which God is present in the human faces of the saints. The Eastern Church also treasures the material and human dimensions of God's presence and action in the sacraments, especially in the triple immersion of the candidate in baptism, anointing him or her both with holy oil and with the aromatic mixture of oil and spices called chrism. Central in her liturgical life is the celebration of the Eucharist, in which Christ speaks in the Scriptures and the preaching and is received in the blessed bread and cup. Christian tradition is upheld in the Eastern Church, not localized solely in the Bible or the head bishop or even in a council but in the lived experience of the whole people of God. The Church is understood as the communion of saints already in the kingdom of heaven as well as all those called into saintly living here and now, in this life, by their baptism.

The Eastern Church, as Evdokimov and Father Lev admit, is often impoverished and oppressed. She is institutionally inept, even chaotic and anarchic. Yet she witnesses to the Kingdom of God in the beauty of her worship and churches. She also has a great patience, a loving indulgence for her sons and daughters, refusing to bind them with legal rigor, preferring to "sin" on the side of freedom and love. These are some of the characteristics embodied in her members whom we encounter in this book.

The Living Icons

From the many figures who have been lights of the Eastern Church in our time, I have selected ten. I wanted to choose from those who truly became part of Western culture and life. The exception is Fr. Alexander Men (1935–90), who spent all of his life in Russia but whose writing and teaching exploded on the scene at the end of the Soviet regime and culminated in his tragic assassination in 1990. The others were rooted in the Russian émigré community of Paris.

Fr. Sergius Bulgakov (1871–1944), first dean of the St. Sergius Theological Institute, was the most prolific, creative, and controversial theologian in his time. A participant in the return and reawakening of intellectuals to the faith and the Church, he collaborated with Berdiaev and others in the well-known collection of essays, *Vekhi* (Signposts), which proposed the rediscovery and renewal of Christian thought and life. The son of a priest and himself a seminarian, Bulgakov lost his faith and clung to Marxist thought until his reading of classic Russian authors such as Soloviev and Dostoyevsky rekindled his hunger for God. From a brilliant start as a professor of political economy at Moscow University, he returned to the Church after several conversion experiences documented in his autobiographical sketches. After political experience in the Second Duma and a major role in the important reforming Church Council of 1917–18, he was ordained a priest and soon after left Russia forever, joining the exodus of thousands to the West. Father Bulgakov was much criticized, even condemned, for his treatment of Sophia, Divine Wisdom, in his writings. I will not focus as much on his substantial writings as on his life of prayer and work as a priest. His ideas about the unity of the Church are the foundation for the restoration of Christianity's witness in our world.

The lay theologian Paul Evdokimov (1901–70) spent years in humanitarian service, which was always a ministry of the gospel. He brought the urgency of suffering and the questions of modern life to his teaching and writings. The monk Gregory Krug (1908–69), academy and salon trained in painting, printmaking, and drawing, led a quiet but rich spiritual life, full of personal struggle and artistic accomplishment. He left little in print but a body of iconography unparalleled in creativity yet deeply rooted within the Tradition, which he helped to restore.

Fr. Nicolas Afanasiev (1893–1966) is an important yet ignored figure who rediscovered the ancient self-understanding of the Church through his historical and canon law studies. His thinking shaped the Second Vatican Council and the contemporary identity of many churches. Fr. Lev Gillet (1893–1980) is among the greatest twentieth-century spiritual teachers, not only through the many books written under the pen name the Monk of the Eastern Church, but also through his ecumenical pilgrimage from Benedictine monastic life to pastoral work in France, England, Lebanon, and Switzerland as an Orthodox priest and monk.

Most unusual is Mother Maria Skobtsova (1891–1945), an image of the complexity of a life of faith in this era. Poet, painter, political activist, married and twice divorced, mother of three children, she became a nun later in life and then directed hostels for the care of the poor and marginal during the depression in Paris. Active in the Resistance, she was herself a martyr-victim of the Nazi concentration camps, sent there for hiding and attempting to save Jewish neighbors.

Finally, Frs. Alexander Schmemann (1921–83) and John Meyendorff (1926–92) both came to America as young adults and spent the rest of their lives as the foremost scholars and interpreters of the Orthodox Church in America and the principal contributors to American religious life and the relationship among Christian churches. Father Schmemann is well known in the liturgical renewal movement for his rediscovery of liturgical theology and for his lyrical writing on the Eucharist, the spiritual content of the liturgy, and the church year. He was a seminary dean, an ecumenical expert, and a much sought after spiritual father. Father Meyendorff was an internationally respected Byzantinist, with Schmemann an architect of the Orthodox Church in America, an influential ecumenical leader, and also a beloved confessor and counselor.[19]

The lives of many of the figures here are entwined. Let me give just a few examples. Paul Evdokimov was among Father Bulgakov's students in the first class to graduate from St. Sergius Theological Institute.[20] Father Lev also attended Bulgakov's classes, though he was not formally enrolled.[21] Mother Maria was a spiritual child of his, and Father Afanasiev also studied under and later taught with Father Bulgakov. Afanasiev, in turn, was a close friend and colleague of Evdokimov and the teacher of Father Schmemann, directing the latter into his own "eucharistic ecclesiology." Schmemann later would craft a distinctive approach that he called "liturgical theology."

These scholars subtly but profoundly influenced each other. Often there is explicit citation; at other times, however, the direction, the spirit, the style, and even the very language serve as the reference. Take, for example, Father Afanasiev's *Trapeza Gospodnia* (The Lord's Supper, 1952), an explosive critique of eucharistic practice among the Orthodox, and his posthumously published *Tserkov Dukha Sviatogo* (The Church of the Holy Spirit, 1975), an exposition of the ancient and formative eucharistic ecclesiology of the primitive church. The impact of Father Afanasiev's thinking, forged from his training in canon law, church history, New Testament studies, and liturgy, is evident in Father Schmemann's posthumously published major work, *The Eucharist: Sacrament of the Kingdom* (1988), as well as in his other writings. Father Schmemann's remarks, in the public defense of his doctoral thesis, "Introduction to Liturgical Theology," at St. Sergius Theological Institute in 1961, with Fathers Afanasiev and Meyendorff as examiners, echoes his teacher's dismay at what the liturgy had been allowed to become, and this with substantial theological, not to mention cultural, defense. Although he would frequently note scholarly objections to details of Afanasiev's eucharistic theology, it is worth noting how imprinted the eucharistic nature of the Church and the churchly character of the Eucharist were in

Father Meyendorff's thinking. Regularly, the Eucharist was the measuring rod of the Church's health in his writing, as evidenced by his editorials in the official publication of the Orthodox Church in America, *The Orthodox Church,* and in his research and lectures.

Father Lev was the rector of the first French-language Orthodox parish in Paris, dedicated to the Transfiguration and St. Genevieve, a community which included the Evdokimovs, the Losskys, the Kovalesky brothers, and Elisabeth Behr-Sigel and her husband, Nicolas. The parish met for liturgy first in the Russian Christian Students Movement offices at 10 rue Montparnasse and later in the Lutheran Church of the Holy Trinity in present-day Boulevard Vincent-Auriol. Louis Bouyer, later a Catholic priest of the Oratory and an important liturgical theologian, also attended services there.

As one follows the history of the Russian emigration, this inter-weaving of friendships and careers is not so surprising. Most of the young people of that emigration were active members of the Russian Christian Students Movement, in which Fathers Bulgakov and Lev, among other clergy, were important spiritual leaders, teachers, and confessors. From this association and the St. Sergius Theological Institute, further points of contact and cooperation emerged in the Fellowship of St. Alban and St. Sergius, an Anglican-Orthodox fra-ternity, the first ecumenical fellowship of its kind anywhere. There was also participation in the fledging years of the association that would become the World Council of Churches and in the more hu-manitarian ecumenical group, Comité Inter-Mouvements pour L'ac-cueil des Évacués (CIMADE), in which Evdokimov worked for over a decade. These connections continued for years. The icons of Father Gregory adorned the chapel of Mother Maria's nursing home in Noisy-le-Grand; Father Afanasiev's student, Alexander Schmemann, became the dean of the American seminary and a leading figure in the liturgical movement internationally; and Fr. John Meyendorff succeeded Schmemann as dean of St. Vladimir's Seminary and be-came one of the primary links between Orthodoxy and the academic community and churches of the United States. Though not all in-termarried or related by family and sometimes passionately dis-agreeing with each other, the lives of most of these figures were interlaced, not only by common situations of language, culture, and emigration, but also by the Great Depression and World War II.

Even more deeply, they were connected by a communion in faith, in sacramental and church life.

I intend nothing sentimental or sacrilegious in calling these individuals "living icons." Each Christian is created in the image (*eikon*) and likeness of God and the life in Christ. The presence of the Holy Spirit is understood through the Eastern Fathers to be a process of *theosis*, a divinizing or deification, becoming more and more like the image in whom one is made and baptized. The description for many monastic saints in particular, *prepodobny*, means "very much like, quite similar to . . . God," this being but one of many working definitions or descriptions of holiness, of sainthood.

CHAPTER TWO

St. Seraphim of Sarov

An Image of Holiness in Our Time

St. Seraphim of Sarov was canonized in 1903, with significant support from Tsar Nicholas II and his wife, Alexandra, both of whom were present at the canonization. St. Seraphim is a key to the more open and creative understanding of the path of the gospel, the life of communion in God. This seems a paradox, for he lived in one of the worst periods of church life in Russia, when living tradition was hardened into categories and formulas, many of which haunt Eastern Christianity to this day. Under Peter the Great, the patriarchate of Moscow was ended and the Church became a branch of the state, governed by the appointed procurator general, a layman, who presided over the synod of Russian bishops. Throughout the Petrine period and the reign of Catherine II, monastic life, already in spiritual decline, became the target of deliberate suppression. More than three quarters of all existing monastic communities were closed, and stringent regulations controlled the establishing of any new ones.

Yet in a time of erosion, the sparks of renewal were struck. St. Paisius Velichkovsky (1722–94), who had graduated from the Kiev Theological Academy, entered monastic life on Mount Athos and began his Slavonic translation of the *Philokalia*, literally "The Love of Beauty." This collection of texts from the Fathers edited by St. Nicodemus of Mount Athos became a classic of Eastern Church spirituality and eventually was translated into Russian. The wandering Russian Christian of the famous *Way of the Pilgrim* purchases a battered copy in the first chapter of his account and carries it along with a Bible in his knapsack as his entire library and the sum of his possessions, reading in it of the "prayer of the heart." St. Tikhon of Zadonsk (1724–82), a remarkable bishop and later hermit monk, also lived in this period. He read widely in the classics of the spiritual life, including those by Western authors, conducted an extensive correspondence with those he counseled, translated the Psalter and the New Testament into Russian, and contributed greatly to the renewal of liturgical life and prayer through his writings, particularly after his death.

Prokhor Moshnin, later to become Father Seraphim, was born on July 19, 1759, in Kursk, the youngest of three children, to Isidore, a builder, and his wife, Agatha. Seraphim's father died the following year, having nearly completed the construction of a church in Kursk. Seraphim's mother, known for her generosity to the poor and suffering, raised him in her own deep faith and love for one's neighbor. As a child, Prokhor encountered the sacred and miraculous numerous times. His vita records a miraculous fall from a building scaffold without injury and his recovery from serious illness after the wonder-working icon of the Mother of God of Kursk was carried in procession past his home, this after his seeing the Virgin in a vision at his sickbed. The hagiography of Seraphim's early years is replete with standard elements such as a passion for the Scriptures and the Fathers and for reading in church at services. Though the home of the wonder-working icon and thus a site of pilgrimage, there was no monastic community in Kursk. A pilgrimage to the Lavra, or monastery of the caves, the first site of monastic life in Russia, brought Prokhor in contact with an elder who confirmed the young man's monastic vocation, sending him off to the monastery of Sarov, near Tambov and Nijni-Novgorod. The bronze pectoral cross that is seen around Seraphim's neck in virtually every icon was given to him with a blessing by his mother when he left home to enter monastic life. After his death it was found among his relics at their exhumation before his consecration. His relics were rediscovered in 1988.

Prokhor was received into the novitiate at Sarov on November 20, 1778, the eve of the feast of the Entrance of the Mother of God into

the temple, by Abbot Pachomius. He was remembered by fellow
monastics as tall and strong, talented in many lines of work, and
always full of joy and enthusiasm for life. He worked in the monastery bakery, was particularly gifted in woodworking and carpen-
try, and was given the office of reader for services. Only a few years
into monastic life he was struck down again with a severe illness,
from which he was healed by a visit of the Mother of God and the
apostles Peter and John, much like St. Sergius of Radonezh. The Virgin told the apostles of Seraphim, "He is one of ours." On the feast
of the Virgin's Dormition, or falling asleep, August 15, 1786, Prokhor
was tonsured a monk and given the name Seraphim, after the fiery
angels who surround the heavenly throne. He was ordained a deacon later that year and in 1793 a priest. While serving as a deacon on
a Holy Thursday, he saw a vision of Christ entering the monastery
church, surrounded by the cherubim and seraphim, blessing the celebrants and congregation. He celebrated the liturgy daily for many
years and received communion at every liturgy he attended, an
atypically intense eucharistic devotion for the time. Before his death,
Abbot Pachomius entrusted a nearby convent of sisters, Diveyevo,
to Seraphim's pastoral care in the future.

In 1794 Seraphim asked permission from Pachomius' successor,
Abbot Isaac, to live in a hermitage some five kilometers from the
monastery, in the woods by the Sarovka River. Several other monks
had also obtained permission for the eremitical life in the woods.
Perhaps no other phase of Seraphim's life is as well known as these
hermit years. He read through all the Gospels each week, along with
the rest of the daily offices and his own prayer rule. He kept a vege-
table garden and chopped his own wood. For Seraphim, the Sarov
forest became a desert, that is, a place of encounter with God and
struggle with himself. He named various forest locations Nazareth,
Bethlehem, Gethsemani, Tabor, and Jerusalem to assist his Scripture
reading and prayer. He returned to the monastery every Saturday
evening for the vigil and for the Sunday liturgy at which he communed. He would then go back to his hermitage with a week's
supply of bread, obtaining the rest of his food from his garden and
foraging in the woods. A popular lithograph shows Seraphim sharing his bread with an enormous black bear. Paul Evdokimov identifies this as a trait of the ancient desert fathers and mothers, such as

Francis of Assisi and Jerome. The animals and birds could detect in the holy ones the original scent of Paradise, the presence of one "very similar, very much like," the Lord himself.

In the forest Seraphim wore the simple unbleached peasant's smock and boots in winter and birch bark sandals in summer. This clothing, common to farmers and workers of the time, became his habit. In the desert of the Sarov forest he prayed for a thousand days and nights standing or kneeling on a large rock, as he is so often portrayed in icons, especially that of Fr. Gregory Krug reproduced here. He also did battle with the forces of evil, as did the desert monastics of the past. During his hermit years, Seraphim was attacked by three robbers who beat him nearly to death. Visited again on his apparent deathbed by the Mother of God and the apostles Peter and John, he once more heard her words, "He is one of ours," and again miraculously recovered. However, the scars of the attack would never leave him. He became prematurely aged, his hair and beard becoming white, and the damage inflicted by the beating left him a hunchback and in need of a cane or staff for the rest of his life. The last years of his hermit period were passed in complete silence and isolation. He no longer returned to the monastery for the feast day and Sunday services.

In spring 1810 the monastery's ruling council and new abbot ordered him to return to community life. This he did, but his manner of living the common life was once again a break from the ordinary. He became a solitary within his cell, in the midst of the monastery buildings, venturing out only at night to the church; his meals and even Holy Communion were brought to him. He communicated with no one and was not seen except at a distance on his evening walks. This isolation was extreme even for monastic life. Just as suddenly, in summer 1815, after the local bishop's futile attempt to visit him, he opened the door of his cell to a young couple, the local governor and his wife. From that day until his death on January 1, 1832, his door was constantly open, his life transformed into a nonstop ministry of counseling, prayer, and healing for thousands of people who flocked to Sarov—Orthodox Christians and non-Orthodox—from all over the country. But even here there were unusual elements. His monastic cell was filled with candles lit as prayers for many who visited and wrote to him. He dispensed pieces of blessed bread, almost a reenactment of the Lord's feeding of the crowds by the multiplication of the loaves and fishes, a vivid testimony to the "bread of life" of the Eucharist, as Evdokimov observes.

Seraphim seemed to straddle modern times and the ancient days of the desert fathers. Seraphim appears to have discerned the complex psychosomatic causes of the sicknesses of Michael Manturov and Nicholas Motovilov, both of whom became his close friends and assistants. He proceeded to heal both of them only after a therapeutic dialogue in which he evoked, or better, provoked, from them a confession of faith in the power of God to heal their diseases. Motovilov, who later would be the confidant of a theophanic revelation, was commanded by Seraphim to stand on his paralyzed legs and walk. In a kind of spiritual psychotherapy, Seraphim cut through all the denials and defense mechanisms of these two, insisting, though, that he was but an instrument, a medium through which the healing power of God was revealed at work in their sufferings. As in the Gospels, having been healed, Manturov and Motovilov were quickly put to work by Seraphim, who had a healthy sense of the sacredness of labor. They became coworkers in many aspects of Seraphim's ministry, taking charge of building a mill and the churches of the Diveyevo convent.

With many others who came to him suffering either from physical diseases or from a wide range of emotional disturbances such as depression, guilt, or delusion, Seraphim displayed a marvelous gift of discernment. He could very quickly "read" through the accounts the suffering person presented, finding the deeper roots of their malaise and inviting them to face them to be forgiven and thus healed by God. Even when people were unable or unwilling to tell him their troubles, he could see within their hearts and relate their situations without their uttering a word. A monk visiting and observing this was amazed and recorded Seraphim's gift of discernment of souls. Throughout the years of his ministry to the suffering, Seraphim never stopped his ministry of prayer. Regularly visitors would have to wait hours and occasionally a day or more until Seraphim opened the door of his cell after a marathon of intercession.

The biographers of St. Seraphim—Donald Nicholl, Valentina Zander, Irina Gorianov, Lazarus Moore, Paul Evdokimov, and Elisabeth Behr-Sigel, among others—all rely on the same sources: chronicles kept by the Diveyevo nuns, reminiscences by monks of the Sarov monastery, and recollections of numerous pilgrims to Seraphim's cell. There are so many anecdotes, so many details to encounters with this little holy man, that they cannot be recounted here. His great love for children is noted endlessly, how he would hide in the tall grass and bushes from adult visitors but then allow himself to be "found" by their children with whom he would play and sing. Seraphim became in every sense the father of the Diveyevo nuns, even revealing vocations to many of the young women of the region who visited him. His care for them was warm and affectionate but occasionally unusual. He would sometimes ask great efforts and sacrifices of them and sometimes dissuade them from what they believed to be their chosen course in life: some who deeply desired monastic life he directed into marriage, others the opposite way. Michael Manturov's sister Helen was a special spiritual child of his who entered the Diveyevo community and held an important position of leadership there. Seraphim's conversations with her shortly before her death at the age of only twenty-seven are extraordinary in their discernment of the fear but also the joy of dying in Christ. Another of the sisters, Mary Miliukov, could be called Seraphim's favorite. At her death, it seemed that his own daughter had died.

Seraphim's own dying was remarkable, for it was preceded both by efforts at reconciliation with all those around and by his chanting of the hymns of Easter, even though it was the end of December, right after Christmas and just before Epiphany. Evdokimov recognizes in St. Seraphim's year-round use of the Paschal greeting a sign of the Resurrection as the very heart of the Christian life. Seraphim called each person he met *Radost*, "My joy," and to each he would then proclaim, "Christ is risen," no matter what the season. His fellow monks found Seraphim kneeling before the icon of the Mother of God in his cell, the book of the Gospels open before him, the pages smoldering from the candle that had fallen on them. Though his body was still warm, his heart had stopped and they could not revive him. His funeral was like an Easter celebration in the middle of winter, and almost exactly seventy years later, the services of his glorification at Sarov in July 1903 were, as he foretold, like an Easter celebration in the midst of summer greenery and heat.

There is, at least in my reading of everything I could find on St. Seraphim, a strong sense of the magical. I do not mean superstition or the occult but the wonderful childlike quality of certain fairy tales, ones whose words transport us back to our own childhood home and feelings of great joy and light. Over the years after the Sarov and Diveyevo monasteries had been destroyed by the Communists, the forest flattened, all signs and memories of Seraphim and his monks and nuns obliterated and even his relics apparently gone, still there were beautiful stories about his continuing presence. Soldiers were greeted by a smiling little man in a white smock, lost travelers guided in howling blizzards by a little old man in white. Peasants would bring fresh pine boughs into the antireligion museum in the former Kazan cathedral where some believed the relics might have been kept. To the guard who could not understand the gesture of the branches, the visitor would say, "These are for the little father, they remind him of home." Then, after glasnost, when a wooden case in the antireligion museum was opened, there was the bronze cross, the remains of his monastic habit, and an ecclesiastical document identifying the remains as his relics. St. Seraphim's relics were found, and he returned, as he said he would, to Sarov and to his beloved Diveyevo, where a monastery has been opened again. The procession bearing him back traveled by train, by truck, and on foot, a pilgrimage that many thought could never happen.

Breaking the Molds, Transcending the Boundaries

Although St. Seraphim would appear to have traveled the institutionalized path of asceticism, entering into monastic life and then the ordained priesthood, both his person and his life overturn the stereotypes and myths that have accrued to "spirituality" and to holiness in the modern period. For this reason many of the figures profiled in this book were drawn to St. Seraphim, and several contributed insightful studies of his life and teaching. Evdokimov often wrote about him. In a study of the history and place of saints in Orthodox tradition, Evdokimov holds up St. Seraphim's character and fidelity to the gospel, finding in him a pattern for holiness in our time.[1] Perhaps the best-known incident, recorded by Motovilov, richly illustrates both Seraphim's personality and position.[2] On a snowy winter afternoon, in a field outside his hermitage in the Sarov forest, St. Seraphim not only allowed Motovilov to see the luminous results of being in the presence of God, in communion with him, but also enabled Motovilov to share in this experience himself. In their conversation St. Seraphim emphasized his simple yet precise expression of holiness, that it was for everyone and was what God deeply desired. Holiness, he said, consisted in "acquiring the Holy Spirit," that is, living within the community of the Trinity. Motovilov described almost blinding light, warmth despite the winter cold, a beautiful fragrance, and above all, indescribable joy and peace, exactly what the New Testament indicates is the real presence of the Spirit.

That he was a priest and monk and Motovilov a layperson meant nothing in the domain and power of the Spirit. This is witnessed by what one might call the pilgrimage of St. Seraphim's life. Healed miraculously by the Mother of God in his childhood, the recipient of numerous visits by her and other saints, the seer of visions of Christ at the liturgy, St. Seraphim at first appears to conform quite neatly to the category of monastic saint. But on closer inspection, the categories of priest, monastic ascetic, even *staretz,* or spiritual father, are all transcended and transformed. Though he never left the monastic life, he became a hermit, a mystic, a recluse, and the target of much misunderstanding, hostility, and abuse by members of his own monastic community. Then his interior transformation became visible. The door of his cell was open to all, and every day many visited for his blessing, for his counsel, for the pieces of blessed bread he offered. He listened, counseled them, gave them holy water, and anointed and laid his hands on them in blessing. Although still a monastic, he no longer wore the formal habit but a simple peasant smock and bark shoes. His isolation from others ended, he belonged to the world. Through him the monastery opened to the world, a prefiguring of the wonderful openness of the monks of the Optina monastery to so many, including Dostoyevsky. Though still a priest, no special treatment was demanded, and he communed with everyone else at the monastery's liturgy.

Although he was rooted in the customs of the Russian Church and monastic life, St. Seraphim was a model of holiness, a living icon in his own time who extends the possibility of communion in the Lord to every person in every situation in society. Any prestige accruing from status, ordained or monastic, is obliterated. Also demolished are any stereotypes of what holiness looks like, of what ascetic practices are necessary. He fasts, reads the daily offices, attends the services in the monastery church and receives communion, and lights so many candles before his icon that the monks fear he will burn down the monastery. He keeps all the rules. Yet his life and his words make it clear that these are but means to an end and never an end in themselves. When one has recognized the Holy Spirit, one ceases to say prayers or keep the rules, for the Spirit takes over, making all of one's life prayer. "Acquiring the Holy Spirit," he said, "is the whole point of the Christian life," and "if one is saved," becomes holy, "thousands around will also be saved." These are the most quoted of all St. Seraphim's words, and they contain his amazing openness to God and to all people. St. Seraphim welcomed everyone, clergy or lay, married or monastic, wealthy or poor. Each person was his "joy," every being illumined by the Spirit and the Risen Christ.

His continual reading of the Gospels brought Seraphim to the amazing "evangelical inversion," the turning upside down of things that Christ works in all human situations. For him the always disconcerting *metanoia,* or transformation of life, was essentially one of utter simplicity. Seraphim's whole person and all his dealings with people were marked by joy and love. This little man, huge in holiness, is very accurately depicted in the very moving last section of Mother Maria's essay, "Types of Religious Lives." In this essay the "evangelical" type or radical life of the gospel is described as giving away to others the love one receives in abundance from God. The Johannine measure echoes here: if we cannot love the neighbor whom we can see, it is impossible to love the God we cannot see.

We now turn to persons of faith from our own time. We come to look for their vision, the experience of those who, as Evdokimov said, did not just say prayers but "became prayer, prayer incarnate." In them we will see as in a mirror the image of what is also possible for ourselves; lives "very much like God."

CHAPTER THREE

Sergius Bulgakov

Political Economist and Priest, Marxist and Mystic

In his words at the funeral service for Fr. Sergius Bulgakov in July 1944, his bishop, Metropolitan Evlogy (Georgievsky), said: "Dear Father Sergius, You were a Christian sage, a teacher of the Church in the purest and most lofty sense. You were enlightened by the Holy Spirit, the Spirit of Wisdom, the Spirit of Understanding, the Comforter to whom you dedicated your scholarly work."[1] This was the faithful yet creative professor of theology whose prayer at the beginning and end of most books was, "*Maranatha,* Come Lord Jesus!" This was the priest whose ministry at the altar, in confession, and in prayer Fr. Alexander Schmemann marveled at, calling him "a prophet and contemplative of the mystery, a guide to the magnificent domain on high to which he beckoned us by his flaming fire, by his spiritual authenticity, by the image he left us of himself."[2] Metropolitan Evlogy also said of Father Sergius, "Because your theology was the fruit not only of your brain but also of the hard trials of your heart, it was perhaps inscribed in your destiny to be misunderstood, accused."

In the son of a priest and seminarian who lost his faith, in the former Marxist professor of political economy become priest and theologian, Metropolitan Evlogy found not only the first dean of his theological institute, St. Sergius, but the first Orthodox thinker who would try in a comprehensive way to establish an encounter between the Church's Tradition and the world of the twentieth century. As

Paul Valliere emphasizes, Father Bulgakov was the first twentieth-
century Orthodox theologian who engaged the modern world and
its culture with the Tradition of the Church, and he did so in a manner more radical than any of his contemporaries in either the Eastern or the Western churches: "Bulgakov's dogmatic theology . . .
says yes to Church Tradition, yes also to the world, yes to theology,
yes also to the humanities, yes to God, yes also to humankind."[3] His
was a theological mind bold enough to try to formulate in positive
terms the Incarnation, which the Council of Chalcedon over a millennium and a half earlier could only describe as "without separation,
division, confusion." In the struggles of his heart and difficult life,
Father Bulgakov would attempt to draw out, in thousands of pages
and dozens of sermons and talks, the meaning of the Incarnation:
Bogochelovechestvo, as Valliere rightly translates it, "the humanity
of God," as the very core of Christian faith.[4]

Boris Jakim, the foremost translator of Father Bulgakov into
English, dares to characterize his style as "mystical lyricism," eventually creating in his voluminous writings a panorama so broad that
it might in turn be called a "mystical epic."[5] Nikita Struve puts
together in rough fashion the figures that express the enormous productivity of a man who lived in destitution, his health so poor that
in his fifties he was thought to be terminally ill.[6] Despite the poverty
and two operations for throat cancer that robbed him of his voice,
despite the infighting of the Russian emigration's competing ecclesiastical communities and groups, despite fierce attack even from
colleagues who respected him, not to mention the Moscow patriarchate's criticism of his work, Father Bulgakov nevertheless produced
a corpus of astonishing content and even more amazing size. His
little trilogy on the Mother of God, the angels, and St. John the Baptist runs over 750 pages of dense text and the large trilogy some 1,500
pages, and along with this he produced smaller studies of the Eucharist, Sts. Peter and John, the Apocalypse, the icon, his classic catechetical book, *The Orthodox Church,* his many articles in journals
and collections, his lectures, his letters, and more than 1,200 pages of
never published journals, sermons, prayers, and other works. As
the theologian Constantine Andronikov, his French translator, observes, no theologian in the Eastern Church had produced a body of
thought comparable since the fall of Byzantium, and this is to bracket

apart all the writings in sociology, political economy, philosophy, criticism, and theology before his forced exile from Russia in 1923 and all his work as a delegate to the Sobor, or Great Council, of the Russian Church in 1917–18.[7]

There is no doubt that Father Bulgakov's work, even in translation, presents formidable challenges. So much shaped by the German intellectual heritage of the nineteenth century, his prose is difficult: long and convoluted sentences reminiscent of the battle one has with such diverse giants as Hegel, Marx, and Weber. Yet deeper than this is his immense learning, his thinking grounded not only in philosophy, psychology, Russian and western European literature, and economic and social theory but also in the church fathers and the theology of his time. One should not be surprised to read his essays on Picasso's art, his citation of theological writers from England, Germany, France, and the United States and from all denominational backgrounds and specializations. One would have to admit that with the exception of only a few, the depth and breadth of his scholarship are unsurpassed among Orthodox teachers and scholars of any field, particularly theology.

He was, after all, the product of a "Silver Age" of learning and the arts in Russia, a veritable renaissance in many disciplines, especially philosophy and theology. When one considers his peers, the lack of comparison to anyone in our highly technologized and overspecialized time is all the more astonishing. His friend and mentor was the brilliant theologian and scientist Pavel Florensky, who would be executed in the former monastery of Solovki, turned into a Soviet prison camp. He was close to many who were exiled or able to migrate to the West. He collaborated and taught with philosophers such as Nicolas Berdiaev, Lev Shestov, Lev Karsavin, Nicolas Lossky, and Simeon Frank; with historians and social scientists such as George Fedotov, Pierre Struve, and Anton Kartachev. The poet and social activist Mother Maria Skobtsova was his spiritual child. The theologian Georges Florovsky was his teaching colleague at St. Sergius and with Vladimir Lossky his opponents in the controversy over the orthodoxy of his writings. He was the spiritual father and close friend of Sister Joanna Reitlinger, who with Leonid Ouspensky and Fr. Gregory Krug led the movement of renewal and return to tradition in iconography. Then in the Russian emigration there were the

far better known cultural icons Chagall, Kandinsky, Bakhst, Dia-
ghilev, Balanchine, Chaliapin, Nijinsky, Prokofiev, Rachmaninov,
and Stravinsky, to mention but a few.

I mention the latter renowned figures simply to provide perspective and context for Father Bulgakov and his colleagues and students,
to locate them amid what others refer to as a "pléiade" or even "pan-
theon" of gifted individuals of the Russian Silver Age. It is a puzzling, disturbing fact that the contributions not only of Bulgakov but
of most of the rest of the theologians mentioned here are now in
eclipse, neither studied in Orthodox institutions nor discussed with
any regularity in scholarly writings, never really brought into the
mainstream of theological endeavor in the West, a tragic consequence
of Orthodox ecclesiastical conflict, as Rowan Williams suggests,
the turning of a younger generation or different school—Vladimir
Lossky and Georges Florovsky—upon their elders or opponents,
the desire to escape controversy, eventually indifference, perhaps
even self-loathing.[8] Even when academic heads of theological institutions express reverence for Father Bulgakov, this does not mean he
has been integrated into their courses and reading lists and research
projects. But it is my conviction that he should be read for the first
time, or read again, and not only by those studying theology. For
in Father Bulgakov we not only find amazing originality at work
within a tradition (something of a feat in itself) but we find as much,
if not more, in the witness of his life.

A Flight from the Church, Back to the Church

I was born in a priest's family, and Levite blood of six generations flowed in my veins. I grew up near the parish church of
St. Sergius, in the gracious atmosphere of its prayers and within
the sound of its bells. The esthetic, moral and everyday recollections of my childhood are bound up with the life of that parish
church. . . . Until I was an adolescent I was faithful to my birth
and upbringing as a son of the Church. I attended the parochial
school in my native town, Livny, for four years and was then sent
to the Theological Seminary in Orel for three years. In early adolescence, during my first or second year at the Seminary, I went

through a religious crisis, painful but not tragic, which ended in my losing religious faith for many, many years. . . . How did I come to lose my faith? I lost it without noticing it myself. It occurred as something self-evident and unavoidable when the poetry of my childhood was squeezed out of my life by the prose of seminary education. . . . In losing religious faith I naturally and, as it were, automatically adopted the revolutionary mood then prevalent among the intelligentsia. . . . [E]ven as a Marxist in a state of spiritual barbarism, I always longed for religion and I was never indifferent to faith.[9]

The author of these lines later described both his ordination and life of prayer in far different terms.

On Pentecost, 10 June 1918 I was ordained a deacon. If one could express the inexpressible, I would compare this first ordination to a burning flame. The most striking moment occurred when I passed through the Royal Doors and approached the Holy Table for the first time. It was like going through fire, scorching, cleansing and regenerating. It was like entrance into another world, into the kingdom of heaven. It initiated for me a new state of being in which I have lived ever since. . . . The experience of the second ordination [to the priesthood] was even less describable than that of the first—I can only keep silent about it. Bishop Feodor addressed his sermon to me in the sanctuary, which moved me deeply. . . . There was a general rejoicing and I felt a kind of serene triumph, a sense of eternity.[10]

Sergius Nikolaievitch Bulgakov was born in 1871 to Fr. Nicolas Vassilevitch Bulgakov and Alexandra Kosminitchna Azboukina, in the village of Livny, in the province of Orel.[11] His father was not the rector of a real parish but of a cemetery church, which had a cantor for services rather than a choir and whose subsistence was in the form of *treby*, fees paid for the priest's celebrating the memorial service (*panikhida*) for the dead, as well as other liturgical services. Not only in childhood, but also through much of his life, Father Bulgakov would live within the priesthood and in great poverty. His family of origin was also marked by the scourge of so many Slavic families, alcoholism, which contributed not only to his father's death but also to that of two older brothers. Given the extreme poverty of the rural clergy, particularly that of a cemetery chaplain's family, as well as high infant mortality rates, Bulgakov's family was also scarred by the emotional illness of his mother. It is remarkable, in light of these experiences, that his own marriage to Elena Ivanova Tokmakova, with whom he had three sons and a daughter, was a very good one. Despite the painful loss of their three-year-old son to kidney disease in 1909, the turmoil of forced emigration with temporary separation from each other and the family in exile, and unrelenting destitution, Bulgakov and Elena enjoyed almost fifty years of a deep and joyful marriage, dying within months of each other in 1944.

As was expected of the sons of priests, Bulgakov entered the provincial seminary of Orel, but there his crisis of faith—not helped by the highly formalized, closed system of theological education—propelled him first into the preparatory school at Yalets and in 1890 to Moscow University's Faculty of Law. Though more at home in the humanities, particularly literature and philosophy, Bulgakov asserts in his autobiographical notes that like many other young intellectuals, law and the social sciences appeared to provide a better point of departure for changing society. His intellectual gifts were nonetheless recognized by his professors, and on completion of his undergraduate and master's degrees in 1894 and 1897, respectively, he was invited to teach there as a lecturer and from 1898 to 1900 went to Germany for postgraduate studies. During this period, Bulgakov, like his peers, espoused the Marxist perspective, believing social democracy to be the best path for the transformation of Russia. It is worth noting that later he would characterize his assimilation to Marxist thought as "a saddle fitting a cow," not a good fit in any way, although he favored democratic socialism as the best form of government and economic organization. His 1900 study, *Capitalism and Agriculture*, already put him at odds with orthodox Marxist theory and in particular, as Williams points out, with the more recent positions of Lenin and Plekhanov regarding the inability of peasant farmers owning land in common to be a potent political force.[12] For Bulgakov, the cultural factors of Russian personality and life were far too complex, and he also found in data on international agricultural organization and production other reasons to doubt the perspectives not only of Marx but also of his Russian interpreters.

While he was not granted the doctorate for his study, it opened a faculty position for him in political economy at the Kiev Polytechnic Institute. His work *From Marxism to Idealism,* chronicled his passage there from 1901 to 1905, and in the first decade of the century he also was involved in the Union of Liberation, an association for social and economic change. He worked with figures as diverse as Peter Struve, Nicolas Berdiaev, and Vyacheslav Ivanov, and with the latter two he established several journals. He served as a deputy in the Second Duma in 1907, representing the Orel province, and this experience soured him on any thought of a career in political office. His movement away from ideological Marxism took him to a somewhat generalized religious and philosophical dimension, guided by Dostoyevsky, the subject of a well-received open lecture in 1901. His autobiographical notes, which he used without attribution as an illustration of faith as a personal experience of encounter with God in one of his books, chronicle a gradual return to faith, first inspired by the transcendent beauty of nature.

I was twenty-four years old. For a decade I had lived without faith and, after early stormy doubts, a religious emptiness reigned in my soul. One evening we were driving across the southern steppes of Russia, and the strong scented spring grass was gilded by the rays of a glorious sunset. Far in the distance I saw the blue outlines of the Caucasus. This was my first sight of the mountains. I looked with ecstatic delight at their rising slopes. I drank in the light and the air of the steppes. I listened to the revelation of nature. My soul was accustomed to the dull pain of seeing nature as a lifeless desert and of treating its surface beauty as a deceptive mask. Yet, contrary to my intellectual convictions, I could not be reconciled to nature without God. Suddenly in that evening hour, my soul was joyfully stirred. I started to wonder what would happen if the cosmos were not a desert and its beauty not a mask or deception—if nature were not death but life. If he existed, the merciful and loving father, if nature was the vesture of his love and glory, and I the pious feelings of my childhood, when I used to live in his presence, when I loved him and trembled because I was weak, were true, then the tears and inspiration of my adolescence, the sweetness of my prayers, my innocence and all those emotions which I had rejected and trodden down would be vindicated, and my present outlook with its emptiness and deadness would appear nothing more than blindness and lies, and what a transformation it would bring to me![13]

A few years later he would experience an epiphany, the encounter not just with a masterpiece but with a person depicted there.

In 1898 a new wave of intoxication with this world came upon me. I experienced "personal happiness." I met the West for the first time. My admiration of its culture, its comfort and its social democracy was boundless; and then suddenly a wonderful encounter with Raphael's Sistine Madonna took place in Dresden. It was a foggy autumn morning. I went to the art gallery in order to do my duty as a tourist. My knowledge of European painting was negligible. I did not know what to expect. The eyes of the Heavenly Queen, the Mother who holds in her arms the Eternal Child, pierced my soul. I cried joyful yet bitter tears, and with them the ice melted from my soul, and some of my psychological knots were loosened. This was an esthetic emotion, but I was then still a Marxist, but was obliged to call my contemplation of the Madonna by the name of "prayer." I went to the Zwinger gallery early in the mornings in order to be there before others arrived. I ran there everyday to pray and weep in front of the Virgin, and few experiences in my life were more blessed than those unexpected tears.[14]

But it was not until a sunny autumn day in 1908 at the hermitage of St. Zossima that he actually returned to the sacramental life of the Church.

I had come there as a companion of a friend. Secretly I hoped I might meet God. But my determination deserted me and while I was at Vespers I remained cold and unfeeling. When the prayers for confession began, I almost ran out of church. I walked in deep distress towards the guesthouse, seeing nothing around me, and suddenly found myself in front of the elder's cell. I had been led there. I intended to go in another direction but absent-mindedly made a wrong turn in the confusion of my distress. A miracle had happened to me. I realized it then without any doubt. The father, seeing his prodigal son, ran to meet me. I heard from the elder that all human sin was like a drop of water in comparison to the ocean of divine love. I left him, pardoned and reconciled, trembling and in tears. Feeling myself returned as on wings within the precincts of the Church. At the door of the chapel I met my surprised and delighted companion, who had seen me leave in a state of acute distress. . . . The next morning at the Eucharist I knew that I was a participant in the Covenant, that Our Lord hung on the cross and shed his blood for me and because of me; that the most blessed meal was being prepared by the priest for me, and that the gospel narrative about the feast in the house of Simon the leper and about the woman who loved much was addressed personally to me. It was on that day when I partook of the blessed body and blood of my Lord.[15]

So crucial to his understanding of the meaning of his life were these mileposts of his conversion that Bulgakov included them, anonymously, at the beginning of his 1917 study, *Unfading Light*. Yet another and perhaps the most moving of his autobiographical writings is also presented in this volume, again anonymously, but given its power, I think transparently. In summer 1909 the Bulgakovs lost their eldest son, Ivan, only three years old, to nephritis, a horrible experience for any parents, all the more unspeakable because of the agony of the child: his fever due to the infection, his pain and crying, and finally his death. In an "intimate letter," sometimes addressed directly to his dead child, the anguish of a young father and mother are particularly moving, as they experience the compassion of God through the bitterness of their child's suffering and death.[16] The child's suffering was a crucifixion, not only of his love for his son, but also of the very thought of God as love. Yet precisely here, where all of Christian faith appeared to be going over the edge into the abyss of pain and loss, Bulgakov describes the epiphany both he and his wife experienced. She blurts out that heaven has opened to take their boy. He admits that for the first time in his life he experienced God's love, not the self-absorbed love humans have, but that of Christ, which penetrates even the wall of feeling that cut him off from others. This was by no means the only time that Father Bulgakov would record the irruption of God into his life. During serious illness just after exile from Russia in 1921 in Crimea, he would write of his hope of experiencing the light of the Transfiguration, of seeing the Kingdom of God in power before his death.[17]

Return to the Father's House

As Williams describes it in his commentaries to his translations of several texts from Bulgakov, these years between roughly 1905 and 1917 were a time of tremendous ferment for Bulgakov.[18] Not only did he turn from Marxist thought and politics to a more reflective, although critical, position, he also "returned" in a profound and again critical way to the Church. Having broken with the desiccated scholastic theological training of the seminary of his youth, very much the "Babylonian Western captivity" later to be described by Florovsky, he deepened his reading not only of the Fathers but also of church history and of contemporary theological and philosophical writers such as Troeltsch, Harnack, and Maurice. He published essays on primitive Christianity and apocalyptic faith and socialism, became active in a Soloviev society in Moscow, and held a chair in political economy at Moscow University from 1906 to 1911, from which he resigned in protest over lack of academic freedom. In this period there was the profound influence of his friend Fr. Pavel Florensky, who was also teaching in Moscow and was the author of a radical effort in what might be called "symbolist" theology, *The Pillar and Column of Truth*.[19]

Another watershed was the 1909 publication of the now famous collection, *Vekhi,* in which Father Bulgakov and six others wrote about the position of Christian intellectuals in a Russian culture and society rapidly reaching the revolutionary boiling point. Williams has translated his contribution, a lengthy essay titled "Heroism and the Spiritual Struggle," in which the vague ideals of the intellectuals are rejected in favor of the modest, personal commitment of the individual, a path of conversion and commitment for which Bulgakov uses the traditional term for monastic obedience: *podvig*.[20] One can only wonder whether much later on Father Bulgakov's own student, defender, and frequent popularizer, Paul Evdokimov, was not moved by this description of the almost invisible ascetical dimension in everyday life to speak about the calling of all the baptized to a kind of "interiorized monasticism," no matter their actual status in life. Their common source is very likely in Dostoyevsky, in the figure of Aliosha in *The Brothers Karamazov,* the young, idealistic monastic novice sent back into ordinary life by his spiritual father, the exemplary Father Zossima.[21]

When Father Bulgakov was forced to leave Russia in 1923, his exile took him first to the Crimea, then briefly to Constantinople, then to Prague, where a substantial émigré community had gathered. It was in the mid-1920s that he began active priestly work with the Russian Christian Students Movement and taught at the Russian Law Institute, opened as a kind of university-in-exile in Prague with support from many Czechoslovak intellectuals, President Tomas Masaryk not the least of them. When a theological school was to be opened in Paris, Metropolitan Evlogy, exarch of the Russian Orthodox diocese in western Europe, asked Father Bulgakov to serve as a professor of theology and assume the office of dean of what would become the St. Sergius Theological Institute. This he did in 1925, and the first graduating class, which included Evdokimov, arrived in 1928.

Father Bulgakov would spend the rest of his life at St. Sergius, a fixture both in its classrooms and most especially in the chapel, formerly the chapel of a German Lutheran Mission in Paris. He and his family lived in a tiny faculty apartment on the grounds. He attended and gave papers at ecumenical conferences of the WCC in Lausanne, Oxford, and Edinburgh. In 1927 he was a cofounder of the new ecumenical association between the Orthodox Church and the Anglican Church, the Fellowship of St. Alban and St. Sergius. He also traveled to the United States in 1934 at the invitation of the Episcopal Church, lecturing at Columbia University and Seabury-Northwestern Seminary in Evanston, Illinois, and visiting many other Orthodox and Western parishes in between.[22]

In his nineteen years in Paris Bulgakov produced an unbelievable series of books, beginning with *Peter and John* (1926), *Icons and Their*

Veneration (1931), and *The Orthodox Church* (1935), which was trans-
lated immediately into French and English as a primer for Western
Christians. *The Wisdom of God* (1937), a synopsis of his approach to
Sophia written in his own defense, was also published in English and
French. Then there is the smaller trilogy—*The Burning Bush,* on the
Mother of God; *The Friend of the Bridegroom,* on Saint John the
Baptist (1927); and *Jacob's Ladder* (1929), on the angels—as well as
the great trilogy—*The Lamb of God* (1933), on Christ; *The Comforter* (1936), on the Holy Spirit; and *The Spouse of the Lamb,* on the
Church, published posthumously in 1945. Also posthumously published was *The Johannine Apocalypse* (1948). In addition to writing
and lecturing and other public engagements, Father Bulgakov was
a much sought after confessor and counselor. From 1939, Father
Bulgakov was deprived of his full speaking voice, having had his
vocal chords removed because of cancer of the throat.[23] Somehow he
was able to develop an audible whisper that enabled him to continue
teaching, although he was allowed to celebrate an early morning
daily liturgy, with a small group of friends, family, students, and
spiritual children participating. As dean and professor he taught and
shaped an entire generation of theological students at St. Sergius,
many of whom served as priests and bishops in the Church.[24] What
he accomplished in the last two decades of his life, despite great illness, poverty, attacks on his writing, and other deprivations, is truly
remarkable.

A "Living Icon"

Fr. Sergius Bulgakov is an icon in many ways. He is an image of
Russia, from the years leading up to the revolution to the present.
All of the tensions and contradictions of rebellion and conservatism,
love for tradition and creativity, conflict and openness, reverence for
a person and vicious attack on one—all these are found in and
around him. He left the faith in which he was raised, in revolt against
its inability to respond to the questions of both his head and his
heart, only to return to Christian tradition as an adult, slowly wend-
ing his way back as a pilgrim. His adherence to the Church's Tradi-

tion was complete but not blind or legalistic. He found precisely within the Tradition the creativity and dynamism that enabled the gospel of the Kingdom to meet every age and every circumstance still as the gift of freedom and peace and joy. Yet in sharing this almost unbelievable openness of Christian faith to the world, he immediately encountered the rigidity of those for whom Christianity was an enclosed and set system. For the most part his conflict was with his fellow Russian Orthodox émigrés, but he faced off more than once with Protestants, particularly at the ecumenical conference at Lausanne in 1927 and on the importance of the Mother of God. In what Valliere sees as his effort to place Orthodox Christianity "in dialogue with modern civilization," his attempt to understand the "humanity of God" effected in the Incarnation, Father Bulgakov found himself charged with heresy at worst and pitied for useless theological speculation and "system building" at best, even by friends and supportive colleagues.[25] It is hard to understand how a theologian who had written so much, who had been so active in ecumenical work and in the students' movement and more broadly in both émigré and French intellectual life, was forgotten so quickly and so totally ignored in the half century or more since his death.

The closer one looks, the clearer it becomes that Bulgakov represents not only the Russia he had to leave in forced exile but also in many ways the conflicted situation of the Church in the twentieth century, of the Christian in the modern age. St. Seraphim of Sarov may indeed be an image of the transformations a soul must pass through, the transcendence of all categories and positions, the simple and direct humanity that that true holiness looks like. Perhaps Father Bulgakov, teacher of the Church, faithful pastor and saint though he most certainly is, serves as an image of the other, the struggling side of this "new being," of the "hidden holiness" of our time. He both agitated for change and became the victim of the forces he sought to incite. Sadly, he is little known or read today, despite the towering achievement of his writing. Even less known is his life of prayer and priestly service, a radiance of holiness long since overshadowed by condemnations, most of them without grounds, of his theological work. The reputation of being attacked and even condemned for his writings raises the nagging question of Father Bulgakov's status not

only among theologians, but generally in the Orthodox Church.
Deans of the two prominent Orthodox theological institutions in the
West recently addressed these issues.

Father Bulgakov and the Deans

In a long tribute published on the centenary of Father Bulgakov's
birth in 1971, the then dean of St. Vladimir's Theological Seminary,
Fr. Alexander Schmemann, left his estimation in "three images."[26]
Having entered St. Sergius as a student during the last four years of
Bulgakov's life, Father Schmemann remembered him as a priest, as a
man of prayer, and finally as celebrant of the liturgy. In all of these
his gifts as confessor, counselor, and preacher are reverently evoked;
even his personal holiness, his communion with the other realm, the
Kingdom, is depicted without embarrassment, this last aspect a monumental and rare thing for the always unsentimental opponent of
ostentatious piety that Father Schmemann was. Yet it is telling that
none of the "images" are of Father Bulgakov as teacher or scholar.
Father Schmemann devotes substantial space to this, concluding, as
would another dean decades later, that Bulgakov's work had yet to
experience serious study and evaluation, something he hoped would
occur in the future. For himself, though, the central element of Sophia
was completely unnecessary for the accomplishment of Father Bulgakov's overarching aim, namely, the meditation on the Incarnation
in all aspects of life and culture. The authentic source of all his theology, as Father Bulgakov himself stated it, was the eucharistic
chalice, that is, the Eucharist, communion with Christ in the liturgy.
For Father Schmemann, his teacher's authentic sanctity and greatest theological contribution was to be found there, in the sacrament
of the Kingdom. After his operations for throat cancer, when Father
Bulgakov celebrated the liturgy early each morning at a side altar, an
icon of Holy Wisdom, by his spiritual child, Sister Joanna Reitlinger,
hung above him. Sister Joanna, in her memoir of his last days, recalls the intensity of prayer by both celebrant and congregation at
these early morning services. It was during the Nazi occupation of
Paris, a time of terror, killing, and many great privations. Father

Schmemann recalls that Father Bulgakov was clad in lightweight white vestments, because of his health. Juliana Schmemann recalls the extraordinary qualities of these 7:00 A.M. liturgies. His hoarse whisper was audible enough for those attending to make the usual responses. Father Schmemann, then a seminarian, regularly attended. He noted that Father Bulgakov's style was not a model of elegance, but even in his stiff, sometimes abrupt gestures it was possible to glimpse something of the very origins of this liturgical worship, stemming all the way back to the priests of the Old Testament:

> He did nothing but follow the well-established ritual, traditional in all its details, yet one had the impression that the liturgy was being celebrated for the first time, descending from heaven and reaching earth and the dawn of time. The Bread and Chalice on the altar, the candles' flames and incense smoke, the hands raised in prayer to heaven: all of this was not just a "service." There was something of a unity with all of creation, something pre-eternal, cosmic, what the words in the liturgy "awesome and glorious" suggest. It was not by accident, it seems to me, that Father Sergius' writings were weighted down with the very language of the liturgy, Slavonicisms, so often vibrating with liturgical praise. For his theology, at its very depths, was precisely and above all litur-gical, the revelation of an experience received in divine worship, the transmission of this mysterious "glory" which pervades all of liturgy, of the "mystery" in which it is rooted and of which it is an "epiphany." The manifestation of God but also of the world such as God created it, of the divine origins of creation, destined to be filled with God, when God will be "all in all."[27]

The best pages of his thousands, Father Schmemann concluded, were not those attempting to define Wisdom, by nature incapable of defi-nition, not those that dealt with this "hypostasis" of God, but the sentences and paragraphs that reflected the light and joy of his experience and of his liturgical vision. All of the thousands of pages of dense, "mystical lyricism" of Father Bulgakov's grand theological "system" was, in Schmemann's opinion, his own "fall" and but the Pyhrric victory of so much German idealism, so much Hegel and

Marx and other theorists covering over the true gifts of theology
Father Bulgakov had received at the altar, in prayer, from the Bible,
like some kind of camouflage.

Almost twenty-five years later, Fr. Boris Bobrinskoy, present
dean of St. Sergius Theological Institute where Father Bulgakov also
served as dean and professor, held this enigmatic "Russian Origen,"
as Father Bulgakov has been called, in one of the most positive contemporary assessments. In the annual academic convocation lecture
there, he straightforwardly acknowledged not only Bulgakov's theological brilliance and creativity, but refered to him as the "visionary
of Wisdom," the very element for which he was so vehemently attacked.[28] It would be useful to have Father Bobrinskoy's nuanced,
deft French text also in English, for he is able to pinpoint some of the
most neuralgic aspects of the never concluded, never clarified debate
about what Father Bulgakov really intended by the centrality of
Sophia in his writing, both the Divine uncreated Sophia and the created Sophia, the very action and presence of God throughout creation.

Perhaps, Father Bobrinskoy implies, precisely in the difficulty of
finding exact language and precise boundaries in the Holy Wisdom
in Father Bulgakov's writings that we arrive at the ineffability of the
encounter between God and creation. Just as it is impossible to ex-
haustively define the Incarnation, so too it is equally impossible to
define the nature of God's relationship with his creation. Consider
that in the Old Testament this relationship is expressed in the pil-
lars of fire and cloud in the Exodus, in the fire and smoke on Mount
Sinai, in the mercy seat and Ark of the Covenant in the Tabernacle
and later in the Temple at Jerusalem. The Lord reveals himself constantly, not only through his "word," spoken by his prophets, but
also through the instructions and deeds of angelic messengers. Then
there is the figure of Wisdom in Proverbs and other of the sapiental
literature, seemingly at once a created manifestation of God but
described also as the personalization, one might say a kind of pre-
incarnation of God among humankind. One cannot simply attack
Father Bulgakov for what was already in the Old Covenant, a rich,
complex, and mysterious figure, that of Wisdom.

Father Bobrinskoy quite rightly then underscores that what Father Bulgakov was struggling to express is the inexpressible, that
which can only be communicated in the icons, in the sacraments, in

the liturgical texts, chants, and sacred space such as the sweep of the dome of Hagia Sophia in Constantinople. In the icon of Holy Wisdom one can say, as astute commentators including Eugene Trubetskoy and Paul Evdokimov have, that "two worlds" intersect, or better collide. In the mysterious purple of the even more mysterious figure of Wisdom in the Novgorod icon, is neither darkness nor light.

> In its ultimate fullness, the icon represents the economy of salvation, God's Wisdom in its totality. The purple places us at the "beginning," at the source of creation. It is thus the first statement of the Bible: "Let there be light." It is the preeternal dawning, and this explains the color purple that rises up above the abyss still without life or light. From this abyss, God draws out being.[29]

The color is mysterious, as are the figure of Wisdom in this well-known icon and the halting, struggling words not only of Father Bulgakov but also of Paul Evdokimov, his student. Their efforts are to describe the indescribable but nonetheless palpable presence of God in creation. Holy Wisdom is also associated with Christ, with the Woman of the Apocalypse, clothed with stars, with the Mother of God, and with the Church, and all of these suggest that for Father Bulgakov there was never any question of posing a fourth person of the Trinity, of creating a dogmatic novelty but of a prayerful contemplation on the Shekinah, the glory of the Lord alive in the world: At most this was theological opinion, mystical pondering, and nothing worthy of the accusation of heresy.

Father Bulgakov's intellectual and spiritual quest, Father Bobrinskoy asserts, led him to the very peaks of the most inaccessible divine mysteries, to a vision that in fact Saint Benedict and Saint Gregory Palamas, among others, were given of the penetration of all the cosmos, of all of creation by the life, the energy, the being of God which cannot be seen or described. Perhaps, he says further, using the very words of Vladimir Lossky, the author of the pamphlet that condemned Father Bulgakov in 1936, the Holy Spirit "who cannot be seen except in another person, who hides himself, concealing even his own appearance" might be the key to grasping the *kenōsis,* the self-emptying, the hiding of Divine Wisdom in creation. With others who were students of Father Bulgakov, Father Bobrinskoy echoes

the more forgiving feeling of even Vladimir Lossky toward the end
of his life, namely, that eventually "the polemics about sophiology
would one day find a denouement in the work of another generation
of theologians."[30]

The other dean who has at least in print taken on the work, if not
the person, of Bulgakov is Fr. Thomas Hopko, dean of St. Vladimir's
Seminary. First, in his introduction to the revised translation by
Lydia Kesich of Bulgakov's classic, *The Orthodox Church,* he enu-
merates what he believes are examples of Bulgakov's errors, much
like the young Vladimir Lossky.[31] Although in the introduction as
a whole he praises Father Bulgakov's optimism and fidelity to Christ,
the Church, and the Tradition, he nevertheless must also provide
summary identifications, with little elaboration, of several respects
in which Father Bulgakov was "mistaken." These include his chapters on the sacraments and liturgical services that Father Hopko
fears those grounded in Father Schmemann's renewal of liturgical
theology will find disappointing and shocking, largely because of
the Western influence they exhibit, possibly also the illustrative
symbolism attached to specific parts of the eucharistic liturgy. The
admittedly brief account, often extremely descriptive, that Father
Bulgakov was providing essentially for Western readers unfamiliar
with the liturgical practice of the Eastern Church may account for
his reliance on the symbolic approach, stated in terminology with
which Westerners would be more familiar rather than the internal
evidence and interpretation from the liturgy itself. Certainly less
elegant than Schmemann's, nevertheless Bulgakov's chapters are of a
catechetical nature and nowhere as problematic as other scholastic
texts of either Russian or Western production. But it is Bulgakov's
eschatological and apocalyptic musings, characterized as a "type of
Christian universalism," that cause greater problems for Hopko.[32]
From his criticism it would appear that Father Bulgakov did not
comprehend correctly the Fathers' opinions about God's mercy and
love being experienced as torment by the damned, who inflict on
themselves sorrow and pain because they choose not to accept God
and his compassion. But one wonders whether Father Bulgakov's
reflections on the *apokatastasis,* the merciful raising of all creation
by God after purification, has been considered here in its radicalism

but as others such as Olivier Clément and Evdokimov stress, *not so much as doctrine* but as the object of prayer, of hope, and of reflection. Suffice it to say that the idea of universal salvation has always been a matter of contention in the Church, but nothing prevents one from at least contemplating and praying about it.

More recently and again paradoxically, Father Hopko assessed Father Bulgakov's significance and errors in response to an essay by Myroslaw Tataryn.[33] He lists individuals who either attacked or ignored Father Bulgakov's theology—from academic figures such as Serge Verhovskoy, Vladimir Lossky, and Florovsky, who published critiques or attacked him in the classroom, to Meyendorff and Schmemann, who rejected him mostly by avoiding mention of him in their writings and teaching, to Sophie Koloumzine, the noted leader in Christian education, who in her youth had Father Bulgakov as a spiritual father and whose sole response to his effort to explain his work was the idea that it was unnecessary. The marshaling of these figures along with the claim that Father Bulgakov's thought has had little or no influence on Orthodox or any other theology, that the response from his own Orthodox theologians has been either to attack or to ignore him—all of this seems to be a rather heavy-handed response. Furthermore, it sounds extremely curious in light of Father Hopko's apparent recognition of Father Bulgakov's greatness. And once again Father Hopko feels it necessary to point out both Father Tataryn's and Father Bulgakov's errors, this time in the understanding of *kenosis.* Perhaps the nearly contradictory attitude here is symptomatic of the reaction to Father Bulgakov within the Eastern Church. Valliere also observes such ambivalent responses, over the years, to Father Bulgakov's work.[34]

However, all these deans of Orthodox theological seminaries, whatever their individual approaches, hold up Father Bulgakov as a true treasure of the Church, regrettably painted with accusations of heresy, even more sadly (and unjustly) ignored by subsequent generations of scholars, teachers, and students within the Church. The West cannot be blamed for this, as so few of the recognized giants of Orthodox theology in this century are well known. More often than not it has been scholars of the West, such as Jaroslav Pelikan, Paul Valliere, Kris Groberg, and Robert Slesinski, who have explored the genius and contributions of the thinkers of the Russian emigration. Even given the scope of Russian studies, however, the volume of publications is not overwhelming.[35]

By Jacob's Well

Father Bulgakov's openness to the modern world, especially to the cultures and the churches of the West, was a distinctive feature of his life, and this receptivity became the mark of others around him in the Russian emigration, though by no means all. He participated in ecumenical conferences at Lausanne (1927) and Edinburgh and Oxford (1937), delivering a highly controversial paper at Lausanne on the necessity of the place of the Mother of God in liturgy and theology.[36] The same instincts led him to be a founding member of the new interchurch association the Orthodox belonged to, the Fellowship of St. Alban and St. Sergius. As in the gatherings of the Russian Christian Students Movement, so too in that of the Fellowship, Father Bulgakov sought to define the identity and work of each group as ecclesial, by organizing the meetings around the cycle of liturgical services, the Divine Liturgy of the Eucharist being at the very center of every day's activities. At meetings of the Fellowship from the outset, the Eucharist was celebrated each morning, using alternatively the Anglican and Orthodox rites and upon the same altar in the chapel of the retreat house at St. Albans. From these much smaller instances of "churching" would later come the adoption of celebrating the Eucharist using various of the rites of the represented churches (Lutheran, Orthodox, Anglican, Reformed) at meetings of the Ecumenical Conference in Amsterdam in 1939 and then in succeeding meetings in the postwar period.[37]

Always a "pioneer," as Zernov characterizes him, in the midst of this period and surely based on the Spirit-filled liturgical and communal experiences of both the Russian Christian Students Movement and the Fellowship, Father Bulgakov began to focus also on the issue of the deeper ecclesial communion (*koinōnia*) of apparently divided Christians. This article, "By Jacob's Well," appeared in 1933 both in *The Restoration of Christian Unity* and in English translation in the *Journal of the Fellowship of St. Alban and St. Sergius*.

Almost seventy years later, it remains both a stunning example of Father Bulgakov's fundamental understanding of Christian faith, the Church, sacraments, and Christian life and a continuing lightning rod for conflict and controversy. For Father Bulgakov, the present situation of divided churches places us by Jacob's well, where to a woman *outside* of the Jewish ecclesial community, a Samaritan, Christ affirms that the time has come when true worship will take place, neither on the Samarian mountain nor in the Temple at Jerusalem but "in spirit and in truth" will the Father be worshiped (John 4:21–23). He contrasts this wondrous word of Christ about the Church universal with the "harsh, unbending, unrelenting institutionalism of the one saving Church here," a contradiction of the freedom of the Spirit who "blows wherever he pleases" (John 3:8). One would expect then the immediate wall of separation, the economy of distance to be put forward: *extra ecclesiam nulla salus,* the Orthodox Church is the one and only true Church.

Father Bulgakov asserted this in his principal catechetical work, *The Orthodox Church,* but here he raises an astonishing claim.

> There exists between the Church and the Churches not only a relationship of mutual expulsion but also one of concordance. This unity is simultaneously something already given and something we must attain to. No single historical Church can so confine its attention to itself alone as to ignore the Christian world beyond its own limits. Even heresies and schisms are manifestations taking place only within the life of the Church—for pagans and men of other faiths are not heretics and schismatics to us. One can picture differently the ways to Church unity, but its very existence already assumes the fact of actual unity. The Church is one, as life in Christ by the Holy Spirit is one. Only, participation in this unity can be of varying degrees and depths.[38]

Tragically, it is not primarily a love for the Church and a truly ecclesial love that impels Christians. In both East and West there is also the continuing will for division. Father Bulgakov said this in 1933, but it holds true today. Yet what he confesses here is that the Spirit still keeps even those who have been divided from one another by doctrine, worship, history, and other factors in at least a partial unity with each other. He details quite specific examples of this: unity in public and personal prayer, in the Creed and the Word of God, in the spiritual life, the union with Christ, even in the sacraments. Rules of the Church, that is, conciliar decrees of the fourth and fifth centuries that prohibited divided Christians from praying with each other, "have not been canceled formally, although life itself cancels them." What were measures formerly of defense now have nothing from which to defend the Church. Rather, Father Bulgakov argues, there is the miracle of numerous relationships among all kinds of Christians: marriages, friendships, and the miracle of the "great joy which is bestowed on us in our time by the Holy Spirit and a new revelation of the universal Pentecost." "Faith in Our Lord, love for him, worship directed to him"—these are realities by no means restricted to any one Christian community.[39]

Increased awareness of this weighs on us in the modern era, when older forms of separation are disappearing. In a groping, hopeful, but unsure manner Christians in the twentieth century have begun to work with one another, study together, and pray together. When we lift ourselves to Christ in prayer we are one with him. How then can earthly barriers still divide us? Some barriers remain. Some are merely matters of custom and language, others deeper, such as the veneration of the Mother of God and the saints that still divides Protestants from Catholics and the Orthodox. However, in time, Father Bulgakov felt, even such obstacles would begin to erode.

There was for Father Bulgakov no surer sign of the breaking down of hostile walls of division than the sense of oneness in Christ too powerful and beautiful to describe, and this was experienced numerous times in these infant days of ecumenical contact. Father Bulgakov specifically mentions the sense of a new Pentecost felt by those at the 1927 Lausanne conference, a spiritual communion before there was any possibility of shared eucharistic communion. He was by no means the only one to note this overwhelming presence of the Spirit in these gatherings. Others who participated—Zernov, Evdokimov, Behr-Sigel, Mother Maria Skobtsova, Father Lev, Basil Zenkovsky—echo his profound experience of something new, good, and beautiful happening as Christians who were formally divided gathered to pray, study, and converse. Later Evdokimov would make the phrase "ecumenical epiclesis" part of his theological vocabulary.

Father Bulgakov further pointed, almost exactly like the metropolitans Filaret and Platon and Father Lev, to the way in which the saints of the East, for example, Sts. Seraphim of Sarov and Sergius of Radonezh, had become gates into Orthodox spirituality, just as in the Russian emigration, Genevieve of Paris and Francis of Assisi had become bridges to the Western tradition. The communion of saints in heaven is not divided by schisms and heresies but national or other delineations. There is no appeal to sentimentality here, no social or political agenda for unity either, no arguments for conserving resources and avoiding duplication. Neither does Father Bulgakov pretend there are no doctrinal disagreements among Christians. It is, I think, crucial that his first and most basic approach to the unity of the Church is precisely that of the principle, *lex orandi, lex credendi.* Even the acts of councils in defining what is and what is not believed come only after liturgical prayer and in the continuation of the same. His colleague, the church historian Anton Kartashev, concurred that there was no precedent for theological debate and negotiation as means of reconciliation. He was one of the few to support Father Bulgakov's second radical proposal in "By Jacob's Well," that eucharistic communion could be a means toward the restoration of unity, not just its final goal.[40] The proposal was specifically that Christians who recognized their unity in faith and with the blessing of bishops of their churches could share in the Eucharist. Father Bulgakov had in mind here the members of the Fellowship of St. Alban and St. Sergius and most likely participants at other ongoing ecumenical conferences, that is, Christians whose common prayer, study, and work powerfully drew them to actual unity in faith and therefore communion in the holy things. They would serve as a "kernel," a kind of seed from which further unity among divided Christians could grow. In a different way, a student of both, Paul Evdokimov, would argue that only the heart that could sing the Virgin's "Yes" to the angel and chant her *Magnificat,* a "liturgical being," could overcome the academic-dogmatic *non possumus:* "we are not able."

Hesitation, fear, and pointed opposition, however, from both Western and Eastern sides dashed this proposal. Father Lev salvaged from "Jacob's Well" Father Bulgakov's idea of a "spiritual communion,"[41] and the Fellowship developed prayers for this when one could not receive at a eucharistic celebration. Reaction then, as now, was sharp. But should the very idea be dismissed as heretical, disorderly, completely without precedent or merit? Almost thirty years later, Fr. Nicolas Afanasiev, another student and colleague of Father Bulgakov, by the 1960s a professor at St. Sergius and a widely known proponent of the early church's eucharistic ecclesiology, would present a radical reading of the divided Church and the restoration of unity in a manner resonant of Father Bulgakov's boldness. In an essay dedicated to the memory of Pope John XXIII, the "pope of love," he would argue that there is no one, exhaustive stance on the great schism and the nature of the non-Orthodox churches in Orthodoxy. Despite the *Filioque,* the development of papal authority into a universal rather than local and symbolic-servant ministry, despite later doctrinal expressions such as the Immaculate Conception and the Assumption, the Churches of the East and that of Rome in the West remained "churches." More recently this has been expressed as "sister churches." This term has been used despite hostile reactions by some Orthodox bishops and theologians. Most recently it was central in the much attacked Balamand Statement and has been used consistently by Ecumenical Patriarch Bartholomew I and Pope John Paul II, among other bishops and theologians. The conviction that the Orthodox and Catholics are sister churches is rooted, again, not in mere sentiment but in the "given unity" Father Bulgakov spoke of, a unity that at least in part continued after division in prayer, in faith, in the creed, in the Scriptures, in the saints and the spiritual communion with God, and even in the sacraments. All too often it is the dogmatic differences to which Christians are sensitive. The unity in the faith they continue to share is overlooked, deemphasized, perhaps explained away. Father Bulgakov went as far as claiming that in our time there were no longer heretics in the general sense of the term, namely, those who specifically denied the Trinity or the christological dogma in principle. Perhaps here there has been slippage since the time of his writing. Yet, he was quick to point out, very much in a patristic manner, many who were nominally Orthodox were in practice heretical, acting out one or another of the ancient heresies. When Christianity is so cut off from life that existence becomes secularized, is this not a form of Manichaeanism? Is it not only possible but also actual that Christ's humanity is forgotten in favor of his divinity?

And perhaps in this sense it will be found that we all are heretics in various ways. Yet it by no means follows from this that Orthodoxy and the Orthodox do not exist. It only shows that heresy, as such, impairs though it does not destroy life in Christ and in his Church. The notion of heresy, as of a division, only exists within the limits of the Church and not outside it, and it implies a defectiveness in Church life . . . for even the heretics remain in the Church, and it is not given to us to know to what degree they are condemned because of their heresy.[42]

Even with respect to the sacraments, Father Bulgakov warns against "confessional fanaticism," which would deny the presence of Christ and power of the Spirit and hence the validity or reality of the sacraments outside of Orthodoxy, in either the Catholic Church or those of the Reformation. Although he does not mention it in the essay, there is ample precedent in the Fathers, Basil the Great and Augustine in particular, for this generous understanding of the Church's extensive reach and for the conviction that God transcends not only the canons but even the sacraments. In practical terms, the more rigorous ecclesiology of St. Cyprian was countered by the actions of St. Basil and others in reconciling bishops, priest, and laity who had gone into schism in their times. While it may be that some of the Reformation churches lack bishops in apostolic succession, others retain this, and following theologians such as Bishop Theophanes, we have no right to flatly declare the sacraments of another church to be ineffective, lacking in divine grace. Christ does not divide himself, nor does he "deprive this flock of his grace although it has been separated from the fullness of Church life."[43]

Perhaps the hope expressed by Fathers Bobrinskoy, Hopko, and Schmemann concerning serious study of Father Bulgakov is beginning to be fulfilled. Rowan Williams has not only provided several of Bulgakov's writings for the first time in English, but along with them has crafted a study of Bulgakov, his person and ideas, that is perceptive and critical.[44] Fr. Michael Meerson has produced a farreaching review of the renaissance of theological thought of which Bulgakov was a part, and Catherine Evtuhov has probed the earlier part of Bulgakov's intellectual development.[45] Yet undoubtedly Paul Valliere's masterful study of Russian theology in the modern era is the most important contribution.[46] The almost two hundred pages he devotes to Bulgakov's life and principal writings constitute the most concentrated study in any language of Bulgakov, even if it does not submit Bulgakov's most controversial ideas about Divine Wisdom to exhaustive criticism. Valliere identifies the principal aim of Bulgakov's theological work: namely, to bring biblical faith and Christian tradition into conversation with modern experience and the modern world. It is not so much an effort to trim tradition of that which offends its contemporary critics as a profound and creative effort to allow the Tradition to speak with power in the present age as it had in earlier historical periods. In particular for the Eastern Church, whose theological productivity and creativity had been stunted from the end of the medieval period, Bulgakov sought to demonstrate that tradition which is explored, prayed, debated is alive. He sought to examine arguably the core doctrine of the Incarnation in ways previously unexplored, namely to follow the implications of God's entering into time, space, and human bodily existence, the "humanity of God." And he attempted to assess the full, positive meaning of the christology of the Council of Chalcedon not only for God but for human beings as well. In short, when the assessment of theology in the modern era is made, the insight and creativity of Father Bulgakov, despite his shortcomings, rank him with the other masters of our time, such as Tillich, Barth, and Rahner. Finally, Antoine Arjakovsky has sketched Bulgakov's importance for Western theology and the impact of his focus on Divine Wisdom in a perceptive recent lecture.[47]

Holiness: A Longing for the Kingdom

Here again is a claim that is audacious but rings with the freshness, the freedom, and the goodness of the Kingdom. I think Father Bulgakov's unreserved zeal for the unity of the Church lay neither in his mastery of Scripture, the Fathers, or church history nor in his deft scholarship in philosophy and theology but in his eschatological experience and perspective. This is not to make of him some stereotypic wonder worker or visionary but to underscore what has been said of him by many who knew him.[48] He is remembered foremost as a priest, as one who radiated the love of Christ in his ministry, whether celebrating the liturgy, hearing confessions, counseling, teaching, or writing. They saw in him something of the Kingdom, his life and work a living sign of the gospel. In his published autobiographical notes, as several earlier citations make clear, Father Bulgakov very often encountered the power and the beauty of that "other world," which is the new age, the Kingdom. So many of his writings conclude with the cry of the Book of Revelation and the early Church: *Maranatha,* Amen. Come, Lord Jesus. Another colleague compared him to the great paintings and sculptures that both loved, so beautiful that they seemed to be transparent, with only what is good, what is love, shining through.[49]

If this was so evident, even to opponents and critics of his thought during his life, then the radiance, the almost Paschal character of death crowned this existence led in communion with God. Sister Joanna Reitlinger, one of those who cared for Father Bulgakov in the weeks before his death, wrote a memoir of his dying.[50] After celebrating the liturgy on June 5, 1944, the second day of Pentecost, the feast of the Holy Spirit, and the anniversary of his ordination, Father Bulgakov suffered a stroke. He was not discovered until the next morning, unconscious, by his son. He lingered in a state between consciousness and unconsciousness the last forty days of his life and finally died on July 12. Published after her death in 1988, Sister Joanna's recollections, written during the forty days and completed in London late in 1945 and early 1946, are a vivid chronicle not only of his dying but also of the life that led up to it.[51] Four women, Sister Joanna and two other nuns, Mothers Blandine and Theodosia, and E. N. Ossourgina, were his principal caregivers during this time, with family members and Fr. Kyprian Kern also visiting and keeping watch. There is no need to recount all the details she records. During his periods of near full consciousness, Father Bulgakov attempted to speak to them, much of the time successfully. He also tried to write, but his handwriting proved illegible.

Some five days after the stroke came the event that crowns the account. After what appeared to be a struggle and a mysterious conversation with someone unseen, Father Bulgakov's face, much like that of St. Seraphim of Sarov, became a "single mass of light." While describing this wonderful sight, which in its most intense manifestation lasted several hours, Sister Joanna did not hesitate to call it the "unfading light," the title of his early work and a name that evoked the "Gladsome Light" sung of at vespers, Christ, the light of the world.

This account and other memoirs were kept undisclosed for almost fifty years after Father Bulgakov's death. It draws heavily on the lives of the saints and the vocabulary of the liturgical texts, which see death as a "dormition," a falling asleep and passover, a Pascha into the arms of Christ, into the communion of saints, into the kingdom of heaven. Christ's own Pascha and that of the Mother of God are portrayed in the icons of those feasts and contemplated in the hymns and verse for the services of those days. Sister Joanna does what is perfectly natural for one who lived the year and her life in terms of those texts, and as an iconographer, she was shaped by the icons of the light in Christ's Resurrection and the Virgin's Dormition, that is, her death. Her account is neither sentimental hagiography nor a medical record. It is devoid of sensationalism, and much of the end of Father Bulgakov's earthly existence is framed by the wonders of his pastoral ministry, his joyfulness, his loving concern for others. It is not a coincidence that in photographs of him in the last years of his life there is more than a passing resemblance, not in details but in spirit and impression, to St. Seraphim. There is of course the pectoral cross both wore, the long hair and beard of the Russian priest. More than anything else, however, there is the sparkle in the eye, the gleam of the smile that envelopes the entire face, a joy about to burst forth in warm, loving greeting: "Christ is risen, my joy!"

In the end, Sister Joanna remembered much the same image that Father Schmemann did, an image of one who, in his busy life of teaching and writing, in his serving of the liturgy and ministry of confessing and counseling, was already living somewhere else, already in prayer breathing the air of the Kingdom, seeing it around him here and now. The theology school deans agreed when they said that whatever future scholarship would make of his "system," of all the books he wrote, the real fire burned in him as one who was "very much like . . . God." That Father Bulgakov kept this light alive, kindled at his baptism, given more fuel in his ordination, through personal sufferings, through forced immigration, great poverty, accusation and condemnation, and other small indignities he wrote about, is his singular miracle.

In as yet unpublished reminiscences of a number of figures of the Russian emigration, Fr. Basil Zenkovsky, who knew him for over forty years, leaves a complex and very human portrait of Bulgakov. Both his creativity as a thinker and his boundless compassion as a pastor are memorably sketched. So too, however, are his personal failings. Despite his great openness to ideas, there were limits to what he could incorporate in his thinking. There was also his inability to accept criticism, the self-understanding as an intellectual that distanced him from others, his difficulty in expressing affection for those close to him. Neither those who idolize Father Bulgakov nor those who dismiss him will be comfortable with the portrait. Yet it is the life and person we encounter in our time that I am aiming at profiling here.

In living an ordinary life extraordinarily, Father Bulgakov is the first living icon, an image of holiness in our time but not because he perfectly fit the mold of a Russian Orthodox saint. This he most certainly did not, and the very inclusion of him here will make this book unwelcome to some. For them, he will always be a "heretic" and perhaps a controversial theologian of the emigration, whose ruminations on Wisdom were at best dubious. Yet he was also grasped by another love.

> Orthodoxy seems somehow to have lost this [expectation and longing for the coming of Christ] not in dogma but in fact, under the overwhelming burden of its historical heritage. . . . Tradition has ceased to be "vital" and has become the depository of the faith, to be preserved but not developed creatively. Yet Orthodoxy demands not the mere possession of the inherited wealth of faith and life, but prophecy and apocalypse—a call and a promise. In this sense apocalypse implies a concern for the history of the present and the future as well as that of the past. The Church has no continuing city on earth but seeks one to come. Orthodoxy implies inspiration, the eros of the Church, her yearning for the

Bridegroom, the feeling proper to his Bride. It is creativeness directed toward the final goal, the expectation of the End. It is not cowardly fear of life and flight from it but the overcoming of all givenness, the longing for a new heaven and a new earth, for a new meeting and life with Christ. All this is ineffable and sounds like music in the soul; it is like a symphony of colors, like art and poetry. It is an eager expectation of the promise. "Even so, come, Lord Jesus."[52]

CHAPTER FOUR

Maria Skobtsova

Woman of Many Faces, Mother in Many Ways

A Rich Life, a Complex Person

There are few figures in our time as radical, as unusual, and as complex and rich as Elisabeth Pilenko, who later in life, on her monastic tonsure, would become Mother Maria.[1] For all the unusual gifts she possessed—a poet's discernment, a revolutionary's passion, a mother's tenderness—she reveals most of all in her life the struggle to follow Christ, to put his gospel into practice, in short, to make holiness incarnate, real in human life. Born in 1891 in Riga to a family rooted in the Ukrainian aristocracy, she was a promising poet, a gifted amateur painter and craftsperson, a theological student in St. Petersburg when women studying theology were virtually unheard of. She became entangled in the revolutionary movement and frequented the literary circles gathered around the poets Alexander Blok and Vyacheslav Ivanov. She married impetuously when young, had a child, and then saw the breakup of this first impulsive relationship in divorce. During the turmoil of the revolution in Russia, she served as mayor of Anapa, her family's ancestral country village on the Black Sea. There she was put on trial by the retreating White Army for sympathizing with the Bolsheviks. Not long after, when the civil war had shifted in favor of the Bolsheviks, she was almost executed along with other alleged counterrevolutionary sympathizers and escaped only when she bluffed a close connection to Lenin's wife.

With thousands of others she made the exile journey west, and in circumstances of almost unbelievable poverty and discomfort managed
to reach Istanbul and then Paris. During the trip into exile, she married Daniel Skobtsov, who had been the military judge before whom
she was tried in Anapa. Two more children came from this marriage,
a daughter who was to die of meningitis as a child in Paris and a son
who was to die in the concentration camps with the last chaplain of
her hostel, Fr. Dimitri Klepinin.

> At the Last Judgment I will not be asked whether I satisfactorily
> practiced asceticism, nor how many prostrations and bows I have
> made before the holy table. I will be asked whether I fed the hun-
> gry, clothed the naked, visited the sick and the prisoner in jail.
> That is all I will be asked.[2]

Liza seemed to fit in nowhere in her time or world. Or perhaps
she fit in everywhere. She married impulsively, passionately. She
doted on her children, even if briefly. She experienced, as did many
other exiles, a poverty she had never known earlier in life. Liza was
drawn away from family and from intellectual life toward the many
suffering people around her in the Russian emigration. Trips osten-
sibly to give educational presentations almost immediately became
intimate exchanges of pain, encounters with the living dead. Instead
of cultural enrichment or fund-raising, Liza found herself doing
basic social work and spiritual care of a pastoral sort. But in her
Orthodox milieu there was no place for women to do diaconal work.
True, the widowed Duchess Elisabeth, only canonized in the last few
years by the Russian Orthodox Church, had formed a community
of nuns who cared for the ill and abandoned within Moscow in pre-
revolutionary days. However, the revolution swallowed her up as a
martyr, just as it consumed her community and the beginnings of
renewal in the Russian Church in the Great Council of 1917–18.
The only models of monastic life the new Mother Maria saw were
traditional convents that had escaped the revolution, in Estonia and
Latvia, and with these she had no identification. They seemed anach-
ronisms, indulgent luxury for which she had little sympathy while
there was such urgent need, such suffering. In fact, in the substantial
body of writing of various sorts that remains from her, the essays

about a new kind of Christian life, a new way of living out the gospel, and, in particular, new forms of monastic community form the most fascinating and yet most radical and threatening elements of her inheritance.

Thus, from her monastic profession in March 1932 and for the next twelve years until her arrest and deportation to the Ravensbrück concentration camp, where she would eventually die in the gas chambers, she lived an unusual existence as nun, diaconal worker, counselor, administrator of several residences, not to mention fundraiser, cook, and writer. Despite the hesitation of friends such as Nicolas Berdiaev and the young priest Lev Gillet, who was newly entered into the Orthodox Church and who would later be her chaplain, but with the blessings of both her spiritual father, Father Bulgakov and that extraordinary bishop of the Russian diocese in Paris, Metropolitan Evlogy, she fashioned in her own way what he had perceptively suggested. Her monastery became the world around her, so Metropolitan Evlogy would describe it in his memoirs. Her life became a *kenosis*. She was to establish several hostels for the homeless, the helpless, the ill and marginal in Villa de Saxe, Rue Lourmel, and Noisy-le-Grand, with support from a number of the leading figures of the emigration.

> Christ, in ascending to heaven, did not raise with himself the Church on earth. He did not halt the course of history. Christ left the Church in the world and the Church has remained as a small portion of the yeast which makes the entire dough raise. Put differently, within the limits of history, Christ has given the whole world to the Church and she has no right to refuse to spiritually lift the world, to transfigure it. And for this, the Church needs a powerful army, and this is monasticism.[3]

Two Loves

Mother Maria came to see that monastic life is nothing if not the incarnation of love for God and love for one's neighbor. In the very history of monasticism, she suggests, as the movement spread to different geographic areas, with different climates, cultures, languages, even foods, as a living reality monasticism adapted to its new environs. It found ways to flourish outside the deserts of the Near East and the provinces of the Byzantine empire. Lenten fare of the Mediterranean such as olives and hummus gave way to potatoes and "kapusta" (sauerkraut) in the North, just as palm branches became pussywillows.

> Put another way, today the monastic has to struggle for what is essential, for the very soul of monasticism, rather than the abstraction of the external forms of this life, creating new ones. . . . Monasticism is necessary but most especially on the road of life, at its very heart. In reality for the monk or nun, there is only the monastery of the whole world. Here is the "newness" of the "new monasticism," its meaning, cause and justification! And it is important for the monastic to grasp this quickly. There are many who must, despite their fear, become innovators. What is new here is not so essentially for the sake of novelty but because it is inescapable.[4]

Despite her largely negative response to monastics of the traditional style, Mother Maria did not have the time or the inclination to engage in extended theological criticism. It was her conviction that today they had become almost a luxury, inaccessible to most who were seeking God. It would be like the preferred treatment for, say, tuberculosis, she would write: a well-equipped sanitarium in the mountains, with plenty of fresh air, good food, exercise, and rest. Most of the immigrants and the working class in a time of economic decline who were suffering physically, emotionally, and spiritually had to content themselves with cramped, stuffy rooms in tenements, with meager, bad food, with all the other very real scourges of poverty and their consequences: abandoned spouses and children, alcoholism, depression.

So too with the Church in such times. Left here in the world by Christ, the Church is but a small morsel of the yeast that can raise the whole batch of dough. Christ has given the whole of the world and its history to the Church, Mother Maria asserted, echoing the thought of Soloviev and Berdiaev and her beloved Father Bulgakov. In both the time before Christ, that of the Old Covenant, and the "new age" inaugurated by his death, resurrection, ascension, and the Spirit's descent at Pentecost, all of creation, all the human world of society, institutions, culture, relationships was, in the divine plan, being "churched." This was the Russian's notion of *tservkovenlie,* the "churching" of life. How can the Church refuse to build up this world spiritually, to transfigure it? For Mother Maria, monasticism had been placed in the Church as a powerful corps, a veritable army to help in this transformation, not as a flight from an evil cosmos.[5]

For Mother Maria, the classical vows of obedience, chastity, and poverty professed by the monastic define monasticism, not the details of monastic life, the riassa or habit or number of services or buildings. Monastic practices are for her the "historical envelope," which can change, which always has but relative value as the means by which one lives out the monastic vocation in the vows.[6] Obedience promised to God and enacted toward a superior, particularly in Eastern monasticism to a spiritual father or mother, or *staretz,* will today be lived out also as obedient service to Christ through the work of the Church in the circumstances of modern life.[7] In particular, the monastic's vow of poverty, the wisdom of God, and the surprising way of the Kingdom will place the monastic in and with the poor of the world. It should be noted that Mother Maria's entire monastic experience was rooted in the chaos and suffering, the turmoil and poverty of the Russian emigration in France during the Great Depression and then in the occupation during World War II.[8] As in situations of the past, for example, the cases of many of the desert fathers and mothers and later that of Sergius of Radonezh, Nilus of Sora, and Francis of Assisi, monastics worked not only to support themselves but also to clothe, shelter, and feed the suffering.

For Mother Maria, poverty or "nonacquisition," should not be limited to the material plane but deepened. One who is materially poor can be a treasure source of spiritual gifts.[9] In fact, being "poor in spirit" is more precisely what is vowed by the monastic, and such is the sole pathway of the common life of the catholic entity that is the Church.[10] To be poor in spirit is to be able to say with Christ, "Father, into your hands I commend my spirit." The monastic does not preserve what is essentially safe in some kind of "interior cell" but in fact as the older saying has it, gives away what is essential, sacrificially, as did Christ on the cross.

All of this leads to one thing, the necessity of the monastic being active in the world outside[,] . . . in all forms of activity such as social work, and welfare, spiritual assistance[,] . . . consecrating his or her force to the work, to the humanity of Christ in others, not acquiring but dissipating, giving away recklessly for the glory of God.[11]

The title of the posthumous collection of Mother Maria's writings, *The Sacrament of the Brother,* accurately summarizes not only her view of the Christian life in general but also her passionate conviction about monasticism in the modern era. It is taken from St. John Chrysostom's saying that after the liturgy, there is another liturgy, celebrated not on an altar of stone or wood but on the altar of flesh and blood, that of our neighbor, hence the "sacrament" of the brother and sister.

"Types" of Religious Lives: "Synodal" Piety

A very similar, if even stronger, expression of what might be called Mother Maria's "agapic" vision both of Christianity and of monastic life is put forward in the unpublished manuscript from 1937 recently found in the archives of Sophie Pilenko, Mother Maria's mother, by Hélène Arjakovsky-Klépinine, "Types of Religious Lives."[12] Mother Maria was not only a gifted poet and critic of Russian literature but also an insightful student of theology. In this essay she prefaces her examination of various approaches to the Christian life by qualifying her methodology of identifying "types." An empirical individual might well find elements of several of the types in himself or herself. Further, the types she will inspect are specific, not only to Russian Orthodoxy, but also to various periods and events and their consequences. They are not exhaustive either. Yet having said this, there is the implication that the particular types investigated clearly have corresponding types in other faith traditions as well as cultures and historical situations. In other words, there is an eye here to universal categories of religiosity.

The "synodal" type is really a critique of the low level to which all aspects of ecclesiastical life sank in Russia from the time of Peter the

Great until just before the revolution, in the period of ferment and renaissance that culminated in the still understudied Great Sobor of Moscow in 1917–18, prematurely terminated by Bolshevik persecution and the violence and turmoil of civil war. Many today, not only Russians, will feel the pinch of Mother Maria's perceptiveness. There are her sketches of churches tucked into garages and private homes, makeshift iconostases and liturgical objects, and an almost indistinguishable line between Christianity and various forms of Russian culture: foods and feasts and other customs, monarchism, White Army loyalties, in short, nostalgia for a time and place both lost. But the fantastically opulent cathedrals, operatic choirs, window-rattling basso profundo deacons, encrusted altar vessels, gilt-covered icons, and damask vestments of the prerevolutionary era also fall within this type and her incisive analysis. So too does she write of what is even more tragic, of love for tradition turned into fanatic adherence to and obsession about minutiae of ritual and texts, of aggressive, almost violent hatred for anyone outside the self-determined parameters of "authentic" Orthodoxy.

In much of her painful depiction, faith has been amputated from the reality of human beings, liturgy ripped from life, God and neighbor left far from the demands of religion. Tradition became frozen in the synodal period and type of piety, sacraments and liturgy hardened into dead ritual, the married clergy a segregated and mistreated class, the celibate-monastic clergy even more an elite from which bishops were selected. The edifice of Russian Christianity, like the enormous bell of the tsars in the Kremlin, so large it could not be hung or rung, cracked too by premature cooling, was so immense and so officially connected to the state and to culture as to be lifeless and only an institution to many. The authentic life of the gospel, true, continued, but here and there in figures like Philaret of Moscow and Seraphim of Sarov, Tikhon of Zadonsk and John of Kronstadt. Faith also survived in a much more massive way in the local church, in the parish, and in the simple adherence of ordinary people to the services of the liturgical cycle and year, to the icons and feasts. Such a bloated, cultural Christianity or civil religion as the synodal piety also gave birth, Mother Maria emphasizes, to an "intense atheism," a massive exodus from Christianity, which in fact set the stage for the revolution. One thinks of the virtual loss of the Russian intelligentsia—

artists, scholars, politicians—to personal faith, the observance of ritual obligations throughout the year and one's life maintained for correct appearance and for civil order. It is also important to remember the return of so many alienated intellectuals in the first years of the century, of Bulgakov and Berdiaev and Frank and other contributors to the collection *Vekhi,* the renaissance of which Zernov has written. The synodal type of religiosity, she continues, was by no means restricted to the pre-Sobor years of churchly decline in Russia. It continues to "thrive" among the Russian emigration, particularly in the exclusive jurisdiction that in fact called itself the Karlovsky Synod, when it assumed the role of a church-in-exile from that left behind under Bolshevik rule and harassment in Russia.

"Ritualism": The Religion of Rubrics

In the "ritualist" type, Mother Maria identifies first the various ritualistic obsessions of the Old Believers, for example, their fixation on the number of fingers used in signing oneself with the cross, the number of times a liturgical chant was to be sung, the exact wording of the texts of the service books. These people did in fact preserve much that was precious in Church Tradition, one might say, despite their fetishes. One thinks for instance of their preservation not only of ancient icons but also of traditional methods in iconography over against the stylistic decadence of the 1600s on. But Mother Maria again extends her analysis from these "old ritualists" to the ritualist impulse of the wider Orthodox community. Every detail of worship is prescribed and every detail becomes as important, actually more important, than the whole action of prayer: the exact dimensions of the sign of the cross and depth of lesser and great bows and prostrations and when and how many times all these are to be made in church. It makes no difference if the text of the psalms or hymns being chanted are intelligible due either to their being in Church Slavonic or the speed of their execution, no matter that much of the eucharistic liturgy is recited in a whisper and behind closed doors and curtains of the iconostasis. The ritualist takes particular pride in the complexities of the services of the Lenten season and of Holy Week, is masterful in knowing the fasting rules and precise in cooking for them. Such ritualism is not without acts of love and goodness, special collections for the poor, baked goods for prisoners.

> But the basic motive for such activity is that it is prescribed, that it enters into the general rhythm of his life, it becomes a part of the ritualistic concept of things. In this sense he has a greatly developed feeling of obligation and obedience. Thus his relationship to a person is determined by a self-imposed obligation and not on a spontaneous feeling of love toward him. . . . This soul is not looking for a challenge—it is afraid of its unbearable burden, it can no longer either seek anything or become disenchanted. The severe and rarefied air of sacrificing love is beyond its strength. If life passed it by and gave it no external well-being, no external stability, then it turns toward an internal well-being with a special zeal, toward complete assurance and legitimacy of its inner world.[13]

Just a few lines after these, Mother Maria thinks out loud about the close connections between such a ritualist consciousness and the absolute dictatorship of "the Party," herself a former proponent of the revolution and nearly a victim of it too. The basic questions to be put to strict ritualism, however, are:

> How does it respond to both of Christ's commandments about love for God and love for people? Does it have a place for them? Where is there within it a person to whom Christ condescended? If it can be imagined that occasionally there is an expression of its own kind of love for God, it is difficult to see in what way it expresses itself in love for people. Christ, who turned away from scribes and Pharisees, Christ who went to sinners, prostitutes and publicans, can hardly be the teacher of those who are afraid to soil their pristine garments, who are completely devoted to the letter, who preserve only the statues and who govern their whole life by them. They consider themselves spiritually healthy because they observe everything that is prescribed by spiritual hygiene, but Christ told us, it is not the healthy that are in need of a physician, but the sick. Actually, today we have two citadels of such an Orthodoxy: traditional Orthodoxy, statutory, patristic and fatherly:

Athos and Valaam—a world removed from our fuss and our sins, a world of faithful servants of Christ, a world of God's way and contemplation.[14]

Why the nearly sarcastic mention of these two monastic centers by one who at the writing of this essay was a tonsured monastic herself?

And what do you suppose upsets this world of sanctity the most? Is it the present calamities, which are tearing us apart, the new teachings, heresies perhaps, the needs, the destruction and persecution of the Church, the martyrs in Russia, the trampling of belief throughout the whole world, the lack of love? Is this what alarms these islands of the elect the most, these summits of the Orthodox spirit? Not at all. What alarms them as the most important, the most vital and the most burning issue is the question of the New or Old Style in Divine Worship. This is what splits them into factions, for which they condemn those who think otherwise. . . . It is difficult to speak about love in light of all this since love somehow is outside of either the New or Old Style. . . . And there is something threatening and ominous here, precisely because in Athos and Valaam the ancient centers of traditional Orthodox spirituality, a person can find an answer only to one question out of all which are raised by life: whether the Church must live by the New or Old Style. Instead of the living God, instead of Christ crucified and risen, do we not have here a new idol, a new form of paganism which is manifested in arguments over calendars, rubrics, rules, prohibitions and the Sabbath which triumphs over the Son of Man. Idolatry in the world is frightening when it betrays Christ in the name of the state, the nation, the social idea, the petit-bourgeois conformity and well-being. Still more frightening is the idolatry within the Church when it replaces Christ's love with the preservation of the Sabbath.[15]

"Aesthetic" Piety

The richness of Mother Maria's analysis and its timeliness do not halt here, for there are still further "types" she proposes for reflection. In delineating the "aesthetic" type she reflects on the mixed character of human consciousness. While in Dostoyevsky's words "beauty will save the world," and beauty is of God, not all can appreciate it, not all express it identically. Thus we find the emergence of what might be called a connoisseurship of things sacred, of very specific settings of the parts of the liturgy, specific schools of composition, of iconography, architecture. Paradoxically, in the beginnings of a rebirth of faith in the early years of the twentieth century in Russia, with the cleaning and revealing of the icons of Andrei Rubliev and Theophanes the Greek, with the liturgical research of Skaballanovich and the writings of Andrei Grabar and Eugene Trubetskoy, there also developed an elitist aesthetic approach that, according to Mother Maria, "displaces the spiritual and eventually pushes out everything else." But such a type is by definition, by the immense amount of education and investment of time required, limited to a very few. However, those few are among the most influential, leaders not only in academic but also in ecclesiastical life. It is striking that, an artist herself, Mother Maria discerns in this aesthetic form a hidden block to any future development or creativity, whether in liturgical music, iconography, architecture, theological, or philosophical work. The best that can be expected is a kind of curatorial attitude, a preservationist mode to all that is material in Christian heritage and life. Once again there is estrangement of such an aestheticism from real life, from people torn apart by revolution, immigration, and poverty. They cry to Christ for mercy.

> But between Christ and the crowd will stand the preservers of Christ's seamless robe and will announce to the crowd that hate and struggle has distorted your faces, that your daily labors have destroyed your gift to admire beauty. But life itself is great beauty, which cannot be seen by those who have not been tested by it. Sweet singing, emotional chanting, the odor of incense, the beatific, semidormant sensation wrapped in beauty will cloud over the sorrowful image of Christ, will force the stifling of laments, will force heads to bow and force hope to be forgotten. For some this comfortable piety is a temporary lullaby; others will be repelled by it, leaving a great chasm between the Church and real life. The aesthetic custodians of that piety will guard that chasm

in the name of harmony, in the name of rhythm and order and beauty. The profane, secular ones, left on the other side, will not try to leap across the chasm because they will be left with pain, struggle, misery, the horrors of life, and they will stop believing that it is possible and necessary to come toward the Church even with such heavy baggage. . . . Perhaps those eyes capable of seeing love will be able to see how Christ himself comes out, quietly and invisibly, from the sanctuary of the altar, protected by a splendid iconostasis. The singing continues to resound, clouds of incense still rise; the faithful are overcome in their ecstatic contemplation of beauty. But Christ goes out to the church porch and mingles with the crowd of the poor, the maimed, the cast-off, the embittered, the holy fools. Christ goes to the streets, to prisons, to hospitals and into the shacks. Christ again and again gives his life for his friends. How can we compare our beauty and our ugliness to his eternal truth and beauty? Doesn't our idea of beauty look ugly compared to his eternal beauty? Or conversely, does he not deem his divine image, a reflection of eternal glory and beauty in our ugliness, in our miserable life, in our festering sores, in our crippled souls? He will return to the churches and bring with him all those called to the wedding banquet, gathered from the highways, the poor and the maimed, the prostitutes and the sinners.[16]

How vivid a description of the reckless love that Mother Maria herself put into practice in the hostels and the settlement houses she established—criticized both by fellow nuns and one of her chaplains, Father Kyprian, as well as the laity for her maverick monasticism, for sitting in cafés and bars late into the night talking with despairing people, for missing services in order to forage for food at the Les Halles markets and prepare it for the soup kitchens in her houses.

Relentless in her critique, Mother Maria will not leave the aesthetes alone as mere romantics and escapists. They are destructive in promoting an idolatry namely, "when the Church's splendor, beautiful singing, good order of services becomes an end in itself, displacing Christ himself." The aesthetes turn Christ's servants and successors to the apostles, the priests, into servants of the cult, that is, priests in the pagan meaning of the word. The clergy are not judged by their love for the flock, for the one lost of the ninety-nine, but for their singing voices, their knowledge of the *Typicon,* their smooth movements around the altar. How shocking it is, she reflects, when in Soviet Russia all is prohibited to the Church except the liturgical services and when this is the sum total of what fearful, suffering souls find in the church buildings and in the clergy and their fellow worshipers. In this case, where there is no love for an actual person, it would be better if services were banned outright and Christians would have to again discover catacomb existence.

"Ascetic" Obssession

The last of the types that Mother Maria holds up for critical scrutiny is the ascetic. There is nothing original or specifically Christian about asceticism, for it is to be found in Hinduism and Buddhism long before the appearance of Christianity. She proceeds to ask some probing questions about just this historically and anthropologically universal phenomenon, questions that are often avoided by Christians as if to spare their own tradition from careful self-scrutiny, questions that very recently Father Men posed in numerous lectures and articles and a massive series of books on the great world religious traditions. I will bypass this fascinating line of inquiry here.

Yet within the Christian tradition of asceticism Mother Maria identifies as fundamental the necessary struggle involved in attaining the kingdom of heaven, of the individual soul, the immense matter of "my" salvation. Throughout the ascetic literature it is possible to follow this central theme not so much as a thread but as the core, the axis, the entire purpose of the Christian life. Anything and everything else is and must be made secondary. If actions are performed, even to help others, it is essentially out of obedience and for the salvation of *my* soul, whether

I clean out stables, dig for potatoes, look after leprous persons, collect alms for the Church or preach Christ's Gospel—I must do all these things with the same conscientious and attentive effort, with the same humility and detachment, because all these things are tasks and exercises which enable me to curb my will, a difficult and rocky road for the soul seeking salvation. I must constantly exercise virtues and thus I must perform acts of Christian love, but that love must reflect obedience, for we are called and commanded to love, and we must love. . . . Love is the same kind of pious exercise, the same kind of activity, as any other external act. One thing only is important—it is my obedient stance before God, my deification, my turning toward the full experience of his eternal Good. . . . How can I even think that I can give something to the world, I, who am nothing, stained by original sin, corrupted by personal vices and sins?[17]

Anyone familiar in the least way with the ascetic, especially monastic, literature of either the East or the West will quickly recognize the spirit Mother Maria so accurately evokes. This is, after all, a sincere denial of self, a relentless and consistent view of everything tainted by sin and of the need to valiantly struggle through both the evil and the good. Even the good is compromised by the evil. Even the loving kindness extended to the suffering is done not so much to or for them but for God, in obedience to his command, despite our feelings or those of the suffering around us. Quite rightly, Mother Maria observes, this is a "strange and frightful holiness," or better, an imitation of the same, devoid of the very compassion that is the heart of God, the Lover of Mankind, *philanthropos,* as the liturgical texts of the Eastern Church so regularly call him, the God, who loves us, as Evdokimov so often reminds us, in the apt description of Nicolas Cabasilas, with an "absurd love" (*eros manikos*).

The words of the apostle Paul in his first letter to the Christians at Corinth—"but if I have not love, I am nothing"—stand as an indictment of the egoism of such an ascetic consciousness, and in fact there is a counterstream to it not only in the ascetical literature but also in the lives of countless holy women and men within this tradition. Mother Maria's psychological assessment of the dominance of the "I" in this asceticism, not only in the past of tradition, but particularly in our time, a century of overwhelming suffering and misery around us, is most astute. She inventories them all, the afflictions of her time and ours: writing in 1937, she acknowledged already the threat of war, the extinguishing of freedom by revolution, of which she was herself a part, and dictatorship, economic depression, and its results of unemployment, hunger, the breakup of families. Yet if all this could be summed up and likened to a plague, the human response is not quite like the proverbial feast during such a catastrophe. Such would be a prelude to spiritual enlightenment and change, a "courageous despair." No, in the present plague

> one as a rule counts one's daily earnings and in the evening goes to the cinema. There is no talk of courageous despair because there is no despair—there is only complete satisfaction and spiritual peace.... And every fervent prophet, every preacher will face a quandary: on which side of the café table shall he sit, how will he bless today's stock market gains, how will he break through, trample and destroy this sticky, gooey mass surrounding the soul of today's philistine?[18]

Among all the varieties of egocentrism thriving in contemporary society the spiritual variety is for Mother Maria the most disturbing. For it walls us off from the universe, makes us spiritual misers. The more miserly we are, contrary to ordinary expectations, the greater becomes our spiritual emptiness. This is Mother Maria's "strange law of the spiritual life," one to which she will return in presenting the authentic gospel type of Christianity.[19] This law states that "everything that has not been distributed, everything that is saved, everything not lovingly given away somehow degenerates, burns up."

The Gospel Way

After this penetrating look at the various "spiritualities" of her fellow Orthodox, an examination that is exact and even ruthless, Mother Maria at last dwells on the "evangelical" type of spiritual life, a radical return to the gospel and not the associations we would currently bring to the adjective, such as emotional worship or various denominations who label themselves as such.

No matter what the state of life in society or in the Church, the gospel way of life is always alive in the bosom of the Church, through the work of the Holy Spirit. In trying to precisely characterize the evangelical type, Mother Maria speaks of its desire to "Christify" all of life. This is neither the "inoculation" of a culture with a certain dosage of Christian morality, ritual, or art, the "Christianizing" of a people and way of life, nor the crude meaning associated with the churching of life, the subordination or adjustment of everything to the liturgical cycle of the year and services and other rules.

> "Christification" is based on the words, "It is no longer I who live, but Christ who lives in me." The image of God, the icon of Christ which truly is my real and actual essence is the only measure of things, the only way given to me. . . . Christ gave us two commandments: to love God and to love our fellow man. Everything else, even the Beatitudes, are merely elaborations of the two commandments which contain within themselves the totality of Christ's Good News. . . . It is remarkable that their truth is found only in their indissolubility. Love for man alone leads us to the blind alley of anti-Christian humanism and the only way out of it is, at times, to reject man and love for him in the name of all mankind. But love for God without love for man is condemned. . . . These two commandments are two aspects of a single truth. Destroy either one and you destroy the whole truth.[20]

The core of the Good News is love—God's love for us, our love for him, and our love for each other. Love of God and of neighbor are so entwined, so much part of the same reality that they cannot be separated or pitted against each other. One cannot love the neighbor without loving God, something our own recent past still struggles to comprehend. But equally, it is not possible to love God without loving and serving our brother and sister. Mother Maria again perceives a "peculiar, monstrous egoism" in attempting to love the neighbor without sensing in him or her the image of God. As with some of Dostoyevsky's characters so also with ourselves today, how easy is it for the concrete flesh and blood person before us to be disregarded in favor of the greater cause, the abstract person who represents all such homeless folk, people who are sick, abused, mentally ill. The unique person before us may smell, be unattractive, ungrateful. So how much more rewarding and noble it is to work for the cause, this poor soul, Mother Maria writes, becoming a "sacrifice upon the altar of the abstract idea, the common good, the earthly paradise, etc." Whether in the name of the proletariat, the nation or even the Church, such love for the neighbor is doomed because it is without the very source of every person and without the glory that every person is, namely, the living God.

Probing more deeply, Mother Maria notes that there are two kinds of love, one that takes and one that gives, and this is true in every direction, love for a friend, family, children, scholarship, art, one's country, one's ideals, even God. Even in the most selfless love we could think of, that of a mother for the very children she carried within herself and to which she gave life and birth, both kinds of love are not only possible but also actual, present. (I suspect there is much self-examination and indictment by Mother Maria in these lines, for as two who knew her, Sophie Koloumzine and Elisabeth Behr-Sigel told me, Mother Maria's own children were ignored regularly, received no letters or visits or gifts, while she was off raising funds for the suffering, giving lectures, caring for those in her hostels.) A mother may love in her children, not so much the singular beings they are, but in fact various aspects of her own self, her own "I," which then separates her not only from these who are her own but also from others. What may appear to be self-sacrificing may actually be its opposite.

> Only that maternal love is truly Christian which sees in her child a real image of God inherent not only in him but in all people, given to her in trust, as her responsibility, which she must develop and strengthen in him in preparation for the unavoidable life of sacrifice along the Christian path, for that challenge of bearing the cross facing all Christians. With this kind of love the mother will be more aware of other children's misfortunes, she will be more attentive to their neglect. Her relationship with the rest of humanity will be in Christ as the result of the presence of Christian love in her heart. This, of course, is the most radical example.[21]

These words, like others in the Gospels, are "hard sayings," most likely alienating many who hear them. They may also contain the self-revelation, struggle, and pain of the writer's own heart. Yet within the radical challenge they present there is clearly not just Mother Maria's own situation but the experience of the reader of how cruel, selfish, and narrow love can be—parental, marital, familial, ethnic, class, and even that of a religious community. What is distinctive and even disturbing in Mother Maria's passionate words is the further demand she recognizes in the commandment of love, namely, that one deny oneself. It is not enough to renounce as monastics do in their vows, control over material things. The gospel's demand cuts even into the life of the spirit.

> Renunciation teaches us not only that we not greedily seek advantages for our soul but that we not be stingy, that we always be extravagant in our love, that we achieve a spiritual nakedness, that our soul holds nothing back, that we not hold back anything sacred and valuable which we would not be ready to give up in Christ's name to those who need it. Spiritual renunciation is the way of holy foolishness, folly in Christ. It is the opposite of the wisdom of this age. It is the blessedness of those who are poor in spirit. It is the outer limit of love. . . . According to material laws[,] . . . if I give away a piece of bread, then I became poorer by one piece of bread . . . [and by extension] if I give my love, I have become impoverished by that amount of love, and if I give up my soul then I become completely ruined and have nothing left to save. . . . According to the law of the spirit, every spiritual treasure given away not only returns to the giver like an unspent ruble but it grows and becomes stronger. He who gives receives back in return; he who becomes poor becomes wealthier. . . . In turning away from the exclusive focus upon Christ in a genuine act of self-negation and love, one offers himself to others. . . . [T]hen one meets Christ himself face-to-face in the one for whom he offers himself and in that communion he unites with Christ himself. . . . [T]he mystery of union with man becomes the mystery of union with God. That which was given away returns. The love which was expended never diminishes the source of that love, because the source of love in our heart is Love itself, Christ. . . . Here we are speaking about a genuine emptying out, in a partial imitation of how Christ emptied himself by becoming incarnate in humanity. We must likewise empty ourselves completely, becoming, so to speak, incarnate in another human soul, offering to it the full measure of God's image which is contained in ourselves.[22]

The Liturgy of Living

It is not just in the pages of the New Testament that Mother Maria perceives this image of God's self-emptying love, becoming what we pray for the other. Contrary to some of her critics, her radical thinking here is by no means estranged from the Church and the liturgy. In fact, her faith and her practice of loving service to the neighbor were rooted in these. With the little time she had to herself she sewed vestments and painted and embroidered icons for the chapels of her hostels. She is remembered, standing transfixed during the Paschal Vigil, her face illumined by the candle she was holding, true tears of joy streaming down her face. Father Gregory later made exceptionally beautiful icons for the chapel of her nursing home at Noisy-le-Grand. The exquisite faces of the Mother of God and of Christ, the dominant icons on the iconostasis, capture much of Mother Maria herself: peace, sadness for all the suffering, immense longing to comfort. These were recently bequeathed to the chapel of the sisters at Znaménié monastery in Marcenat and appeared in beautiful reproduction in a volume published on the thirthieth anniversary of Father Gregory's death in 1999. Hélène Arjakovsky-Klépinine, daughter of the Lourmel hostel's chaplain, Father Klepinin, showed me a precious souvenir of Mother Maria, the marvelous embroidery of the Allied invasion of Normandy, based on the Bayeux tapestry, which she did in the Ravensbrück camp with threads improvised from rags and insulation. Mrs. Arjakovsky-Klépinine also showed me the design of the last icon Mother Maria embroidered at the camp, now lost, the Mother of God embracing her son, the Lord, not as a child but as the suffering crucified victim—both images of consolation, of the cross and resurrection in the midst of a death camp.[23] For Mother Maria, the self-giving love of God is present and constantly revealed in the Eucharist. Raising the Bread and Cup after the consecration, the celebrant sings: "Your own of your own, we offer You, on behalf of all, and for all."

If . . . this sacrificial and self-giving love stands at the center of the Church's life, what then are its boundaries, its limits? In this sense one can speak of the whole of Christianity as of an eternal offering of a Divine Liturgy beyond church walls. . . . It means that we must offer the bloodless sacrifice, the sacrifice of self-offering love not only in a specific place, on the one altar of only one temple, but that the whole world, in this sense, becomes the one altar of the one Temple—and that we must offer our hearts under the species of bread and wine, so that they may be transformed into Christ's love, that he may abide in them, that they may become hearts of Godmanhood, and that he would give these hearts of ours as food for the world, that he would commune the whole world with these sacrificed hearts of ours, in order that we would be one with him, that we not live but Christ would live in us, incarnate in our flesh.[24]

Mother Maria was not able to gather a monastic community around her for very long. With the exception of Father Klepinin, who shared her fate in a concentration camp, her chaplains and her fellow nuns eventually chose other locations or were compelled by the economic and social conditions to go elsewhere. It is no discredit to say that her singular personality and lifestyle may have played a role. Two women who knew her, extraordinary in their own lives, gave personal accounts of her idiosyncratic, perhaps even eccentric and difficult personality. Sophie Koloumzine described the bohemian, unusual style of dress Mother Maria affected, even before her monastic profession. "She worked by cleaning people's homes and businesses," Mrs. Koloumzine reported, "and often received in addition to payment various material gifts. From scraps of felt and velvet she received from a tailor, she created a hat that to her was the height of fashion, yet turned heads in the train car where we sat." "How she loved children, mine especially," Behr-Sigel remembered. "And yet she had a distinctly negligent relationship with her own, even though she loved them passionately."

Later on, her monastic habit did not prevent her from smoking and from loud conversation with the intellectuals who met at her hostel: Nicolas Berdiaev, Constantine Mochulsky, George Fedotov, and Father Bulgakov, among others. Her relationship with one of her chaplains, the severe, traditional priest-monk and later noted liturgical scholar Father Kyprian Kern devolved nearly into personal warfare. None of the sisters who came to join her remained. Within the Russian émigré community, there were many who loathed everything she was and did: her unkempt appearance, her forays into the Les Halles markets begging cast-off provisions, her late-night excursions into cafés and bars looking for the homeless. Some even felt she had done herself and those around her in by sheltering, even hiding Communists and Jews.

Even though her thought about a renewed monasticism may sound superficially like a call for rejection of the contemplative and liturgical life lived apart, in favor of a life of radical social action for the poor and suffering, such an appraisal is not completely accurate. Her own charismatic vocation was to put herself limitlessly at the disposal of those in great need, usually with the help of volunteers raising funds, gathering food and preparing it, and sheltering the homeless, emotionally crushed, and other wounded souls in her hostels. She eventually worked with her chaplain and fellow martyr Fr. Dimitri Klepinin to provide documentation to hide French Jews during the Vichy government's roundup. Sophie Koloumzine described how Father Klepinin, a close friend, would inscribe an almost microscopic letter "T" somewhere on the baptismal certificates he prepared for those he and Mother Maria were hiding, this symbol standing for the Russian word for "Linden," meaning "fake." Mother Maria even went out to the Vélodrome d'Hiver in the summer heat to be with the thousands of Jews held in horrendous conditions in this cycle racing park in July 1942.

Not only in a time of great suffering from revolution and displacement, economic hard times and war, she held a radically incarnational understanding of Christian discipleship. To love Christ was to love and serve him very concretely, in the face, in the arms of the marginal, even repulsive and needful other. But to judge Mother Maria as simply an evangelical activist would be to overlook her thoroughly eucharistic spirituality, her profoundly ecclesial soul, and her "becoming prayer" (Evdokimov). Reminiscences of Mother Maria describe her radiant, attentive presence at the liturgy, in conversations with others both at cafés and at her hostels, also with energy enough to contribute essays to the periodicals of the émigré community, now our avenues to her person and ideals. Mother Maria affirms the monastic desert as the heart of God who is "Love without limits," as her friend and former chaplain, Father Gillet, put it, but she could not separate this love from that of the neighbor. As

Metropolitan Evlogy, her bishop, the one who received her profession and encouraged her unusual lifestyle said, her monastic place would be the "desert of human hearts."

Mother Maria also points us to a fundamental reality, one obscured in continuous disputes about "modernism" and "traditionalism" in the Orthodox Church and throughout Christianity, namely, that the Christian's commitment is *not* primarily to a heritage, to structures of the past, or even to visions of what the future should be. Rather, each Christian, monastic or cleric or layperson, is called to real life, life in the Church and the world as we find it, an encounter with God, oneself, and the neighbor in need. The echo of St. Seraphim of Sarov is unmistakable here: "That I am a monk and you are a layman is of no importance[,] . . . rather that we are both in the light of the Holy Spirit. . . . Acquire peace, and thousands around you will be saved."

In short, for Mother Maria, this was the true gospel *metanoia,* that is, the profound transformation of oneself and the world through love, prayer, and work. The Russian Revolution, she wrote many times, produced terrible sufferings, wreaked havoc on the Orthodox Church. Yet, paradoxically, it (as well as other catastrophes like the forced emigration, the Great Depression, and even World War II) could be seen as gifts from God, radical liberations from so much weight. These horrors also free us, she insisted, to once again know God and ourselves and each other simply, directly. And then, as today, the situations of our world free us to be the heart and hands of Christ for the neighbor. As Metropolitan Anthony (Bloom) has said, "Mother Maria is a saint of our day and for our day, a woman of flesh and blood possessed by the love of God, who stood fearlessly face-to-face with the problems of our century."[25] She pushed the traditional borders of monasticism and church life well past their former limits. Everything about her, her personal life and relationships, her audacious ideas spoken or put down in writing, even the statement of her clothing and demeanor as a "monastic in the world," all pushed the envelope hard but did not break out of it. As so many of her friends and colleagues in the Russian emigration, she dared to live within what Fr. Alexander Elchaninov called the "absolute freedom" of the Eastern Church.[26] As a Christian witness of our century, truly a living icon, her life and deeds put that freedom and courage before each of us, both as defiant challenge and as loving invitation.

CHAPTER FIVE

Lev Gillet

The Monk in the City,
a Pilgrim in Many Worlds

A Complicated Man, a Wandering Monk

The whole teaching of the Latin Fathers may be found in the East, just as the whole teaching of the Greek Fathers may be found in the West. Rome has given St. Jerome to Palestine. The East has given Cassian to the West and holds in special veneration that Roman of the Romans, Pope Gregory the Great. St. Basil would have acknowledged St. Benedict of Nursia as his brother and heir. St. Macrina would have found her sister in St. Scholastica. St. Alexis the "man of God," "the poor man under the stairs," has been succeeded by the wandering beggar, St. Benedict Labre. St. Nicolas would have felt as very near to him the burning charity of St. Francis of Assisi and St. Vincent de Paul. St. Seraphim of Sarov would have seen the desert blooming under Father Charles de Foucauld's feet, and would have called St. Thérèse of Lisieux "my joy."[1]

Among the remarkable people of the Russian emigration was the iconographer Sister Joanna Reitlinger.[2] For the chapel of the now closed St. Basil's House in London, she created an unusual series of icon panels that bring to life the vision of the "one, holy, catholic and apostolic Church" incarnate in holy men and women, despite the centuries of schism and distance[3] (These and the rest of the iconography of St. Basil's have been transferred to the monastery of Christ the Savior in Brighton-Hove, East Sussex, England. See photos in the illustration section.) On one wall, assembled before the rounded dome of the Great Church of Holy Wisdom of Constantinople are Anthony the Great and Dorotheos, Gregory the Theologian, John Chrysostom, Gregory of Nyssa, Nicholas, Athanasius and Macrina. On the opposite wall, in front of St. Peter's in Rome, are gathered Benedict, Genevieve of Paris, Leo the Great, Martin of Tours, Augustine, and Monica and Irenaeus of Lyons, among others. The gathering of these and other saints of the Church, East and West, as well as that in Father Lev's text above are icons not only of what he taught and wrote but also of who he himself was and the Christian, churchly life he tried to live.

In a century in which the great schism and other divisions of the churches continued to separate people of faith, a century of wars and depressions and rapid social change, there also was the surprise of the ecumenical movement, the sometimes feeble, sometimes defiant urge to recover the original unity of the Church. As with his friends Paul Evdokimov, Father Bulgakov, and Mother Maria, Father Lev became a kind of pilgrim between the churches, truly the citizen and inhabitant of various worlds.

Living in both Western and Eastern monasteries, then among the Russian émigrés and the homeless of Paris and later London, Beirut, and Geneva, the little monk had a large soul, an amazingly expansive and diversified life. His lifelong friend and biographer, herself part of the sweep of church history in this century, Elisabeth Behr-Sigel, has captured something of his quixotic character and nonconformist life. In her biography she refers to him, as I have here, as the "monk in the city," an apparent contradiction pregnant with meaning, and as a "pilgrim" in many worlds.

He most certainly was a monk, both of the Western Church's Benedictine order and of the Eastern Church, but for a relatively brief time resident in a monastic community. Father Lev had the soul of a pilgrim. In his long life he was never tied down to one occupation, position, or place. Born on August 6, 1893, on the feast of the Transfiguration, in Saint-Marcellin, Isère, France, his early life saw service in combat in World War I and university studies in philosophy and psychology. He produced the first French translation of Freud's *On the Interpretation of Dreams,* underwent psychoanalysis, and acquired a lifelong sensitivity to the complexity and the suffering of the soul, as Freud called it. After the war he entered the Benedictine order at Clervaux abbey in Luxembourg. His monastic profession took him to Farnborough abbey in England, where he served and worked under one of the leaders of the liturgical renewal movement, Dom Ferdinand Cabrol. Singled out for further study, he was sent to San Anselmo in Rome, where he made deep friendships with two monks with whom he would be a cofounder, at least in spirit, of the mixed Eastern-Western church monastery of Chevetogne in Belgium.

Later in life, work as priest and scholar would take him across Europe and to the Near East. He would be a member, albeit briefly, of a fledgling monastic community in the Ukraine and a priest in a mission near Nice. After entering the Orthodox Church, he was rector of the first Orthodox French-language parish in Paris. He served as chaplain in a number of locations: to Russians and others held in French prisons, at Mother Maria's hostel, and at St. Basil's House in London. In between and after, he was an itinerant preacher and retreat master, spiritual father and adviser to bishops, priests, monastics, church youth movements and many individuals. He supported himself at various points in his life, not so much by clerical appointments and stipends, but by freelance writing, editing, translating, and research. And if nothing else, he was a go-between, a traveler between numerous "worlds," that of the past century and the present, that of the Western Christian churches and tradition and that of the East, between clergy and laity, intellectuals and artists and ordinary working people, and, most significantly, between an apparently secular, even Godless world and the reality of God and the Kingdom, one he experienced in an intense, even mystical manner. Several of his most widely read books took the form of dialogues between the soul and the Lord, prayer "out loud."

> So then, Lord, it is this? It is truly this? It is only this? This is the whole law and all the prophets? To love with one's whole heart. . . . To love Him who first loved us, to love everything that He loves, all men, all women, all creatures. . . . Yes, my child, that is it, and that is all. Everything "else" has value only inasmuch as

it is the expression, the carrying out—under so many various forms—of that initial impulse which is my limitless Love. . . . The heart transplants, which in our day have become possible, are a wonderful sign of a spiritual reality. To give one's heart to another, to accept the heart of another. . . . It is the parable of limitless Love's triumph.[4]

For years, many of Father Lev's writings were published under the pen name "a Monk of the Eastern Church," a device first contrived to avoid controversy but later continued because of the anonymity and perhaps also the mystery it afforded. Father Lev was in many respects a wanderer. He took a path seldom pursued for a Western monk, far to the East, to a small and experimental Byzantine Catholic monastery in what was then Galicia, now Ukraine, Uniov, near Lviv. He made his permanent monastic profession to and was later ordained by that remarkable bridge figure, Metropolitan Andrei Sheptytsky. But Father Lev was a Westerner, a Frenchman, and it became apparent that his place in the effort to create contact between the churches of the East and the West was back in the West, not Uniov in Galicia. From there he returned to France, first to a mission among Russian immigrants and then to Paris, where he attached himself to the Russian émigré community. Eventually the singular bishop of that western European diocese, then of the Moscow patriarchate, Metropolitan Evlogy, received him into the Orthodox Church and its priesthood, simply by concelebration in the eucharistic liturgy in the Trubetskoy home-chapel in Clamart on May 25, 1928.

From that point onward, Father Lev served in the Orthodox churches in Europe and in the Middle East. A Westerner always, he nevertheless was surely a priest and "monk of the Eastern Church." In this he was a precursor, with Behr-Sigel, of many others from the Western churches who would become part of the Eastern Church in the twentieth century, to some a curious, even suspect phenomenon. Nevertheless, as Evdokimov and Mother Maria and many of the Russian émigrés came to understand it, the destructive Bolshevik revolution also had a very positive outcome, the return of Eastern Orthodox Christians to the West, the opening of contacts of prayer, study, and common work between them. Perhaps surprisingly, there appeared pilgrims from the West to the Eastern Church, men and women whose love for the Church would repair and create bridges between the divided churches.

After a long life, just such a pilgrim, Father Lev, was buried from the Greek Orthodox cathedral in London by his friend and younger colleague, Metropolitan Anthony (Bloom) of the Russian patriarchal diocese of Sourozh. In addition to all the prayers of the Orthodox funeral service, one from the Roman Missal was also read by Metropolitan Anthony. Even in death, Father Lev kept trying to live in an undivided Church. He understood himself to be a priest of the Orthodox Church, but this did not prevent him from ministering to Christians all across the spectrum, preaching in Hyde Park as well as Protestant churches in London and elsewhere, giving retreats to Orthodox, Anglicans, Roman Catholics, and Protestants as well, in short, serving all of the people of God, as if there had never been schisms.

It is characteristic of the enigmatic character of Father Lev that after his death a longtime colleague at St. Basil's House, Helle Giorgiadias, would claim, in print, that he had never left the Catholic Church and had, as some detractors had thought much earlier, "infiltrated" the Orthodox Church almost as a spy.[5] This was her reading of an impassioned exchange when interviewed in his eighties about people and events in the effort to build bridges between East and West in the 1920s, efforts such as the establishment of a Benedictine monastery at Amay in Belgium, whose vocation was to be outreach to the East. Father Lev was one of the cofounders, along with Dom Lambert Beauduin and Dom Olivier Rousseau, of Chevetogne, although he was never to live in this community, which still exists today and is known internationally for having both Eastern and Western monastic communities and churches. Father Lev exclaimed in this exchange that he had always considered himself "a catholic priest in full communion with the Slavic Orthodox Church."[6] This was hardly the revelation of some deep, dark secret of ecclesiastical espionage, although the actions of several in the 1920s, particularly Bishop Michel d'Herbigny, with special "faculties" for work in Russia and points East, might suggest this.

With his singular personality, bordering at times on the eccentric, Father Lev's statements could with some effort be stretched into this

interpretation, for in letters to his family and former colleagues in
the 1920s and even toward the end of his life, he spoke in the idealistic terms of one who recognized the schisms of the churches but
believed that the consequent walls of separation could be overcome
in many ways: in prayer, in holiness, in the living out of a fully ecclesial life. It is important to note that such a vision of catholicity, of
unity despite division, was hardly unique or for that matter peculiar to Father Lev. It clearly was the perspective of his longtime
friends Paul Evdokimov and Elisabeth Behr-Sigel, friends who dearly
loved him but differed profoundly among themselves in other important respects. It was a vision as well as a goal for others of the
remarkable Russian religious renaissance, such as Fathers Bulgakov,
Afanasiev, Meyendorff, Schmemann, and Men.[7]

Father Lev seems to shatter every typology of personality. He was
intense and passionate, extremely private and revealing at the same
time. He is described as childlike and open, most accessible yet often
difficult, brooding, even cranky. Though his thinking was straightforward, his friendships deep and lasting, and his attitude warm and
outgoing, he remained an enigma, even to those who knew him well
and over a lifetime. This is the sense left in Behr-Sigel's immense
biography of Father Lev, based on almost sixty years of friendship
and correspondence, now available in English translation. Yet in this
man of apparent contradictions, there was an amazing resolution or
transcendence of conflicts that would destroy and divide. Just as
Father Lev was moved and transformed by the spirituality of the
Russian Orthodox Church and its clinging to the *kenōsis,* Bishop
Kallistos Ware has described the monk of the Eastern Church as a
most "kenotic" personality himself. Bishop Kallistos cites an early
letter of Father Lev:

> The more I examine myself, the more I see that a life devoted to
> constructing and organizing, a life which produces positive results
> and which succeeds, is not my vocation, even though, out of obe-
> dience, I could work in this direction and even obtain certain
> results. What attracts me is a vocation of loss—a life which would
> give itself freely without any apparent positive result, for the
> result would be known to God alone; in brief, to lose oneself in
> order to find oneself.[8]

With such a long life and voluminous literary output, Father Lev's person and work are difficult to capture succinctly. Clément chose to examine what he considered the central themes in his thinking, realities that not only shaped this extraordinary monk-priest, but that he lived out: the life in Christ, a universality without relativism and God as One who suffers with us.[9]

In the Presence of a Suffering God: Love without Limits

We shall look first at Father Lev's sense of *intimate communion* with a God who not only was "kenotic," the One who suffers with us, the Book of Revelation's (Bukharev and Evdokimov's "Lamb immolated from the beginning of the world") but also "Love without limits," the One whom he often called "Lord Love."[10] While Father Lev was trained as a scholar and published much in that vein, for example, his studies on the "Jesus Prayer," on the concept of the Messiah and the relationship between Judaism and Christianity, on the liturgical year, its lessons, texts, and feasts, many of the books published under his pen name stem from retreats and conferences he gave. Whether focused on the Good Shepherd, the burning bush, the Holy Spirit, a dialogue with Jesus, or the presence of God during a typical working day, all are, in a sense, the revelation of what prayer sounds like, a look into communion with God, and, conversely, a glimpse of God's attitude toward us. I would say further that not only do they reach out to actual listeners at a retreat; they also are a view into Father Lev's internal discourse and relationship with God and his pastoral way with people.

It is not so much the exegesis of the burning bush of Exodus 3 that concerns Father Lev. Rather it is God as fire that burns but does not consume.

God is fire. God is love. God is a self-propagating emotional power, a fire that shares itself. Centuries after Moses beheld the flames of the burning bush, this same fire merged with the tongues of flame at Pentecost, and with the fire that burned within the hearts of the disciples at Emmaus. In saying that God is a fire of love we are certainly stating a truth that plays havoc with many of our ideas, in fact almost all our ideas.[11]

Here we are at the root not only of Father Lev's intentions in a retreat in the late 1960s at Pleshey but also of much of his ministry, namely, to counter worn out, even wrong ideas of God that all sorts of religious teaching and experiences have planted in people with the startling truth found in the Scriptures. In addition, it seemed that from his earliest years working with refugees and particularly the Russian Christian Students Movement, Father Lev was particularly interested in those outside the Church, outside Christianity, outside conventional religious faith of any kind. Speaking to retreatants during the "death of God" era, he observes that perhaps the very word "God" has become overburdened with false meanings. "God" is also all too abstract, too empty a term for many. Why not simply identify him with what is the supreme reality for us, love, and speak of and to the "lord of Love" or "Lord Love"? The Exodus text's narrative is no mere coincidence here, for Moses asks the burning bush for a name, his name.

> You ask what my name is. I am Being. I am the Being whom you see in being at this very moment. Look before you. You see the bush that burns without being consumed. You see fire. The Being I am is a Being of fire. These flames proclaim my love. But look more carefully. My fire does not destroy. That which it burns it purifies and transforms into itself, makes part of itself. And my flame has no need to be fed. It imparts itself, gives itself. I am the Gift that never ceases to give itself. . . . I am Limitless Love.[12]

Weaving in the Eastern Church's vespers Psalm 103 (104), Father Lev expands on the eternal, limitless nature of Love who is God, tracing the cosmic and communal linkages implied in creation. From the mountains and the rock badgers to the storms, the oceans, and every man and woman, within them all God, limitless Love, lives. And there should be no alarm that the Trinity and Jesus Christ have not yet been mentioned, for in Moses' time God had not yet revealed himself as Trinity or become flesh, and yet there still was Lord Love. In the story of the prophet Hosea and his prostitute-wife, Father Lev suggests that the "spontaneous reaction, the first response to the discovery of Limitless Love" is hope, a door of hope opened to each of us, no matter who we are and what we may have made of our lives.

Limitless Love calls us back as beloved, puts a ring on our finger, opens the door to communion with him, to the marriage feast.

In the text Father Lev admits that for him it was a major change to start not with our love for God, our obeying the command to love him, but rather the other way around, that is, with the overwhelming Love that God has, that God is, for us. "I have come to show you, for you are greatly loved," is the angel's message to the prophet Daniel (Dan. 9:23). The letters of John affirm this. But Father Lev pushes even further to the passion, the suffering of God for us and to love us.

> Divine Love is comparable to the atmospheric pressure surrounding us, which sustains each being and also exerts pressure from all sides. Love lays siege to each being and seeks to discover an opening, a path leading into the heart, by means of which Love can permeate everywhere. The difference between the sinner and the saint is that the sinner closes his heart to Love while the saint opens himself to this same Love. In both cases the Love is the same and the pressure is the same.[13]

Limitless Love is for all, both the devoted and the indifferent. Hosea woos back his unfaithful wife and again betroths her in love. Another prostitute, Rahab, saves the Israelite spies and is in turn saved from the destruction of Jericho (Heb. 11:30–31). The scarlet thread she hangs out her window spares Jesus himself who welcomed those cast off by the church of his time: tax collectors, the woman caught in adultery, possessed men, lepers, those considered punished by God with sickness and seizures. The tax collectors and prostitutes would be the first to enter the kingdom of heaven (Matt. 21:31). Father Lev reminds us that not only does Rahab become part of the line of David and therefore of the genealogy of Jesus, but included in the same are others who similarly lived and loved "outside the rules," Tamar and Bathsheba, not to mention King David himself.

A pattern emerges here and is intensified in Father Lev's reflections of the "clean" versus "unclean" dilemma of the apostle Peter, in his vision at Joppa (Acts 10:15). There is a different and, we could say, far more radical ethic at Horeb, of the burning bush, of Limitless

Love. Our own view of what is right and just is in conflict with that of Limitless Love. Love abolishes the Law, the standard, the ethic by which we human beings insist on measuring things, seeking justice. What has replaced the Law is Christ. We now do what is good, truthful, right, *not* because the opposite are against the Law, but because Christ died and rose for us. Such is not "situational ethics" but a parting of ways with legalism. And it is more. Here we begin to see the deeper radicalism of Father Lev, not unique to him by any means, in fact part of the mind of the Eastern Church, as expressed not only in liturgical texts and rites but also in the reflections of writers such as Dostoyevsky. In God's eyes, what may seem "irregular" to us, even to the clergy, may in fact be "regular," that is, right with God. And the opposite holds as well. The one so apparently within the community of the righteous, so careful in fulfilling ritual and other details, may be in "inner truth," very much removed, "outside" the assembly. The greatest sin is, as Christ himself stressed, not the violation of a rule but the action against love or without love.

Father Lev pushes the limits.

> The ethic of Limitless Love demands that we should be able to recognize the presence of God in the very sin that the sinner commits. . . . You must not think I mean that God approves of the sin or encourages the sinner. I simply mean that even in an act of sin God is, to a certain extent, present. . . . [E]verything that happens—the bad act as well as the good—has its roots in the being of God. Only because God gives us our being (or rather lends it to us) are we in existence at the very moment when we commit a sin. At that very moment God could withdraw our being from us, could destroy us. But he holds us in the existence we have received from him, even when that existence turns against him. Moreover the Lord Love, in his infinite mercy, allows sin to contain certain positive elements.[14]

Father Lev gets quite specific here. The illicit sexual relationship is not justified or redeemed by the bit of tenderness, the small moment of self-giving or of compassion. Yet this "spark" from the burning bush is the sign that Limitless Love has entered this relationship.

God is present even in the connection between a prostitute and her client, between two lovers. God continually is "showing forth his compassion in ways that are so often unexpected and always new. Even when one cannot stop, cannot escape from the limits of his or her behavior, there is room, there is openness on Love's part. No one is excluded or thrown out." The Eastern Church, Father Lev argues, as does Evdokimov and their teacher, Father Bulgakov, knows the limitless compassion of God, and thus confession is more healing than punishment, more the joint commitment of confessor and penitent in prayer to find God's way so that the sinner can hear Christ's words: "Rise, pick up your bed and walk. . . . Your sins are forgiven. Go, and sin no more."[15]

It is not fidelity to a code, conformity to a standard, but the often difficult effort "to act as God acts in respect of this sinner and this sin; in other words, I try to love him, or her, out of it."[16] This is threatening to many, for it confronts us with a God who is quite unlike us, free to forgive, to love, to brush offenses away, without any shock or vengeance. It is the same insight that Evdokimov brings back from the Fathers: the reality that God does not compel anyone to love him but knocks at the door of our hearts, waits as a beggar in his "absurd love," even desiring to "share the bread of our suffering." To think with the mind of Christ, to see with the eyes of God, is to transform the person and situation before us.

> To love, with all one's heart, as oneself; the Gospel transmutes all of the law and the prophets into that. . . . It is a matter of offering our whole heart to Love, a heart which is pure as a wine is pure, a heart unadulterated and whole, a heart which is not divided or shared. And in the light of this it might perhaps be useful to revise our contemporary understanding of purity, or more precisely, of chastity. Too often we think of chastity in negative terms, as no more than a matter of abstaining. But a chaste heart, a pure heart, is a whole heart, an integrated, total heart which offers itself to God or to men in its wholeness. The real sin against purity is to offer (or to seem to offer) to God, or to a man, or to a woman, a love which is falsified, a love that is not or cannot be integral, a heart that is not "whole."[17]

As in St. Peter's vision, Father Lev suggests, today we see a great
sheet unrolled before us with all sorts of creatures and things that, to
our conventional religious and moral sensibilities, appear "unclean,"
ways of life and situations we think we should ourselves reject while
also distancing ourselves from those who are involved in them. He
specifically refers to drug addiction, homosexuality, and abortion,
which remain as real now more than thirty years later. But Father
Lev hears these words from the Lord Love:

> There are, among these particular things, some I have already
> purified entirely. Others I am purifying at this moment. But I can-
> not purify or pardon without an inner change in the sinners. I ask
> you to participate in my work of purification by your prayer, by
> your sympathy for the sinner (not the sin), by your adoring dis-
> covery of my absolute Purity acting secretly in the very midst of
> the visible impurity, so that it shall be consumed in my flame. . . .
> Separate the entirely negative element from the positive element
> existing in all faults. . . . Assimilate everything which in the sinner
> comes from me and continues to be mine, and unite yourself to
> me in my effort to transfigure that which is not of me. Enlarge
> your heart to the dimensions of my heart.[18]

Here is a hope that indeed "all will be saved," an impulse both of
faith and love that sees, like St. Gregory of Nyssa, Origen, and in our
own time, Father Bulgakov, the promise of an ultimate *apokatastasis,*
a final resurrection of all into the Kingdom.[19] How irritating this is,
how maddening and how absolutely wrong in the minds of so many
within the Church. How soft, messy, disorderly this approach, this
attribution of attitudes to God. How much more awful a world it
would be if such an ethos became widespread. Perhaps already over
a generation, actually more than a half century ago, Father Lev was
deluded by the permissiveness of the culture around him, distorted
by the psychological and psychoanalytic theory he studied in graduate
school, confused by the complex, troubled people around him in
Paris, Beirut, London, Geneva, and so many other places. Or better,
could it not be that Father Lev, so drawn to the Church of the East
and her preservation of Tradition, perceived here the living and open,

creative and free movements of the Lord Love, transcending rules and stereotypes, always seeking the soul that is lost.

Father Lev concludes the retreat on the burning bush, which I have closely followed here, with the incident toward the end of the apostle Paul's adventures during his journey as a prisoner to stand trial in Rome, toward the end of the Acts of the Apostles, 28. The soaked, shivering survivors of the shipwreck are received with "great kindness" by the barbarian inhabitants of the island of Malta. A huge fire is made so that they can warm and dry themselves. Moreover, the Maltese take the survivors back to their homes, after the emergency services are delivered, for food, rest, and other care. If we are truly servant of the Lord Love, Father Lev says by way of conclusion, then like the residents of Malta, we too will seek out the survivors wherever they may be, drenched and paralyzed by rain and cold, bringing them fire, the fire of our love, the fire of the burning bush, of Limitless Love.

A God who is limitless love, who suffers with his creatures, who reaches down to help, forgive, and save them but without threat or compulsion, a God "absurd" in his affection for us, violating, apparently, not only our sense of fairness but his own law and its implications, such a God is the only God found in the writings of the monk of the Eastern Church. Repeatedly, the same themes surface throughout Father Lev's retreat talks, later written down and published.[20] Two such small collections, printed together under the title *In Thy Presence,* in particular exhibit his distinctive approach and insights. In the first of these, "Limitless Love," it is again the One in the burning bush who addresses us, who reveals a name other than that we usually and unthinkingly use, "God." So "Lord Love," "Limitless Love" makes the first movement toward us and shows himself to be, at one and the same time, beyond our expectations and ideas of a God and yet closer to us than we are to ourselves.

This God is the Triune God, the Father, Son, and Holy Spirit revealed by Christ. However, as Behr-Sigel points out, it may well have been the cumulative effect of working and conversing with so many outside of Christianity, either because of membership in other traditions and communities of faith such as Judaism, Islam, and Buddhism or because of estrangement from Christian faith by experiences of the past and the present that Father Gillet deliberately sought to take another, simpler and more basic path. It is not so unusual a path in the modern era at that, choosing ordinary language, events, and experiences of everyday life to communicate the same Truth of God and his love proclaimed in the Scriptures, liturgy, icons, and theology of the Church's tradition. Father Lev was looking for what Emil Brunner called a "point of contact," what Peter Berger refers to as "signals of transcendence," very basic, even "prototypical human gestures," in which the Holy One is present, encounters, and is encountered by us.[21]

Much of what we heard in the talks on the burning bush is here again, but also new and different reflections. Over and over, the personal character of Lord Love, his relentless seeking us out to share in his love, his constant suffering with us—these are keys on which Father Lev plays, answering very likely to the hunger and frustrations he himself experienced and which he encountered in the people around him, religious and secular. To those who would prefer God in his heaven and all else in place as a form of faith, he reminds us of the active work of God in seeking us and overturning our plans.

> Limitless Love forces open doors. Perhaps I had not achieved some sort of peaceful coexistence with God. Perhaps I had succeeded in believing that, as far as my soul was concerned, I was more or less "in good order," and so had come to feel more or less at rest. . . . And now all those presuppositions have been turned upside down by a divine intrusion. God asks something from me that I am quite unprepared for. It is like the news of an unwanted child. . . . To listen to this demand, to take the costly decision, ah, but why? Everything seemed to be going so well! Must I have new uncertainties and anxieties? . . . And now limitless Love wants to erupt into my life. It comes to upset everything in it. It comes to break up what seemed stable and to open new horizons to which I had never given a thought.[22]

Here and there are the faces of men and women Father Lev listened to and consoled: a woman worried at only the loss she perceives in her aging, a lonely young émigré fearful of the future in a new land, the very pious Christian with prayer books and Bible in hand, running to church, the beautiful girl with so many lovers, the convict he cared for as prison chaplain, the mother who lost her child, the victim of the concentration camp (perhaps the memory here of his beloved Mother Maria?), the alcoholic, the drug addict.[23] There are brilliant small reflections on the significance of a look, a smile, on prayer, on bearing within oneself the spark that kindles the fire of limitless Love in others, and a perceptive meditation on the gift of women to the rest of humanity.[24]

What is more, without descending to the constricting level of "recipes," Father Lev suggests how one can live an authentic life in God in the very ordinary tasks of everyday life. Particularly in the second collection, "Thy Presence Today" the emphasis is as much on the "today," as on "presence." There is a treasure of detail here: the beginning of waking up; the act of washing, dressing, reading, and writing; leaving home for the workplace and those encountered there and on the trip; the simple gesture of the outstretched hand and the clasping and shaking of same; the meals shared or eaten by oneself, the cleanup; finally, the return home to the darkness of night, to the stillness of a house late in the evening, to sleep. How closely this follows the quite mundane schedule of Father Lev during his many years at St. Basil's House in London that Behr-Sigel describes. Yet without giving it a name and without laying it out in programmatic form as a technique (as in manuals of "spirituality" today), Father Lev here suggests the ways in which the life of any person can be "churched," made incarnate with the presence of Christ, be, in St. Seraphim's phrase, an acquiring of the Holy Spirit.

It is not without coincidence that the one who in so many of his writings used the pen name "a Monk of the Eastern Church" and who throughout his life, at least according to his friends and colleagues, consistently understood himself precisely as a monk, in actual practice spent relatively few years within a monastic community. In a fairly long life, he resided in Benedictine and the Uniov Eastern Church monastic communities only from 1920 to 1927, concluding in a brief stay in Nice, in a mission house for the care of Russian refugees. For the rest of his nomadic life, there would hardly be any permanent position and no monastery to which he belonged. One is tempted to conclude that it was principally Father Lev's impatient spirit, the wandering impulse within him that kept him on the move. However, for the many Orthodox dispersed in the West by exile and emigration, permanent monasteries were for a long time impossible and more a dream than anything else. Archbishop Anthony (Bloom) recounts this in an interesting article about his own long monastic life without a monastery.[25] Mother Maria Skobt-sova visited monastic communities that survived the revolution in Estonia and Latvia but found these to be essentially museums of past practice. She was convinced that there could be a renewed monasti-cism in the world, and her bishop, Metropolitan Evlogy, remarked that indeed the streets and the city of Paris and her hostels had be-come her monastery.[26] One can only speculate on the conversations and exchanges of ideas about the way to follow Christ, to live the gos-pel life in the midst of so much turmoil and suffering in the moder-nity of the twentieth century, between Mother Maria and Father Lev who was chaplain at her hostel in Rue Lourmel from 1935 to 1938. The essence of those conversations can be found in many of the texts cited from Mother Maria, quite a few of them from essays precisely on the possibilities of a renewed monastic life today.[27] I would argue that the daily form of Christian living in the presence of Christ that Father Lev lays out here as well as in other places also is rooted in his own nomadic and worldly, primarily urban, monasticism.

It is not surprising that Paul Evdokimov would have devoted so much thought throughout his teaching and writing to this same matter of how to live out the Christian life, as one's ancestors in the faith had for so many centuries of Christian history. But it was im-possible to simply re-create, repristinate the past, to force third- or thirteenth- or eighteenth-century conditions and practices into the life of the twentieth century. Borrowing from the insightful ideas of the eighteenth-century monk and bishop St. Tikhon of Zadonsk, Evdokimov spoke of an "interiorized monasticism," what St. Tikhon had referred to as "untonsured monasticism."[28] One can fuss about descriptions and labels and their implications, whether even the mention of monasticism is appropriate for a universal understand-ing of holiness or possibly a dilution of this singular vocation. Nevertheless, what Father Lev insisted on throughout his preaching and writing was not a "spirituality" of unusual practices and "mys-tical" experiences. Rather, he appears to have assimilated what so many of his beloved Russians understood and urged as the church-

ing of life, the elimination of cultural religiosity, and what Mother
Maria would typify as aesthetic, ritualistic, or ascetic forms in favor
of a "gospel" way of life, a "lived-out" or "experiential" faith as
Evdokimov expressed it. While his vision of the life in Christ is not
without feeling, very much communal, with others and for them,
Father Lev's presentation of this pattern is within the tasks and
details of ordinary living. What Father Schmemann termed the
"sacramental vision of the world," really an eschatological one, in
which every encounter was a possibility for seeing Christ and following him, Father Lev too envisioned such a "paradise of the
moment," in which all of everyday was the arena for holiness.

Living in the Una Sancta

Last, what stands out so strongly, particularly in a time of retro-
gression and revision, is Father Lev's astonishing openness, the
incarnation in his thought and ministry of the absolute freedom of
Orthodoxy of which Father Elchaninov, Soloviev, and Berdiaev and
so many others of the Russian experience knew. Many years later, in
a journal entry that would find its way into his volume *Conjectures
of a Guilty Bystander*, Thomas Merton would write:

> If I can unite in myself the thought and the devotion of Eastern
> and Western Christendom, the Greek and the Latin Fathers, the
> Russians with the Spanish mystics, I can prepare in myself the
> reunion of divided Christians. From that secret and unspoken
> unity in myself can eventually come a visible and manifest unity
> of all Christians. If we want to bring together what is divided, we
> cannot do so by imposing one division upon the other or absorb-
> ing one division into the other. But if we do this, the union is not
> Christian. It is political, and doomed to further conflict. We must
> contain all divided worlds in ourselves and transcend them in
> Christ.[29]

In a remarkable manner, Father Lev accomplished just this union
and communion. Such a realization was the fruit of his own "return
to the sources" and his complex and painful pilgrimage, not only

from the Western Church to the Eastern Church but all of the many
side trips, one might call them, he also pursued over the years: his
exploration of the Judaic roots of Christianity, his fascination with
the traditions of the Orient, his willingness to listen to the voices of
what Evdokimov called "principled atheists," those with serious
criticism and questions of faith. Critics note that Father Lev was
himself a romantic, constantly disappointed, however, by the realities of those people and communities with whom he easily became
infatuated. Above all there was his powerful attraction to the Russian émigré community in France. He rhapsodized over the Eastern
Church, loved her adherence to the Tradition, the greater presence
in her, at least as he saw it in the 1920s, of the faith of the undivided
Church of the first millennium. Not without reason did he so deeply
fall for the Paris Russians, for among them, in Metropolitan Evlogy,
in Fathers Bulgakov and Elchaninov, in the spirit of Soloviev and the
person of Berdiaev, in Pierre and Evgraf Kovalesky, Nadia Gorodetsky, and Evdokimov did he experience the tremendous creativity
of a Tradition that knew itself in the suffering of persecution and
exile and yet was able in great freedom to be open to the rest of
Christendom and the world.

> O strange Orthodox Church, so poor and weak, with neither the
> organization nor the culture of the West, staying afloat as if by a
> miracle in the face of so many trials, tribulations and struggles; a
> Church of contrasts, both so traditional and so free, so archaic and
> so alive, so ritualist and so personally involved, a Church where
> the priceless pearl of the Gospel is assiduously preserved, some-
> times under a layer of dust; a Church which in shadows and silence
> maintains above all the eternal values of purity, poverty, asceti-
> cism, humility and forgiveness; a Church which has often not
> known how to act, but which can sing of the joy of Pascha [Easter]
> like no other.[30]

As Behr-Sigel's biography shows, the Eastern Church was big of
heart and free enough to accept the complicated, emotionally vacil-
lating, and restless pilgrim monk of the West as one of her own. And
in the Eastern Church, Father Lev was not spared any of the weaknesses or eccentricities he recognized her to possess. The best of his

intentions were often disregarded not only by Russian but also by Greek bishops, in Paris, Moscow, Jerusalem, and Istanbul. Even the Arabs, for whom he was to acquire a deep attachment, could be immensely disappointing to him. He was to find the hardening of canon law and episcopal authority and pure inertia wherever he went in the Orthodox world and even where Orthodox had moved and settled in the West. One can only wonder what he would have made of the chaotic and contradictory chacter of Orthodoxy here in the United States, with the curious blend of traditionalism and obsession with technology, the confusing overlapping of and conflict among jurisdictions allegedly in ecclesial and sacramental communion with each other. Time after time, Father Lev's ideals of the catholicity of the Church, her fullness and universality, her freedom and fidelity to the Lord and his gospel were seriously challenged by the actual clergy and laity with whom he lived and worked. Although Behr-Sigel does not conceal his discouragement and depression over the sad, sinful realities of the Christians who comprise the Church, her biographical sketch and Father Lev's own writings leave us with something more than dashed hopes and dreams of a reuniting Church.

In the end, Father Lev's life and his preaching suggest an attitude of hope over against a very messy ecclesiastical landscape. Both Clément and Behr-Sigel underscore his exceptional openness, a catholicity of heart, a universality and immense freedom without his ever being a relativist. To a large degree, Father Lev's life and ministry were on the margins of the institutional Church. Most of his efforts to obtain canonical recognition for groups wanting to enter Orthodoxy or use a Western rite for liturgical worship within an Orthodox jurisdiction proved unsuccessful. In the cases of Charles Winnaert and Evgraf Kovalesky, the inability of Father Lev to gain canonical acceptance for their efforts to form a Western Orthodox Church was hardly due just to his own ineptitude. In fact, he was rather astute ecclesiastically, as the voluminous correspondence he conducted, employed by Behr-Sigel in her biography, would indicate. All too often personal idiosyncrasies and obstinate attitudes probably did more to prevent acceptance than anything else.

It is also likely that Father Lev consistently fell between the ecclesiastical cracks himself. Thoroughly a Westerner, a Frenchman, and formed in the Roman Catholic Church, though he became fluent in

Russian, completely assimilated in Orthodox theology and liturgy, and something of a cultural cosmopolitan, he really could not be taken as "one of our own" by any of the jurisdictions to which he was attached, whether that of the Lviv diocese and Uniov monastery of Metropolitan Andrei Sheptytsky, the Western European exarchate of Metropolitan Evlogy, or the patriarchates of Moscow and Constantinople to which he was later connected. He was never formally excommunicated by Metropolitan Andrei and was never asked to formally renounce anything when received into the Orthodox Church by concelebrating the liturgy and confessing the creed.

Perhaps despite all the small details of his personality and disappointments of his ecclesiastical activity, <u>Father Gillet is nevertheless a kind of sign of both the schism and its healing.</u> There is a well-known statement, attributed both to Metropolitan Platon of Kiev and Metropolitan Filaret of Moscow, cited by none other than Metropolitan Evlogy of Paris:

> Men like St. Seraphim of Sarov and St. Francis of Assisi and many others have in their lives accomplished the union of the churches. Are they not citizens of the same holy and universal Church? At the level of their spiritual life they have gone beyond the walls which divide us, but which, in the fine expression of Metropolitan Platon of Kiev, do not reach up to heaven.[31]

At the beginning of a new millennium and century, many of the ecumenical hopes of Father Lev's youth and mature years, of those now seemingly golden years of contact and cooperative work especially after World War II, are in tatters. At best there appears well-intentioned but ineffective and unconnected gestures. Pope John Paul II's consistent appeals are for the most part ignored or fiercely rejected by many Orthodox bishops, theologians, and clergy just as theirs are apparently ignored by the Vatican. Several Orthodox churches, notably those of Georgia and Bulgaria, have left the WCC, and the participation of others such as that of Russia is suspended for the duration of negotiations and changes in the body's makeup and structure. The voice of the <u>exclusivist or traditionalist perspective within Orthodoxy</u>, that which recognizes nothing, no sacraments, priesthood, church, no grace whatsoever outside its own boundaries, is aggressive and loud, on Mount Athos, in other monastic centers such as Trinity–St. Sergius and Valaam. Any prayer with non-Orthodox Christians is condemned by appeal to the canons' prohibition against worship with heretics. Rebaptism of converts is required, as well as a range of other divisive and isolationist strategies such as use of the old calendar, use of Greek and Slavonic in liturgical services, and a host of other practices many of which are of relatively recent origin or are cultural rather than theological in nature. Sadly the response to such aggressive defining of what is authentic Orthodox belief and practice has recently been weak, overly cautious, or nonexistent.

Father Lev is not alone in witnessing otherwise. His closest friends and comrades, to a person, embodied the freedom of the Eastern Church: fidelity together with great love and openness to the world and the churches, speaking and acting as if the schism had never been or was by their very gestures being healed by the Holy Spirit. Many have been mentioned in this chapter, some are the focus of other chapters in this book, still more fall outside our view here.

However, we find in Father Lev's deep faith, persistence, and creativity, despite his discouragement and counterproductive ecclesiastical functioning, a sign of hope for ourselves. Despite all the personal weaknesses and failures, despite even the grand chaos, what Evdokimov termed "ecclesiastical anarchy," Father Lev (and his comrades) loved Christ and the Church and nurtured that love in whatever ways were possible. He remains a sign of what can be said and done, under the most trying circumstances.

CHAPTER SIX

Paul Evdokimov

Worldly Theologian, Man of the Church

Rediscovering and Reevaluating a Theologian

A saint is not a superman, but one who discovers and lives his truth as a liturgical being. The best definition of man comes from the Liturgy: the human being is the one of the *Trisagion* and of the *Sanctus* ("I will sing to the Lord as long as I live"). . . . It is not enough to say prayers; one must become, *be* prayer, prayer incarnate. It is not enough to have moments of praise. All of life, each act, every gesture, even the smile of the human face, must become a hymn of adoration, an offering, a prayer. One should offer not what one has, but what one is. This is a favored subject in iconography. It translates the message of the Gospel: *chairé,* "rejoice and be glad, . . . let everything that has breath praise the Lord." This is the astonishing lightening of the weight of the world, when man's own heaviness vanishes. "The King of Kings, Christ is coming," and this is the "one thing needful."[1]

It is now more than thirty years since the death of the Orthodox theologian Paul Evdokimov. Tomoko Faerber-Evdokimoff, his widow, has been responsible for the new editions of his works, and several of these continue to appear in new printings.[2] Several collections of his essays have been published, also through her indefatigable efforts.[3] During his lifetime, many of his writings were translated, and the following English editions of his work have been published: *The Art of the Icon* (1988), *The Sacrament of Love* (1985), and *Woman and the Salvation of the World.* (1994). The Paulist Press English translation of what Clément has called his "masterpiece," *Les âges de la vie spirituelle,* titled *The Struggle with God* (1966), had long been out of print, but Fr. Alexis Vinogradov and I revised the translation and *Ages of the Spiritual Life* was published by St. Vladimir's Seminary Press in 1998. A special number of the French journal, *Contacts,* commemorating him, "Paul Evdokimov, Témoin de la beauté de Dieu: Vingt-cinq ans après," number 172, appeared in 1995.

But just who is this theologian, fully a Russian yet writing only in French, thoroughly Orthodox but at home in the churches of the West, a scholar yet writing lyrically as a poet? He was one of a group who displayed enormous creativity, working within Church Tradition while pressing beyond theological borders—Berdiaev, Bulgakov, Gillet, Afanasiev, among others, and after them, Schmemann and Meyendorff. He is both a theologian of the Church and of the world. He is fully a teacher of the Church, always turning to her Tradition, revealing hidden treasures. At the same time, he constantly reaches into his twentieth-century world and speaks from experience in it. Participating in many aspects of life, public and private, momentous and mundane, he was spouse, parent, widow, Resistance member, counselor, administrator of hostels caring for the suffering and the marginal. He was a scholar and teacher, and in all of these vocations he was, as he put it, a "priest" of the universal, baptismal priesthood. In all things, he was, again in his own words, a "liturgical being," an "ecclesial soul." He spoke the language of our era, experienced and grappled with many of our problems: war, discrimination, political upheaval, and poverty, both economic and spiritual. Yet he was spiritually beyond the immediacy of our world's concerns, never overcome by them, not seduced with easy solutions. He constantly challenged the meaning of history, such as the Russian Revolution, as well as the seemingly impossible difficulties of the present, such as the misery in the Third World and developed nations' indifference to it. As the other persons of faith we are encountering here, Paul

Evdokimov presents us not only with a creative, challenging, and beautiful body of writing. He also presents us with a life of holiness, lived fully in the Church and in the world.

Sadly, many of Evdokimov's distinctive characteristics as a theologian also make him difficult to appropriate today. Much of this difficulty has to do with the present state of theology—overly academic, with virtually no ties to liturgy or to the community of the faith, and with primarily a critical, even adversarial orientation to Tradition. Such a climate is less than receptive to the liturgical, patristic, and iconographic richness of Evdokimov's theology, even its poetic qualities. In such wealth, he is most faithful to Church Tradition as the best Orthodox theologians of this century have also been. Evdokimov is singular in his compassion for the life of our time, and his life bears vivid witness to this. He expressed the Church's Tradition in innovative, elegant, and accessible ways. Yet by itself such an endeavor cannot succeed. Ultimately (and he understood it this way) the ecclesial theologian speaks within a community of meaning, to those who want to hear a word of meaning for life, not simply a loose assembly of critics.

As rich as Evdokimov's theological work is, it nevertheless faces resistance and rejection today, despite his effort to encounter the modern reader. Such is the case of theologians who choose to remain within the Church and the world while at the same time eschatologically moving beyond them, the mark, some would say, of authentic and classic theological work. All the aspects of his thought we will inspect here can be gathered together in what is the central motif of this essay, his stance and vision within and beyond Church and world. Fr. Alexander Schmemann was very much like Evdokimov in this dialectical position, and he saw it as exactly the place for the Church and her teachers to be in our time, within and beyond, in Pauline terms (and example), yet perfectly appropriate to God, *theoprepis*.[4]

A Life Within and Beyond

Evdokimov was both within and beyond the various worlds in which he lived: the Church and modern society, Orthodoxy and the

West, theology and culture. His belonging "within" is easier to understand, his being "beyond" somewhat more mysterious, because it
is eschatological. For him, this being beyond the boundaries was neither alienation nor rebellion but a sign of the very mystery he sought
to proclaim in his writing and life, the reality of the Kingdom of God
to come and at the same time powerfully present.

Evdokimov is a "witness to beauty," as Clément characterizes
him, a perceptive interpreter of the liturgy's poetry, choreography,
and music, of the icons' shimmering light and color, a riveting nar-
rator of the Church's teaching. On the same pages that he unpacks
Isaac the Syrian, Gregory of Nyssa, and John Chrysostom, he is discerning in his estimation of Marx, Nietzsche, Freud, and Jung. He is
at home with the urgency of Dostoyevsky and Gogol, Sartre and
Camus, Augustine and Thérèse of Lisieux. His essays resonate with
the suffering and resentment of the Third World as well as the excess
of European and North American affluence. These same texts brim
with contagious joy, rooted in the experience of martyrs and ascetics,
ancient and contemporary. He reveals our age's gifts, even, as Simone
Weil noted, the purification of faith brought by atheistic question-
ing. In an essay on sanctity, he argues that struggle, not resignation,
lies at the heart of the spiritual life, an experience universal to people
of conviction today.

Unlike Weil, Evdokimov was always at home in the Church,
acutely aware of her members' sin and of numerous mistakes in her
dealings with the world. Prayer was as natural as breathing for him,
so he was remembered. He was a child and a teacher of the Church
without hypocrisy or arrogance while at the same time perceiving,
as his close friend Fr. Lev Gillet and others did, the genuine
obstacles to and opportunities for faith, those that authentically
exist within oneself, those coming from outside, from the culture and
society, as well as those indeed raised by the Church herself.[5] He
understood the tragedy of the Russian Revolution to be providential, for in it he saw the resurrection that accompanies the cross, a
chance for Orthodoxy to be broken out of its long isolation, to
once again stand alongside the Western churches. In some respects,
his conviction about ecumenical reunion, for him a divine gift and
imperative, separates him from those Orthodox whose ecclesiology is radically exclusive. Evdokimov is among those who follow

Khomiakov's principle: "We know where the Church is, but we cannot be sure where it is not."[6]

Within and Beyond Orthodoxy

Though there are significant differences among them, Evdokimov
belongs with his Orthodox confreres who desired to share ecclesial
life with the West, his own teachers Nicholas Berdiaev and Sergius
Bulgakov, his friends Fr. Lev Gillet and Elisabeth Behr-Sigel, and
Fr. Nicholas Afanasiev, among others. Their strong personalities
often clashed, and they disagreed, as Aidan Nichols points out, yet
Evdokimov concurred with them that in its own renewal, Orthodoxy could build up the entire Church by sharing its lived Tradition
with the West.[7] In turn, Orthodoxy could recognize in the faces of
the West the original diversity and unity of the early Great Church,
realizations lost to the East through its historical isolation and ethnic factionalizing. With Father Lev he cherished a passion for the free
catholicity of the undivided Church and with him and others worked
for the recovery of this churchly communion.[8]

Precisely out of love for the Church, Evdokimov, like many of his
Orthodox colleagues, did not hesitate to identify abuses and affirm
normative ecclesial patterns. His criticisms, free of polemic, do not
deny what is wrong in, say, the abandonment of frequent communion and privatization of worship, clericalization, ethnic factionalizing, formalized theology, legalistic rigorism. These are identified,
but Evdokimov emphasizes the ideal, underlining the experience of
all celebrating and receiving the Eucharist, pointing out the interdependence of clergy and laity and the clergy's charism of service,
lifting up constantly the vocation of all the baptized, drawing attention to the urgency of living out the liturgy in one's status and role
in life. Passionately committed to the healing of the Church's divisions, Evdokimov consistently acted as though there were no schism,
according to his friend, the theologian Nikos Nissiotis. He did not
deny historical reality but strained beyond divisions toward the
divinely willed unity of the churches, consistently affirming the
actual unity in diversity, the *koinōnia* of the Church's first millennium. This sense of the original and ultimate unity of the Church

was shared by very few, among them the founder of Chevetogne, Dom Lambert Beauduin, and, of course Father Lev the ecumenical pioneer and ecclesial maverick. Some critics dismiss Evdokimov's perspectives generally, not just his ecumenical ones, as impractical, romantic, reckless, defective, even dangerous. Other figures of the time have been pasted with similar labels: Bulgakov, Afanasiev, Congar, Bouyer, Daniélou, de Lubac, to mention but a few. Evdokimov was in good company when it came to being both within and beyond the Church and the world. His own bishop, Metropolitan Evlogy, Father Lev, Mother Maria, his teachers Berdiaev and Bulgakov—all were criticized for their efforts to embody the Church's Tradition in living and contemporary forms: Metropolitan Evlogy for allowing such diverse creativity to bloom and for uniting with the ecumenical patriarchate for the pastoral good of his diocese, Father Lev for pursuing the ideal of catholicity in the Church, Mother Maria for making her untypical monastic life a service to the suffering people around her, Berdiaev and Bulgakov for exploring the depths of Tradition and connecting it with modern life.

Within and Beyond Ecumenical Issues

In his most comprehensive work, *L'orthodoxie*, Evdokimov provides a startling theological example of this within and beyond. Titled identically to his teacher Bulgakov's book introducing the Orthodox Church to the West, Evdokimov surpasses his mentor in presenting a sweeping yet probing tour.[9] He presents classical Orthodox ecclesiology: the Church is the life of the Holy Trinity among humankind, centered in the liturgy and prayer, in the experience of the Incarnation and the Kingdom, and then, secondarily, the Church consists in theology and ecclesiastical structure. He places the Eastern Church ecumenically, *among* the churches of Rome and the Reformation. Cutting through doctrinal and historical division, he argues, from the Fathers, that schism does not invalidate the life of God always flowing in the Church's sacraments and ministry. The Holy Spirit is not fenced out by the canons. For him, the Mother of God is the icon of the truly ecclesial soul, for only her *fiat* of prayer enables one to receive the ecumenical *epiklesis,* the Spirit's gift of unity.[10] Evdokimov is disturbing yet refreshing in his recognition, from deep within the Tradition, that the Church is not just historical but also charismatic and eschatological. The despairing *non possumus*—"we cannot"—of the ecumenical dialogues and their impasses are shattered by his vision that goes charismatically and eschatologically far beyond theological and ecclesiastical boundaries.

Evdokimov's understanding of the Church, of the schisms, of the Holy Spirit's restoring "communion in the holy things" is so profoundly rooted in Tradition that it is radical. Like those in Constantinople in 1054, he seemed, figuratively, to refuse the bull of excommunication. In his view, even error and sin could not obliterate the presence of the Holy Spirit among those who confessed Christ and his sacramental life in the Church. Evdokimov continued Soloviev's and Father Lev's creative yet disturbing ideas about ecclesial reunion. He developed a typology of the division of apostolic charisms among the churches, emphasizing their validity and unity in diversity while acknowledging their interdependence and the tragedy of their continued separation from each other. He spoke, leaning on Soloviev, of the "Pauline" (Reformation), the "Petrine" (Roman Catholic) and "Johannine" (Orthodox) churches being incomplete alone and fulfilled only in communion with each other, as in the millennium before the schism of 1054.[11] Yet he never advocated "full communion" by compulsion, scholarly consensus, or vote, so profoundly incarnational, charismatic, and eschatological was his ecclesiology. It would never be sufficient for the churches to merely combine resources for humanitarian work, or streamline their administrational structures for economic efficiency and call such achievements "unity." For him, the schisms would be healed by the Holy Spirit's "ecumenical *epiklesis*" and the conversion of the churches, Mary again the model. Only when the churches turned again toward each other and became icons of prayer would they receive the gift of restored communion in an "ecumenical Pentecost."[12]

A Life and Witness of Service, Within and Beyond

One's life is the arena in which salvation occurs, and such was the case with Evdokimov's remarkable journey of service and teaching in the Church but for the life of the world. Pavel Nicolaievitch was born in St. Petersburg on August 2, 1900, and died on September 16, 1970.[13] His life transversed more than two-thirds of the twentieth century and was molded by its events. After his colonel father's assassination in 1907, he was raised by his mother, a woman of profound faith, in a rich ecclesial life. After cadets' school, he began theological study at the Kiev Academy in 1918, but in the upheaval of the revolution he emigrated with his family, arriving in Paris in 1923. Along with Russian émigrés of every background, he worked in numerous jobs, far removed from his family's status and the academic career on which he had embarked. He drove taxis, washed railway cars, was a chef's assistant, and worked the night shift at Citroën. Yet in 1928, with the aid of a scholarship, he completed his theological degree at the St. Sergius Theological Institute, the newly opened Orthodox theological school in Paris. He was in the founding leadership of the Association of Christian Russian Students, also in the late 1920s. In 1927 he married Natasha Brunel, a teacher of Italian, and they had two children, Father Michel, now professor emeritus of comparative literature at Poitiers and an Orthodox priest, and Nina Pecheff-Evdokimov. In 1942 he completed a doctorate in philosophy at Aix-en-Provence with a thesis on Dostoyevsky and the problem of evil. The implicit theology of such masters as Dostoyevsky and Gogol would be a lifelong interest. He published *Le mariage, sacrement de l'amour* in 1944, an examination of the sacramental nature of marriage, of the home as *ecclesia domestica,* and of married life as vocation, as enactment of the universal priesthood of the baptized.[14]

During the occupation, Evdokimov was active in the Resistance, particularly with Protestant friends in CIMADE. His was a ministry of service: the hiding, protection, and aided escape of Jews, political prisoners, and other targets of Nazi oppression. With his wife's death in 1944, Evdokimov's life took what would appear to be another unusual turn. He did not seek ordination to the priesthood but remained a lay theologian. Despite his doctorate and two books, he did not enter French academic life after the war but continued diaconal work. He was the director of a CIMADE residence, first in Sèvres and later in Massey. Originally a hostel for war refugees and displaced persons, in the 1950s and 1960s it became a Christian house of hospitality for Third World students and other immigrants and for troubled youth and an assortment of other marginal people. Although never ordained, Evdokimov was the spiritual father of these households for two decades. As the remembrances eloquently describe him, he was always available for conversation, for quiet, compassionate listening, for fatherly advice.[15] He exercised a liturgical leadership in the community, presiding at table prayers and vespers in an ecumenical chapel at the hostel in Sèvres. In his memoir he identified his work as an exercise of the priesthood of Baptism, of the liturgical vocation to which all were called, lay or ordained, married or monastic.[16]

Evdokimov not only wrote with brilliance about the life of the Christian in the world, he lived out that calling most remarkably. The untypical witness of Pope John XXIII comes to mind, along with the theologian-pastor Dietrich Bonhoeffer and Father Lev. There is the witness of Mother Maria who adapted monastic life to a ministry to the suffering and who died as a martyr in Ravensbrück.[17] One thinks too of the hermit Charles de Foucauld, of Bede Griffiths, the English Benedictine planted in India, of Brother Roger Schutz of Taizé, of the American Trappist Thomas Merton, and of the American Orthodox theologian Alexander Schmemann, who connected, in a manner much like Evdokimov, the beauty of the world with the beauty of the life of the Church. Living the Church's faith and then reflecting on it in view of the complexity of our time seems to have put these individuals beyond ordinary ecclesiastical and theological categories, although faithfully still *within* them. This is precisely where one has to locate Paul Evdokimov. In an apparently contradictory manner, he remains within the Orthodox ecclesial and theological experience yet moves beyond it, not only in ecumenical work, but also in thinking and writing in a decidedly creative and worldly way that never abandons the Church's Tradition. Thus he speaks from within the Church. Yet in the actual targeting of his writing and his own activity, he is beyond ecclesial parochialism and situated within the social realities of our time, where the authentic ecclesial mission should be taking place.

Evdokimov was involved practically in ecclesiastical, ecumenical, academic, and diaconal work. In addition to the years of counseling and administration for CIMADE, he taught at the Ecumenical Institute at Bossey, along with Nikos Nissiotis. Engaged in youth work since the late 1920s, he participated in the establishment of the international Orthodox youth movement Syndesmos in 1953 and began teaching on the faculty of the St. Sergius Theological Institute while also offering summer theological conferences and programs for adult theological education, with Clèment. He was remarried, in 1954, to Tomoko Sakai, and in 1958 published his singular study of the place of woman in the faith and Church, *La femme et le salut du monde.* In 1959 he received the doctorate in theology from St. Sergius Institute for *L'orthodoxie,* a veritable treasure trove from which he would continue to bring out things old and new for the rest of his life.

Divine Philanthropy, the Theological Core

More than any of his texts, *L'orthodoxie* shows that what is sometimes criticized as Evdokimov's "pointillist" methodology is not at all a disordered dabbling with theological details. Rather, like his mentor Bulgakov, he reveals the freedom within the Tradition of the Church. He roots the myriad elements of the Church's life in her fundamental reality, the life of the Holy Trinity and the Incarnation. It is Evdokimov's grounding in the Tradition and his wonderful freedom within it that permits him to creatively speak of these theological basics as "anthropology." Here one perceives the real core of his entire theological vision, God's philanthropy, for like Nicholas Cabasilas, his thought is rooted in God's "foolish love" (*manikos eros*) for humankind. Very much like Berdiaev, Bulgakov, and Father Lev, Evdokimov primarily understood theology as the contemplation of God's suffering for his children, his limitless love.[18] It is in this sense that he can divide *L'orthodoxie* into, first, "anthropology," that is, God's action for us, and, second, "ecclesiology," God's living with us in the community of the Church, in the ecclesial life of scripture, prayer (above all the liturgy of the Eucharist), and the icons. Finally, he considers the "eschaton and last things," the presence and mission of the Church in the world, as the new eon, the rupture of time by the Kingdom. Seemingly disparate components are thus knit together in the unity of the divine and the human, in liturgy and life. From within her treasure, Evdokimov finds the force to push the Church out beyond herself, to be God's life, for the life of the world. At the same time he insists that the world is not to be rejected but finds its completion beyond itself within the Kingdom to come, already present within the Church. This dialectic pervades his writings. Whether examinations of "light" in the Scriptures, of the theological meanings of color and form in the icon, of the presence of God in apparent absence, of the shape of lived-out holiness in a figure like St. Seraphim of Sarov—each subject he treats is always referred back to the Incarnation and to the Kingdom. Each is a meeting of the Divine and the human, of the philanthropy within God reaching out beyond to invite, never coerce, reciprocal love from humanity.

Evdokimov's productivity continued into the 1960s. He was appointed an official observer at the third session of Vatican II in 1964 and is judged to have had some impact on the shaping of *Gaudium et spes,* the *Pastoral Constitution on the Church in the Modern World.* He published *Les âges de la vie spirituelle,* perhaps his finest work on the spiritual life in 1964, and in the mid-1960s the number of his journal articles continued to grow. In the late 1960s came his studies of the Orthodox Church's particular handing on of the Tradition with respect to the Holy Spirit, Christ, the life of holiness lived in prayer and the liturgy, and the icon and the theology of beauty it expresses (*La prière de l'Église de l'Orient,* 1966; *La connaissance de Dieu selon la tradition orientale,* 1968; *L'Esprit saint dans la tradition orthodox,* 1969; *L'art de l'icône. Théologie de la beauté,* 1970; *Le Christ dans le pensée russe,* 1970). Entwined with the themes of these monographs were Evdokimov's explorations of the unique *agapé* of God, his "kenotic" or emptying love, called *manikos eros, l'amour fou,* "absurd love," by Cabasilas, the fourteenth-century Byzantine lay theologian.[19] Although we shall examine Evdokimov's understanding of interiorized monasticism as an illustration of his simultaneously churchly and worldly theology, it would not be inaccurate to say that Evdokimov made divine philanthropy his central theological motif, God's infinite compassion and desire for our joy.[20]

Beyond Ecclesial Barriers: Mary and the Spirit

Evdokimov's love for the Church and understanding of her nature flowed into a passionate concern for the restoration of her unity. He suggested distinctive contributions Orthodoxy could make, proposing, in particular, approaches from within the Tradition to move beyond such formidable impasses as the *Filioque* and doctrines of Mary's immaculate conception and assumption. His firm footing within the Tradition gave him freedom and enabled him to push beyond fossilized formulations and ecclesiastical barriers to recover the truth of the Church's teaching, obscured by schism and polemics. Evdokimov was able to map out a course that could be steered through the debris of disagreement, back to the originally shared doctrinal truth. He sought to proceed beyond the impasse regarding the immaculate conception and assumption while at the same time returning to the essential teachings these dogmas intended to proclaim from within Scripture, liturgy, iconography, and piety. Evdokimov clarifies what these two dogmatic formulations really aim at: the embodiment in Mary of the truth of the Incarnation and basic Christology and the sharing of humanity in the divine life through the Paschal mystery. In elucidating the foundational affirmations, Evdokimov reinterprets these Marian dogmas and their intent within the Tradition of the Church. His efforts reduce some of the misunderstanding and imputed disagreement that has divided the churches. At the same time, he sought to share the treasure of Mary, especially with churches of the Reformation, thus seeking to move beyond objections not only to her but to the sacramental, incarnational, and iconographic realities of the Church she expresses.

Evdokimov also confronts the *Filioque* controversies. His analysis of the mutuality of the Trinity and his consequent argument of a *Spirituque* to accompany the *Filioque*, thus preserving the relations within the Trinity, are too complex to summarize here. Nevertheless, we again find in his work the pattern of within and beyond. Working from within the Trinitarian proclamation of the Scriptures, liturgy, and Fathers, carefully unraveling the initial intentions of the proponents of the *Filioque*, Evdokimov is able to urge the discourse beyond the usual philosophical ecclesiastical boundaries to offer not so much a solution as a fuller Trinitarian perspective, in which what was divisive no longer divides. Crucial here is his emphasis on the telos, or end of the Divine Trinitarian economy, namely, that the mutual *agapé*, love within the Trinity, flows out beyond God, in *philanthropia*, love for all mankind.

In the face of contemporary infatuation with social action, Evdokimov consistently affirmed the inseparability of sanctification from service, thus of liturgy from ministry to the neighbor. God does not demand the distortion or abuse of what is human. Never, according to Evdokimov, is prayer, liturgy, fasting, or any other religious action merely a formal requirement but always a free action of love, done in interaction with God and the rest of the ecclesial community.[21] There is no room for compulsion or mere formalism. As an authentic Orthodox spokesman, he nevertheless ventured far beyond the boundaries and isolation self-imposed by some Orthodox, for both theological and ethnic reasons. Evdokimov, as other émigré theologians already noted, remains faithfully within the Orthodox perspective but reveals just how this vision extends, by its very ecclesial, catholic character, beyond, to the rest of the ecumenical Church and to the world that God made, loves, and seeks to save. He also shatters many stereotypes in which the West still indulges, caricatures of Orthodoxy's doctrinal stagnation and ritualistic formalism. For championing just this living, free, and joyful character of Tradition, Evdokimov has evoked suspicion and outright rejection from hypertraditionalist rigorists in Orthodoxy.

Having established linkages of prayer, study, and service with Christians of the Reformed and Lutheran churches earlier in his life, in his later years Evdokimov forged strong ties with Roman Catholics, first through personal friendship with Dom Célestine Charlier and in writing for his journal, *Bible et vie chrétienne,* then through his work at Vatican II and through teaching at l'Institut Supérieur d'Études Oecumeniques of l'Institut Catholique in Paris. It was at a meeting of the French Mariological Society that he presented his last paper, a profound contemplation of the relationship between the Mother of God and the Holy Spirit, her divine maternity through the Holy Spirit's power. Drawing on the Scriptures and the Fathers, Evdokimov offers a creative reflection on Mary's role, both in the economy of salvation and in the life of the Church. It is a mariological contribution of considerable ecumenical import, bridging not only disagreements about the Mother of God but also other, even thornier divergences on the nature of the Church. In Mary, he argues, we have a double icon: of incarnational salvation in process, of divine grace and human assent meeting. At the same time, in Mary's *fiat* and the Holy Spirit's power, that is, in her divine maternity, we have an icon of what cannot be seen, of the divine paternity, of the Father's love and the Spirit's life-creating power, shown in the God become human through this faithful handmaid. On his return from the conference, Evdokimov added a concluding paragraph to this extraordinary piece, "Panagion et Panagia, le Saint-Esprit et la Mère de Dieu," on the eve of his sudden death.[22] In contemplating Mary as an icon of the Father's love through her maternity, Evdokimov affirms the incarnational and sacramental character of the Church, a bearer while also a receiver of divine grace, a fundamental ecclesiological principle much debated ecumenically.[23]

Theologian of the Church and the World

The generation of Paris-rooted theologians has drawn to an end. Only Olivier Clément, Fr. Boris Bobrinskoy, and Elisabeth Behr-Sigel are still active. Fathers Afanasiev, Kniazeff, Schmemann, and Meyendorff, along with Nicolas Zernov, Lev Zander, and Constantine Andronikov, are gone. With the passing of these earlier theologians, it might seem that with them, Evdokimov is superfluous, just the voice of another time. Some have maintained that he is not an original contributor but at best a "gifted popularizer." What does Evdokimov have to say? In many ways, he is as pertinent now, perhaps even more so, than a generation ago. He sought to appropriate for the rest of the world the distinctive contributions of the Russian Church and her spirituality without sentimentality or the urge to repristinate a lost time and place.[24] Similarly, his revealing of the Church's riches is devoid of the ecclesial chauvinism sometimes present in Orthodox circles. The Tradition of the Church, as dynamically experienced in the liturgy, icons, the "mind" of the Fathers, and in the saints' paths toward holiness—these are perceptively interpreted and shared. Moreover, his proclamation of the core of Christian faith is made, quite intentionally, to a culture seeking spiritual truth but repelled by religion of the traditional sort, and all too easily attracted by vendors of alleged holiness. In retrospect, essays like his appeal to the churches from 1950, his article (with Clément) on the preparation for an ecumenical council, or his varied pieces on the pursuit of sanctity, the art of prayer, and the "foolishness" of God's love are striking for their freshness, for the absence of ecclesiastical jargon and banal piety, and for their relentless honesty, both to Tradition and to the modern world's mind.[25]

In locating Evdokimov on the theological map and evaluating his contribution, it is helpful to recall his time and contemporaries, as well as examine the substance of his theological craft. Despite some differences in detail, he is very much in the company of Berdiaev, Bulgakov, Father Lev, and a number who preceded him, including the enigmatic nineteenth-century theologian Alexander Bukharev, who left monastic and priestly ministry for married life, the equally unusual Pavel Florensky, and the philosopher Vladimir Soloviev.[26] He shared their freedom to move creatively yet faithfully within the Church's Tradition, pushing beyond, as did the church fathers, to probe more fully God's revelation. Occasionally, this entailed returns to images and issues long ignored. Bukharev had incurred harsh criticism for probing the connection between Church and world, between the faith and the real life of Christians, their marriages and families, social and economic existence. In Bulgakov's case, it was exploring the figure of Divine Wisdom that became the target of attack. This signaled the intense uneasiness of his fellow Orthodox with Bulgakov's radical freedom in expressing the Church's faith to the modern mind and in such an inquisitive and creative manner. Such remaining within but pressing beyond provoked intense criticism, formal accusation, and censure by the Moscow patriarchate but also later exoneration. Bulgakov's name still evokes discomfort and critique among many Orthodox theologians. The same was later true, though less dramatically, for Afanasiev's "eucharistic ecclesiology."[27] Even within their own Orthodox circles, Evdokimov and his comrades were often criticized, unjustly, for "modernizing," accused of moving away from the Tradition, when in fact their accomplishment was only to push beyond more recent theological encrustations, to return to the sources. Their radicality lay precisely in their profound knowledge of the Tradition and fidelity to it, which afforded them enormous freedom in theological expression, the freedom of the life of the Kingdom. Their alleged novelty was actually restoration of earlier perspectives, now long obscured. Such would later be the fate of Fr. Alexander Schmemann in urging a return to the liturgy as the *theologia prima* and to the Eucharist as the core of ecclesial life. Paul Evdokimov was characterized by his contemporary, the equally gifted lay theologian Vladimir Lossky, not without certain sharpness, as "Orthodoxy's Protestant." Evdokimov's deep regard for the Reformation's rediscovery of the freedom of the gospel would have made him proud of such a label, I suspect.

For Evdokimov, this evangelical and hence theological freedom is rooted in the Holy Spirit's continuing presence in the Church. For him, as for his comrade, Father Afanasiev, it was always "the Church of the Holy Spirit," the title of Afanasiev's major work in ecclesiology. As Father Meyendorff would insist repeatedly, authentic Tradition is living, constantly finding new ways of expressing the unchangeable Truth. Thus one could remain within the Tradition while pushing beyond its boundaries, bringing the faith of the Church to the world. The worldly character of Evdokimov's life immediately distinguishes him and is an embarrassment, possibly even an impediment, to some extreme traditionalists while a characteristic of great attractiveness to still others. Although too much of an old world, cosmopolitan type to call him a countercultural figure, Evdokimov is nevertheless surprising, even refreshing, as a theologian both of the Church and of the world. He consistently speaks in different language, with a tone quite different from other theologians. One catches, for example, some of the same relentless passion for speaking the Church and the gospel honestly to the world as Rahner, Moltmann, Pannenberg, or Schillebeeckx, but more poetically and in elegant prose rather than the heavier, abstract academic style. For just this quality of his work, some critics still regard him as a gifted popularizer but nothing more, a characterization that is most inaccurate.

As a theologian, Evdokimov was always grounded in a lived faith, enacted in liturgy and prayer. He does not simply echo the Fathers but expresses their "mind," at once so genuinely humane and spiritual. For him, it could not be faithfulness to the tradition to mimic fourth-century ascetic practices in the midst of early twenty-first-century Paris or New York. The challenge is to discern the forms beyond the historical and cultural borders of a particular era while remaining within the authentic spirit of the Tradition. So, like the early desert monastics, prayer and service of the neighbor remains constant, while elements such as dress, the details of fasting, and the length of liturgical services should find the forms appropriate to Christians of our time and their life, exactly the path taken now for more than thirty years by the monks, nuns, and lay companions of New Skete in upstate New York.[28] Evdokimov argues for living Tradition, forms appropriate both to God and to the age, not simply unqualified preservation of the past. Not only abuses and misunderstandings, but the whole life of the Church is constantly being transformed by the Holy Spirit, a power not to be resisted. For Evdokimov, there are no theological justifications for continuing the balkanization of Orthodoxy into ethnic jurisdictions, perpetuating clericalist authoritarianism or introducing majority-vote democracy. Throughout his writings, with both reverence and integrity, Evdokimov identifies that which needs renewal or even removal in the life of the Church, yet he always recognizes the Church as more than an institutional arrangement, capable of constant engineering. Rather, like Father Schmemann in particular, Evdokimov calls for the transformation, the true churching of Christians, the authentic asceticism and martyrdom of being the Church in the modern age.[29]

In supporting the integrity of the Church's Tradition while at the same time recognizing the failings of her members, Evdokimov did not avoid controversial issues, among them, the role of women.[30] He did not support the ordination of women to the priesthood and defended this position not only by appeal to Tradition but also by arguments about the division of charisma between Christ and the Holy Spirit and between men and women in the economy of salvation and in the Church.[31] Yet at the same time, in the same writings, Evdokimov is a bold voice against the accumulated misogyny in the Church's history and for the unique gifts and callings of women in the Church, not only in marriage and monastic life, but in teaching and diaconal ministry. He presents the Mother of God as an archetype of the feminine, paralleled by John the Baptist as the masculine archetype, both reflecting the image and likeness of God, both alongside Christ in the classic *Deisis* icon, the image of the Church's economy of salvation. He develops the unique relationship of Mary to the Father and the Holy Spirit through her "yes" to divine maternity. Evdokimov emphasizes her as a type or model for the incarnational calling, the Christ-bearing vocation of the Church as a whole and of each individual Christian.[32]

A compelling account of Evdokimov's perspective on the Church in the modern world is found in the 1950 open letter to the churches. In it he captures secular culture's rigorous criticism of the Church, and he takes these challenges seriously, recognizing their sources in Marx, Nietzsche, Freud, Sartre, and Camus and in lived experience: the horrors of war, oppression and poverty, racial and ethnic hatred and violence. Rather than call for an abandonment of the Church in the many failures of her members, in their arrogance, he challenges the Church to truly become again what she is, communion with Christ. By this he understands a return to the fullness of her liturgical life of prayer and her mission of "incorporation" with the world, the Church's being, as the Eucharist, real bread for the life of the world. This is Evdokimov's incessant claim, expressed in the biblical images of salt, light, fire, food, and drink, that the Church is life transformed in Christ and that this is all the Church has to give.[33] He suggests that the establishment of a chair of atheism in every theological faculty would keep things honest. If, like the martyrs of the earliest days, the Church showed herself to be in constant conversation with Christ, there would be no mistake about her reason for being. He understood, for example, that the best liturgical renewal would be neither excision nor innovation but restoration of the ancient mode of celebration: in the language of all, by all of the assembly, in the fullness of the liturgy's hymns and prayers, in the completeness of the communion of all in the Eucharist, precisely the perspective of later liturgical theologians such as Aidan Kavanagh, Frank Senn, and Alexander Schmemann.[34] Evdokimov explicitly voiced such a perspective for transformation most explicitly not only in the liturgy but also in its necessary consequences, namely, the life of service to the neighbor, the "sacrament of the brother," as John Chrysostom called it. Not only was this Evdokimov's own experience, the exercise of the baptismal priesthood wherever one found oneself, it was also the understanding of Church in the world he promoted in his theological work.

From the Desert Monastics to Our Day:
"Interiorized Monasticism"

One should not be surprised that Evdokimov would focus on marriage and monasticism, only to reveal startling connections and elements. In examining marriage and its distinctive spirituality, only he would choose to inspect its distinctive martyrdom and asceticism. He is the only theologian in recent or even longer memory to bring marriage and monastic life into such close connection, thus revealing not only common points of struggle but also how these two apparently opposite forms of life complement each other.[35] In this he pays tribute to Bukharev and Father Lev.[36] One of his principal gifts to our understanding and practice of the spiritual life is his identification of monasticism's radical witness to the Kingdom, its eschatological maximalism, and his application of this to the whole of the Church. This recognition was not original to him but had earlier been stressed by John Chrysostom and Basil the Great and more recently by Tikhon, Bukharev, and Schmemann, among others.[37] Evdokimov even uses St. Tikhon's own expression for this: "interiorized monasticism." With only a few exceptions, this most inventive of his theological contributions, truly a spirituality at once primitive and contemporary and for all Christians, has been scarcely studied.[38]

In a manner startling to churchly sensibilities both inside and outside of Orthodoxy, Evdokimov suggests that the spirituality of monasticism, while being lived out very particularly, that is, in celibacy, community of goods, obedience to the superior, and constant prayer, is at root not unique or even restricted to monastics. Following Chrysostom, Basil, and other commentators, he claims that the form of discipleship preserved and enriched by the second- to sixth-century desert monastics is, in its essentials, universal for the Church. Monasticism, he argues, was in its origins an evangelical and ecclesial impulse, an eschatological passion given by the Holy Spirit for constant renewal. Monastic life, in earliest expression and down through the history of the Church until today, is nothing more than the Paschal mystery being lived out in great intensity. In its historical and cultural context, monastic spirituality was a response of struggle and witness, a nonbloody *askesis* and *martyria* after the persecutions, in a situation of churchly domestication to the culture, a time of disintegration, as Kierkegaard was to call it.[39]

The monastic impulse was paradoxical: to heal by painful transformation of self, to save the world by flight from it, only to enter more deeply into combat with the Evil One in the solitude of the desert, to begin living in Paradise here and now.[40] It is the Holy Spirit's renewing the life of the Church, truly charismatic therapy. This divine healing is always personal: *conversatio morum,* the conversion of one's whole self and life.[41] The early monastics did not seek to escape the world but to encounter it more intensely. To do this, though, they had to reclaim radical ecclesial existence, and in post-Constantinian Christendom, they had to again go apart, as the first disciples of Jesus.[42] As Douglas Burton-Christie amply documents in his study, the early monastics' spirituality was far from self-centered, as is the case with so much that passes for "spirituality" in contemporary culture.[43] Rather the intense life of prayer, particularly in the Scriptures, the rigorous scrutiny of self over against the biblical and liturgical word, was for the building up of the neighbor and the self into Christ. This is what Evdokimov calls the true therapeutic of ascetic struggle, none other than Jesus' own response to the temptations of the Evil One.[44] Through the vows of poverty, chastity, and obedience, the Christian renounces the domination of material wealth, selfish carnality, and the ego so as to receive authentic freedom: life with God.[45] Here he leans heavily on the brilliant nineteenth-century Russian theologian Bukharev, who himself moved from the monastic back to lay life while affirming the connections between the two. False identity is exchanged for one's true identity in God. One becomes both cross bearer (*staurophore*), a classical appellation for the monastic, and Spirit bearer (*pneumatophore*), an agent of the Holy Spirit for the sanctification and the salvation of the rest of the community and of the world.[46] Such transformation is worked out through the charisms of the spiritual life: discernment, impassibility, silence, vigilance, repentance, humility, and joyful dying, easily recognizable as the essentials not just of monastic existence but of universal Christian discipleship.[47] The charismatic, evangelical, and liturgical life Evdokimov sketches out in classical monasticism is not only for reappropriation by contemporary monastics, as readings in the work of Merton, Kelty, Cummings, and Louf would clearly indicate. For Evdokimov, this pattern of Christian living can be received and lived in our culture. It will be "interiorized," not so much privatized but simplified, adapted to the texture and tempo of existence in our time. Monasticism in particular and spirituality in general must never devolve into antiquarian re-creation, like our "interpretive" historical sites, with characters in authentic period dress and dialect. There is simply no room in Ev-dokimov's vision for what some traditionalists would identify as the only authentic examples of monastic or more general ecclesial life, namely, versions that are eccentric, nostalgic flights backward in time, and there are both parishes and monastic communities of this sort. Fasting today should not be a slavish replication of the dietary practices either of the Egyptian Thebade or the northern Russian lavra but would involve restraint from modern excesses of either indulgence or meticulousness in consumption. Clearly, the striving for silence entails direct combat with and flight from the relentless, enveloping sound of our culture and its technological possibilities. Dependence on alcohol, drugs, stimulation, even sex and work is ripe for ascetic struggle and reordering. So too the management of one's surplus income, relationships, and especially time are most appropriate sites for an asceticism of faithful simplicity and churchly wholeness.

Evdokimov would not recognize interiorized monasticism as a historical facsimile, an intellectual fantasy, or a repertoire of spiritual techniques. The life of the first monastics, as their *Sayings* and ac-companying literature teaches, was most concrete, a true collision of flesh and blood with the Spirit. Evdokimov fondly and frequently quotes the ancient monastic dictum: "Shed your blood and receive the Spirit."[48] Thus the paramount elements of the spiritual life be-queathed by the early monastics are, not surprisingly, those of the Church's liturgical life: the common reading, singing, praying, hear-ing and teaching of the scriptures and sharing of the eucharistic Bread and Cup.

Clement of Alexandria shows that we must nourish ourselves on the seeds of life contained in the Bible as we do in the Eucharist (*Strom.*, 1, 1). It is Origen who fixed the meaning of the "eating" of the Scriptures (P.G., 13, 130–34) and tradition has followed him. We consume "eucharistically" the "Word mysteriously broken" (P.G., 13, 1734; John Chrysostom, *In Gen. Serm.*, 6.2; Gregory Nazianzus, *Oratio, 45*, 16). St. Jerome says: "We eat His flesh and drink His blood in the divine Eucharist, but also in the reading of Scripture" (*Eccles.*, 3, 13). St. Gregory Nazianzus compares the reading of the Bible to the consummation of the paschal lamb. This eucharistic manner of consuming the Word presupposes the *epiklesis* of every reading. . . . At the time of the liturgy, the people are convoked first to hear and then to consume the Word. This hearing builds up the people of God, forms the eucharistic preparation for consuming the Word incarnate, and for entering into substantial communion with the Word.[49]

To this "liturgical existence" is joined the royal, priestly, and prophetic life of service. Each Christian is called and anointed to such service by baptism and confirmation and chrismation.[50] There can be no self-centered salvation *(Solus Christianus nullus Christianus).* Many are saved by an individual's conversion to Christ (e.g., St. Seraphim). So the Church cannot be dissected into those who act and those who are passive. It consists of those ordained to teach and preside at the liturgy and serve as pastors as well as the faithful. Together they are the royal priesthood, the holy people called to be the salt, yeast, and the light for the life of the world. Many of the dead-end disagreements of current ecumenical dialogues find authentic resolution in Evdokimov's ecclesiological vision from within the Tradition: the Church is always conciliar, "sobornal." Authority in the Church is never just from above, held by the clergy, but centered in Christ, enlivened by the Holy Spirit, in a community always including both pastors and people. The Church's identity and truth are best expressed in the eucharistic assembly.[51]

From the inheritance of the desert monastics and all who have followed them, the Christians of today receive and make their own the same eschatological maximalism, interiorizing the same urgency for the Kingdom. Now it is to be lived out in offices, schools, living rooms, and kitchens as well as in church.[52] The Trinity is present at the same eucharistic table and in the same Scriptures read and prayed.

The same Lord is there to be served in the neighbor. In his own writings, Fr. Michel Evdokimov emphasizes that his father's vision of interiorized monasticism always involves an "interiorized ministry," a vocation of service to God and the neighbor, through the liturgy and the Church and beyond, in and toward the world.[53] For every Christian, the sacraments of initiation confer the dignity of prophet, priest, and king.[54] Every profession and state in life can be a form of this universal priesthood. In the liturgy, such a priest "makes of everything a human offering, a hymn, a doxology."[55] Then, in daily life, in the "liturgy after the liturgy" of St. John Chrysostom, such a Christian is

> freed by his faith from the "great fear" of the twentieth century, fear of the bomb, of cancer, of communism, of death; [his] faith is always a way of loving the world, a way of following his Lord even into hell. This is certainly not a part of a theological system, but perhaps it is only from the depths of hell that a dazzling and joyous hope can be born and assert itself. Christianity in the grandeur of its confessors and martyrs, in the dignity of every believer, is messianic, revolutionary, explosive. In the domain of Caesar, we are ordered to seek and therefore to find what is not found there—the Kingdom of God. This order signifies that we must transform the form of the world, change it into the icon of the Kingdom. To change the world means to pass from what the world does not yet possess—for this reason it is still this world— to that in which it is transfigured, thus becoming something else— the Kingdom.[56]

So the early monastics' pattern is a model for all Christians. Evdokimov confirms their wisdom, later Luther's, about "vocation." The world becomes a monastery, every state in life is a vocation, all areas of work are places for the exercise of the universal priesthood, each Christian is *monachos,* the one who alone seeks only God. The "alone" here means not in isolation but solely, only God. And for Evdokimov, such a single-minded goal is always ecclesial and sacramental, which is to say, liturgical and communal.

Liturgical Existence: The Way of Holiness Within and Beyond

Like Afanasiev, Kern, and Schmemann, the Eucharist is for Evdokimov the very heart and life of the Church.[57] The liturgy is the fundamental icon of the Kingdom—the mystery and miracle of heaven and earth meeting, of the divine becoming human, transforming all creation.[58] Like Maximus the Confessor, Nicholas Cabasilas, and so many others, Evdokimov writes a commentary on the eucharistic liturgy and on the rest of the liturgical life, not only in *L'orthodoxie,* but also in a beautiful essay on the life of prayer, *La prière de l'Église d'Orient,* and in an exquisite examination of the life of holiness. The liturgy is at the heart of his work on the theology of beauty and on the icons, *L'art de l'icône,* at the conclusion of which are superb meditations on the principal feasts and icons of the liturgical year. Occasionally, as at the conclusion of *L'orthodoxie,* Evdokimov cannot be restrained any longer by words. The vision must be described iconographically. The beauty within the Church irresistibly beckons beyond, to the light of the Kingdom.

Perhaps a place should be allowed for an image which can say much more than words. In the interior of Orthodox churches one can see the iconostasis, a wall which separates the sanctuary from the central nave, the Kingdom from the world. In its origins, this was a low barrier which separated the people from the altar in order to maintain necessary order during church services. In the passage of time, the genius of the liturgy has adorned this line of separation with certain icons in their proper place and sequence, covering the entire surface of the iconostasis. The Christ of the *Deisis* icon is enthroned at the center, shining forth, and all around Him stand the saints, who sing and who reflect His light. This assembly makes us see with sharpness the wonderful metamorphosis: what was in the beginning a wall of separation has become a bridge. Christ establishes by his saints the passage—the Pascha—for each and every one of us into the Kingdom. Each and all are invited to deepen the luminous presence of Christ, this birth and second coming by the Spirit's breath, and it is a miracle that through this spirit-bearing Nativity and Parousia of Christ in us—already the Kingdom—that our separation can be changed into a connection, a unity. The Orthodox, the Catholics, the Protestants, walking on the way of holiness toward the terminus, which is Christ, can find themselves once again to be living icons, reunited on the iconstasis of the Temple of God, the royal door, opening to the depths, the abyss of the Father.[59]

There are so many themes that Evdokimov handled with such finesse and affection. Some of these I have mentioned briefly, such as his work on the Holy Spirit and the Mother of God, his understanding of God's "foolish love," his traditional yet radical thinking about the reunion of the churches, his centering on the eucharistic core, the liturgical nature of the Church. There are others: his deft treatment of theological dividers such as the *Filioque* and the Marian dogmas, the Petrine office, the ecumenical goal of full communion. I have not been able to delve into these at length. Given the unusual course of his life, his focus on myriad issues, and his great ecclesial freedom, it is not surprising that there should be criticism, not only of his method and his chosen topics, but also of his conclusions. There remain those in Orthodoxy who are repelled by the very freedom he found precisely within the Tradition of the Church, a dynamic communication he knew to be true and vivifying. For such as these, Evdokimov could never be traditional enough. His ability to discern between the different expressions of spirituality from one age to another would appear to violate what some understand as the timelessness of Tradition, that is, an invariable conformity, in substance and details, both interior and exterior. His pushing beyond, while remaining within Tradition, is not recognized for the eschatological vision it sustains but is suspect, rather, as mere innovationism, a capitulation to the restlessness of modern consciousness. Still others would fault him for not being radical or free enough, for staying too much within Tradition and for not venturing out far enough, for not moving outside the community and its faith heritage. Much current theological debate rages on about patriarchy, hierarchy, ethnocentrism, misogyny, and racism in the doing of theology, in liturgy and in church life. Here Evdokimov would be guilty of not having something more radical to say about issues that are highly controversial now, such as the place of women in the Church, the language with which we speak of God, the deepening crisis of authority in the Church, to note just a few.

One could not claim that Evdokimov has a solution acceptable to viewpoints dominant in the Church and culture today. Yet he reveals the truth of the Tradition in its beauty. He provides a rich vision of ecclesial being. Here I have been able to dwell at length on only one, his view of an inheritance of spirituality from the past. After all, the "ages" of the spiritual life of which he wrote are also the ages of the Church's life. The "interiorized monasticism" he described is no "method" of spiritual exercise as the old manuals used to prescribe, no museum shop reproduction but a living pattern of Christian holiness, proven in Tradition, one that has served regularly as a source of renewal. His interiorized monasticism bears within the fullness of the Church's Tradition, but he shows that this churchly, liturgical life of holiness can and should be lived beyond ecclesiastical, historical, and cultural boundaries. Evdokimov's gift is to reveal how one can live within the Church in great freedom and joy, without being imprisoned. Moreover, he demonstrates in his writing and life how remaining within urges one beyond to the world, in compassion and loving service, whatever one's place in life. Here, I think, can be found the authentic inclusivity of the Church, an eschatological openness quite unlike the pathetic attempts of many churches today to be all things to all people.

In Evdokimov, an Orthodox Christian to the core, one finds the evangelical passion for holiness lifted up by some of the Western churches, particularly those of the Reformation. He was able to find and delight in what some desert monastics called the paradise of the present, the Kingdom from beyond very much within everyday life, God in the neighbor's face. Here we find the most convincing evidence of Evdokimov's theological singularity, of his faithful speaking from within the Tradition and the twentieth century, and of his eschatological position precisely beyond where we are so likely to draw both ecclesial and cultural boundaries. Here is his relevance to our time. His vision is rooted in the Eucharist and extends to a life of praise, a lived liturgy of holiness in which there is never a conflict between communion and service, in which one becomes prayer, in everything.

CHAPTER SEVEN

Gregory Krug

Artist of the Icon, Theologian of Beauty

Other than a collection of notes on the relationship of icons to the feasts and theology of the Church, all of which form only a very slim volume, George Ivanovitch Krug produced no body of writings.[1] He produced no volumes of theology and did not achieve substantial changes in church life such as eucharistic revival or the granting of autocephaly in the manner of Fathers Bulgakov, Afanasiev, Schmemann, and Meyendorff. He was not a sought after preacher, teacher, retreat master, or pastoral counselor as were Fathers Lev and Men. And he was not a social activist and organizer of humanitarian assistance, as were Mother Maria and Evdokimov.

But like the rest, in the phrase of Evdokimov, he was truly an "ecclesial being," one who did not simply say prayers but "became prayer." This he did as a master of the "theology of beauty," by being perhaps the century's premier artist of the icon, but also as a monk and most basically as a person who struggled hard throughout his life—with the upheavals of emigration from revolutionary Russia and settlement in two foreign countries, with the poverty of the émigré population and of the Great Depression, with severe depression and other emotional troubles, with the horrors of confinement in a psychiatric hospital during the German occupation of Paris, and finally through the monastic vocation during the last twenty years of his life. Sensitive and gifted artistically, he was trained in several media: watercolor, oil, etching, printmaking, and drawing. He came

to the making of icons in adulthood, just as he came to the Orthodox Church. Nevertheless, his was a simple, quiet life of prayer,
study, and work, an authentic "ecclesial existence," both as a layperson and, later, as a monk. Drafted into the making of icons out of
sheer need and the lack of trained iconographers, he created a body
of iconography of singular originality and unsurpassed beauty. While
some of his icons have deteriorated because of the conditions of their
locations and the limited materials he used, given the poverty of the
depression and post–World War II France, those that remain, both
in situ and in photographed documentation, are among the finest of
the contemporary efforts.

Father Andrew Tregubov, himself a gifted iconographer and priest
in the Orthodox Church in America, with assistance from Alexander Solzhenitsyn's Russian Social Fund, traveled around France in
the early 1980s with the iconographer Elisabeth Ozoline, who had
known Father Gregory, and worked with his colleague in iconography, Leonid Ouspensky, to document his icons, particularly those
in church settings. The fruit of this endeavor of preservation through
documentation is an extensive collection of slides of the icons of
Father Gregory. Father Tregubov has presented many lectures across
the country and taught courses using these slides. With the assistance
of the Diocese of New England and its then hierarch, Bishop Job
(Osacky), himself an iconographer, a selection of twenty-two plates
with a page of reflection on each was published.[2] Father Tregubov
notes in his introduction that such a publication makes more widely
accessible and permanent Father Gregory's now hidden and disappearing but magnificent gift to the Church and the world, namely,
his "theology in color," the face of God in the faces of Christ and the
Mother of God, saints and angels. Given the technical precision
needed to accurately reproduce Father Gregory's work, I simply
make reference to this and to another collection of reproductions
mentioned below for a meaningful overview of his ability to communicate the beauty of the Kingdom in his icons. The sampling presented here is limited to several of the icons Father Gregory made
for the church of St. Seraphim of Sarov in what was an orphanage
and is now a retreat center and hostel in Montgeron, outside Paris.

More recently, on the thirtieth anniversary of Father Gregory's
death, his monastic colleague and caregiver during his final illness,

Father Barsanuphius, edited a collection of eighty-five reproductions of his iconography both in his own skete of the Holy Spirit at Mesnil-St. Denis and in Mother Maria's nursing home chapel of the Mother of God, the Joy of All Who Sorrow, at Noisy-le-Grand, now in the chapel of the Monastery Znaménié at Marcenat.[3] This collection included a biographical sketch. Father Barsanuphius also edited a collection of articles published about Father Gregory from 1969 to the present, a wealth of reminiscences and information about his life, artistic training, and work. A conference on Father Gregory was held in June 1999 at the Sorbonne, sponsored by the Research Group on the Russian Emigration (GRER).[4]

An Artist's Life, a Soul's Journey

To regard Father Gregory only as an artist, albeit a "sacred" artist, would be to severely diminish the scope of his work and life. In many ways, though not a teacher, writer, or lecturer, his own soul's journey is itself a rich, moving icon of faith in our times.

Much like others in this volume, Father Gregory was a man of contrasts, one in whom contradictory qualities existed side by side. Though an artist by training, first in his native Estonia and then in Paris, he was repelled by most modern art, particularly abstract art, favoring Soviet realism and American illustration. By all accounts, he was wonderfully intelligent and an attentive listener, full of joy and sensitive in welcoming every guest to his small hermitage, or skete. He was unusually well read in art history, iconography, architecture, and theology, if not formally educated other than in studio art. Yet he was also reclusive, given to emotional reactions, stubborn in certain behaviors such as dealing with doctor's orders and medications. He would not allow anyone to watch him work on his icons. He was devoted to his Russian culture and Church, even to Russia itself despite Soviet rule. He was thoroughly committed to the Tradition of the Church, from the canons on iconography to the liturgical prescriptions of the *Typicon*. This was consistent from his youthful membership in the 1930s in the Paris Confraternity of St. Photius, an association dedicated to retaining ecclesial communion with the patriarchate of Moscow and to communicating the

Orthodox tradition and faith to the West. His close friend, the lay theologian Vladimir Lossky, was a founding member of this group. Yet at the same time Father Gregory used all sorts of materials in his iconography in a nontraditional manner. As Father Barsanuphius observes, Father Gregory would use the decomposed egg white as well as the yolk for his tempera paints. Later on in his work the boards for the icons were coated not with the usual layers of gesso, that is, powdered lime or alabaster, but with casein, "cheese" as he called it. He would use linseed oil that had aged to the point of being rancid to enhance the drying action of the varnish or olifa that seals an icon. He would employ all sorts of materials for pigments, including garlic, ground coffee, and shoe polish. He mixed pigments, loaded with toxic substances, in his bare palm. His hands would often be absent-mindedly wiped on his hair or his monastic habit. He would continue to retouch icons even after the final varnish had been applied to seal the work. These are among the reasons that some of his iconography has deteriorated and cannot be restored or repaired.

Even a casual inspection of the reproductions of his work leads to the conclusion that Father Gregory was careful about adhering to the canonical forms even in minute details for depicting various feast icons and icons of Christ, the Mother of God, the angels and saints. Yet he would allow the Tradition of the Church to guide but not imprison his iconography, particularly in the creative and expressive quality of many of his frescoes, especially those for the church of Fr. Euthymius Wendt's chapel in Moisenay. There Father Euthymius, the superior as well as the architect of the chapel and a student and spiritual son of Father Bulgakov, commissioned him to do icons of Divine Wisdom. He insisted despite Father Gregory's theological and artistic objections that he paint Divine Wisdom in a trinity of representations, as the Angel of Fire, then as a variant of the *Deisis,* the Throne of Heaven, with the Mother of God in the center painted directly on a column of the church, with her parents, Sts. Joachim and Anna, the "ancestors" of God, taking the usual places of the Virgin and St. John the Baptist, and finally the Wisdom of the Cross.[5] Father Gregory and Father Euthymius filled the chapel with the echoes of their "discussion," yet in the end these unusual frescoes were completed. Even in more conventional icons, the size of the hands and the head, the immense tenderness of the faces, the vibrancy of colors—all seem to explode the iconographic forms, making the work of other iconographers seem dull by comparison, mere copies. In the church of St. Seraphim, he made extremely large icons of Christ and the Mother of God for the icon screen and had Christ holding a closed book, all of this so as to focus the children's attention on them and make them as accessible as possible. Further, as Father Barsanuphius also points out, in his extraordinary attachment to St. Genevieve of Paris, Father Gregory spoke of her as one would speak of an intimate friend. Even when she was not even asked for, he would include her in an icon screen or in a fresco of otherwise Russian saints, even depicting a meeting between her and her contemporary in distant Syria, the famous St. Simeon the Stylite, a meeting that occurred only in spirit and through messages conveyed by pilgrims.

An Unusual Child, a Gifted Youth, a Time of Trial

George Ivanovitch Krug was born on January 5, 1908, in St. Petersburg, his father of Swedish background and a Lutheran, his mother Russian and an Orthodox Christian, neither particularly active in Church life. Valentine Marcadé includes a number of childhood anecdotes, most likely related by his sister Olga Ivanovna, that indicate his independence of spirit and imagination. His recitation of the Our Father during bedtime prayers at the greatest volume he could muster was because God was so old, so deaf, and so far away that otherwise the prayers would not be heard, or so the little George had inferred from the way in which God had been presented to him.

There are also tales of fearless yet risky behavior as he grew older, a near drowning when swept off in the current on a raft in the Neva River, a wild ride on his skis down a mountainside in Estonia. He changed from a quiet, docile, almost "model child" whom his mother called by such nicknames as "chicken-brain," "owl's eye," and "toad-neck."[6] With many others, his family fled to the then still free Baltic republic of Estonia, where he completed his secondary education at Narva. George continued art training in watercolor technique with the painter N. V. Semionov, then graphic arts at the Tallin School of Art, particularly printmaking and etchings. Some of his etchings of urban scenes were purchased from a show of the school's best students' work by the National Museum, dark views of houses and streets yet with light leading the eye beyond to something, somewhere else than the darkness. In 1928 he studied in a private academy in Tartu with Glinka, learning oil technique. He immersed himself in keyboard studies at the same time, even presenting a Bach recital that drew very favorable reviews. Yet he abruptly gave up the piano after the same concert.

Moving to Paris, the Western center of the Russian emigration, in 1931, George studied with D. N. Milioti, who had taught at the Russian Academy briefly in existence under the leadership of Tolstoy's daughter, Tatiana Lvovna. Among other young artists he met Leonid Ouspensky, who would become a lifelong friend and an important iconographer and scholar of iconography. Invited by the painter Somov to his summer home in Normandy, he perfected his draftmanship, and a number of sketches remain of the countryside and later of Paris street scenes. He also worked on illustrations for one of Gogol's novels. There was much of promise and of great expressiveness in his work during the early years in Paris. However, several decisive turns took place there too.

A significant encounter occurred in 1924 with Lev Liperovsky, physician and later priest, at a gathering of the Russian Christian Students Movement at the Pskov-Petcherskii monastery in Estonia. In the company of so many other young émigrés, George must have discovered for the first time a living faith, expressed in the liturgical worship, especially in the Eucharist, inspired by many who themselves had come to rediscover the faith they had abandoned in pre-revolutionary Russia. George, who was still living in Estonia, was led to the Orthodox Church and became what Evdokimov so often called an "ecclesial being." Long before he entered monastic life in 1948, he attended services, receiving communion at every liturgy and serving as a reader.

Having already begun the study and painting of icons in Estonia, in the French capital and its environs he continued his iconography training with Sister Joanna Reitlinger and A. P. Feodorov. He and Ouspensky were commissioned to create the iconography for the Three Saints Church in Rue Petel in 1935. They also collaborated on a chapel dedicated to the Virgin's Protecting Veil (Pokrov) at the

Russian Grosrouvre farm, in Monfort l'Amaury in Yvelines.[7] At
Three Saints one can still see their second marvelous cooperative
effort in this church, done between 1959 and 1961; both painted frescoes in the nave and in the altar area and the double iconostases.
Running the entire width of the church, above the two iconostases,
is Ouspensky's series of feast icons in fresco, the one festal event, the
raising of Lazarus, running into the next, the Palm Sunday entrance
into Jerusalem, moving right into the Last Supper and the Crucifixion, and so on, an ingenious nod to the end of our historical time
in the kingdom of heaven. Around the perimeter of the back are
Father Gregory's frescoes of the apostles. Now partially obscured
by music stands and lecterns are two assemblies of saints and angels
by Father Gregory, processing toward the royal doors, oriented
toward the holy table and the center of eucharistic worship in the
church.

During the later 1930s George, "Doudik" to his friends, developed
a number of symptoms of emotional illness. As Father Ozoline,
Anne Bogenhardt, and his friend Leonid Zuroff report, he became
more and more "feverish" in his activities and external comportment.
He also became more withdrawn from people, painting all night and
then destroying what he had made. He seemed to be gripped by a
great fear and by the sense that some sinister force had gained control of him. His precarious, even alarming emotional state troubled
his family and friends. His sister believed his intense spiritual life,
disorganized and without a spiritual father, was also part of the problem. With his consent and for his own protection, she hospitalized
him at the psychiatric hospital Sainte-Anne, on November 6, 1942.
He remained there until July 1, 1943. Again in 1944 he was unable
to respond emotionally to his mother's death, two years after the
sudden death of his father in Estonia, and he was again hospitalized
by his sister at Sainte-Anne for his own protection.

George Ivanovitch was hospitalized during a terrible period, the
German occupation. The patients barely survived, especially when
the Nazi occupiers deprived them of food, as the mentally ill were
but another category of those deemed "unworthy" of life and in line
for extermination. The patients at Sainte-Anne were reduced to eating even the weeds and grass that grew in the courtyard, where they
were allowed for air and exercise. Yet in the midst of this hell, in the

phrase of a twentieth-century saint, the Russian monk Silouan of Athos, George Ivanovitch did not despair. He assiduously continued his art, doing countless portrait sketches of his fellow inmates. These his sister picked up on her weekly visit and then took from one Russian parish to the other to sell, to buy food for her brother that he shared with his asylum mates. Catherine Aslanoff, Vladimir Lossky's daughter and the godchild of Father Gregory, underscores the deep respect and tenderness in these drawings.[8] They attest to his love for his fellow inmates and what one might even call a ministry of compassion, while he himself suffered in a dark night of the soul. Much points to some kind of depression rather than a deeper, decisive psychopathology. His gradual restoration in his spiritual father's care bears this out.

Healing and Peace in Monastic Life

On his release from Sainte-Anne, Father Gregory lived with his sister. Eventually he found a home in the parish of the Holy Trinity in Vanves, just outside Paris. Living in a room next door, he served as the reader for services there, became a regular communicant, and found in the pastor, Sergius Schevitch, a spiritual father. In addition to Olga, Father Sergius had visited George at Sainte-Anne and eventually obtained his release, gifted as he was with care for the suffering and willing to take responsibility for the newly discharged patient.

For a long time, George was unable and unwilling to paint icons, as a result of the shock of his internment and feelings of unworthiness. Father Sergius persisted, however, with prayer and encouragement. It was he who urged George to take the step toward monastic profession and finally on the first Sunday of Lent in 1948, the feast of the "Triumph" of Orthodoxy in the end of iconoclasm and veneration of the icon, tonsured him and clothed him in the monastic habit with the name Saint Gregory of Kiev, a monk and iconographer of the twelfth century. Under Father Sergius' care and in the path of monastic life and the liturgical cycle of Holy Trinity parish, Father Gregory recovered not only his emotional stability but also his ability to again paint icons.

In 1950 Father Gregory took up residence in a small hermitage and chapel of the Holy Spirit in Mesnil-St. Denis, near Versailles, a property that had belonged to Fr. Andrei Sergueenko and a small community gathered around him.[9] This small skete would be his workplace and his home until his death from stomach cancer after a long illness, on June 12, 1969. After his death, despite stringent laws governing burial sites, permission was obtained to bury him outside the skete chapel. The iconography of the chapel, built of fieldstone, was completely done by him and is perhaps the most beautiful and expressive of his work. Another masterpiece is his iconostasis and fresco of the Trinity behind the altar in the church of St. Seraphim at Montgeron. The recently completed church of the monastery of the Sign (Znaménié) in Marcenat has the iconostasis Father Gregory originally made for Mother Maria Skobtsova's nursing home chapel at Noisy-le-Grand. The former residence of Nicolas Berdiaev, in the Paris suburb of Clamart, possesses a small house chapel of the Holy Spirit with all the iconostasis icons—those of Christ, the Mother of God, St. Nicholas and the Descent of the Holy Spirit, the angels Michael and Gabriel, the row of the feast icons and those of the royal doors, the evangelists and the Annunciation—done by Father Gregory in the early 1950s, in excellent condition and of brilliant color and expression. The Church of All Saints at the St. John the Baptist monastery in Tolleshunt Knights, U.K., the Church of St. Mary Magdalene in the Hague in Holland, and the Church of the Mother of God of Iversk in the summer colony at Montmartin-sur-Mer in Normandy all have iconostases and other icons of Father Gregory.

From the time of his monastic profession until his death twenty-one years later, Father Gregory lived the dual existence of a monastic and an iconographer. He spent weekdays at the skete and came to the Vanves church for the vigil on Saturday evening and Sunday liturgy. Catherine Aslanoff recalls attending Saturday evening vigil at Vanves parish, where her father also had Father Sergius as his confessor. After the services, Lossky and Father Gregory, who were friends from the days of the Confraternity of St. Photius, would converse. Lossky said afterward that he always put his research and writing to Father Gregory. Lossky was then working on his dissertation on the negative or apophatic theology and knowledge of God by the thirteenth-century German mystic, the great Dominican

Meister Eckhart. Father Gregory, though he had never formally studied philosophy or theology, "understood every nuance with such finesse," Lossky later recalled.

He never asked for or accepted payment for his work and often reworked his icons, to the chagrin of his spiritual father. He would often give away an icon to someone who had admired it. Although it is not the custom for Russian iconographers to sign their icons, Father Gregory's work had various "signature" elements, such as the size and shape of the hands of Christ or the Mother of God. Toward the end of his life he always included a white border around the red line that inscribed the halos of the figures.[10] Father Tregubov reckons that altogether more than 550 icons came from his hand. Many of his early works were lost long ago and the number of small, portable icons he made that are in private hands is difficult to render precisely. Obviously, any iconographer ends up painting the same or virtually the same subjects for both churches and individuals. True, there are variations in depiction permitted by the canons and by various schools and traditions, of Christ, the Mother of God, the angels and saints, and the feasts. In the depiction of the Mother of God, something particularly dear to Father Gregory, there is considerable creativity, a great deal of variation, and yet it is always the very same woman, whose glory is obedience to the Word of God. Aslanoff feels that in each icon of the Mother of God, no matter if they were repetitions of the classic types—Hodigitria, "the one who points the way," Umilenie, "tenderness," or Znamenie, the Mother of God of the Sign—there is a new hymn to the Virgin. Each time he painted her, there would be "astonishing, unexpected, striking differences in the depiction of her person, the rhythm of the drapery of her clothing, the proportions of the lines, the colors and most of all the expression of the faces and the light which always emanated from these."[11]

> It is necessary to say that in the Church there is no limitation which impedes all movement, which takes away freedom in the painting of icons. Icons are not just copied, mechanically reproduced, but are born, the one from the other. Thus one can explain the infinite variety which is the very nature of icons, a variety which does not at all break their familial unity, one could say, and

which allows, without depriving them of mobility and suppleness, the transformation of their representations, the keeping of their unity and internal integrity without allowing the icon to dinstintegrate into a multitude of representations which are unconnected and alien to each other.[12]

In his notes Father Gregory writes of the veneration of icons as "a flaming torch the light of which is never extinguished."[13] Even when there is hostility and indifference to the icon, its light does not fade, cannot fade, for it comes from the light of the Transfiguration on Mount Tabor. Despite his deep commitment to the Church's teaching on icons, Father Gregory was not only in principle but also in practice extremely free and creative in the expression of the truth of the Tradition.

Father Gregory's "Notes"

Perhaps one of the most intricate of Father Gregory's notes on icons and their relationship to the liturgical feasts deals with the icon of the descent of the Holy Spirit at Pentecost. Carefully reviewing the scriptural lessons for the feast, he observes that there have been two different ways of presenting the descent of the Spirit iconographically. He insists, however, that the Mother of God not only can but should be present, at the center of the assembled apostles in the upper room, as the Acts of the Apostles in fact reports it, for the outpouring of the Holy Spirit in the day of Pentecost. Here Father Gregory, though standing in one stream in iconographic tradition, nevertheless runs directly against the opinion of other specialists in iconography, including Ouspensky, who argues that the deeper theological meaning of the Pentecost icon is lost if the Mother of God appears at the center of the apostles and not the empty seat or altar symbolizing the presence of Christ. Father Gregory is eloquent in his argument.

It seems that the rationale for this representation resides in the actual event of the feast, the indisputable and incontestable participation of the Mother of God in the assembly of the apostles who received the Holy Spirit in the Upper Room. . . . What is the meaning then? . . . Why was the Mother of God present there and why did she receive the Holy Spirit in the tongues of fire? It would appear that this was the will of the Holy Spirit himself who had already sanctified her by his coming at the Annunciation. . . . There was an interior, spiritual necessity determined by the direct, personal will and by the authority of the Holy Spirit and the Holy Trinity as a whole. Why then do we hear so little of this in all the texts of the Pentecost services and only in the accounts of her life and in the reading from the Acts of the Apostles? Here again we could listen to what St. Innocent (of Gerson) says: "Do we not have here the mystery that is far from being solved, that of all glory." But the glory of the Mother of God cannot be affirmed until the end. It cannot be affirmed just as the glory of the divine Light, just as the royal fullness cannot be affirmed, equal to the divine dignity, of the dignity of the Mother of God. She cannot but sparkle in the solemnity of the feast of the Holy Spirit, the feast of the Holy Trinity. For who among human beings can be filled with a greater plenitude of the wealth of the gifts of the Holy Spirit if not the Mother of God who is "more honorable than the cherubim," the "Queen of heaven," of whom a liturgical hymn says "that if she so desired she could have a power equal to the divine power." We must believe that the feast of the Holy Spirit has been for the Mother of God precisely the accomplishment of the fullness of the gifts necessary for the ministry of the Church and for the ministry of the Mother of God in the Church, at the same time containing and surpassing every ministry of angels or of human beings, even that of the apostles. The place of the Mother of God in the Church is a singular, royal one. She, the Queen of heaven and earth, contains in herself a high power and every ministry, that of the angels and of human beings. In the icons where she is represented with the apostles, she is at the center and as it were the head of the apostles. The gathering of the apostles surrounds her and she appears to be the cornerstone of the assembly. Almost always she is seated upon a throne apart and this marks her royal dignity as Queen. . . . Could it be otherwise? In the liturgical hymn verses the Holy Spirit is said to rest upon the apostles as on the head of all humanity. Would the Mother of God be

deprived of that dignity, of that election? Is it that she is not able
to be the head. It really seems as if the fullness of the feast would
not be there if she were not present.[14]

Father Gregory continues, unfolding a lyrical and nuanced meditation on the Church, which of course the Mother of God and apostles represent, as the abode of the Holy Spirit. Part of this reflection
concerns the unity of the Church, inherent in her holiness because
of the unity of God as Trinity, Three-in-One. His words have special relevance today, when ecumenical hopes for the reunion of
the divided have been diminished, if not dashed, when positions
have hardened, particularly within the Eastern Orthodox churches.
How striking Father Gregory's words are when one considers how
committed he was to his "Mother" church, that of the patriarchate
of Moscow, and how faithful he was to the entire Church Tradition.

And the destruction of the unity of the Church, one could say, is
the destruction of the house of God, the destruction of the sanctified habitation of the divine. And every sin which seeks to
destroy this unity of the Church is hostility toward her holiness
and originates in eternal darkness. Every heresy and schism in the
Church is the destruction of the image of the Holy Trinity in her,
the image which is imprinted in her, which gives birth to and
keeps alive the indissoluble unity of the Church. What a heavy
responsibility falls on those who do not act zealously for this
unity, who do not love it or, what is worst, become the enemy of
her unity.[15]

It is not surprising that Father Gregory's beautiful vision of the
place of the Mother of God—in the icon of the feast and at Pentecost, in the midst of the apostles—echoes that of his friend, Vladimir
Lossky, especially in the latter's essay on her, "Panagia."[16] The particular focus on the Church's character of "catholicity" (*sobornost'*)
is also shared by the two, one an iconographer and monk, the other
a scholar and theologian.[17] Father Gregory sums up not only the issue
of the inclusion of the Mother of God in the Pentecost icon but also
the much larger reality of her being an icon of the Church and, moreover, a living presence and mother within the life of this communion.

The unity of the Mother of God and the apostles, at the Ascension of the Lord as well as at Pentecost, is unchangeable and the final, definitive event in her life saw them together again at her Dormition. Here their reassembling from all the corners of the universe is irrefutable. Each of them was borne by the Holy Spirit from the place of his ministry to Jerusalem and the apostles once again formed an assembly around the Mother of God. With the bodiless powers, the angels, and the women who assumed the apostolic ministry, they celebrated her funeral and carried her body to the place of burial. Here again we find the same close kinship which places the Mother of God among the apostles, on the Mount of Olives as on Mount Zion and in the Upper Room, filled on the day of Pentecost with the fire and the breath of the Holy Spirit. In all the life of the Church it is difficult to present the smallest apostolic action without the presence of the Mother of God. It is also impossible to represent the catholicity, the universal communion of the Church without her participation or to ignore her participation wherever the Church's catholicity is expressed. This is so because the ministry of the Mother of God in the Church embraces everything. The Mother of God as Queen of the heavens and the earth cannot be apart from even the slightest activity of the Church, whether that of angels or of human beings and there is no manifestation of the Church's catholicity that is not filled with the fullness of her blessing. It is for this reason as well that the fullness of the apostolic assembly gathered in the Upper Room on the day of Pentecost, the fullness which has shaped the apostolic nature of the Church, does not occur without her participation.[18]

Those who knew Father Gregory remember him as a somewhat shy but warm and friendly monk. Elisabeth Ozoline remembers his round, radiant face, with no beard but a moustache and hair that framed his face, uncut according to monastic tradition and often flowing free from beneath his monastic cap, around his shoulders. He enjoyed Father Schevitch reading the Fathers and lives of the saints to him while he worked, but later, when this was no longer possible, he preferred listening to classical music while painting.

Stories about his eccentric behavior abound, some quite fascinating and true, others inaccurate and corrected by Father Barsanuphius in his recent volume. Contrary to what Anne Bogenhardt reports in her catalog of his works,[19] Father Gregory did not subsist only on chestnuts and mushrooms he gathered in the woods and from fruit from a medlar tree by his skete. He ate whatever was placed before him, rapidly. Neither did he refuse medical care for his many afflictions—arthritis, neuritis, hypertension, angina, diabetes, the cancer that took his life—because this was in conflict with the monastic state and submission to the will of God, as Valentine Marcadé writes.[20] He needed help to take the medication his doctor prescribed at the correct intervals, not all at one time, as he was accustomed to doing. Again, the best testimony to Father Gregory comes from Father Barsanuphius, his fellow monk and his caregiver in the last years of his life. There is no need to exaggerate Father Gregory's ascetic practices to create for him a kind of holiness comparable to that of classical monastic literature or the lives of saints. As Father Gregory's life indicates, he had suffering enough and much with which to struggle in terms of emotional and physical health, poverty, the upheavals of exile, the depression, the war, and most of all the immense inner battle with his own soul.

Icons: The Meeting of God, Face-to-Face

While never well known, even in the Orthodox world, today Father Gregory's person may be said to remain in hiding, even as his iconography becomes more widely appreciated and recognized and as more is published and translated about his life and his notes on icons. However, the icon is not a puzzle. Despite the apparent effect of the iconostasis, particularly in the classical Russian style in which it is accompanied by a curtain over the royal door in the Orthodox church, the icon does not conceal God, the saints, or the Kingdom from us. Neither does it intend to divide the clergy from the laity, the people of God from things sacred. Quite the opposite: the icon has been called a "window into eternity," "theology in color," a doorway into transcendence. In Evdokimov's superb study of the icon's theology, the icon exists because of God's creation, because of God's wish to dwell in this, particularly among his children, and even more so because of the wonder of the Incarnation, the almost unthinkable and impossible action of God becoming part of his creation, of God becoming human, taking on flesh and blood, a body, a life, subject to time and place, to exhaustion, hunger, sickness, pain, and ultimately death.[21]

In the end it may be that his icons are the best route in which to most completely encounter Father Gregory. To that purpose we move at last to the three magnificent icons reproduced here in the illustration section courtesy of St. Vladimir's Seminary Press, publisher of Father Tregubov's collection of Father Gregory's work. All three come from the chapel of St. Seraphim of Sarov in Montgeron. Originally the property, a small estate with a mill, Moulin de Senlis, housed an orphanage for children whose parents had died during the revolution, the depression, and World War II. Sophie Mikhailnova Zernova (1899–1972), sister of Nicolas Zernov, chronicler of the Russian religious renaissance, was herself a University of Belgrade graduate in philosophy, an active member of the St. Seraphim Brotherhood, and the Russian Christian Students Movement's traveling secretary. Her work paralleled that of Mother Maria in providing legal assistance to émigrés, finding work for them, and working in the field of child welfare. She was the founder of Centre d'Aide aux Émigrés Russes (1935) and from 1939 on headed the home for orphaned and abandoned children. In 1959 a young architect, Nikita Kovalenko, built an octagonal chapel of brick, modeled after a Romanesque church in Bulgaria. Under the soaring hemispherical dome the symmetry of the arches of this classic building was embraced by Father Gregory. I visited it myself and was amazed at the light and spaciousness of the Romanesque lines. While the fresco icons that Father Gregory created for the chapel of the Holy Spirit at his own skete are wonders of iconography, it must also be admitted that the fresco of the Trinity behind the altar and the ensemble of panels in the Montgeron iconostasis must rank among his most beautiful.[22]

Prompted by the realization that small children, the orphans, would be meeting their Lord, his Mother, and the saints in this holy place, Father Gregory created in the two principal icons of Christ and the Mother of God figures of both astonishing presence and tenderness. The two principal icons are quite large, almost 3 feet by 4 feet (37" x 45"), as is that of St. Seraphim, to whom the chapel at Montgeron is dedicated. There most likely is much more to the story behind these icons than either I or Father Tregubov, who has photo-graphed and written and lectured about them, are aware. Yet in clos-ing this profile of Father Gregory, it seems only right to reflect on the theology of beauty he created in his icons.

On entering the St. Seraphim chapel in Montgeron, one is imme-diately enclosed in the warmth of the symmetrical brick walls and bathed in light from the windows surrounding the dome above. The icon screen into which these large icons are set is richly carved yet simple, not at all monumental. The icon screen consists only in the lower row or story with these large icons and above it a single row of roundels, each 22 inches in diameter, containing a miniature *Deisis,* or Prayer, collection, Christ in the middle, flanked by the Virgin and John the Baptist, the archangels Michael and Gabriel, and the apos-tles Peter and Paul.[23] This is indeed a simple selection; in larger screens this row can contain many more angels and saints.

But of all the icons on the screen, one's eyes are drawn first and foremost to those large ones of the Mother of God, to the left of the central royal doors, and that of Christ to the right. Theologically, the icon of the Mother of God represents Christ's first coming, born of her and held tenderly in her arms. The icon of Christ himself, hold-ing the gospel book and blessing, clad in a lapis lazuli outer robe with the brilliant red stole of his high priesthood visible on his right shoulder, is that of the Pantokrator, the Lord of All, coming again at the end of time. In between these two icons is the altar, on which rests the gospel book, and where the Eucharist is celebrated, the two principal modes of Christ's coming to us and being with us now, his word and his body and blood in the sacrament of the Eucharist.

As in all icons of Christ, the Greek letters of his name, IC XC, "Jesus Christ," are on either side of his figure while in the cross inscribed in his halo are the Greek for the words of the Lord from the burning bush to Moses, his "Name," *Ho on,* "I Am who I Am." In many icons of Christ the gospel book will be open, with a passage inscribed and clearly legible, for example, "Come to me all you who labor and are heavy-burdened and I will give you rest," "I am the Light of the world." But here the book is closed. There is no spe-cific or special message for these children. As in all of Father Greg-ory's icons, very little is imposed on the one who comes before them. There is no attempt to find the precise New Testament phrase for the orphans, no effort to teach them intellectually. There simply is the face of God, which seeks those who enter the church, grasping them but ever so tenderly, looking at them with love, the One who is Love, Jesus. Likewise, the icon of the Mother of God, the type called Glikophylussa, literally "sweetly kissing," or Umilenie, "tenderness." The cheeks of the Mother and her Child touch. He clasps her with both arms. She holds him in her left arm, her hand looking much like a chalice, her right hand also open, both points us to him and stretches toward him in prayer, for us, with us. The brilliant lapis lazuli blue that Father Gregory used here does not overwhelm us, as in the outer cloak of Christ, blue there witnessing to him as God, the "man of heaven." In the icon of the Virgin the heavenly blue is hidden by the reddish brown *maphorion,* or outer cloak, her humanity, symbolically, not just concealing divinity but being permeated by God. Mary is thus icon of the Church and of each believer, filled with the Holy Spirit, made again into what each was orginally created to be, "in the image and likeness of God," "very much like, similar to . . . God." The Greek letters, contracted on either side, proclaim her Maria Theotokos, Mary, the Bearer and Mother of God.

Icons have various levels or dimensions of meaning. Here we have Christ and the Virgin but also the first and last comings of Christ. We have the Mother and her divine child, but we also have the Church and each Christian. We have the Bearer of God, but we also have what we are to become, each of us ourselves giving birth to God in our actions, in our love for each other. In both icons, the faces speak of the "limitless Love" that God both is and has for each of us. And yet both icons also draw us in to loving God and his saints, our brothers and sisters, and into the imitation of that Love, loving the saints who are around us in our daily lives. It goes without saying that icons in the Eastern Church are didactic, tools of teaching, and inspiration, moving us to prayer and contemplation. Yet they are so much more: maps to follow, patterns that direct us how to live.

Perhaps it is in the icon of St. Seraphim that we see this expressed both simply and intensely. Quite a few commentators have said that this is the quintessential icon of Seraphim, expressing his identity and his life, teaching, and work more effectively than any other. Admittedly there are others. I am very fond of the classic Russian print of

St. Seraphim feeding his daily visitor, a huge black bear. There is also a beautiful icon of the repose of St. Seraphim, kneeling before the Mother of God's icon in his cell, his hands folded on his chest, his falling asleep so peacefully, so gently, his dying while lost in prayer. There is also the well-known portrait of Seraphim done during his lifetime in 1832, preserved in the New Diveyevo convent in Rockland County, New York.[24]

Father Gregory's icon of St. Seraphim is placed on the icon screen at Montgeron in the space just to the right of the side or deacon's door, very often the location of the saint or feast to which a church is dedicated. Identical in size to the two principal icons of Christ and the Mother of God, it too commands attention as one enters the chapel. Again, Father Gregory very likely had in mind the small children who would have come here for daily services and prayer, for the face of St. Seraphim, while clearly derived from his portrait, is marked by calm, joy, and the tenderness that characterized all the iconography in the chapel. Father Gregory has in his typical way stripped many of the details that are present in other icons. Gone are the bear, the log cabin hermitage, the pine trees of the Sarov forest. One almost has to remember that St. Seraphim is kneeling here on his famous rock, one that became almost his church, his place of daily prayer for over three years, a thousand days and nights, as the account goes. The stone in the forest by his hermitage has become heaven, we may say. St. Seraphim, though a priest and a monk, here wears the simple cotton smock and bark shoes of a peasant. In his hands, extended in prayer to Christ, are the *chotki,* the prayer rope on the knots of which one repeats the prayer, "Lord Jesus Christ, Son of God, have mercy on me, a sinner." Around his neck is the bronze cross his mother placed there when he left home to enter the monastery. When his relics were miraculously found in 1988, this same bronze cross was among them and, along with documents, confirmed that the relics were St. Seraphim's.

The entire figure of St. Seraphim glows in an incandescent white that is Easter, like his use, year-round, of the Paschal greeting. Each he met was greeted with "Christ is risen," and called, no matter what his or her name, "My joy!" (*Radost'*). Behind Seraphim is not the gold that in Byzantine icons connotes heaven. Rather the glowing background is the Sarov forest, his hermitage, his monastery in nineteenth-century Russia, but also the world, our world now all become heaven. Christ has entered and is present. Seraphim's halo penetrates two levels of heavenly blue, the first filled with rays of divine light, of grace, the second, that immediately around Christ, a deeper, richer blue like that of the bright nights of summer in the far north. While Father Tregubov does not like to make much of it, I am especially struck by the way in which not only the figures of Christ and Seraphim incline toward each other, but also their halos touch, meet, open to each other. This is what communion with God looks like, this is what Evdokimov meant in all of his rich phrases: "becoming prayer, incarnate," our becoming "liturgical beings," "ecclesial person," "Christified creatures." The inscription reads "Saint Seraphim, Prepodobny—the One very like God." This is Seraphim the monk of Sarov monastery, who is also Prochor Moshnin of Kursk. But somehow the person and life of St. Seraphim are, like this icon, so transparent to the light of Christ that they almost fade, inviting us into that light. I think again here of the face of Motovilov in the snowy meadow, glowing just as St. Seraphim's, and the Batiushka's, the little father's, words that it makes no difference who you are, you too can acquire the Holy Spirit, and if you do everyone around will too. Before this icon, I am not given a historically detailed description of St. Seraphim or a precise account of his life and teaching. Yet I receive the essence of the saint. I too am invited not just to say prayers but to become what I pray, to become prayer incarnate.

At Sarov the immense complex of monastery churches and buildings is long gone, as is the convent St. Seraphim established. Until very recently it seemed as though even the saints' precious relics were gone in the turmoil of the revolution. Yet, almost miraculously, his relics have been found and were taken back to Sarov and Diveyevo in procession. At Montgeron the orphans are also gone, grown up and with families of their own, passing into their later years. When I visited several years ago the current residents were refugees from the embattled former Yugoslavia. Inside the stately gate and through the busy courtyard of the estate one came to the St. Seraphim church and one could enter if the lady with the key could be found and would loan it. While Father Gregory has disappeared from his skete and the Orthodox scene of Paris, despite their often inferior materials and location and lack of care or restoration, his icons remain in several churches there as well as other places, including people's homes. Not unlike St. Seraphim in the Montgeron icon, Father Gregory has become transparent, a pointer to the beauty of God in his icons. They are his theology, his sermons, windows into the Kingdom created and opened by his hand.

CHAPTER EIGHT

Nicolas Afanasiev

Explorer of the Eucharist, the Church, and Life in Them

A Source of Eucharistic Ecclesiology

The Church was established by Christ at the Last Supper and came into existence on the day of Pentecost, when the first Eucharist was celebrated by the disciples. . . . On the day of Pentecost, the disciples were filled with the Spirit. . . . The disciples become "one body" in the Eucharist, which is accomplished in the Spirit and through the Spirit. . . . The Eucharist is the center towards which everything aims and in which everything meets. The Body of Christ is realized only in the Eucharist.[1]

Thus, in a manner criticized as "one-sided" and "exuberantly" so by commentators such as Kallistos Ware, John Meyendorff, John Zizioulas, Peter Plank, and John Erickson, Fr. Nicolas Afanasiev begins his challenging study, *The Lord's Supper* (Trapeza Gospodnia), one of the sharpest statements of his effort to return to the eucharistic ecclesiology of the early Church. While an ecumenical gathering of his contemporaries, including Gregory Dix, Louis Bouyer, Henri de Lubac, Jean Daniélou, Bernard Botte, I.-H. Dalmais, and Yves Congar, similarly rediscovered the Church's identity best expressed in the eucharistic assembly, Afanasiev did so distinctively and uncompromisingly. As Aidan Nichols notes, Afanasiev's studies in eucharistic ecclesiology were the only works of an Orthodox theologian

to be mentioned in Vatican II's working sessions and drafts and embodied in the Constitution on the Church, *Lumen Gentium*.[2]

Decades later there is no doubt that the reigning ecclesiological
paradigm is that of *koinōnia/communio*.[3] Neither does such an
approach to understanding the nature of the Church lack its critics.[4]
While communion ecclesiology in general is not rejected, certain
aspects are debated, and Afanasiev's vision has been among those
subject to serious criticism. Among others, Erickson has noted what
would appear to be a eucharistically narrow rooting and perhaps
self-serving reading of ancient Church history in Afanasiev's writing.[5] Bishop Kallistos (Ware) consistently credits Afanasiev (along
with Schmemann and Zizioulas) with recovery of the basic understanding of the Church as the eucharistic assembly.[6] Yet he too finds
problems in Afanasiev: one-sidedness, exaggerations of Ignatian
and Cyprianic ecclesiologies, as well as some applications of ecumenical eucharistic practice suggested by Afanasiev toward the end
of his life.[7]

Fundamental to this revisiting of Afanasiev is my conviction that
his work has significantly shaped our understanding of the Church
and, perhaps more important, our life as Christians by returning to
the source, the Eucharist. Yet the greatest criticism of Afanasiev's
vision is his alleged overemphasis on the completeness of the local
eucharistic community, often understood by some commentators
exclusively as the contemporary parish, and the insufficient weight
he supposedly gives to the links between the local church and the
universal Church. There are, as suggested, still other criticisms such
as those of Metropolitan John Zizioulas, including his alleged lack
of attention to the bishop and his supposedly overfunctional view
of the ordained ministry.[8] There are also those for whom many
aspects of a eucharistic or communion ecclesiology are problematic,
as responses to the *Baptism, Eucharist, Ministry* document of the
Faith and Order Commission of the WCC indicate.[9] Robert Jenson's
insightful study points out specific troubles of particular church
bodies but also what he understands to be the greater and deeper
rifts.[10]

So there has been criticism of Afanasiev's work, even by those
who recognize his contributions and share his basic insistence on eucharistic ecclesiology.[11] I want to argue here that Afanasiev's ground-

ing of the Church in the eucharistic assembly has become normative in theological discussion, even though his name is not always mentioned. Further, I contend that Afanasiev is sometimes unjustifiably accused of exaggerations or deficiencies. Most frequently, he has been taken to task for positions he did not hold, most notably that the local Church fairly well comprises the ecclesial reality, the larger expressions of the Church being merely quantitative collections and the universal Church merely an ideal. Furthermore, most critics pay little or no attention to Afanasiev as a person and to the significance of his personal witness and teaching for the Church and a number of important colleagues and students.

In his posthumously published *Church of the Holy Spirit* are elements that refute many of his critics: a pneumatological dimension to his ecclesiology that does not contradict the basic eucharistic foundations, a view of the Church that recognizes the importance of baptism and of the bishop and other ordained ministries, and the eucharistic core including unity in the faith.[12]

Afanasiev can be criticized for certain features of his work. It is likely, for example, that in arguing for the eucharistic basis of the Church, he contrasts the most extreme features of Ignatius and Cyprian to highlight eucharistic ecclesiology.[13] However, the terrain with which he is concerned has always proved to be precarious in the history of the universal Church, not only among very conservative Orthodox. One need only recall the negative first reactions to Vatican II's rediscovery of the Church as more "the people of God" and less a rule-based institution, more a "communion" than simply a hierarchy of clerical authority. In his critique of certain ecclesial realities Afanasiev evoked strong, mostly negative responses, both in his time and today. He attacked misunderstandings of eucharistic preparation and piety that resulted in lack of participation. Colleagues of his, such as Frs. Kyprian Kern and Louis Bouyer and his student Fr. Alexander Schmemann, shared in his conviction about what had been the ecclesial and eucharistic norm: *epi to auto*. Both then and now, there has been opposition to their suggestions for liturgical restoration, for example, the fully audible chanting of the prayers of the liturgy by the celebrants, preaching at every liturgy and on the lectionary texts, fuller congregational participation in singing, and, most important, regular reception of communion by the faithful. It cannot be said that these liturgical practices are observed throughout Orthodoxy today or that they are approved of as faithful to the Church's Tradition even by church leadership.

Afanasiev remains controversial. His critics not only point out his alleged deficiencies but also reveal, in a very striking way, the continuing resistance to his fundamental vision on the part of both theologians and ecclesial leaders. As I show, it would appear that for some the grounding of the Church in the Eucharist with all this entails for Afanasiev—baptismal identity, charismatic vocation, unity in faith, the bishop and other ordained ministries, and acknowledged, explicit communion with the rest of the churches—is still somehow insufficient. While it is understandable that Afanasiev's courageous exploration of the ecumenical consequences of eucharistic ecclesiology with Rome (not without criticism of the same) would draw fire, it is puzzling indeed why the attitude toward his more basic vision remains neuralgic. Such an eminent canon law specialist as Archbishop Peter (L'Huillier) of the Orthodox Church in America observed that Afanasiev's eucharistic ecclesiology is crucial simply because it is *the* ecclesiology of the Scriptures, of the early Church, of the ecumenical councils, in short, the authentic Orthodox vision of the Church, her eucharistic heart, her ordained servants, and the whole baptized priesthood of the people of God and their mission in the world.[14]

Not only in the dogmatic constitutions on the Church but equally in the new *Catechism of the Catholic Church*, in the *Baptism, Eucharist, and Ministry* document, and in the writings of two very different theologians whom he taught—Fathers Schmemann and Meyendorff—the gathering of all the faithful around the Scriptures and the eucharistic table has become the very "icon" of the Church's identity. The new *Catechism* does not hesitate to echo the radical proposition of Afanasiev's vision, namely, that "the Eucharist makes the Church."[15]

A Churchly Life, a Eucharistic Personality

The circumstances of Afanasiev's life shaped him and his work. Born in Odessa in 1893, son of an attorney, he and his younger sister were raised by their mother and grandmother after his father's early death. His vocational interests turned from medicine to mathematics, which led him to artillery school and then service in the civil war caused by the revolution. Afanasiev, like Evdokimov, found himself swept up in the horrors of the White Army's losses and eventual flight. Like so many others, young and old, he experienced the upheaval and loneliness of exile. Along with it came the turmoil of emigration and the internal conflicts within the Russian Church and competing Russian intellectual and political circles in Europe. With marriage in 1925 and the completion of his doctoral studies and degree at the University of Belgrade in 1927, Afanasiev began secondary school teaching in Macedonia, then teaching canon law and church history from 1930 on at St. Sergius Theological Institute, the newly established Orthodox theological school in Paris. There he would be a colleague of the émigré scholars with whom he had studied in Belgrade, among them Frs. Sergius Bulgakov and Basil Zenkovsky and Bishop Cassian Besobrasov, all of them creative thinkers in dogmatic theology, philosophy and education, and New Testament exegesis, respectively, key figures in the religious renaissance that had begun in Russia in the earliest years of the twentieth century.

After priestly ordination, on the day after the old calendar Christmas, January 8, 1940, he began pastoral work among émigrés in the south of France, then took on the Russian parish community in Tunis for the remainder of the war, even through blockade and attack. He returned to teaching at St. Sergius in 1947, and to a great deal of consultation work in canon law and active involvement in the liturgical weeks and ecumenical activity.

To his initial training in canon law and ecclesiastical history, he added work in the Fathers. This eventually emerged in numerous articles in the Russian-language theological journals based in Paris. Like Evdokimov, Schmemann, and Meyendorff, he deliberately published in French-language journals, leaving the confines of Russian as one permanently settled in the West. There were numerous demands on his time and therefore constraints on research and writing. Always tottering on the edge of bankruptcy and impoverished, fund-raising was essential for St. Sergius Institute's survival, and Father Afanasiev devoted himself to all this as well as teaching and administration. As a canon lawyer, he was constantly drawn into consultant work with his own diocese and various bishops. Many of his articles in French from the end of the war until his death were responses to questions raised in ecumenical conferences, such as the Orthodox canon law regarding marriage and excommunication from and reconciliation with the Church. All this was in addition to his basic work in eucharistic ecclesiology, which also led him to important and radical positions regarding the relationship of the clergy and the laity in the Church, the question of power, particularly that of bishops, and a rich, challenging theology of the universal priesthood of all the baptized, his contribution to the "rediscovery" of the Church as the "people of God." Evdokimov was to echo this last theological emphasis, joining it to his own emphasis on interiorized monasticism, the pattern of spiritual life that was for all, not only for monastics.

These activities, combined with confession and pastoral care, the usual liturgical obligations, and the long interruption of the war and his poor health, makes it almost a miracle that he produced a formidable body of writing. Principal among his writings is the posthumously published "Church of the Holy Spirit," his doctoral thesis and the core of a much larger work on the Church, other portions of which exist as separately published articles. This work presents his understanding of the Church far more extensively than any other, including his widely translated and read essay, "The Church Which Presides in Love," and the lesser-known *The Lord's Supper*.[16]

Afanasiev lived to see his perspective on eucharistic ecclesiology shape the teaching documents of Vatican II. He also participated in the nullification of the mutual anathemas of the great schism of 1054, propelled by the meetings of Ecumenical Patriarch Athenagoras I and Pope Paul VI in the last year of his life, on December 8, 1965. His wife, Marianne, tenderly describes some of the details of his last months in a biographical sketch. He was able to assist in the baptism of his grandson, given his own name, Nicolas. He also was fortunate to have a publisher accept his major work, *The Church of the Holy Spirit*, and he eagerly began to prepare the manuscript from the monumental work he had planned. Just a few weeks before his death, he awakened his wife, excited, asking if she had not heard the entrance of a young man into their room, perhaps, she wondered, the angel sent to take him home. His last weeks were spent in the hospital and even near the end, she says, his great fear was that if he recovered he would not be able to celebrate the liturgy, so profound was his love for his priestly vocation. Perhaps it was not delirium or hallucination, his frequent reports of seeing the "young man" again during his last days in the hospital, waiting for him, sitting on the corner of his bed or in the hallway, amid the poor, the suffering, and the other lost ones going to and fro there. Marianne remembered his desire to see the blue sky, and when she opened the hospital room's curtains, despite the gray, overcast sky of Paris in December, there was a tiny patch of blue, with a weak bit of winter sun peering through, a last glimpse of the sun and sky so dear to Father Afanasiev from his sun-drenched Odessa childhood on the Black Sea.

He fell asleep in the Lord on Sunday, December 4, 1966, the feast, on the old calendar, of the Entrance of the Mother of God into the Temple, a feast of the Advent period and the special day of the Russian Students' Association so important to so many in the early years of the emigration. In an obituary memorial to him, Father Schmemann underscored the "hidden fire, a truly consuming love for the Church" that was the foundation of all of Afanasiev's work and urged the translation and publication of his major writings for English-speaking readers.[17] As early as 1954 Schmemann underscored the significance of his teacher's book, *The Lord's Supper*, in an essay that in retrospect serves as both preview and program for his own writing in the years to follow.[18] Later, in what many consider his masterpiece, *The Eucharist*, Father Schmemann calls it a "splendid though not yet fully appreciated work," citing it several times in the first chapter and echoing Afanasiev's perspective throughout.[19] The impression many have when seeing the face of Father Afanasiev in the few photographs of him that remain, particularly the one in this book, is of a joyful yet winsome, shy man. In fact, those who knew him, Father Zenkovsky in particular, recall his deep humility, his feeling that he had never accomplished what he might have been capable of doing in scholarship and above all his intellectual and personal integrity. Some remember even a kind of inferiority complex, a sense on his part that his vision of the Church would never be realized. Yet of all the luminaries of the emigration, he is the only one cited by name in Vatican II, and his influence is larger than he could ever have imagined.

The Lord's Supper: Excavation, Diagnosis, Challenge

There is no doubt that despite any personal reticence, Afanasiev's style and point of view are incendiary, and *The Lord's Supper* is important as an early statement of his vision of eucharistic ecclesiology. What Afanasiev sees as the Church's identity and structure bears consequences for its actual practice, and the decadence of the Church's current practice is more than theological error but profound spiritual sickness. Yet there is a significant by-product of inspecting this early and still fairly inaccessible text.[20] On closer view, it becomes clear that Afanasiev does not hold the positions for which he is most often attacked, that of overemphasis on the eucharistic centrality of the Church, or hyperlocalism, as Zizioulas and Kallistos Ware most often fault him, or "Orthodox congregationalism," as Nichols puts it.[21] I argue here that Afanasiev's understanding of the ecclesial nature of the Eucharist and the eucharistic essence of the Church not only challenges us but even more, as it identifies what has gone wrong, allows us to perceive the healing of both ecclesial sickness and schism.

The Lord's Supper was completed on November 13, 1950, in a period of significant productivity for Afanasiev. The first part of a monumental ecclesiological study, his *Church of the Holy Spirit* had been finished only recently. Plans for and parts of the never completed second portion, *The Limits of the Church*, were being written and were later published.[22] *The Lord's Supper* appeared in 1952 as the second and third volumes of a series put out by St. Sergius Institute titled *Orthodoxy Today* (Pravoslaviya i Sovremenost). The compact work of about one hundred pages was rigorous in scholarship, drawing on much of Afanasiev's earlier research and thinking, yet it was also written to be accessible to more than the academic theological community. It is divided into three sections: a historical sketch of eucharistic ecclesiology, the concelebration of clergy and of all the faithful, and the reception of communion. Throughout there is both trenchant analysis and impassioned urgency, hallmarks of his style. Ecclesial-liturgical practice, or better, abuse in both understanding and enactment, is dealt with explicitly. Afanasiev attacks the "unchurching" of liturgical celebration, its detachment from the whole assembly. He tracks the disappearance of roles for the faithful through developments such as prayers, particularly the eucharistic prayer, or *anaphora,* rendered for the most part inaudible by the celebrant's near-silent recitation and the iconostasis becoming a wall-sized barrier, with a curtain added over the central royal doors, so that much of the action of the liturgy was hidden from the faithful.

These are "reductions," as Schmemann would later call them, of both liturgy and Church by clericalization, sacralization, and individualization. The most obvious result was the practical transformation of the liturgical assembly into a noneucharistic gathering, even though the liturgy of the Eucharist was still the normal service of Sundays and feasts. Other than the concelebrating clergy, there was, especially for the laity, infrequent communion, sometimes but yearly, a pattern that endured in much of Orthodoxy. Afanasiev chronicles the slippage of the Eucharist from the central, defining action of the Church to merely one of many services performed (by no means the most popular) and documents the theological rationalizations for this.[23] One can read a similar boldness and fervor in his colleague at St. Sergius, Fr. Kyprian Kern, who similarly identified the erosion of eucharistic ecclesiology in an important study in 1947.[24] Chief among Kern's objections is the privatization of the Eucharist, its distortion into an intensely personal and rare act. The communal nature of the eucharistic liturgy and in fact of all ecclesial services was overturned and transformed, to the Church's great detriment, into private devotions: baptisms, marriages, funerals, and as memorial services for the deceased, the most frequented rites by the Russian Orthodox. Father Schmemann recalls that in his experience of growing up in and being educated in the Russian gymnasium in Paris, yearly communion was an important "Russian custom" to be followed faithfully.

The privatization or individualization of the Church's worship is, for Afanasiev, the greatest of its modern pathologies. As the work of other theologians sharing his vision witnesses, this was truly an ecumenical phenomenon, by no means restricted to the Orthodox

Church. Yet Afanasiev's study is not just a diatribe against abuses. Primarily it is constructive, a forceful statement of the ideal of the Church as witnessed in the Scriptures, in the teaching of the Fathers, in the very texts of the liturgical celebrations themselves, and in the canons of the councils. One can easily read related versions of eucharistic ecclesiology in Afanasiev's colleagues, Father Bulgakov and Evdokimov.[25]

At the outset, as in the lines quoted at the beginning of this chapter, Afanasiev asserts the pneumatological character, that is, the relationship of the Holy Spirit to the Eucharist, to all the offices of the church, from liturgical presidency to preaching, teaching, and diaconal service and to the baptismal priesthood of all. The Church is a creation and constant action of the Spirit. As Evdokimov was fond of saying, the coming down of the Holy Spirit (*epiklesis*) is perpetual in the Church, especially in the Eucharist.[26] This inherent attention to ecclesial pneumatology is elaborated in Afanasiev's much longer and extensive study, *The Church of the Holy Spirit,* and is a pervasive quality of both that work and *The Lord's Supper.* To those who would fault Afanasiev for "reducing" the Church to the celebration of the Eucharist, it is crucial to take account of the *whole* of his vision, as expressed across the breadth of his writing. One cannot but be struck by the significance he gives to the Holy Spirit's action in establishing not only the episcopate and presbyterate, but, even more basically, of creating the royal priesthood of the faithful.[27] The Church is where the Spirit is and *omnis gratia,* "all grace."[28] And it is only through baptism that the Holy Spirit consecrates, by washing, anointing, and tonsuring, all of the faithful as kings, prophets, and priests. The whole of the second chapter of *The Church of the Holy Spirit* is given to a detailed examination of the initiation rites.[29]

Far from ignoring the importance of the ordained ministries and the place and necessity of the bishop in particular, Afanasiev argues that it is precisely the "rupture" of these from the eucharistic liturgy, the development of clerical authority apart from the liturgy, that ultimately led to the ascendancy of law, canon law, and ecclesiastical power rather than divine love as the ruling principles in the Church.[30] Thus when we concern ourselves with the eucharistic ecclesiology and its claims, it is necessary to recall the substantial concern of Afanasiev for the baptismal and charismatic identity of all the members of the eucharistic assembly, laity as well as clergy. His eucharistically centered understanding of the Church, then, not only includes but indeed requires the Spirit's work in baptism.

"When You Gather in the Church"

In the first chapter of *The Lord's Supper,* the New Testament witness and that of Justin Martyr and the Church of the first centuries are vigorously examined, revealing the centrality of the eucharistic liturgy. The Acts 2:44 description of the apostolic eucharistic assembly, *epi to auto*—"always everyone and always together for one and the same thing"—becomes the defining characteristic of the Church. Afanasiev asserts here and throughout the communal nature of not only liturgical worship but also all ecclesial life. Even the chief pastor sits on his *cathedra* only in the assembly, and only as a member of it can he be the head.[31] Afanasiev states the eucharistic-ecclesiological identity so radically as to become provocative.

> Christianity is the "Church of God in Christ." Whoever confesses Christ also confesses the Church and whoever does this, also confesses the Eucharistic gathering. Christianity apart from the Church is something that never was and never can be. "There is no salvation outside of the Church." These words of Cyprian of Carthage have a eucharistic sense. Any other way is a path of individualism.[32]

A cluster of claims are made in the first chapter, "When You Gather in the Church," almost all of them later challenged by Afanasiev's critics. He specifically refuses to idolize the ancient Church, observing that the Church cannot be limited to one period and that no perfect or ideal moment ever existed.[33] He meticulously dissects the developments in the liturgy over the centuries, tracing changes sometimes obliquely indicated in the texts of ecclesiastical authors such as Eusebius and Hippolytus, in the canons of councils as well as other documents, such as the report of the confiscation of ecclesiastical property, particularly liturgical objects by Roman officials in North Africa in 303.[34] In this last text the entire body of the clergy is described as assembled in the church building, occupying exactly the places and roles they would during the liturgical celebration. The eighteenth canon of the Council of Nicaea is carefully analyzed for its decrees on the manner of distributing communion, asserting a new order, namely, communion of the clergy down the hierarchy— from bishop to presbyters to deacons—rather than the older pattern of the deacons immediately assisting the bishop in bringing the Bread and Cup to the presbyters.[35] The impetus for much change in the eucharistic liturgy appears to be the setting of the Great Church of Constantinople amid the ceremony of the Byzantine emperor and his court. "Solemn simplicity was not sufficient for an imperial Church," Afanasiev summarily states.[36] Yet he does not, as one might expect, condemn the enrichment of the liturgy wholesale. Rather he recognizes the understandable human desire to expand and beautify worship.

In both *The Lord's Supper* and *The Church of the Holy Spirit,* as well as in other essays such as "The Church Which Presides in Love" and "Una Sancta," Afanasiev seeks normative patterns in both the teaching and practice of the first centuries.[37] Thus he stresses the Pauline ecclesiology of *koinōnia.*[38] Also, there is his insistence on the "oneness" of altar, presider, celebration—one bishop, one Eucharist in each local church.[39] Over against a "universal ecclesiology" attributed to Cyprian, he recognizes the more primitive "eucharistic ecclesiology" of the local assembly, a distinction that Zizioulas and others claim he exaggerates and misunderstands.[40]

However, Afanasiev never pits the one, universal Church of God *against* the local church. Rather he argues that in the earliest centuries the universal communion of the Church of God was recognized, as, for example, in Irenaeus, but was experienced first and foremost in the local assembly to which one belonged throughout life. Afanasiev does not conflate the universal Church with the local, nor does he reduce the reality of the Church to the local assembly by affirming the ecclesial fullness of the latter. A longer citation shows, I contend, no confusion of local and universal in Afanasiev.

The multitude of local churches was *not* dispersed, it was united. The union was something absolutely *sui generis:* the unity was not the result of separate parts reuniting, but it was the unity of one and the same Church. Each local church united in itself all the local churches because it possessed all the fullness of the Church of God, and all the local churches together were united, because they were always this same Church of God. Though a local church did contain everything it needed within itself, it could not live apart from the other churches. It could not shut itself in or refuse to be acquainted with happenings in other churches: for anything that happened in other churches, as well as in its own, happened in the Church of God, the one and only Church. All the multitude of local churches forms one union founded on concord and love. Every local church must be in concord with all the other churches, because within the Church of God, ever one and only one, there can be no discord. This means, empirically speaking, that every local church accepts and makes its own anything that happens in the other churches, and that all the churches accept everything that happens in each fellow-church. This acceptance (its regular designation is the word *reception,* or *receptio*) is the witness of a local church indwelt by the Church of God, witnessing the work being done in other churches also indwelt by the Church of God—the Spirit bearing witness of the Spirit.[41]

This passage from "The Church Which Presides in Love" is to be found almost verbatim in the first chapter of *The Lord's Supper.* The Church's oneness in local multiplicity is the essential vision of eucharistic ecclesiology.[42] It is not Afanasiev's aim to romanticize a "golden age" of either the liturgy or ecclesial existence. On the contrary, by rigorous scrutiny of the offices and structure connected to the Eucharist, he is testing the principle "lex orandi, lex credendi" and formulating his own, most scriptural and patristic version of the Slavophiles' concept of the Church's catholic nature, or *sobornost'.* It also should be noted that Afanasiev's presentation of eucharistic ecclesiology is his response both to the actual and decadent conditions of ecclesial life in Orthodoxy and to the ecclesiological positions of the pre–Vatican II Roman Catholic Church and Reformation churches. Particularly in the ecumenical dimension, he quite explicitly counters the arguments for papal authority and primacy of the Church of Rome, as well as the Protestant rejections of ecclesiology. It is the separation of the structure and organization of the Church from the Holy Spirit and the Eucharist at which he sets his sights, a theological distancing he detects not only in Rome and the Reformation churches but in his own Orthodox Church as well.[43] Afanasiev cannot accept the conclusions of Harnack and others that the catholic tradition is essentially the hardening of law and structure when the eschatological intensity of the first centuries of Christianity has diminished.[44] It is important to recall his strenuous protest, particularly in *The Church of the Holy Spirit*, against the triumph of "law" over the Spirit in both churches of the West and the East.[45] For him, the only authentic "power" in the Church, the only way in which the local churches, as well as clergy and the faithful, should relate to each other is Love, not simply social equilibrium and respect but the presence and power of the One who is limitless Love.

Concelebration: The People with the Bishop

In the second chapter of *The Lord's Supper*, it might appear that the argument is chiefly about liturgical rubrics and Afanasiev's preference for a return to the simplicity of the liturgy before its later Byzantine encrustation. Yet there is more than rubrical significance in the question of who presides, and such considerations lead to the service or diaconal qualities of the offices of pastoral leadership. In *The Church of the Holy Spirit*, Afanasiev submits the development of bishop, presbyter, and deacon to sustained investigation in the Scriptures, the Fathers, and the councils.[46] In *The Lord's Supper*, however, the concern is, as the study itself, far more succinct and practical.

Chief among Afanasiev's emphases is the communal nature of the Eucharist and the Church and the participation of the whole assembly in the eucharistic liturgy, and, by extension, in the rest of the life of the Church. There is continuity with the perspective of *The Church of the Holy Spirit*.[47] Again, the assertions are practical and audacious. There can be no eucharistic gathering where there is no Church and there can be no Church without the Eucharist.[48] For Afanasiev, eucharistic assembly means participation. There can be no Eucharist (and hence no Church) without both presider, that is, pastoral leadership, and concelebrants.[49]

Clearly, many other works are done by and in the Church in addition to the Eucharist—baptism and chrismation, preaching and teaching, the works of love in caring for the sick and suffering—but, as Schmemann would later also argue, all refer back to and draw meaning from the eucharistic center.[50] The charge by critics that Afanasiev would erroneously turn all contexts of eucharistic celebration into "Church"—in hospitals, in the field by military chaplains, at schools, camps, and youth gatherings, and, for that matter, in monasteries—is a curious challenge indeed. Do not the very intercessions of the liturgical litanies include all these places and the people in them? Was not the émigré theologians' stress on *votserkovenlie*, ecclesialization or churching, precisely such a vision of the Church's embrace of all of life?[51] In describing the profoundly ecclesial character of the Russian Christian Students Association, and later the Anglican-Orthodox Fellowship of St. Alban and St. Sergius, both Zernov and Behr-Sigel underscore the definitive impact of these being punctuated by the daily offices and marked especially by the celebration of the Eucharist, a liturgical shaping in which Fathers Bulgakov and Lev had an important role.[52]

The different places or roles in the liturgical assembly are not according to honor or any other political or social or economic status, Afanasiev insists, but with respect to the ministry of each, which is a gift of God. In the "priestly act of worship," there is no division of the assembly. It is not, as it appears later in history and today, that some, the ordained, "celebrate" while the rest, the laity, merely attend. The one who is gifted with presidency of the liturgy and the community in love must be at the head, but there can be no presidency without the assembly, no Eucharist without the Church.

Unlike some contemporary efforts in liturgical renewal, often drastic, minimalizing, and iconoclastic, Afanasiev's endeavor is at once less detailed, more conservative and profound.[53] Thus his critique of the concelebration of numerous priests is not an attack on clergy roles in the eucharistic celebration or, despite his many comments on it, a call for radical removal of embellishments added to the Eastern Church liturgy from the Great Church of Hagia Sophia and the Byzantine imperial court.[54] Afanasiev's aim is even more basic. He was writing in a time when, in his émigré Russian Orthodox milieu and certainly outside it, in the rest of the churches, one could say there was a "eucharistic famine," what Afanasiev will describe as a tragedy.[55]

It is the people of God, in all its fullness, that celebrates the sacraments of the Church. The gathering, which is the essential element of the *ekklesia* has been forsaken. There is, in fact, no gathering. There are only sacred acts which are performed by those who are ordained.[56]

Afanasiev's aim, like that of so many of his colleagues, was nothing short of a serious displacement of the prevailing liturgical (and pastoral) ethos in order to restore the Eucharist to its preeminence and reinvigorate a very different yet ancient ecclesiology. Like others in the liturgical renewal movement, East and West, close to fifty years ago, he championed the then radical vision of participation, that is, ecclesial concelebration by both laity and clergy through prayers, singing, and receiving of communion at each liturgy.

Now apart from the later teaching in both the East and the West that grew to support changes in liturgical practice, providing rationales for rare reception of communion, silent praying of the *anaphora*, quite against the localism charges of his critics, Afanasiev explicitly identifies the development of the parish as a semi-independent part of the Church, with its priest as liturgical president as one of the most crucial detours from the Church's ancient vision and practice.[57] The Church was most intensely herself when laity and clergy gathered around the bishop as the sole presider at the Eucharist.[58] Such was the fundamental principle of ancient ecclesiology. Eucharistic presidency—"in Love," including preaching and leading the assembly in prayer and administering the holy gifts—was the only basis for the ongoing role of the bishop as chief pastor and of the local church as possessing ecclesial fullness but not being complete unless attached, in communion, with the other churches.[59] In recognizing the essence of the bishop and his ministry in eucharistic presidency, quite contrary to the criticism of Zizioulas, among others, Afanasiev gives emphasis to the presence and role of the chief pastor. He also unequivocally affirms that the local church can *never* stand by itself. Rather the local church (not originally equivalent to the contemporary "parish") is constantly in communion—eucharistic, teaching, diaconal—with the rest of the churches and with the universal Church. The fullness of the Church was there in the local church, but the local church never exhausted the Church universal, catholic, and one.

Much of the criticism of Afanasiev is leveled at his supposed hyperlocalism, an exaggerated view of the self-sufficiency of the local church that diminishes not only the larger Church of God but also the place and work of the bishop. Yet, if read carefully, *The Lord's Supper* and *The Church of the Holy Spirit* categorically reject any kind of "eucharistic congregationalism," as Nichols describes it.[60] Afanasiev most specifically calls for the implementation of certain renewals promulgated at the Great Sobor of Moscow in 1917–18, which the revolution thwarted.[61] To enhance the oneness of the eucharistic gathering of the bishop's church, there would seem to be two possible routes. One could emphasize, in addition to already existing ways, the parish's eucharistic gathering as an *extension* of the bishop's gathering. Already several liturgical elements both express this and call for further work, such as the necessity of an *antimension,* the cloth containing sealed relics and bearing on it a representation of the burial of Christ, signed by the bishop on the altar for the celebration, and the mentioning of the bishop by name in the litanies. Other canons echo the eucharistic "oneness" in additional ways: only one liturgy can be celebrated by each bishop or priest on a given altar on a given day; there can be no liturgy without the presider and minimally one congregant.

This "extension" form of eucharistic ecclesiology has become, at least in part, the model for contemporary Orthodox church bodies in America and elsewhere, as for the Roman Catholic and other churches of the catholic tradition, among them the Anglican and Lutheran. There are many other outgrowths of this model of unity in diversity of eucharistic gatherings, of episcopal pastoral leadership grounded in eucharistic communion. Among these would be regular visits and presiding at the Eucharist in parishes by the bishop; regular gatherings at least of representatives of the clergy and laity of the diocese not primarily for business but for the Eucharist, prayer, teaching, and fellowship; regular communication among the parishes and with the bishop by publications and other means; and regular cooperation in educational and diaconal activities as an outgrowth of the eucharistic communion among the parishes, within the local church, here meaning the diocese and not the isolated parish. Afanasiev suggests that the alternative to this would be the strengthening of the parish itself as a local church, with the pastor a quasi-bishop, much like the effort of establishing *chorepiskopoi* in earlier times. The diocese would then become a district of local churches.[62]

The great difficulty would appear to be the qualification I stated above about the first of the two models, namely, that "in part" the diocese is composed of parishes whose eucharistic gathering and hence life are extensions of the bishop's church and closely linked with it by various eucharistically based connections. Not only due to Reformation-rooted changes in understanding of ordained ministry, ecclesial structure, and procedure, congregationalism has emerged as a dominant mode of parish life across the churches in America. All of the weight of Orthodox conciliarity, of eucharistic ecclesiology and the importance and authority of the bishop, has not prevented various kinds of isolationism—ethnic, political, economic, congregationalism—from flourishing both in parishes and in individual dioceses. To describe and analyze this ecclesial fragmentation, due only in part to the canonization of ethnic-based jurisdictions among the Orthodox, while fascinating and crucial (in light of the efforts of SCOBA at Ligonier, Pennsylvania, in 1994 and the negative reaction of Ecumenical Patriarch Bartholomew I to efforts at ecclesial unity), is beyond this chapter's scope. Yet it is necessary to observe that Afanasiev's ecclesiological affirmations should not be restricted only to his own context, the émigré Russian Orthodox Church of the late 1940s and 1950s, even though that is his principal target. The relevance of his ecclesiological probing and challenge remains, not just for the Orthodox, but across the churches, given the ecumenical work of the last several decades and the hopes for the second millennium.

In America, as students of church life have been noting, allegiance to one's family or ethnic church body appears to be weakening in what may be a further stage of secularization in an otherwise apparently religious society. Yet it is not only a question of individual or familial ecclesial belonging that is much on the horizon here. Rather the ecclesiological issues also include relations among parishes within a diocese, within a national church body, and among church bodies or denominations. And the conflicts in American church bodies cannot be construed only along the lines of interest-group agenda or the controversies of the "culture wars." The rifts run much deeper, down into the bed of tradition and faith. Self-commissioned studies of several denominations suggest that it is hardly just a matter of diversity in faith but of genuine conflict and confusion. Afanasiev's view of eucharistically rooted ecclesiology is a great help here, underscoring that unity inheres in the very constitutive action of the community's thanksgiving and praise, proclamation and intercession, confession and communion with the Lord. The eucharistic assembly, with all concelebrating in their office and place, is not only a reflection of the Kingdom, an "eschatological icon," it is also the pattern to be constantly returned to in resolving conflict, in renewing the life of the Body.

"*Communion and Participation*"

The last section of *The Lord's Supper* is in many respects the most passionate and radical of Afanasiev's challenges. The immediate target of his criticism appears to be the infrequent, perhaps only annual reception of communion by the faithful in the Orthodox churches of his time. He lifts up the intense "preparation" for communion established among the Russians, *govenie,* including confession, increased attendance at services, fasting, abstinence from alcohol and sexual relations, reconciliation with enemies, mostly in the Lenten season, but also before important life events. Now while he does not make this sustained preparation the butt of his attack, he underscores the problems such practice creates. The aim and many of the specific ingredients are in fact the regular elements of the Christian life, heightened in awareness and intensity, especially in Lent, as a way of leading all back to their regular observance. Yet it is the intensity and seriousness of the preparation that imply not the transformation to more regular practice but the opposite, their rare practice, connected with a rarely performed sacred act, receiving communion.

Where such a practice and its ethos endure, the Sunday Eucharist thus becomes an observed, nonparticipatory event. The liturgy is conducted by the clergy presider(s) and choir, and few if any receive communion, while the prayers of the liturgy and teaching that the Church is a eucharistic assembly continue. This constitutes for Afanasiev the "eucharistic tragedy" of our time.[63] The New Testament's

proclamation and witness, "always everyone and always together,"
epi tô auto, has devolved into "not all and not together," "each one
for himself, separated." Afanasiev rejects both the idea of "spiritual
communion" and the later development of the *antidoron* (blessed
but not consecrated bread) as canonizations of decadent practice,
that is, regular abstinence from communion and not theologically
defensible. Christ said, "Take and eat, take and drink, . . ." and this
was not meant "spiritually" but actually, materially. Justification for
not receiving is a denial of the very action of the Holy Spirit, a pneumatological emphasis of Afanasiev here in *The Lord's Supper* and
throughout *The Church of the Holy Spirit*, inexplicably ignored by
one of his most consistent critics, Metropolitan John Zizioulas.[64] In
the liturgy, St. Paul's own words state the conditions for participation in the Eucharist: "The grace of Our Lord Jesus Christ, the
love of God the Father and the communion of the Holy Spirit."

Further, Afanasiev explicitly grounds the regular participation in
the Eucharist in baptism, contrary to what some see as a lack of
attention to baptismal implications for ecclesiology.[65] For Afanasiev,
to be in the Church is to be worthy of receiving communion, to be
gifted with participation in the Body and Blood of the Lord. Such
is never a matter of "duty" or canonical "obligation": "As many as
have been baptized into Christ, have put on Christ." In the text of
The Lord's Supper, Afanasiev explicitly emphasized the baptismal
and chrismational foundations of eucharistic assembly, even citing
this Pauline verse which serves as the troparion after baptism and
chrismation, during the procession around the font.[66] In *The Lord's
Supper*, the foundation both of the assembly's concelebration and of
eucharistic communing is baptismal belonging, while in *The Church
of the Holy Spirit*, the pneumatological dimension, the work of the
Holy Spirit on the assembly and individual believer, receives further
emphasis.[67] Not only in the earlier Jewish *havurah* Sabbath meals,
but later in the Christian eucharistic gatherings, there was no place
or understanding for nonparticipatory spectators. Why would one
come, if one did not share in the meal, the very reason for gathering, the very manner of giving thanks, of praying?[68]

The passage of time, though, saw changes, the time of peace for
the Church brought its own "sorrows." Not unlike other theologians, Afanasiev too sees a continual decline in the eucharistic life

of the Church after the Edict of Milan. Canons such as the second canon of Antioch and the eighth and ninth apostolic canons, prescribing the continued presence at the liturgy after the reading of the gospel and the reception of communion, become necessary and later are explained away as "impossible" by commentators such as Balsamon, Symeon of Thessalonika, even down to the early-twentieth-century canonical authority, Bishop Nikodim Milasch.[69] *Antidoron* becomes a substitute for communion. The impossibility of communing at every liturgy, even for the clergy, is supported by appeals to unworthiness, lack of preparation, conscience, circumstances in personal and social life.[70]

> If personal unworthiness was indeed an impediment against receiving communion, then practically no one could ever be admitted to the Eucharist. . . . The eucharistic gathering is the manifestation of the Church in all her fullness and all her oneness. Eucharistic communion is the very expression of life in the Church. If we eliminate eucharistic communion, then what is left of our life in the Church? Is prayer even temporarily able to replace communion? The prayer of the Church is prayer "in Christ," but it is impossible to be "in Christ" apart from eucharistic communion with Him.[71]

Such is the "exuberance" with which Afanasiev reaches his crescendo on the Eucharist making the Church. Both his style and his substance have disturbed critics. Pushing the argument to the extremes, he wonders whether the issues of unworthiness, lack of preparation, and the "impossibility" of receiving at each liturgy do not call the validity of Baptism into question! St. Symeon the New Theologian similarly mused about the validity of the sacraments for the indifferent.[72] Alexander Schmemann would sound many of these passionate arguments again in numerous journal articles and monographs, particularly in an article based on his important report to the synod of bishops of the Orthodox Church in America.[73]

With his colleagues of the Russian diaspora, Afanasiev reveals notable insight about the progressive secularization of the Church, of social life, and, as Peter Berger has emphasized, of the consciousness of the individual Christian.[74] It is here, I think, that the peculiarities of the Russian Orthodox evaporate and the common problems of being the Church in the late twentieth century are encountered by Afanasiev's insight. The cause of the "eucharistic tragedy" of the late twentieth century lies not so much with lack of preparation or unworthiness but rather in the deepening dichotomy of life, the splintering of faith from the "real" life of family, work, and play. Put in the favorite term of the Russians, it is the "unchurching" rather than the "churching" of life, really, shutting the eschatological door, not unlike what Max Weber termed "disenchantment."[75] We can no longer see in our entire life either the preparation for eucharistic communion or the results of such sacred participation. "Spiritual" or pious practice has been partitioned off into perhaps a special season of the year such as Lent or Easter or to moments of particular anxiety or significance. Liturgy itself is compartmentalized, in Schmemann's words, oversacralized, so as not to connect with everyday life. In either case, not only is the Eucharist, but the Church and therefore the expansive wholeness of the Christian life, drastically reduced. The world no longer is perceived as sacrament, as the liturgy presents it.[76] The basic understanding of early Christianity has been lost, namely, that for each member of the Church "there is only one possible life, which through the mystery of Baptism by water and the Holy Spirit, has been given to Christ." The reference is explicit: "All is yours, and you are Christ's and Christ is God's" (1 Cor. 3:22–23).[77]

In assessing the historical devolution of the Church's eucharistic centrality, Afanasiev does not fault only the secularization of the body by the increasing membership of less ardent believers. The proliferation of eucharistic liturgies, from the Lord's day and few major feasts to Wednesdays, Fridays, and Saturdays by the patristic period of the fourth and fifth centuries and later to every day, did not maintain or increase the frequency of communion. The rule became that only some, never all, attended, and then of these just a few actually received. And so the process of eucharistic dissolution continued, with theological justification and support, across the churches until the twentieth century.

It is noteworthy that Afanasiev identifies not theological errors for this process but human behavior and attitudes. While not reducing the process to a sociological phenomenon, he sees a progressive ecclesial deterioration. The institutional character of the Church does not disappear. Neither does its corporate character or its elements such as ordained clergy, liturgical services and sacraments, Scriptures, councils and canons. However, what comes to dominate is individualism, not only in intensely personal pietism, but also in parish life, diocesan activity, even preaching, teaching, and clerical practice.[78] Father Schmemann documented this process throughout his corpus, especially in his still provocative articles from more than thirty years ago on the problems of Orthodoxy and in his study, *The Eucharist*.[79] It is not just an American phenomenon but a much more basic social, political, and psychological development of our time, the rise of the self over against alienated and oppressing institutions and traditions.[80] Afanasiev is volatile in his insistence that the tragedy is individualization, the Eucharist and hence the Church being domesticated into private devotional acts and fulfillment of obligatory rituals, the triumph of self both among the faithful and the clergy, rather than the tumultuous, transforming power of Christ, breaking into this world and our hearts with his Kingdom.

> We profess faith in "one, holy, catholic and apostolic Church . . . but this faith goes completely unrealized in our actual life. . . . We cannot even explain why we profess our faith in the Church. Each one remains a separate atom in relation to all the others whom we do not even know. Often, we do not know those with whom we approach the chalice. We enter the church building for ourselves alone, and not in order to "gather together as church." The neurological center of individualism lies in the Eucharist. The foundational principle of "always all and always together" manifests itself most fully in the Eucharistic gathering, which is the gathering of all for one and the same thing (*epi to auto*) Everyone ministers to God at the Eucharist. Neither separate groups not separate members celebrate: it is the Church that celebrates.[81]

Drawing from the 1 Corinthians text (11:27–33) so often used to support stringent methods of preparation for worthy communion, lest one should eat and drink to one's own damnation, Afanasiev maintains that the privatizing of the Eucharist into an exclusive, personal act of piety and the collective abstinence from regular communion and the disappearance of pastoral leadership are precisely acts of serious self-condemnation. The "most threatening accusation of the unchurching of our church life" is the celebration of the Lord's Supper in an empty church and without participants, just as the "greatest sin" is the same in a church packed with many, with no one or just a few communing.[82]

Both at the time of his writing and subsequently, such obstinence on Afanasiev's part about the eucharistic essence of the Church, the ecclesial nature of the Eucharist, and the domination of individualism have earned him criticism from many quarters. His writings were among those burned as "heretical" under the order of then Bishop Nikon of Ekaterinburg in February 1998. To many nowadays as well in the West, the problem of nonparticipation in the Eucharist he so passionately protests may seem irrelevant, given the reception that has accompanied liturgical renewal. There is no doubt that in the last section of *The Lord's Supper*, "Communion and Participation," and in the concluding pages of that part, this vision is presented in the most forceful, nonnegotiable, even absolute fashion. It is claimed not as merely Afanasiev's own theological opinion but Christ's own desire and the ancient tradition and practice of the Church, witnessed to by the Scriptures, the apostolic fathers, the canons, and the very texts of the liturgical prayers themselves. It is also telling, I think, that despite the good intentions contained therein, Afanasiev cannot accept such efforts at liturgical reform as the call for stripping away later historical accretions to the liturgy or even the sincere commitment of clergy and laity to commune at every eucharistic liturgy.[83] Both attempts are well founded but in the end will amount only to social engineering, tinkering with a far more serious sickness. They will not alter the situation because these too are, in the end, individual acts.[84] The immediate task is not to bring about various changes in liturgical life but to "realize the authentic nature of the Eucharist," which thereby entails rediscovering the Church, one's baptismal calling, and, what is more, the vocation of the Christian life. Significant, though implied, in Afanasiev's ruthless criticism of individualization is more than polemics against pietism, more than a wish to move from the practices of the Russian or any other ecclesiastical past. It is the wager of this essay that Afanasiev's radical ecclesiology, so regularly and undeservedly attacked, still has import for us, not only with Orthodoxy but across the churches.

Continuing Contributions

Afanasiev's confrontation of the assumptions of the popular piety of his time, with both its mindless hyperconservatism and its intense individualization, has been effective even outside that milieu. He was not, as some have understood him, simply a polemicist against ecclesiastical authority, particularly that of bishops and of canon law. Trained both as a canon lawyer and as an ecclesiastical historian, he rather came to recognize the inner charismatic character of the Church's authority and structure. It was neither power nor law, neither the hierarchy of the ordained nor ethical conformity, but the power of love, given by the Holy Spirit to both clergy and laity to be the body of Christ, as the saying of Saint Irenaeus of Lyons that formed the epigraph of *The Church of the Holy Spirit:* "Where the Church is, there also is the Spirit of God and where the Spirit of God is, there is the Church in all her grace."[85]

Afanasiev, as it turns out, was far from alone in leading us back to perhaps this century's single most important rediscovery. Both a student and colleague, Fr. Alexis Kniazeff, later dean of the St. Sergius Institute, has articulated this vision of the churching of life (*votser-kovenlie*) and the world, a theme beloved to Berdiaev and Bulgakov as well as others in the Russian diaspora, a view at once intensely incarnational and inclusive.[86] Many of his contemporaries, both of the Eastern and Western Church, have been shaped by his teaching, even if they disagree with certain aspects of it. Zizioulas and Ware, Schmemann and Tillard, among others, have become the inheritors of his eucharistic and ecclesiological archaeology. His friend and colleague at St. Sergius in the last years, Paul Evdokimov, clearly was moved and deepened by his strong presentation of the universal priesthood of all the baptized. It became a constant component of Evdokimov's thinking and appears in virtually all of his writing, in one or another form. This understanding of the accessibility of

vocation and the ministry of prayer and service and holiness is so
important that it is, in fact, the underlying motif of this book. What
their lives say to us is that we too are invited to become the servants
of the Lord and of each other, "prophets and friends of God," saints.
This is, one might say, the practical consequence of Father Afanasiev's eucharistic ecclesiology. It was his singular gift to uncover the
inherence of the Church in the Eucharist, thus recovering the ancient
yet always new relationship of ecclesial existence and liturgical being.

Throughout his radical attack on decadent practice, Afanasiev
recognized the unchurching at work in his century. For him, this
amounted to progressive privatization, an ecclesiastical consum-
erism, often in the name of piety, democracy, and freedom, but at
root resulting in the erosion of the eucharistic nature of the Church.
This lost, the Church's mission to the world becomes confused or
reduced to simply political and economic justice. Curiously, those
who criticize Afanasiev rarely perceive this important contribution
of his, consistently present throughout his writings: his own critical
appraisal of the Church in modern society. He shared the common
passion of the émigré theologians, not simply to reiterate the sources,
not just to recite the tradition of the Church, but to return to its simplicity and power and connect these with our time.[87]

Beneath the "eucharistic tragedy" of the Church, as well as beneath the sad and scandalous schism of the churches, Afanasiev
detected the loss of the early Church's eschatological awareness, dynamically present in the constitutive actions of eucharistic assembly,
celebration, and communion. Over against the domestication of the
Church into the Roman imperium, later into the Byzantine, Caro-
lingian, Kievan, Muscovite, and other cultures and state apparatuses,
and still later into what we would call denominational enclaves and
private pietism, he is relentlessly committed to the *eschatological
dimension* of the Church's life, contrary to Father Meyendorff's criticism, and for him, this is rooted precisely in the eucharistic gathering.[88] Today it is the common tendency, perhaps temptation, across
the churches to accept this eucharistic ecclesiology and then, taking
it for granted, in effect nullifying its challenge and demands, to proceed to hunt down the next strategy of evangelism and stewardship,
that is, membership growth and fund-raising. If more recently there
has been a fascination in Western culture for "spirituality," this too

is stamped with personal choice and reluctance to become part of a community of faith, with its allegedly imposed doctrine and ritual.[89] Is it not possible to detect, precisely in the manner of appropriating "spirituality," just the individualization of which Afanasiev speaks?[90]

Hence, a second contribution of Afanasiev is his stress on the *communal nature* of the Church and her *conciliar life,* again the image for which is found in the eucharistic gathering. He does not root the Church's identity in the Scriptures alone, in doctrine, the councils and their canons, or even in the episcopal office.[91] The eucharistic ecclesiology that he so vigorously championed, is, as he argues so persuasively in *The Church of the Holy Spirit,* a pneumatological and incarnational reality. The evangelical and charismatic force of Afanasiev, attributable to the eucharistic character of his ecclesiology, is both surprising and refreshing, particularly from an Orthodox theologian (although such are fast unbecoming best-kept secrets, for example, Bulgakov, Schmemann, Meyendorff, and Evdokimov). Afanasiev teaches us that the Church is only demeaned if its divine, Spirit-endowed nature is devalued and subordinated to its legal-institutional, that is, its social and political, dimensions.

Although it lies beyond the limits of this study, I conclude with perhaps Afanasiev's sharpest challenge that remains before us, the *recovery of ecclesial communion.* The provocative consequences of his understanding of eucharistic ecclesiology were summarized in the study he wrote on the schism between the East and West and the renewal of eucharistic communion between them. This essay was dedicated to the memory of John XXIII, whom Afanasiev calls "the Pope of Love," obviously echoing his own view of "presiding in Love." "Una Sancta," published in 1963, is no mere rhapsody to "good Pope John," Vatican II, or the ecumenical movement and was published even before the mutual lifting in 1966 of the eleventh-century anathemas under Paul VI and Athenagoras I. Much of the essay's substance is to be found elsewhere in his authorship: the contrast between universal and eucharistic ecclesiologies, the matter of primacy and the priority of Rome, and, especially problematic for the Orthodox and other churches, the infallibility of the bishop of Rome and the proclaimed Marian dogmas. Afanasiev does not flinch from the realities, which not only are differences but which caused and have perpetuated the schism. Nevertheless, he contemplates that

scene, recorded by Eusebius, of the conflict-riddled relations between
Rome and the East in a much earlier time, over the date of the celebration of the Resurrection. Yet for these divergences, they maintained peace and maintained communion with each other, Anicetus
of Rome even yielding presidency at the Eucharist there to Polycarp,
an action that is an icon of the eschatological character of the eucharistic Church.[92] Despite the real and serious divergences, Rome and
the Orthodox, according to Afanasiev, "have never ceased to be
churches to each other." All polemics of both aside, the mutual recognition of their common ecclesial nature is there to be seen in history, today described in the language of "sister-churches." The sharp
attacks on such ecclesiology and its eucharistic roots continues in
Orthodoxy.

   The bold challenge Afanasiev makes is to confront the present
schism with this pattern from the past. While doctrinal divisions and
other differences should not be wished away, the lack of absolute
agreement while maintaining eucharistic communion is nonetheless
a historical ecclesial reality. It is not just the truth of doctrine that is
at issue in the schism, but also the truth and the power of Love.
Could it not be that the loss of this Love has contributed to the loss
and deterioration of doctrinal truth? In a spirit much like that of the
letters of John (1:4) and 1 Corinthians (13) and in the same boldness
as Bulgakov's proposition of over sixty years ago, Afanasiev argues
that the reestablishment of eucharistic communion between East and
West would be neither a denial of the schism nor a facile use of the
Eucharist to attain ecclesial unity but rather an assertion of the authentic reality of the Church as eucharistic assembly.[93] It would be
an act of faith in the Church, not just saying prayers but becoming
them, prayer incarnate, as Evdokimov eloquently put it.[94] Other
moving words of Evdokimov's also come to mind:

   Mariology carries ecumenical ramifications. Sergius Bulgakov
   considered it to be his particular task to constantly remind others
   of the dogmatic content in the veneration of the Theotokos. The
   tearing of the seamless garment of Christ symbolizes the sin
   against the Mariological integrity (sophrosyne) of the Church. The
   ecumenical problem has its root in the mystery of the Church and
   falls silent at the gates of Mariology. Present-day ecumenism is

still strongly marked by a male spirit and is therefore so non-liturgical. It does not sing; it talks and discusses. The conflict erupts at the deeper level where the confessional "We cannot" (*non possumus*) resounds on every side; it is viewed essentially as a conflict between fidelities to the respective traditions. It suggests the need to recover the dogmatic foundations of ecclesiology by a great return to the patristic sources. No agreement will be reached simply through theological reasoning, but through a praying heart and the Liturgy, through the sacrament of the ecumenical *fiat:* "Here am I; I am the Lord's servant, as you have spoken, so be it" (Luke 1:38).[95]

Father Afanasiev's voice, in all its radical fullness, needs to be heard again, not only in the specialized ecumenical dialogues or conversations of liturgical theologians, but more broadly in the churches. His relentless eschatological vision, despite its alleged one-sidedness and omissions, is a genuine return to the sources, a recognition of the Eucharist in the Church and the Church in the Eucharist. As Alexander Schmemann reminds us, what concerns the Eucharist concerns the Church and what concerns the Church concerns the Eucharist, "so that any ailment in the liturgy reflects on our faith and on the whole life of the Church: *Ibi ecclesia, ubi Spiritus Sanctus et omnis gratia.*"[96]

CHAPTER NINE

Alexander Schmemann

Teacher of Freedom and Joy in the World as Sacrament

"A free man in Christ, a man full of joy"

Human life is the expectation of that which is at the end, and at the end is the joy of the bridal chamber, the joy of the Resurrection. At the end are Mary and John and all the saints; at the end is the wonderful fullness of life. When I see this end, I want to reach it, to move in its direction. I have to make an effort, and when I make an effort my whole life becomes an exercise. I meet a man in whom I am not interested, but I realize that this man has been sent to me by God and the encounter becomes meaningful. I have a meaningless job, but that job is the one by which my body, my spirit, my life are to be changed into expectation. Everything acquires a meaning; everything becomes sanctified, because everything is a step on that long journey to the top of Mount Tabor.[1]

December 13 is the feast of the first canonized Orthodox saint of North America, St. Herman (1756–1817), the missionary-monk of Spruce Island, Alaska. St. Herman planted the church among the Aleuts for more than forty years by prayer, teaching, and service to the suffering. Everything we know about him echoes and witnesses to his personal holiness. He gave a good witness through love for God and for his Aleut neighbor, even in the force of opposition from the Russian-American Trading Company and with little tangible help from his home monastery, Valaamo, or his mother church in Russia. A line from the few writings left behind is usually placed on his icon, summarizing his life and holiness: " ... from this day forth, from this hour, from this minute, love God above all."

Present at St. Herman's canonization in Alaska in 1970 and instrumental in the work leading toward it was another immigrant Orthodox who made America his second home. Transplanted in New York City from the Russian emigration of Paris, Fr. Alexander Schmemann became not only a leader in liturgical renewal, not only a shaper of the Orthodox Church in America, but just as profound an ecclesial soul and just as much an example of holiness in our time as Herman of Alaska. Born in 1921 in Tallin, Estonia, into a Baltic German-become-Russian family, he spent most of his childhood, adolescence, and early adulthood in Paris, passing through the Russian as well as the French educational systems, both *gimnaziya* and *lycée*, and eventually studying at the University of Paris and St. Sergius Theological Institute. At St. Sergius from 1940 to 1945 he was taught by, among others, the church historian A. V. Kartashev, who left with him the historian's consciousness; Fr. Sergius Bulgakov, whose theological work did not impress him but whose priestly gifts very much did; and Fr. Basil Zenkovsky, who provided a model of work in psychology and philosophy, of how to fully appreciate the arts and sciences of the modern world. However, Frs. Nicolas Afanasiev and Kyprian Kern would have the greatest intellectual influence on him. He married Juliana Osorguine in 1943, was ordained a priest in 1946, and began teaching church history at St. Sergius and assisting Father Kern with a small parish in the suburb of Clamart. However, it was exposure to the ecumenical liturgical renewal movement, part of the larger *ressourcement,* the return to the sources, namely, the Fathers, the Bible, and the liturgy, that definitively shaped and nourished him. He was able to encounter many of the preeminent scholars of this revival, not only in reading, but especially in the liturgical weeks at Saint Sergius organized by Kern and Afanasiev. All of this stimulated the approach he would later call "liturgical theology." Firsthand acquaintance with Catholic liturgical and historical theologians such as Dom Botte, Louis Bouyer, Jean Daniélou, Yves Congar, Henri De Lubac and the study of others such as the Anglican Benedictine liturgist Dom Gregory Dix enabled him to find a distinctive place in the rediscovery of the Tradition: the liturgy, the Fathers, and the eucharistic nature of the Church herself. Yet it was a sense of mission that eventually led Father Schmemann, Father Meyendorff, and others to America. There it would be more likely, they hoped, to contribute to an indigenous, nonethnic non-"diaspora" Orthodox Church. Decades later, after much work and against much resistance both internationally and at home, the fruit of this vision, borne principally by him and Father Meyendorff, was the granting of autocephaly, that is, independent status, to the former Russian Metropolia in America by the patriarchate of Moscow in 1970. Coming to the United States in 1951, Father Schmemann began teaching at St. Vladimir's Theological Seminary when it was located in New York City. On its relocation to suburban Crestwood, New York, in 1962, he became its dean and remained in that office until his death from cancer more than twenty years later. On December 13, 1983, St. Herman's feast, he fell asleep in the Lord.[2]

A liturgical scholar, seminary dean, theologian to bishops, literary critic, preacher, and pastor, Father Schmemann is recognized ecumenically for his diverse contributions. His voice is still heard, along with those of the *ressourcement,* but for more than the "Orthodox position" on matters liturgical. Schmemann's singular gift to the Church was his recovery of the fundamental location of the Church's rationale for being, the roots of her life, mission, and expression *in the liturgy,* primarily in the celebration of the Eucharist.[3] He brought back, in other words, the authentic *theologia prima.* At the same time, he accomplished nothing less than a restoration of ecclesiology and a renewal in ecclesial life. In his deft rendering of the various contemporary "reductions" of the Church, he was able to reveal the Church's essential identity, very much like the nineteenth-century Orthodox theologian Alexei Khomiakov and following the eucharistic ecclesiology of his teacher, Nicolas Afanasiev.[4]

Yet in his pursuit of the life of the Kingdom of God in the Church and the liturgy, Father Schmemann never abandoned the world of literature and politics, of culture, society, and historical process.[5] Above all, his keen understanding of the world, his ease in its midst, whether Paris or New York City, his intense delight in the good things of this life were profoundly grounded in the triadic poles of his theology and indeed of his own faith and holiness: creation, the

Fall, and Redemption. He was a superb scholar and teacher, a competent administrator, but a person of faith, another example of holiness in our time.

To listen to Father Schmemann is to be wonderfully startled by the wealth of his humane learning. Though his work as a liturgical historian is well known, his work in other areas is impressive, such as his commentary on the history of doctrine, monasticism, schism, and, beyond ecclesial subjects, the history of contemporary political movements.[6] Of great interest and delight to me, trained in the sociologies of knowledge and religion under Peter Berger, is Father Schmemann's masterful reading of the structures, movements, and consciousness of modernity.[7] More than thirty years ago he provided an unusual counterreading of American society and the place (or lack of place) in it for a community of faith and its tradition. These perspectives on modern America's secularism, its toleration for diversity, pragmatism, and urge to conformity, were later joined by his experience of the social and cultural changes of the 1960s and 1970s. Though he did not live to see the intense radicalizing of issues in the Church in the later 1980s and 1990s, very little would have surprised him.[8]

Teacher of Tradition

Father Schmemann was above all a teacher. The Tradition of the Church, the truth of the gospel, the glory of the liturgy—all this was faithfully transmitted, one could say incarnationally embodied and personally communicated, by him. Tapes of his retreat conferences and lectures capture the forceful qualities of his preaching and teaching.[9] So too do the volumes of selections from the almost three thousand "Sunday Talks" he recorded over the years for Radio Liberty.[10] These talks, on the creed, on the feasts of the liturgical year, and on the Mother of God, intended for listeners in the USSR with little knowledge of the faith, are among the most humane and beautiful of his writings.

Those who knew Father Schmemann recall his pastoral gifts as confessor and counselor. In fact, his passion and faithfulness as a

priest of the Church are evident in every role he filled, whether with
larger groups at conferences, the assembly gathered for the liturgy,
or the individual who came to him as pastor. At his funeral, his colleague and friend, Veselin Kesich, eloquently summed up his priestly
witness throughout his life and particularly in his terminal illness.

> He was a free man in Christ; he was a man full of joy. . . . He
> taught us a lesson on how, in suffering, the power of the eternal
> God may be revealed. He taught us a lesson about power in weak-
> ness. My dear friends, to teach this particular lesson—power in
> weakness—is *the* fundamental lesson: that is the Gospel. The
> Gospel is nothing else but power in weakness. The One who was
> sacrificed in weakness was raised by the power of God.[11]

Father Schmemann was a deeply sensitive, even poetic soul, but
he was never a sentimental person. He had a healthy aversion to the
indiscriminate sentimentality that canonizes everything Russian as
precious, everything done in the liturgy and life of the Church as
sacred. Perhaps the greatest of his gifts was a deep perception of what
was authentic and what was false in Christian life. He was able, as
the New Testament letter of St. John puts it, "to discern the spirits"
(1 John 4:1). His piety was vibrant, not the antiquarian, stereotypical,
formal sort. He served the Church vigorously and practically in a
number of positions. Not only did he teach at St. Vladimir's for
thirty-two years, twenty-one as dean, he was also theological adviser
to the Holy Synod of Bishops and one of the principal architects of
the autocephaly of the OCA in 1970. He worked as theologian
with SCOBA and with various domestic and international inter-
Orthodox groups for theological education and youth work such as
Syndesmos and the Orthodox Theological Society. He promoted
St. Vladimir's Theological Quarterly and helped to create the seminary's annual summer institute for liturgical and pastoral theology,
modeled on the "liturgical weeks" of St. Sergius Theological Institute. The mission of St. Vladimir's Seminary Press, the preeminent
English-language publisher of Orthodox theology, owes much to his
ideals of learning for the whole Church and for the world.

Yet Father Schmemann often met with bitter resistance, hostility,
and rejection from the clergy and laity of his church. Now that selec-

tions from his journals have been published, it is also possible to encounter him in his own struggles with what passes for "religion," with the narrowness, both ethnic and theological, of his church. One can also read here of his coming to grips with his own failings, weaknesses, and frustrations.

> Friday, October 12, 1973: . . . Dean, Protopresbyter, professor: I sometimes feel (especially on a sunny, solitary morning like today) that it has nothing to do with me personally, that it is a poor mask, and yet, 90 percent of my life is determined by these titles. When I take off the mask people are shocked—how can he be himself? When I wear the mask, whatever I say or do is justified. How easy it is to dilute one's personality under a mask and even become fond of it.[12]

There is no neat, proper resolution of either of these. He resists typing either as a hero or as a saint, in the caricatures of these, I mean. Despite his deep misgivings about the conservation of the past as "antiquities," a museum approach masquerading as faithfulness to the tradition, he cautiously but resolutely proposed specific restorations in the liturgy: more frequent reception of communion, the return of baptism to a communal rather than private act, the reasoned abbreviation of texts rather than their rapid recitation to save time. He was not afraid to question the quality of many liturgical texts, especially those light on scriptural foundations and heavy on poetic fantasy. He showed in the chapel of the seminary how the cycle of feasts, the daily office or prayer of the hours, and, most of all, the eucharistic liturgy could be celebrated with dignity and in a manner that allowed the entire assembly to drink from this fountain of divine life. He also showed how liturgy and life could be integrated, over against the tendencies to "reduce" participation in services to yearly "obligations." In his own spiritual life, the journal selections now reveal a very free soul, as Kesich described him, but a most expansive and joyous spirit.

> Holy Tuesday, April 21, 1981: . . . What has Christianity lost so that the world, nurtured by Christianity, has recoiled from it and started to pass judgment over the Christian faith? Christianity has

lost *joy*—not natural joy, not joy-optimism, not joy from earthly happiness, but the Divine joy about which Christ told us that "no one will take your joy from you" (John 16:22). Only this joy *knows* that God's love to man and to the world is not cruel; knows it because that love is part of the absolute happiness for which we were all created. . . . The world is created by happiness and for happiness and everything in the world prophesies that happiness; everything calls to it, witnesses it by its very fragility. To the fallen world that has lost its happiness, but yearns for it and—in spite of everything—lives by it, Christianity has *opened up* and *given back* happiness; has fulfilled it *in Christ* as *joy*.[13]

In a beautiful and incarnational way, Father Schmemann brought everyone and everything in his life into prayer. The formulaic orders of daily prayer were not his practice, but his faculty meetings, counseling, teaching, and lecturing, and especially his reading and writing and time with friends and family—all "became prayer, prayer incarnate," in Evdokimov's phrase. The journals were written in the last decade of his life. In the selections translated and published he looks back, not always happily, on what he had accomplished in thirty years of effort in America. Not long after being "fired" as adviser to the synod of bishops of the OCA he wrote:

Monday, February 1, 1982: If anything became clear during this last month of fuss and work, it is the realization that the time of constant compromises which I have lived with in the church has come to an end. Not on my initiative, a very long period of my involvement and influence in the church as an *éminence grise* has ended. The powers that be have decided to get rid of all counselors, and mainly me. At first I felt—I can't conceal it—that it was offensive, unfair, a rejection of my "merits," etc. But now after a month of fighting with myself; that is, fighting with putting myself at the center of everything, with sadness and mixed feelings in my heart, I feel somehow liberated. Since 1966 I always felt responsible for everything in our Church. And now it is as if someone has taken away that responsibility. At first it was difficult not to give advice, not to interfere. . . . But now it's easy.[14]

St. Seraphim of Sarov. Contemporary icon by Olga Poloukhine,
photo by Hannah Plekon, author's collection.

Fr. Sergius Bulgakov, Paris, 1930s, courtesy of Professor Nikita Struve.

Mother Maria Skobtsova, Paris, 1930s, courtesy of Hèléne Arjakovsky-Klépinine.

Fr. Lev Gillet, London, 1970s, courtesy of Fr. Stephen Platt, Fellowship of Sts. Alban and Sergius.

Interior of former St. Basil's House Chapel, London. Icons by Sr. Joanna Reitlinger, now in Monastery of Christ the Savior, Hove, East Sussex, UK, courtesy of Fr. Stephen Platt, Fellowship of Sts. Alban and Sergius.

Saints of the East (*above*) and West (*below*), frescoes by Sr. Joanna Reitlinger, former St. Basil's House Chapel, London, courtesy of Elizabeth Behr-Sigel.

Paul Evdokimov and Fr. Lev Gillet, Versailles, 1960s,
courtesy of Mrs. Tomoko Faerber-Evdokimov.

Paul Evdokimov, 1968,
courtesy of
Mrs. Tomoko
Faerber-Evdokimov.

Paul and Tomoko Evdokimov meeting Pope Paul VI, Rome, 1964–65,
courtesy of Mrs. Tomoko Faerber-Evdokimov.

Fr. Gregory Krug at his skete, late 1960s, courtesy of Fr. Protodeacon André Chépélov.

Fr. Gregory Krug and his spiritual father, Sergius Schevitch, around the time of his entering monastic life, 1948, courtesy of Fr. André Chépélov and Mrs. Levandovsky.

Icon of Christ by Fr. Gregory Krug, St. Seraphim Church, Montgeron,
courtesy of St. Vladimir's Seminary Press.

Icon of the Mother of God by Fr. Gregory Krug, St. Seraphim Church,
Montgeron, courtesy of St. Vladimir's Seminary Press.

Icon of St. Seraphim of Sarov by Fr. Gregory Krug, St. Seraphim Church,
Montgeron, courtesy of St. Vladimir's Seminary Press.

Fr. Nicolas Afanasiev,
Paris, 1950s,
courtesy of
Professor Nikita Struve.

Fr. Alexander
Schmemann
at liturgy,
1970s,
courtesy of
St. Vladimir's
Seminary
archives.

Fr. Schmemann at communion, 1970s, author's collection.

Fr. John Meyendorff,
1980s,
courtesy of
Mrs. Marie Meyendorff.

Fr. Meyendorff lecturing,
1980s,
courtesy of
Mrs. Marie Meyendorff.

Fr. Alexander Men,
1970s,
courtesy of
Abraham Grossman.

Fr. Men
and his wife,
Natalya,
1970s,
courtesy of
Alan Carmack
and Yakov Krotov.

Contemporary icon of Fr. Men, Russia, 1990s,
courtesy of Alan Carmack and Yakov Krotov.

Continuing in his journal the next day, he plunges deeply into the clericalism so deeply embedded in the church, the desire to retain control over the laity, the means of doing this by "fencing in" the reception of communion, by resorting constantly to rules, office, law.[15] He wondered about the kind of formation a seminary he had worked hard to build up was actually providing for future clergy and lay leaders of the church. He had real doubts about the tunnel vision, the limiting of perspectives such an education was producing, as well as about the fanaticism and intolerance, the obsession with dress and forms and the rubrics that he saw growing around him in the Orthodox Church. He had real doubts about how he had frantically attempted to be "all things to all men" in his life. Only after his diagnosis of terminal cancer does he begin to slow down and recognize what was truly important. One hopes that more of the journal entries, ideally *all* of them, might also appear in print at some time. As with the journals of Thomas Merton, recently published in their entirety, such a genre destroys any idealized, romantic images of a saint, only to enable us to recognize all the more plainly how holiness is the accumulation of many mistakes and inadequacies, numerous eccentricities and imperfections, all shaped, transformed, by God into a new being, a "living icon."

I do not think it an exaggeration to say that the OCA would be a very different, poorer example of faithfulness to the gospel without Father Schmemann's person, work, and life. Many of the choices he made, bitterly disputed at the time, have turned out to be very wise and right in the decades that followed: his insistence on moving to the language of the people in all aspects of church life, his commitment to a truly indigenous church and not an ethnic enclave, his conviction that the call of the gospel was for the "life of the world." Since his death his work has been less than lovingly remembered and listened to, sometimes deliberately ignored or contradicted within his own ecclesial community. His death and that of his colleague Fr. John Meyendorff have left a veritable vacuum in the intellectual and spiritual leadership of the Orthodox churches in America. One senses very profoundly the loss of their strong voices in opposition to the emergence of isolationist and legalistic tendencies, to anti-ecumenical attitudes among the Orthodox in America. Perhaps more than anything what is missing is their courage, the spirit of freedom, joy, and love for the world that so characterized both teachers. It is difficult not to see the current state and direction as regression or even abandonment of the vision of eucharistic ecclesiology and mission that was Father Schmemann's and his teachers' and his peers'.

Father Schmemann was also an active teacher and scholar outside Orthodoxy. He served on several WCC committees and participated in numerous theological groups and delivered many papers at their conferences. He contributed articles to an international array of journals and scholarly collections. He was a signer of the 1975 Hartford Statement, originated by Peter Berger and Richard John Neuhaus, which was highly critical of tendencies in American mainstream churches and culture, a discerning view of the "culture wars" and erosion of Christian tradition to come. He prepared an insightful essay for the collection that interpreted the statement's intent.[16] It is striking to hear what Father Schmemann said at the close of this essay in the context of regressive sectarian and traditionalist tendencies today.

> I know that are those Orthodox who affirm and preach that the Orthodox can and must live in the West without any "reference" to the Western culture except that of a total negation, to live in fact as if the West did not exist, for it is totally corrupt, heretical, and sick beyond repair. To achieve this, one must create artificial islands of Greek or Russian or any other Orthodox culture, shut all doors and windows, and cultivate the certitude of belonging to the sacred remnant. What these "super-Orthodox" do not know, of course, is that their attitude reflects precisely the ultimate surrender to that West which they abhor: that in their ideology Orthodoxy is being transformed for the first time into that which it has never been—a sect, which is by definition the refusal of the catholic vocation of the Church. And there are those who maintain, as I have tried to say, a peaceful coexistence of Orthodoxy with a culture that, in reality, claims the whole man: his soul, his life, and his religion. Both attitudes are ultimately self-destructive.[17]

In such a full life, Father Schmemann was nevertheless able to produce a substantial body of writing. However, much was published in small journals or remains unpublished. His earliest published essays, in Parisian and New York Russian Orthodox journals in the late 1940s and early 1950s, already take up such issues as the centrality of Pascha, the feast of the Resurrection, of the liturgy as the heart of the Church, and of the Church as more than institutional structures, dogmatic and canonical formulations, and national (ethnic) associations.[18] His earliest English-language articles, from the mid-1950s, begin with the festal cycle of the liturgical year and emphasize the Church's eucharistic nature and the Eucharist as *the* sacrament of the Church.[19] His important ecclesiastical-history study, *The Historical Road of Eastern Orthodoxy,* appeared first in Russian in 1954 and in English translation in 1963. This work is still overlooked in favor of his liturgical studies yet is rich in detail on the historical life of the Church, detail crucial to, yet not usually made explicit, in his later ecclesiological studies, such as those collected in *Church, World, Mission* (1979) and the posthumous selections, *Liturgy and Tradition* (1990). Father Schmemann's close scrutiny of the development of the Eastern Church's collection of rubrics, the *Typikon* and the *ordo,* or shape of liturgy, constitutes his *Introduction to Liturgical Theology.*[20] It remains an important early expression of his core teaching about liturgy as the life of the Church, the *ordo* as the Church's self-identification, and liturgy as the sanctification of time and of Christian living. One can read not only the names but also the profound influence of scholars of the return to the sources such as Congar, Bouyer, Daniélou, Rousseau, Dix, Cullman, Brilioth, Botte, Cabrol, Baumstark, Casel, and particularly Afanasiev on Father Schmemann's theology. Of striking significance is his drawing on one of his own lesser-known teachers. Father Kern made an intense indictment of the loss of eucharistic churchliness amid centuries of accumulated piety, devotional acts, individualism, and ecclesial pragmatism.[21] Within a few years, Father Schmemann would be expanding his teacher's judgment not only of this liturgical decline but also of the ecclesial crisis in his very important articles of 1964–65, "Problems of Orthodoxy in America."[22] Now, more than thirty years after its writing and its defense in accomplishment of the doctorate at St. Sergius, it is striking to hear his motivation and boldness in trying to recover the power of the liturgy, this from the preface to the Russian edition:

I am fully aware that I have examined that sphere of church life that has for many reasons remained tacitly untouchable, protected by a kind of taboo, in any event, in the Orthodox Church. This is the sphere of worship, of the liturgical life, the liturgical experience. . . . Until now our theology has strictly respected this taboo, . . . restrained its courage and critique at the sacred doors of the temple, become mute as soon as the first words of the eternal liturgical mystery were uttered. . . . Before those who inspired me to the theological service of the Church, my teachers and fellow students in this service, I must confess that I transgressed this taboo not for the thrill of a cheap dare but in faithfulness to theology and its essential mission in the Church. . . . In recent times it is being admitted that piety and worship have a more direct relationship to theology as its nourishing source, as the "rule of prayer" determining the "rule of faith." However, conversely, it has not been admitted that theology has the sacred right to guard the purity of worship, its faithfulness to its mission and purpose. If theology is indeed the revelation of the Church's experience, in words pleasing to God and through definitions which relate to this experience, and if further, the experience of the Church is given to us, lives within us, first within the mystery of her liturgical experience, then theology should of necessity stand guard over this experience and to the measure of its ability and means <u>preserve it from defilement, distortions and perversions</u>. . . . The taboo to which I just referred has become impotent. Before our very eyes there is a great exodus from the Church. I emphasize, not only a rebellion against her of demonic powers and evil spirits from below, but specifically dissolution of humanity and the Church. In the thunder and noise of technological revolutions, in a world that appears like an asylum or the scaffolding of some amorphous perpetually unfinished skyscraper, the old familiar symbols have ceased to reach the human intellect, understanding and conscience. More accurately, they have become mere symbols, they have lost the ability to be the bearers of the power to transfigure "reality," to insurmountably, forcefully subject this reality to the kingdom of God, the all-embracing goal of the Gospel. . . . In relation to the world (the pious Christian) can be in a state of frenzied apocalyptic pessimism or then in a naïve, all-forgiving optimism. All this changes nothing in his experience of the Church. . . . It is protected, somehow "guaranteed" by a complex, glorious, all-embracing web of symbols, satisfying his religious feelings, and rendering him blind and deaf to all realities. In this special, idiosyncratic world that lives by its own totally independent life called worship, reality, any reality, simply vanishes, is rejected, and disintegrates. It does not exist. Worship has no relation to it, as Pascha does not relate to the accidental date on which it falls as a result of complex calculations. . . . We exit the church and we find the world and everything at the same point we left it two hours ago. . . . We simply left, and then having returned, some of us with a sense of having fulfilled some "religious obligations," others with regret that we must once more plunge into the cold, cruel, evil world. But the miracle of renewal did not take place. There is no awareness that suddenly everything has begun anew, from the beginning, which is near, which is revealed, which is given, which is radiant with the gifts of the Holy Spirit, the kingdom of God. . . . The miracle took place in the temple, the church, closed, guarded, mystical: the consecration of the gifts, the transformation of the bread and the wine into the Body and the Blood of Christ, eternal, always the same, ineffable miracle, concealed from profane eyes in the confines of the sanctuary, covered by the wings of the seraphim, a mystical reality and according to our understanding, having and needing no relation to the profane world.

Father Schmemann, in a rare moment of personal revelation, recalled how as a boy in the Paris Russian émigré community he experienced the dissonance and divergence of the two worlds, that of ordinary everyday life even for an immigrant, that of school, play, family, and work, and that of the services in church. It was not simply the conditions of the emigration, of being in at least two linguistic and cultural worlds, neither was it the effect of the depression or other social circumstances. This was the personal experience he brought to the study of theology and to the vocation of a priest. Theology only intensified the experience and in the end taught him to look for, value, and love only the truth about theology, liturgy, the Church, and human life.

[T]he true meaning of worship is to be found not in the symbolic, but in the real fulfillment of the Church: the new life, given in Christ, and that this eternal transformation of the Church into the Body of Christ, her ascension, in Christ and with Christ into the eschatological fullness of the kingdom is the very source of all Christian action in this world the possibility to "do as he does." . . . Not a system of astounding symbols but the possibility to intro-duce into the world that consuming and transfiguring fire for which the Lord pined and "wished that it were already kindled."[23]

World as Sacrament, Liturgy as Life

Father Schmemann was a most discerning critic, but he consis-tently affirmed the Church's essentials, and he did this not simply as an academician but with the greatest concern for the lived conse-quences, for the relationship of faith and existence, liturgy and life. The finest expressions of these are his volumes on the principal sacra-ments: *Of Water and the Spirit* and *The Eucharist*.[24] The true heart of his teaching was given in them and was also expressed in what has been the best known, most widely read of his books, *For the Life of the World*. The liturgy is presented, not as one more thing the Church does, not just her enactment of historical, colorful, symbolic rites, but as the very presence of God among his people and their ascent to the Kingdom of Heaven. In Father Schmemann's teaching, the classical principle holds, whether in its simpler version, *lex orandi, lex credendi,* or in Prosper of Aquitaine's more precise rendering, *(ut) legem credendi lex statuat supplicandi* (the rule of prayer is the rule of belief).[25] The whole of the day, the night, the year, all of time is sanctified in the liturgy. All of human activity is to be transformed: work, play, eating, sleeping. Every point in human life is a moment of God's saving and bringing us back: from our burial and resur-rection in Baptism, to Chrismation or confirmation, to Christian marriage, the anointing of the sick, and the burial of a Christian. Through the Church's liturgy and ordained ministry all of human life, especially material things—bread, wine, oil, water, words, touch—are directed back to what they were created to be—good in God's sight and, in the case of humankind, his very image and likeness. The consequence of this life of God and with God in liturgy is made explicit. Time becomes the very "sacrament of the world to come," the eschatological icon of God's saving and reclaiming of his fallen creation.[26] Hence follows the mission of the Church, to be witnesses (martyrs) of these things, proclaiming the gospel to all, baptizing all, that is, bringing all into the Church, up into God's Kingdom. Father Schmemann constantly emphasized the paschal or resurrectional nature of the Church, the liturgy, and Christian living, an intense realization within the Eastern Church's experience, exemplified by numerous holy women and men even into our era.[27]

The liturgy, especially the Eucharist, as the procession, the journey of the people of God into the Kingdom is pursued carefully by Father Schmemann in these volumes. The shape of each liturgical celebration, the liturgical gestures, texts, objects used—all are examined, not for the metaphors or symbolized meanings with which they have been endowed by liturgists of the past, but for their transforming power and their proclamation to the liturgical assembly, to each Christian and to those who might enter the worshiping community. The missionary thrust of the liturgy, indeed the missionary rationale of the Church, runs through these pivotal writings and pervades his teaching, in striking contradiction of those who would criticize the Eastern and other liturgical churches for inwardness and incorrect priorities.[28] Frank Senn echoes Father Schmemann in his examination of the Church's primary and traditional mode of evangelization: the liturgy.[29]

Father Schmemann unfolds an expansive, catholic understanding of the liturgy through contemplation of each sacramental element of the eucharistic celebration in his posthumously published *The Eucharist: Sacrament of the Kingdom*. He presents the Eucharist as the paradigmatic form of the liturgy and indeed of the Church, fully appropriating and pushing further the insights of his teacher, Father Afanasiev. In the Eucharist, the Church is assembled by the Holy Spirit to enter and ascend to the Kingdom. This occurs in the whole action of the assembly: by reading, singing, preaching and hearing the Word, by praying for all, by offering in unity the bread, cup, and themselves in thanksgiving and remembrance, and by being joined to the Lord and each other in the holy communion which is the Body and Blood of Christ, his life in, with, and for the life of the world.

Father Schmemann's analysis of the Eucharist is not just a focus on liturgy as one more aspect of Christian faith and life alongside other equal or perhaps more important components. In almost every writing he specifies the connections between liturgy and life. These connections lay in the three "moments" of salvation history he consistently underscored. In a paper given just the year before his death, he expressed these three "acclamations" of faith very powerfully and practically.

> First, God has created the world. . . . To claim that we are God's creation is to affirm that God's voice is constantly speaking within us and saying to us, "And God saw everything that he had made, and behold, it was very good" (Gen. 1:31). The Fathers state that even the devil is good by nature and evil only through misuse of his free will. Then there is a second element, inseparable from the first: this world is fallen—fallen in its entirety; it has become the Kingdom of the prince of this world. The Puritan world view, so prevalent within the American society in which I live, assumes that tomato juice is always good and that alcohol is always bad; in effect tomato juice is not fallen. Similarly the television advertisements tell us, "Milk is natural"; in other words, it is not fallen. But in reality tomato juice and milk are equally part of the fallen world, along with everything else. All is created good; all is fallen; and finally—this is our third "fundamental acclamation"—all is redeemed. It is redeemed through the incarnation, the cross, the resurrection and ascension of Christ, and through the gift of the Spirit at Pentecost. Such is the intuition that we receive from God with gratitude and joy: our vision of the world as <u>created</u>, <u>fallen</u>, <u>redeemed</u>. Here is our theological agenda, our key to all the problems which today trouble the world.[30]

Seriousness, passion, yet good humor, and above all joy pervade this theological vision. Yet there is great discernment too, for perhaps the most prevalent heresy of our day about humanity is described and dismissed here in the earthy terms of alcohol, milk, and tomato juice. In other places in his writings, Father Schmemann uses standard American images of wealth, power, and pleasure: skyscrapers, world fairs, big cars, steaks, cocktails, and romance.

Fr. Stephen Freeman's article

Revealed here is the arrogance of *our* decisions about what is natural and good over against what we, in moral and political correctness,
define as evil. Father Schmemann could identify this human selec-
tivity over against God as precisely the kind of religiosity (politics
and morality) that is not only tolerated by our essentially secular
society but even mandated by it. It is an anthropomorphic and an
anthropocentric religion, surely what Feuerbach had in mind. Yet
it is not the "traditional," that is, the revealed, handed over faith of
the Church, the Scriptures, and the liturgy. It is our way, not God's.

Father Schmemann's effort, as he often put it, using Johannine language, was to "discern the spirits" of the culture, to learn whether
they were of God. This sharp scrutiny of the ethos of both the
Church and the world was always accompanied by the basic *keryg-
mata* of creation, fall, and redemption. Put another way, he saw, as
did the Fathers, not only the Eucharist, but also the Church and the
world as sacrament.

> [I]n the first chapter of Genesis, we find a clear statement of this
> sacramental character in the world. God made the world, and then
> man; and he gave the world to men to eat and drink. The world
> was God's gift to us, existing not for its own sake but in order to
> be transformed, to become life, and so to be offered back as man's
> gift to God. . . . But sin came, breaking this unity: this was no mere
> issue of broken rules alone, but rather the loss of a vision, the
> abandonment of a sacrament. Fallen men saw the world as one
> thing, secular and profane, and religion as something entirely
> separate, private, remote and "spiritual." The sacramental sense of
> the world was lost. Man forgot the priesthood which was the pur-
> pose and meaning of his life. He came to see himself as a dying
> organism in a cold, alien universe. . . . And so the Eucharist is not
> simply a way of discharging our duty of thanks to God, although
> it is that as well. It is not merely one possible relationship to God.
> It is rather the only possible holding together—in one moment,
> in one act—of the *whole* truth about God and man. It is the sacra-
> ment of the world sinful and suffering, the sky darkened, the tor-
> tured Man dying: but it is also the sacrament of the change, His
> transfiguration, His rising, His Kingdom. In one sense we look
> back, giving thanks for the simple goodness of God's original gift

to us. In another sense we look forward, eschatologically, to the
ultimate repair and transfiguration of that gift, to its last consummation in Christ.[31]

Sacrament is hardly just a religious service but the transformation of
each person, of humankind, and of all creation by Christ, through
the Spirit, in the Church, to the glory of the Father. The rule of
prayer *is* the rule of faith. The continuous death of fallen humankind
is continuously trampled down by the death and rising of Christ in
the liturgy. No corner of life is neglected, no aspect of humanity is
spared. All is touched by Christ. "In the world of the incarnation,
nothing 'neutral' remains, nothing can be taken away from the Son
of Man."[32]

Against the World, for the World

Father Schmemann was a teacher of the Church's communion
with God—the liturgy. But the world never departed from his vision.
In fact, it is precisely in his analysis of twentieth-century America,
in his rigorous criticism of the Church's numerous "reductions" in
it, capitulations not encounters with it, and in his vision of what the
Church might be that he was most intensely a "free man in Christ,
a man full of joy." In this, he was most countercultural, most threatening and subversive, in the best senses, and he remains so.

In his evaluation of contemporary American society and culture,
Father Schmemann used the frequently employed term "secularism"
but with a distinctive understanding.[33] By no means was such a secular culture without religion, and only in rare circles could there be
found real antireligious sentiments. On the contrary, secular, one
could add diverse, America is awash with religiosity, but many religious traditions and their communities, not to mention isolated
"spiritual" individuals, are intensely, aggressively self-centered and
autonomous. Religion must conform to the values, the ethos, and the
pace of life of Americans. It must meet their needs, console, encour-
age, and generally support what its consumers demand or expect.

In the jargon of the 1990s, purposeful, enlightened religion is "politically correct," and this can be in liberal or conservative, liberationist or fundamentalist, or lifestyle categories.

Speaking of his own Orthodox Church, but by implication other churches, Father Schmemann charges that a profound capitulation is occurring: surrender to American secularism and its acceptable forms of religious faith and behavior. He catalogs a variety of reductions: of the parish to a fund-raising, voluntary association, perhaps with strong ethnic or class roots; of the liturgy to "Sunday" Christianity, an hour or so that inspires, even "entertains" the parish clientele and attracts new members as well; of the priest to an administrator-executive and a helping-professional; of membership to minimalistic giving and reception of the Eucharist; of the parish's spiritual identity and health to programs for the increase of members and dollars; of the house of God to a plant of buildings for various church activities; of *koinōnia* to the ethos of "togetherness" or "family."[34] All of these reductions and other similar ones are formidable sociological realities. In 1964–65 when Father Schmemann wrote the classic, some would say infamous, articles comprising "Problems of Orthodoxy in America," as well as today, many of these characteristics would constitute a "healthy," "outgoing," "successful" parish, with the same descriptions applicable to the pastor as well.

Not surprisingly, in these accomodations, seemingly so sensitive to members' needs and lifestyles, there is a complete reduction or termination of the personal character of Christian faith. To be sure, Christianity is not restricted to individual salvation. The gospel is to be preached everywhere. Baptism and the feast of the Kingdom, the Eucharist, are for "the life of the world." Yet even in the community of the Church and her liturgy

> the salvation of the world is announced and *entrusted to each person,* is made a personal vocation and responsibility and ultimately depends on each person. . . . The whole world is given—in a unique way—to each person and thus in each person it is "saved" or "perishes." Thus in every Saint the world is *saved* and it is fully saved in the one totally fulfilled Person: Jesus Christ.[35]

Martyria: The Personal Struggle

Father Schmemann's "solutions" to the problems of the Church—the liturgical, canonical-structural, and the spiritual—run provocatively counter to prevailing churchly wisdom. Indeed his call for a "churching," a transforming, a reintegration into an ecclesial community is subversive of the strategies of the church growth movement and of every other market-driven tactic for expansion of membership and revenue.[36] He points to the restoration of real pastoral leadership by both bishops and priests. Return to the baptismal and eucharistic nature of Christian life is accomplished by the restoration of the eucharistic liturgy and daily prayer as the very *core* of human life. The absolute priority of place and love must be for the "holy things" in which we have communion with God and each other (*communio sanctorum*).[37] In these articles, Father Schmemann makes it clear that the clergy have been not just the victims but the principal perpetrators of the many reductions in the life of the Church. For clergy and for all the baptized, the true encounter with the crisis lies not in any program, strategy, or study project. The churching of which he speaks is a personal encounter with Christ, a personal acceptance of the gospel, and a personal confrontation with oneself, one's neighbors (even in the Church), and the world. Father Schmemann notes that his mention of *martyrs,* a stunning thought in America, is hardly a rhetorical flourish.

For if one takes Christianity seriously, be it only for one minute, one knows with certitude that *martyria,* or what the Gospel describes as the narrow way is an absolutely essential and inescapable part of Christian life. And it is a narrow way precisely because it is always a conflict with the "ways of life" of "this world." From the very beginning to become and to be a Christian meant these two things: first, a *liberation* from the world, i.e., from any "reduction" of man, and as such has always been the significance of the Christian rites of initiation. A man is set free in Christ because Christ is beyond and above all "cultures," all reductions. The liberation means thus a real possibility to see this world in Christ and to choose a Christian "way of life." In the second place, Christianity has always meant an *opposition* to and a fight with this world—a fight, let me stress it again, which is primarily, if not exclusively, a *personal* fight, i.e., an internal one—with the "old man" in myself, with my own "reduction" of myself to "this world." There is no Christian life without *martyria* and without *asceticism,* this latter term meaning nothing else, fundamentally, but a life of concentrated effort and fight.[38]

Church: Mission for the Life of the World

It is perhaps startling to hear such conviction about personal conversion and transformation at the heart of Christian life and the Church from an academic theologian, respected pastor, and ecclesiastical administrator. Yet here again Father Schmemann's teaching was exactly counter to and subversive of hardened, untruthful ideas about the Church in his own Orthodox church and beyond. In his ecclesial teaching, Father Schmemann was revolutionary precisely because he was so radical, so faithful to the Tradition. He relentlessly affirmed the conciliarity and hierarchical nature of the Church in the face of clerical domination, demands for lay control, and antiinstitutional as well as anticlerical tendencies.[39] Over against models of representative democracy and clericalist autocracy, he put forward the icon of ecclesial life, namely, the unity-in-diversity and personal distinctions of the Holy Trinity. The Father, Son, and Holy Spirit reveal the unity of persons living in obedient, submissive, and sacrificial love; of the Son to the Father and to humankind, of the Father to the Son and of the Spirit to the world. The Trinity is one but three, joined to each other in love. So clericalism (inclusivism we would add) and any other reduction of the life of the Church to a politicalsocial model are illegitimate and destructive of the Church's life. Both clergy and laity are capable of such inappropriate and antiecclesial reductions.[40] The clergy can be reduced to elected, hired functionaries or can reduce themselves to religious tyrants. Neither is their true office of pastoral ministry to the flock. Laity can be reduced to fund-raisers, administrators, social activists, or passive dues-paying members of a voluntary organization, or to a merely political constituency that acts on majority vote. In none of these reductions is the people of God affirmed, the chosen race, the royal priesthood, and holy nation called out of darkness into God's marvelous light (1 Pet. 2:9).

Father Schmemann cites the nineteenth-century lay Russian theologian Khomiakov on the ever-present tendency in the West (and the East as well) to turn the Church into some *thing,* an authority, a reality external, other, and thus *alien* to us.[41] From this fracture of the Church's communion, this disembodiment, this "reification," quickly flows the fractionalizing of a body, now political into "we" and "they," clergy laity or other more recent variations based on gender, sexuality, ethnicity, and other social-cultural categories, which Father Schmemann did not specify but could well have imagined. The personal, sacramental nature of the Church is so easily demolished in these reductions.

In our time the Church is being reduced to an agency for justice issues, to an experiment in implementing affirmative action ideals, to an institution desperate to attract and hold members and increase revenue through whatever strategies, as long as they are effective. Actions and words need no longer be "appropriate" to God. This is, sadly, an ecumenical fact, true across the churches.[42] Clearly, his attack on ecclesial reduction encompasses the most recent forms. And in his understanding of the personal encounter, that of *martyria* and asceticism, of personal conversion and transformation and struggle, he holds on to the divine-human, incarnational, indeed sacramental identity of the Church. In a paper from 1961, Father Schmemann eloquently proclaims the Church as this divine-human communion.[43] The Church is the sacrament of the Kingdom, the "fullness" of God here and now, the *pascha* or passage, through baptism and the Eucharist into the Kingdom.[44] At the same time, the Church is "increase and growth in faith and love, knowledge and *koinōnia*."[45] So the Church is also a "human response to the divine gift, its acceptance and appropriation by man and humanity."[46] As such, the Church must always be *simultaneously* "God centered" and "man or world centered."[47] The Church reduces, distorts herself if she becomes only one *or* the other, if theocentricity is sacrificed to anthropocentricity or vice versa, if prayer is rejected in favor of practice, *ortho-doxia* (true worship) subordinated to *ortho-praxis* (the works of loving kindness, lit. "true action"). Likewise a fetishistic obsession with rubrics, rules, lesser points of doctrine, and ritual constitutes a reduction, a substitution of the means for its end, an idolatry of the Sabbath rather than true service of God and neighbor. What Father Schmemann wrote more than thirty years ago, primarily about the Orthodox Church, is still penetrating, provocative, and necessary for the churches, East and West, in America today.

> The Church, the sacrament of Christ, is not a "religious" society of converts, an organization to satisfy the "religious" needs of man. It is *new life* and redeems therefore the whole life, the total being of man. And this whole life of man is precisely the world in which and by which he lives. Through man the Church saves and redeems the world. One can say that "this world" is saved and redeemed every time a man responds to the divine gift, accepts it and lives by it. This does not transform the world into the Kingdom or the society into the Church. The ontological abyss between the *old* and the *new* remains unchanged and cannot be filled in this "aeon." The Kingdom is yet *to come,* and the church is not *in* this world. And yet this Kingdom to come is already present, and the Church is fulfilled *in* this world. They are present not only as "proclamation" but in their very reality, and through the divine *agapé,* which is their fruit, they *perform* all the time the same sacramental transformation of the *old* into the *new,* they make possible real action, real "doing" in this world.[48]

Father Schmemann's own *martyria,* his personal witness, and ascetic struggle were faithfully to hold together the whole and the holy communion of Church, liturgy, world, and mission. He taught and lived *the truth* about the Church. He made it clear that no matter how horrible the reductions and abuses, the truth about the Church as the life of God could (and should) be both spoken and lived out. But he also insisted that this could only be done in "holy things" and in a holy life—in the liturgy, in prayer, in works of love, but all of these personally, concretely, by each Christian. One of Father Schmemann's relatives told me a favorite saying of his: "When in doubt, say, do something religious." This was not just advice for a priest, choir director, or worshiper who gets lost or momentarily forgets in the complicated liturgical services of the Orthodox Church.

True, according to Father Hopko, Schmemann's writing and teaching and entire life might be summed up as a "no" to secularism, a "no" to the human construct of "religion," which Karl Barth also rejected, but a "yes" with all his being to Christ and his Kingdom. Yet, for him, because of the incarnation, the coming of Christ into human flesh and blood, into time and space, into the creation, "nothing 'neutral' remains, nothing can be taken from the Son of Man," nothing can be separated or protected or distinguished from God. In a curious, seemingly paradoxical way, everything is of God, of the Kingdom, perhaps one could say "religious" in the deepest, most authentic sense. When Father Schmemann spoke of the "world as sacrament," this was not mere theological lyricism. He was a man for whom nothing human was not also holy, beautiful, and worthwhile in itself.

Many I have spoken to who were blessed to have known, studied, or worked with him, even just dined or spent time with him to witness his singular character. In response to difficult questions about the identity and presence of God, he was able, on a summer's day, to pluck out a blade of grass and proclaim: "Here, God is here, God is this," without the slightest danger of preaching pantheism. The recently published selections from his journal attest to this; so too do the anecdotes, stories, and experiences of him that await publication in a sorely needed biographical study. Yet even in the books and taped talks he left behind there are lively miniatures, small "sacramental" scenes, icons of the beauty and presence of the holy in everyday life: his wondering about all the lives being lived behind the lighted windows of houses he viewed at night from his train; the "icon" of married loved revealed in the elderly Parisian couple, sitting silently, hand in hand on a park bench in the sunlight of an autumn afternoon; the signs of success and security and happiness so much sought after vanishing in the hospital room, on the sickbed; the profound difficulty of fasting ("Just one more sardine"); hilarious descriptions of wanna-be monastics and mystics poring over the *Philokalia* and debating prayer rules, prostrations, and ascetic practices; kindhearted send-ups of meticulously pious individuals tracing enormous signs of the cross on themselves, for all around to see; witty recollections of an international conference on the Eucharist where no one except the celebrating clergy received communion at the liturgy; a perceptive response to the dispute over where to seat Orthodox participants at an ecumenical meeting, not with the "high Church" Swedish Lutherans and Anglicans but with the Quakers; the elderly woman's sad, tragic remark after the long, joyous service of Easter night, "But what if all this really happened, Father?"; equally sad but also humorous vignettes of the attachment to a country, a culture, a life long since disappeared while unable to live with those around one.

Father Schmemann was able to understand and accept all sorts of people: Russian dissidents who almost violently disagreed with each other about how they disagreed with the Party; the intelligent, perennial "seeker," who saw no contradiction in being, at one and the same time, a Christian, Muslim, and Buddhist. Here was a theologian whose reading embraced e.e. cummings, Gide, Julien Green, and Proust, who loved the classics of his beloved Russian and French literature but also devoured biographies, the writings of critics of religion, the very best in culture. His son, the Pulitzer Prize–winning journalist Serge Schmemann, gave a revealing portrait of Father Schmemann in an interview published on the tenth anniversary of his death in the *Moscow Times*.

At home Father Alexander never told us to "go to church," or that "you must fast," or "do it this way," never. Simply, he did what he had to and we found ourselves drawn to those things which were important to him. I can't say we spent as much time in church as he did, but our joy in the services came entirely from him. In our house the guiding principle of churchly life was the example of my father. My father is fasting quietly, without insisting that anyone does so, and instinctively we begin fasting as well, after all, we can't let him fast alone! It was important for him, and thus it became important for us. . . . With him everything was cozy, he was always extremely joyous. If we arose in the morning in foul spirits and saw that he was happy and energetic—with him each day began this way—then his attitude infected us all. . . . He always fought against the reduction of Christianity simply to forms and rules. It, in fact, liberates man from the narrowness of forms and rules and Father Alexander saw in Christianity the freedom of the person and love, and in his lectures, writings, sermons, always sought to reveal the deeper meaning of all things occurring in the Church. He never oversimplified, seeing in each person the very complex arena of struggle between good and evil. . . . [H]is theology was marked above all by the element of freedom. His Christianity is that of Christ, for precisely He gave us freedom. All church rules, after all, can acquire a certain independent life of their own, totally detached from God. Father Alexander knew this all too well, which is why he never began from rules. For him all things begin with faith in God, which leads to an order of life, and not the other way around.

The list could go on and on, for this was a man of the Church, to be sure, but a person of faith who loved the world and people and everything that is good and beautiful in life and the world:

A Christian is the one who, wherever he looks, finds Christ and rejoices in Him. And this joy *transforms* all his human plans and programs, decisions and actions marking all his mission the sacrament of the world's return to Him who is the life of the world.[49]

CHAPTER TEN

John Meyendorff

Defender of Living Tradition

How is the Orthodox Christian to maintain and witness to his faith in the complicated and changing world of the twentieth century? There can be no answer to this challenge of our age without *living tradition*. Of necessity, any Orthodox theology and any Orthodox witness is traditional, in the sense that it is consistent not only with Scripture but also with the experience of the Fathers and the saints, as well as with the continuous celebration of Christ's death and resurrection in the liturgy of the Church. However, the term "traditional theology" can also denote a dead theology, if it means identifying traditionalism with simple repetition. Such a theology may prove incapable of recognizing the issues of its own age, while it presents yesterday's arguments to confront new heresies. In fact dead traditionalism cannot be truly traditional. It is an essential characteristic of patristic theology that it was able to face the challenges of its own time while remaining consistent with the original apostolic Orthodox faith. Thus simply to repeat what the Fathers said is to be unfaithful to their spirit and to the intention embodied in their theology. . . . True tradition is always a living tradition. It changes while remaining always the same. It changes because it faces different situations, not because its essential content is modified. This content is not an abstract proposition; it is the Living Christ Himself, who said, "I am the Truth." . . . The task of living theology, expressing the one and living Tradition of the Church, consists in defining the problems of our day and giving answers in accordance with the requirements of the one truth of Christ's Gospel.[1]

Thus did Fr. John Meyendorff introduce a collection of his own articles and papers, giving it quite deliberately the same title, *Zhivoe Predanie, Living Tradition,* as an important collection of essays published in Paris by theologians of the Russian emigration in 1937. Some of them were his teachers at St. Sergius Theological Institute there, others were members of the cathedral parish of St. Alexander Nevsky, the "Rue Daru" church, where he and his family belonged. All were colleagues of an earlier generation, comrades united if not in particulars then in the overarching understanding of the gospel as the dynamic life of the Church, her Tradition as ancient yet ever new, changing while remaining the same truth. And this passage, along with other specific themes—the importance of contact between the Orthodox Church and the churches of the West in the search for restoration of unity; the impossibility, in fact, the great error of sheltering the Church from the culture and history that surround her; the scandal of multiple Orthodox jurisdictions in America rather than one unified church; the various problems of the divorce of liturgy from life; the identification of religion with ethnic belonging—would be the constant concerns of Father Meyendorff throughout his life, in his various and many roles within the Church. Father Meyendorff was an internationally recognized scholar, his stature only growing through his career, commencing with his Sorbonne thesis, the first studies in many years of the thought of the mystical theologian, St. Gregory Palamas. Yet he was much more than a gifted academician, more even than a respected ecumenical participant and leader within his own church. He was in his own distinctive manner yet another example of holiness in our time, one who both wrote about the gospel and lived it.

When I first met Father Meyendorff, he was at the peak of his many careers. He was the newly appointed dean of St. Vladimir's Seminary, having succeeded Father Schmemann on the latter's death. He had seen the realization of the dream and goal of an autocephalous or autonomous Orthodox Church in America fourteen years earlier, largely through his efforts and those of Father Schmemann.

Born on February 17, 1926, to an aristocratic, Russian–Baltic German family in the Paris suburb of Neuilly-sur-Seine, he grew up in the Paris St. Alexander Nevsky cathedral parish.[2] His students remember his meticulous knowledge of the *Typicon,* the collection of the details and rubrics of the liturgical services of the Orthodox Church, a knowledge he would playfully use to "fence" with Father Schmemann, even during services in the chapel of St. Vladimir's Seminary. "Who told you to do that?" Father Meyendorff once demanded of a seminarian-deacon during a vigil service there. "Why, Father Schmemann," was the reply. "Ah, but what does he know about the *Typicon!*" said Father Meyendorff jokingly (Schmemann was an internationally known specialist in and professor of liturgical theology at the time).

Father Meyendorff's long liturgical experience began when he served as an altar boy at the cathedral. He completed his secondary school studies in Paris and was a 1949 graduate of St. Sergius Theological Institute in Paris. In 1958 he received the Doctorat-ès-Lettres from the Sorbonne for his work on Saint Gregory Palamas and was ordained a priest the next year. He came to America in 1959 and started what would be his lifelong work as professor at St. Vladimir's Seminary, first in New York City and after 1962 in its location in Crestwood, New York. As so many of his articles and essays attest, he was deeply committed to the mission of theological education, not only of priests and lay church leaders at St. Vladimir's, but of all the faithful. Also a student of Father Afanasiev, he assimilated his teacher's emphasis on the calling of all Christians in their baptismal priesthood to do the work of the gospel, to be the Church. Keenly aware of the increasing level of higher education in the American population, he returned again and again in his own writing and teaching to the need for an educated laity. He refused to recognize any conflict between learning and faith, basing his conviction on the example of the Fathers themselves and of the church down through the centuries. The Fathers were graduates of the academies, the universities of their time, steeped in philosophy and rhetoric, knowledgeable about politics, the arts, the science of the times. Thus they were able to use all aspects of their culture to communicate Christ and his gospel. For them, no corner of society, of human life was alien to Christ's transforming presence. Such should be the case in the modern era, especially when on so many fronts the faith and the tradition of the Church were being not only challenged but, as in the Soviet-dominated sectors of the 1950s through the 1980s outright attacked and persecuted. Particularly in the freedom of the West, and of America especially, it was the obligation of faithful Christians to be fully part of their society and culture.

Yet Father Meyendorff's commitment to education was comple-mented by his profound love for scholarship. Few seminary admin-istrators as busy as he, few ecumenical figures as active as he, could boast such a curriculum vitae rich in publications and research awards. What is more, the vocations of teacher and scholar did not prevent him from working in many other places, from being a representative of and spokesman for Orthodox Christianity across the country and internationally. In many ways Father Meyendorff embodied and continued the tradition of the Russian émigré scholars in Paris begun almost on their arrival there after the revolution. Like so many of them who were his teachers, Father Meyendorff was at home in the West, eager to share the gifts of the Eastern Church with Western Christians, completely faithful to the Church's tradition, but like the men and women of the Russian religious renaissance, also apprecia-tive of the West's heritage and intensely interested in authentic ecu-menical study and dialogue, aimed at the healing of the schism.

Part of what was a Russian church in France and a Russian in back-ground, despite the Baltic German family name, he nevertheless was a citizen first of France and then of the United States. He became part of the life of the place where he lived, found a home there, as did many of his fellow Russians of the emigration. He had no patience for the idea of the Orthodox living only in various ethnic enclaves, in some diaspora existence in the new world, always dependent on their "mother churches," elsewhere. In fact, much of his writing was taken up with the theological indefensibility of such a diaspora arrangement and the ecclesiological aberration of multiple jurisdic-tions, that is, church bodies and bishops in the same place rather than a unified Orthodox Church. With Father Schmemann, he was an architect of the autocephaly of the OCA and throughout his career explained and defended this action on the part of the Russian Metro-polia in America and the Church of Russia of the Moscow patriarchate. (Before the granting of autocephaly in 1970, the OCA was formally the Russian Orthodox Greek Catholic Church in America, also the Russian Metropolia.)

Father Meyendorff was not afraid to speak out against distortions of Tradition by those who would claim themselves to be more authentically, more fervently Orthodox. For example, he lamented the fragmentation of the Russians, both the emergence of the Karlovtsky Synod, today better known as the Russian Orthodox Church Outside Russia (ROCOR), and the split between those who remained in the Moscow patriarchate in western Europe and those, who with Metropolitan Evlogy and St. Sergius faculty and students, asked to be under the care of the ecumenical patriarch when continued communion with Moscow was not possible, this in the tumultuous Stalinist 1930s.

Senior Fellow at Dumbarton Oaks, Fellow of the Centre National de la Recherche Scientifique, the National Endowment for the Humanities, and the Guggenheim Foundation, Corresponding Fellow of the British Academy, president of the American Patristics Association and the Orthodox Theological Society of America, he was internationally recognized as a scholar—of Gregory Palamas and Byzantine theology and ecclesiastical history. Having served in its central committee, as moderator of the Faith and Order Commission, Father Meyendorff was much respected in the WCC and in other ecumenical settings. When the Lutheran church bodies in America were preparing to unify, he was invited to present a paper at a theological convocation leading up to the unification. Almost twenty years later, it remains a stellar example of his theological thinking, completely classical, faithful to Tradition yet creative, vibrant, and practical. It is not only a lucid presentation of the possibilities and the crucial importance of the Orthodox-Lutheran dialogue, both nationally and internally, but a perceptive understanding of what constitutes the life of the Church and her ministry, the Eucharist, is sketched out, very much in the spirit of his teacher, Father Afanasiev, who is explicitly recognized along with his own sources.[3] In an understated way, Father Meyendorff also makes clear what is necessary practically for restoration of churchly unity, *koinōnia* or communion in the "holy things." His is no tedious list of doctrines, certainly not adoption of liturgical forms or cultural styles but, as Father Afanasiev and, much earlier, Father Bulgakov insisted, authentic unity in faith and eucharistic sharing. The clarity and simplicity in their conception of how the division will be healed are perhaps far more radical and controversial today, in an era of ever-hardening positions among the churches.

Father Meyendorff was intimately associated with Syndesmos, the international Orthodox youth movement, as a founding member. He taught at, among other places, Columbia University, Dumbarton Oaks, St. Sergius Institute, and the Union Theological Seminary in New York. He also taught at Fordham University, supervised a number of doctoral students, remained an adviser to the synod of bishops, and was very much involved in ecumenical work with other churches. On the feast of St. Mary Magdalene, July 22, 1992, he died in Montreal, after a brief but difficult struggle with cancer. He enjoyed only a few weeks of retirement from the dean's office at St. Vladimir's, in fact had packed off to his summer house at Labelle, Quebec, where he was leveled by the rapidly moving disease. His was an all too sudden departure, and the void created by his death in so many areas, especially leadership, theological expression, and giving voice to the best of the Orthodox heritage, remains deep.

Father Meyendorff's written work alone is a challenge. Surveying it, one moves from Christology to his specialized research on of St. Gregory Palamas (1296–1359), his production of the critical edition of Palamas' *Triads*, his commentary and synthesis of Palamas' importance.[4] There is straightforward historiography, both of Byzantium in particular and of Russian Orthodoxy, the Orthodox experience in America, ecumenical relationships and work, conflicts within the international and the American Orthodox landscapes, within the WCC and the National Council of Churches (NCC) and international political situations, especially those in the years leading up to and including glasnost.[5] He also published the most complete look at marriage in Orthodox theology other than Paul Evdokimov's study.[6] In the editorials he wrote month after month for the national church newspaper, *The Orthodox Church,* Father Meyendorff's voice is sometimes witty, often critical and acerbic, always perceptive. He was not afraid to take on the Orthodox extremists. He was especially critical of the divisive and destructive activities of the Russan Orthodox Church Outside Russia, the synodal church descended from the Karlovtsy synod of bishops who held themselves to be the true Russian church, over against the allegedly Bolshevik-compromised Moscow patriarchate. He also took on the Mount Athos monastics and various adherents to the old calendar for their theological definitions of ecumenical work as "heresy" and for their claims of being the only authentic bearers of Tradition. He did not back off from openly criticizing the Russian bishops who condemned Solzhenitsyn as a traitor. He criticized, up until his death, the ignorance and hostility to learning on the part of so many of the clergy and laity. He was not above admitting to the rifts among theologians, often personality clashes, sometimes powerful disagreements in substance, both in the Paris context where he was born and educated as well as in America. He was a consistent enemy of diaspora as a description of Orthodoxy in America, arguing that "diaspora" is never an appropriate understanding of the one, holy, catholic, and apostolic Church. In view of the sheer volume of Father Meyendorff's work, I leave his more specialized work in Byzantine studies—Christology, spirituality, ecclesiology, and ecclesial history—to other analysts. Some commentary and response to his legacy in these areas has begun, both in a Festschrift and a special issue of the theological journal published by his alma mater, St. Sergius Institute.[7] Two collections of his editorials and articles provide several targets of not only his writing and lecturing but also his active intervention. These are church unity and order, the ecumenical quest for unity among divided Christians, and, finally, the Christian witness, the Church's mission to the world. Last, it is important to consider Father Meyendorff's priestly ministry and his understanding of the Christian life, one of service and holiness. His own example of living the gospel is a precious legacy in addition to all his scholarly and administrative contributions.

Church Unity and Order

The Church of God, because it is "catholic" and "apostolic," is concerned with the whole of humanity, with the whole of the

Truth and with everything positive and good happening in the
world; if we refuse to learn, to listen, to be concerned with the life
and beliefs of other Christians, we will not only miss much ourselves, but we will also be unfaithful to Christ's commandment of
love and to our responsibility to witness to Orthodoxy everywhere. Inasmuch as the various ecumenical meetings, councils and
assemblies provide us with these opportunities, it is our Christian
and Orthodox duty to be there.[8] (March 1967)

However, facing the Roman Catholic and Protestant "openness,"
the Orthodox Church does not—or should not—present the picture of a "closed" world. The Church is open to everything good
because she is truly "catholic": she is closed only to error and sin.
Every human being, created in the image of God, is her actual or
potential child, and should be the object of her love, her attention
and her care. The "heretical" West has, in the course of history,
produced many authentic saints; it has created a tradition of civil
liberties which we all enjoy and which were often lacking in the
Orthodox East; it is involved today in many generous and authentically Christian concerns: all these positive elements are not
"heretical" but essentially Orthodox, and no one today will pay
attention to the message of the Orthodox Church unless we lovingly and openly meet and accept as such the blessings and the
wisdom which God has so obviously bestowed even upon those
who are not members of the one visible Orthodox Church.[9]
(April 1967)

These are direct, honest, and bold words from almost forty years
ago, tragically yet rarely heard publicly from any Orthodox theologian, bishop, or priest today. Fear or caution has made us mute. Yet
Father Meyendorff was not alone a generation or more ago. One
could hear, regularly and just as boldly, the same spirit in his colleague Father Schmemann; from their teachers, Fathers Afanasiev
and Kern; from their contemporary colleagues in theology Evdokimov, Clément, and Nissiotis, among others. Father Meyendorff
consistently was able to bring together the voices that spoke truth-
fully of the gospel, the Church, and Christian life, no matter their
locations. He mentions Fathers Pavel Florensky and Teilhard de

Chardin as theologians alone in their efforts to point to the cosmic dimensions of faith, to see the convergences in science and theology as both seek the truth.[10] Rather than ignore or dismiss the best theologians of the West in our time, like those before him, he would brilliantly set them side by side with the Fathers, applaud their fidelity to the Church's teaching Tradition, whether Karl Barth, Leslie Newbegin, John Macquarrie, or Karl Rahner. Here he weaves together the ecclesiological personalism of Lossky and Rahner.

[W]hat is the *koinōnia* and the "unity" of the Church? Obviously and primarily a unity of man *with God,* and only secondarily a unity of men with each other. If man is a "theocentric" being, any unity outside the "Center" will be defective and perhaps demonic. "A human being," writes Karl Rahner, "is a reality absolutely open upwards; a reality which reaches its highest (though indeed 'unexacted') perfection, the realization of the highest possibility of man's being, when in it the Logos himself becomes existent in the world" (*Theological Investigations,* I, Baltimore: 1965, p. 183). The true *koinōnia* occurs when such an "opening" is really possible. In an essay on ecclesiology published posthumously, Vladimir Lossky also insists on this same anthropological dimension. No Christian ecclesiology, he maintains, is possible on the basis of a secularized anthropology, which necessarily reduces the Church to the level of a human organization. Understood in this sense, *koinōnia* is also necessarily a personal event.[11]

Father Meyendorff inherited from the Russian religious renaissance a number of qualities and resources. Chief among the characteristics were openness, both to the ancient Tradition of the Church, found in the Scriptures, the liturgy, and the Fathers, and openness to the world around, not only the arts, literature, music, and politics, but the rest of the faith communities as well. It is no exaggeration to say that without ostentatiously labeling himself as such, Father Meyendorff was always aware of the ecumenical, that is, the catholic and universal character of the gospel and the Church. "Ecumenical" for him did not primarily mean just the activities of the WCC or the NCC, only large gatherings, common statements, international dialogue groups. For him, it also meant the tragedy of

those baptized in the name of the same Trinity, formed by the same
Word of God, who were nevertheless divided from each other at the
eucharistic table, unable to share the one Bread and Cup of the Lord's
Body and Blood. For him, this division was not so much a theoretical, that is, theological, disaster but a spiritual suffering, a scandal to the rest of the world, a real stumbling block for young people
struggling to believe. He inherited from his own teachers the restored
sense of the Church as fundamentally a eucharistic communion.
Within this vision, he understood the Church not merely as a collection of the canons of various councils, that is, rules to be kept, and
certainly not principally as a hierarchy of power, from the patriarchs,
metropolitans, and bishops on down. He insisted that the clergy and
laity were inseparably bound to one another in the love and communion of Christ, that bishops and priests were the servants of the
people of God, themselves members of that community, and that
their election and ministry was always within and for this assembly.
They were never above or apart from the flock, their authority only
that of Christ, acknowledged, one might even say legitimated, by the
faith and obedience of the people of God.

> [T]he Church is a *single body:* no member of the body can live in
> isolation from, even less, in opposition to the other members.
> Inside the body, however, there is a diversity of functions and
> responsibilities. . . . Since the faith is indeed the sources and the
> goal of Church life, there is no true Orthodoxy without every lati-
> tude being given to the bishops and priests to exercise their min-
> istry *in all aspects of life* of the dioceses and parishes. Of course,
> no one in the Church is infallible—and certainly not the clergy.
> We Orthodox believe that the entire people of God, clergy and
> laity, are responsible for keeping the faith, as well as for the entire
> life of the Church. Every Church function is exercised in the
> community and for the community. . . . Only that authority
> will be authentic and justified which is rooted in service.[12] (No-
> vember 1971)

The Church is not a human organization, ruled by any of the
systems which man may devise—democracy, autocracy, clergy-
rule or laity-rule—but a temple of God, where God and man

meet, where man is being led to eternal life, where God, in his mercy, gives to men and women the privilege of being his sons and daughters.[13] (April 1972)

Father Meyendorff did not hide behind vague descriptions. Rather his approach was that of the historian, always specific in Orthodox parishes and dioceses, always particular even if painful. Regarding what were at that time truly neuralgic issues threatening the unity of the Church, he named several: anticlerical lay fear of priests and bishops controlling parish decisions, finances, even property; the belief that the priest's spiritual leadership exhausted his participation in the life of the parish, that the clergy should be concerned with "spiritual" and liturgical matters only, the "material" realities of the parish, the diocese or church body, being beyond their competence and outside their jurisdiction.[14]

Consistently, he enunciated the ecclesiology of the Eastern Church, one that could be called both eucharistic, as Father Afanasiev termed it, or "sobornal," conciliar, as Florovsky and others preferred to describe it. Crucial here is that no one person or group, including the clergy, is infallible and most important that life is in common, "as a single body," no opposition of clergy to laity or rule of one over the other.[15] True, bishops have the specific responsibility to teach the gospel and preserve the purity of the faith and to lead the assembly in liturgy, with priests as their local representatives and spiritual heads of communities. Yet "the entire people of God, clergy and laity, are responsible for keeping the faith, as well as for the life of the Church. Every Church function is exercised in the community and for the community. . . . Only that authority will be authentic and justified which is rooted in service."[16] This was his approach with respect to the most specific matter of formulating and then accepting a new statute for the regulation of the life of the OCA. But he would insist on exactly the same ecclesial understanding in the matter of electing a bishop for one of the dioceses of the OCA, the procedure here being that ancient one restored by the Great Council of Moscow in 1917–18, providing for the clergy and lay representatives of the diocese to nominate a candidate who would then be canonically elected and consecrated by the other bishops of the Church.[17]

Long before radical politicized perspectives raised other issues, Father Meyendorff would also insist that the people of God, the laity, included both men and women as members of the baptized priesthood of all. There could be no exclusion of women from participation in the life of the church: in parish councils, dioceses, councils, and assemblies as well as the assembly of the entire church body. While Father Meyendorff did not envision the ordination of women as bishops and priests, he emphatically supported the growth of women's participation in numerous other offices and dimensions of church life. To see only the ordained as leaders was to be trapped in a clericalist position incompatible with the authentic ecclesiology of Orthodoxy, in which there are many different charisms or gifts for service.[18]

When one recalls that Father Meyendorff was first and foremost a historical theologian (not just a specialist in Byzantine ecclesiastical history) his strong positions about the Church not being reduced to structures, rituals, and rules, a radical standpoint he shares with Father Afanasiev, become all the more radical. To the taken for granted idea that the Church exists only in division or brokenness, he retorts with a surprising turn of thinking. "Communion with God cannot, as such, be 'divided,'" he writes, but "it can be incomplete and deficient on the personal human level because of man's lack of receptivity to the divine gift."[19] God's openness is his response to our openness. To deny this fullness of revelation, namely, God's continuing to offer to us the gift of communion in its fullness, despite our sin, is, in the astute words of St. Symeon the New Theologian, to "close heaven which Christ opened for us and block the way which he himself has traced out for our return."[20] The implications of our only limited ability to be open, to receive the gift of communion, are startling.

No individual member of the Church can take his membership in the *koinōnia* for granted. Actually, he is constantly in and out, either excluded through his sins, or reintegrated through repentance. But the ministries, the structures—the entire Church "order"—are a given reality, inasmuch as they are functional to the Eucharist. . . . However as soon as "order" becomes an end in itself, it blasphemously creates a new obstacle to the *koinōnia*. Such a blasphemy can be institutionalized, permanently or only temporarily, when the structures (episcopacies, primacies, etc.) are used for any other purpose than that which is theirs, that is, to administer, to secure and to promote the *koinōnia* of man with God and in God with his fellow man. Some of us will see such a misuse of the church "structures" whenever they are conceived as vicarious powers, exercised individually over the eucharistic *koinōnia*. All of us, I hope, will condemn the divisive use of "structures" in the defense of nationalistic, political, racial or economic interest. All of us have sins on our conscience in this respect. No one, I think (and certainly not the Orthodox!), could affirm that his belonging to the Una Sancta is based upon the actual performance of the ecclesial "structures" of the Church to which he belongs.[21]

How radical these words sound today, in an atmosphere (precisely among the Orthodox!) in which mere institutional attachment, that is, simply being within canonical church bodies and observing various rules and rites, is taken to constitute in itself true all that is necessary for authentic Christian living. An absurd, simplistic, and in Father Meyendorff's words "blasphemous" equating of "structures" and *koinōnia* routinely occurs, not only with respect to non-Orthodox Western churches and Christians but even within the communion of Orthodox churches itself. Non-Orthodox churches are dismissed as "heretical," their sacraments and ministries and even prayers "without grace," that is without Christ and the Holy Spirit, and such a position is in turn claimed to be the only authentic one for Orthodox to maintain. Further, in the ongoing ecclesiastical situation that Meyendorff and Father Schmemann termed scandalous, that of the various jurisdictions in the United States, eucharistic and doctrinal unity are celebrated: clergy serve together, all commune with each other, yet there is no practical unity, no common action of the bishops, of the seminaries, of even local parishes. At best, there is ignorance and indifference, at worst, suspicion, vilification, rejection of fellow Orthodox. Here and there one will hear strong words, as in summer 1999 from the heads of two of the Orthodox churches,

Metropolitan Philip of the Antiochian archdiocese in America and
Metropolitan Theodosius of the OCA, admitting the scandal, the sin
lurking beneath ecclesiastical proprieties, arguing that unity is the
only acceptable state. Yet one could also hear in public a diocesan
bishop of one of the jurisdictions say that he wished no contact whatsoever with the other two majors ones, judging them to be hardly
Orthodox if at all because of their accommodations to contemporary American life and liturgical looseness, among other things.

The life of the Church, while not exhausted by or reducible to
"structures," is nevertheless eminently practical. It must be lived out.
Here again Father Meyendorff could admit and openly, publicly
where the Orthodox Church had missed the mark.

The great gap between theory and practice in the historical Orthodox Church of today would be grounds for despair among the
Orthodox themselves, and for nothing but compassionate irony
in those who look at us from outside, if theory were only "theory"
and not a gift of God, if the divine Eucharist were not transforming over and over again our poor human fellowship into the true
and catholic Church of God, if, from time to time, God were not
performing miracles like permitting the survival of the Orthodox
faith in oppressively secular societies or providing for the Orthodox dispersion throughout the West, making possible a universal
Orthodox witness again. To close the gap and thus to become
worthy of the mighty acts of God so obviously performed for our
benefit and salvation, remains for us a sacred duty. The gap cannot be closed through bluffing, lying and boasting about the past
glories of this or that particular tradition, of this or that ecclesial
institution. There is one positive characteristic of the critical age
in which we live: its ability to discern the inauthentic, its search
for existential truth, its search for holiness.[22]

Perhaps in the matter of the Church's life and unity, one could find
none more expansive vision and dynamic than his. For example, he
consistently opposed the remnants of "phyletism," that is, the identification of Orthodoxy with particular ethnic identities and groups,

Slavic, Greek, Arab, or otherwise. The gospel was preached to all, is for all peoples. The striking outreach of the early Russian missionaries to North America underscored this for him. The Alaskan Natives to whom these missionaries came were not transformed into little Russians. The example of Sts. Innocent Veniaminov and Jacob Netsvetov was of indigenizing and acculturating the Christian faith as deeply and quickly as possible, creating, as did Sts. Cyril and Methodius a millennium earlier, alphabets to allow translation of the Scriptures and all the service books into the languages of the people. Here also the practical example of St. Tikhon, the bishop in America early in the twentieth century and later patriarch of Moscow at the time of the Russian Revolution, was also significant for Father Meyendorff. St. Tikhon encouraged the use of English in liturgical services and approved of the translation by Isabel Hapgood of a service book. He also refused to see Christianity in predominantly ethnic terms. It was his urging that brought a Lebanese Arab, Raphael Hawaweeney, to become an auxiliary bishop for Arab Christians in Brooklyn. This same Bishop Raphael encouraged the use of English as well, and his exemplary life has led to his canonization as yet another American saint of the Orthodox Church in May 2000.

For Father Meyendorff as for these pastors before him, there was no appropriate use of the term "diaspora" for Christians except eschatologically. He saw the claim of the see of Constantinople to control Orthodox Christians in "barbarian lands" (the Council of Chalcedon, canon 28) and the claims of mother churches in lands from which Orthodox Christians have migrated to the New World as spurious. The Church is to be continually planted anew, and the Church can never really be identified as "Russian," "Greek," "Syrian," "Serbian," "Romanian," or, for that matter, "American."[23]

Now for Christians, there is no more "Zion" on earth; they long for a "New Jerusalem" in the Kingdom of God. In a sense all Christians are in "diaspora," or in "dispersion," but not because they were expelled from their country, but because "they have no continuing city" here, but "seek one to come" (Heb. 13:14). The Church is always called to manifest and anticipate this Kingdom, the true homeland of Christians [which] ... is wherever the

Liturgy is celebrated, but it is not limited geographically; it is not tied up to any country or city on earth.[24]

Here we encounter the single most frustrating of all the conditions of the Orthodox Church in America, namely, the lack of authentic unity, the maintenance of several bishops in one area, the multiplication of ecclesiastical organizations of the various jurisdictions, the claim even that after more than two hundred years people in North and South America do not yet sufficiently possess the *phronema*, the requisite piety, knowledge, and churchliness to be autonomous, local churches, requiring not only rule by patriarchs far away but even local supervision by bishops and clergy from elsewhere. Even today these sentiments and related ones are still expressed: "a 'Russian' bishop, that is, one from the OCA, could never be accepted by Greeks"; that the various jurisdictions serve very different constituencies of faithful with very different needs. Thus, if this were true, Serbian Americans would be different kinds of Orthodox Christians than, say, Lebanese Syrian Americans, or Egyptian Americans, or Ukrainian Americans, not to mention all those from western European or mixed backgrounds.

Father Meyendorff spoke out even more boldly: for a truly ecumenical patriarchate of Constantinople as a source of unity among Orthodox Christians, not a quasi-papal centralization of authority but a universal bishop with "primacy of honor," who would preside in love as a sign of unity in the churches. Perhaps, he wondered out loud, this would best be effected if in fact the patriarchate of Constantinople relocated from its besieged and harassed location in present-day Istanbul to a freer place. The ancient see of Antioch is no longer located there but in Damascus.[25]

Father Meyendorff did not hesitate to echo and even amplify the bold stands taken by others: Archbishop Paul of Finland's call for autocephalous status for his church from the patriarchate of Constantinople and Fr. Leonidas Contos' call for similar autonomy for other local churches and the end to the situation of "diaspora," the call of Metropolitan Philip of the Antiochian archdiocese in America for a unified church here.[26] With Father Schmemann, he encouraged and then warmly greeted the monastic communities of New Skete into the OCA from the Ukrainian Catholic Church, telling them that they "should properly be called western Eastern Christians."

The Ecumenical Quest for Unity

The future of true ecumenism lies in asking together true questions instead of avoiding them, in seeking the unity God wants instead of settling for substitutes, in invoking the Spirit of God, which is not the spirit of the world. Councils, assemblies, conferences and consultations provide the opportunities for doing so and should not therefore be altogether discarded. However, they will not create unity because unity "in Christ" is not manmade; it is given in the Church and can only be discovered and accepted.[27] (November 1969)

Recently Peter Bouteneff, who worked on the Faith and Order Commission of the WCC in Geneva and presently teaches at St. Vladimir's Seminary, reported that the present climate among the Orthodox with respect to other, non-Orthodox Christians has so degenerated that he himself has been criticized not only for referring to Catholics and Protestants as "Christians" but also for wishing someone a "happy Easter," using thereby a less than Orthodox, questionable, perhaps even "heretical" term for the feast of the Lord's resurrection. Across the landscape of the Orthodox churches not only abroad, in the eastern European lands formerly dominated by Communist regimes, now torn by ethnic, political, and other conflicts, but in America as well a vocal minority has defined such limited boundaries for Orthodoxy that it loses all semblance of catholicity and universality, all the character of a Church that embraces all, and has begun to take on the rigid, exclusive features of the sect type of religious organization.

To be sure, such a hyperorthodox position, such an "integrist" or "traditionalist" perspective, is not new in the Orthodox churches. Such an attitude of supreme self-confidence bordering on self-righteous judgment and condemnation of other Christian communities has appeared in the Eastern Church at many times and places

over the centuries since the great schism of 1054. The list of items that
become embattled issues is long and includes not only liturgical calendars and practice and theological doctrine but also numerous other
aspects of life, down to the very words one uses to refer to feast days,
the liturgical seasons of the year, even to minute elements of everyday life: food, clothing, manners.

There are many places in Father Meyendorff's writings where he
encounters the imperialistic claims of such Orthodox most directly,
even bluntly. Being from the Russian emigration in Paris and later
transplanted to the greater New York area, both locations of intense
conflict among Russian Orthodox jurisdictions, he did not employ
much diplomacy in his critique of the attitudes and tactics of the
Russian Orthodox Church Outside Russia, perhaps historically one
of the most consistent proponents of the "traditionalist" stance described here. When, for example, an ecumenical organization such
as the WCC or NCC made mistakes either theological or political,
he was equally bold in identifying these and opposing them. During
the 1970s, some individuals and groups in the WCC began to call
for a shifting of its concentration away from the difficult work of
exploring doctrinal, liturgical, and ecclesiological disagreements
among Christians (with the aim of recovering unity given by Christ
to the Church) toward what they saw as more urgent social justice
concerns, areas where action, often politically radical or in support
of the same, was called for. Father Meyendorff, while supporting
the WCC's historical aims, was not afraid to criticize this shift
and the conviction behind it that unity in the faith was less important than common action.[28] In the early 1980s he applauded the Lima
document, *Baptism, Eucharist, Ministry,* which was many years in
preparation and led to the WCC and beyond by Faith and Order
theologians, Lutheran Bishop William Lazareth, and Greek Orthodox theologian Nikos Nissiotis. The contribution of the Orthodox
churches' tenacious preservation of a sacramental understanding of
the Church was much in evidence in this important expression of
ecumenical convergence, really the last profound theological effort
the WCC has made in the past two decades.[29] But when erroneous
or distorted charges were leveled at such groups by political conservatives and even by the *Reader's Digest,* Father Meyendorff refused
to be silent and called for truth.[30] Moreover, to those who would

claim that any ecumenical contact or activity was against the canons of the Orthodox Church and a betrayal of Tradition, he was quick to point out that the very mission of the Church required participation.

> As Orthodox we have no right to ignore the world around us; this world requires our presence and our voice whenever it can be heard, precisely because our message is unique and because the Church is the guardian of universal truth.[31] . . . The Orthodox have always believed—and have said so at ecumenical gatherings—that the Orthodox Church is the One Church of Christ to which Christ promised that "the gates of hell would not prevail against it." (Matt. 16:18). . . . Thus, we believe that the "oneness" of the Church is still with us—in Orthodoxy. However, the Orthodox Church has also recognized the sincerity, the devotion, the Christian achievements of non-Orthodox Christians; those who invoke the name of Jesus Christ cannot be considered as foreign to Him and thus foreigners to His Church, especially when they are sincerely ready to listen, to search, to seek unity in Christ. Their quest, their challenge to us, their witness to the non-Christian world cannot leave us indifferent.[32] (January 1973)

Such is a classical vision of ecumenical work. While intercommunion was not possible given the broken communion among the churches, nevertheless Father Meyendorff explicitly supported prayer among Christians seeking unity in the faith. To claim that the canons that prohibit "prayer with heretics" apply always and everywhere the Orthodox are with the non-Orthodox is to misunderstand these very canons, which "had in view conscious apostates from the Church and not sincere Christians who never personally left it."[33] Such an ecumenical view, very much open to the churches and the world, is rooted in Father Meyendorff's ecclesiological vision. As a consequence, one sees this very sound sense of Church and mission reaching out in many different directions. He addressed developments in the American Episcopal Church, historically close to Orthodoxy, directly, honestly, and sensitively, particularly the swift move to ordaining women.[34] He applauded the genuine advances and breakthroughs of Vatican II: the recovery of the "collegiality" of the episcopacy, the laying down of the anathemas of 1054 by Patriarch

Athenagoras I and Pope Paul VI, the emergence of a new atmosphere in the life of the Roman Catholic Church, one of freedom and participation unknown before the Council. Yet he equally identified specific questions on which little change had occurred: the centralization of authority in the papacy, the claims to papal infallibility, adherence to the proselytizing approach to unity in the case of the Eastern Catholic ("Uniate") churches, the inability to recognize the blockade formed by the dogmatization of Mary's Immaculate Conception and Assumption, the lack of attention to the even deeper problem of the *Filioque* in the creed. In the symbolic gestures—Ecumenical Patriarch Athenagoras I in giving Pope Paul VI a bishop's stole (*omophorion*), the pope's visit to the patriarch, the embrace of the two and their praying together in the Holy Land, the return to the terminology of "sister churches" well before the much attacked Balamand Statement of 1993—Father Meyendorff found, despite the omissions and setbacks, a great deal over which to rejoice and give thanks to God in such matters. In 1978, on the election of Pope John Paul II, he reiterated what was his consistent ecclesiological and ecumenical position.

> As Orthodox Christians, we may regret that the Gospel of Christ and His presence is being carried to contemporary mankind in forms associated with institutions and doctrines which we see as incompatible with the apostolic faith. Papal infallibility remains quite unacceptable to us. But we cannot deny the fact that millions of human souls accept the Christian faith, read the Scriptures, study the Fathers, preach the Gospel and attempt to live a Christian life inside Roman Catholicism. This is why the Orthodox Church, while rejecting all errors, never condoned the view that the mistakes and errors, officially accepted by the Great Church of the West, totally deprived its members of the grace of the Holy Spirit. The Orthodox Church has always prayed and hoped not only for the individual salvation of all, but also for the restoration of unity among Christians of East and West in the fullness of Truth and Love.[35]

Not long after Meyendorff called on the OCA, which was in a free society, not in a culture that harassed or officially persecuted Christians, to take a leadership role in responding and reaching out to the initiatives for Christian unity coming from Rome, or anywhere else.[36] He vigorously protested the exclusion of representatives from Western Orthodoxy in the international Roman Catholic–Orthodox dialogues, precisely theologians and clergy and laity who work and live in predominantly non-Orthodox settings, who have had substantial experience in reaching out to the churches and cultures of the West.[37] Now almost a decade after Father Meyendorff's passing, it is hard to see his own church body, the OCA, taking any kind of leadership role, in world Orthodoxy, in ecumenical relations, even in the social conflicts of American society except abortion. Paging through the collections of Father Meyendorff's regular editorial essays, one can hear him on abortion, but also on all the other facets of life: on poverty and racism in America, on disarmament, on the attempts of political candidates to "use" religion both positively and negatively to their advantage, on the frequency of violence in American society, and, as early as 1978, on the dangerous side of the rediscovery of ethnicity.[38] It would be futile to try to label Father Meyendorff politically. What is more significant in his most discerning and perceptive commentary on the life of the Church and the individual Christian in our complex, technological, often antireligious culture is his eschatological insight.

> However, the truly Christian—and perhaps, the peculiarly Orthodox—responsibility today is to show that the solutions to these problems are found in the Kingdom of God, a Kingdom which exists "within" and "among" us since God became man. For the Kingdom of God is not only a reality "beyond," but it is also a living reality in this world. The function of the Church consists not simply in making this world "a little better," but to make the Kingdom of God present among men. The Church does not carry with it a social utopia, but the ferment of a new humanity, a new eternal life for the world. Only in the Kingdom of God and in the person of Jesus Christ himself does one find the norm, the pattern of social action. Only there is the absolute with which one can evaluate any present situation.[39] (February 1968)

Conviction about the absolute of the Kingdom, an eschatological ultimate, left Father Meyendorff free to urge what today might seem to be radical things. He proposed that the Orthodox welcome dialogue with the many evangelicals in America serious about the ancient Church, the Fathers, the sacraments, and the liturgy.[40] Later this would result in the reception of quite a few evangelicals into the Antiochian archdiocese as well as the OCA. Always a proponent of deeper education for the clergy and laity, he constantly pressed for discernment between what is the Holy Tradition of the Church and what was only changeable culture- and time-bound customs. He dared to call for acceptance of "what is great and holy in the Western American way of life in order to welcome it into an integrated Orthodox ethos," while discerning "what is heretical, demonic and dehumanizing."[41] (May 1978)

Here is perhaps one of the most overlooked of his insights. While an outspoken opponent of the idea of Orthodox existing only in diaspora, here in the West, the only authentic Orthodoxy remaining in "mother churches" elsewhere, Father Meyendorff did recognize the "pilgrim" nature of the Church but in an eschatological sense. As a historian and theologian, as a priest for whom pastoral work was of the greatest importance, and even as a Russian who grew up in France only to migrate to America, Father Meyendorff developed a keen sense of "place," I would say of "home."

> [T]here is one striking fact about the Orthodox Church in the mid-twentieth century: she is no more physically absent in the Western world. She is present here both physically and spiritually and we—you and I—are responsible for the efficiency of that presence. She can no more be really called "Eastern" when millions and millions of her faithful are, for several generations, citizens of Western countries, when they speak the language of these countries, when they intend to remain here and to build up the Church and when hundreds of converts join the Church regularly, without any real proselytizing on our part. This Orthodox "diaspora" is obviously one of the most important spiritual events of the twentieth century and it cannot be considered as just an historical accident: a definite will of God entrusts us with the responsibility for a worthwhile message about the True Christian faith; it challenges our claim to be members of the One True Church. . . . Since we claim to possess the Christian Faith in its truly "catholic" (i.e.

all embracing and universal) form, we must accept with love and humility the problems of Western Christianity as our own and search for their Orthodox solution. To think that we will convert America to Byzantine culture or preserve Orthodoxy by locking it up in a nationalistic ghetto, sentimentally attached to the past— be it "Holy Russia" or "Hellenism"—is possible only through self-righteous naiveté. . . . This requires a tremendous effort. . . . It means that nothing but heresy and error should be foreign to us, either in Western Christianity or in the Western world as a whole which has become our world because God has placed us here.[42] (April 1968)

Over and over, Meyendorff warned against the extreme, so attractive in American culture, of either a completely accommodated, secularized version of Christianity, the plague by the way of all churches here, or an equally wrong fanatical "hyper-Orthodoxy," which confuses the Tradition with numerous man-made customs and ethnic and cultural styles, none of which has any theological basis and which always differ from one place and time to another. Father Schmemann was likewise consistent in speaking against such extreme understandings and their practice. Father Meyendorff once pointed with pride to a portrait of one of his ancestors hanging in the dining room of his residence at Saint Vladimir's Seminary. (It was a group of Lutheran clergy visiting him during a meeting of the American Orthodox–Lutheran dialogue hosted at the seminary.) The portrait was of his great-grandfather, also with the Baltic German name "Meyendorff." Father Meyendorff told us that though a high-ranking officer in the Imperial Army, his great-grandfather was the president of the Lutheran Consistory of all of Russia and remained a staunch Lutheran. Given the setting and the group of Lutheran clergy present, this was no mere conversation starter or polite throwaway gesture but a sign not only of his civility but also of his profound sense of the unity of all in Christ. Father Meyendorff's son, the theologian Paul Meyendorff, confirmed this, adding that through marriage to a Greek Orthodox woman, under Russian law in the nineteenth century, all nine of their children were baptized in the Orthodox Church, and this is how the Meyendorffs became Orthodox. The great-grandfather, however, erected a statue of Luther

in the courtyard of his estate in Estonia, a symbol of his own endur-
ing confessional loyalty. I believe that in his scholarly writing Father
Meyendorff retained a kind of sympathy for the Lutheran part of his
roots. In a still relevant article from 1964, he underscores the desire
of Luther and Melanchthon to return to the sources, the Scriptures,
the Fathers, in short, the Catholic tradition of the Church, the Augsburg Confession itself claiming to be nothing else than such a recovery of the ancient apostolic faith of the Church.[43] But the effort of
the reformers was not understood by the Orthodox East, to which
they in fact refer numerous times in the confessional writing and
attempted several times to engage in correspondence.

Nevertheless, Father Meyendorff's assessment again is a manifestation of his essential openness to all that is good and truthful and
beautiful wherever the location. Here in the Western reformation
churches he could recognize what was of the catholic impulse, of the
authentic Tradition of the Church, while at the same time noting the
specific struggle the reformers engaged in, namely, the Augustinian
and later Scholastics versions of theology and ecclesiology. Never
does he dismiss wholesale the historic or the contemporary Protestant efforts as mere "heresy," yet he deftly indicates where their
vision of the Church and that of Orthodoxy part ways. The understanding of *Ecclesia reformata et semper reformanda* in the Orthodox view can apply quite authentically to the "traditions" of the
churches, especially to those instances in which local and historical
usages have come to obscure the apostolic faith and to impede the
gospel in the life of the Church. The Tradition of the Church, however, is beyond reforming, having been handed down by the apostles. Two decades later, in the presentation he made to the conference
preparing for the merger of three Lutheran bodies in America, he
reaffirmed this open and constructive approach, applauding much
that was good not only in the convergence of the Lutheran bodies
and in other ecumenical breakthroughs, such as the then newly
promulgated *Baptism, Eucharist, Ministry*. Yet at the same time he
warned of the ever-present danger of further division inherent in the
post-Reformation multiplication of "confessions" and in the later
emergence, both in Europe and especially in America, of "denominations." "Recovery of unity is neither a matter of accepting docu-

ments or validity of orders but recognition of unity in faith which
is the recognition in each other of the Church, of the Holy Spirit, one
common life in Christ."[44] In fact, by referring to St. Basil the Great's
today startlingly radical approach to reconciling dissident Encratite
communities to the *una sancta,* also the resolution of schism between
those who accepted the Council of Nicaea's creed and those who did
not, often the majority in many places. Even the form of reconciliation varied, in some cases baptism, in others anointing with chrism,
in yet others a profession of faith, the sealing of the reconciliation
being in the celebration and reception of the Eucharist. If one finds
unity in the faith, then the bond is one of Church, of communion.
How radical a view this is today where charges of "heresy" again fly
easily and so often without any warrant.

In addition to his participation in the official Orthodox-Lutheran
dialogue in America, Father Meyendorff wrote extensively on the
unfolding developments in the Roman Catholic Church, especially
during Vatican II and afterward. He applauded every step the Catholic Church took toward returning to the ecclesiology and faith of
the undivided Church. He enthusiastically supported the return to
the Scriptures, the Fathers, and the liturgy as the primary sources
of the Church's life. He pointed out, often for an Orthodox audience
all too set in their prejudices, the unmistakable convergences of practice and faith still existing between themselves and Catholics: baptism, the Eucharist, the saints, the ministry of bishops, priests, and
deacons, monastic life. At the same time he did not flinch from
underscoring those areas in which division would remain unless
there were deep transformation.[45] Mainly these clustered around the
understanding and exercise of the Petrine ministry, the place of the
bishop of Rome in the universal Church not as its infallible and absolutely authoritative head but, as Father Afanasiev characterized it,
"the one who presides in love."[46] Even such a serious doctrinal point
as the phrase added by the West to the Nicene Creed, the *Filioque,*
was slowly being recognized by the Catholic Church as a matter of
great significance for the Eastern Church, no mere bit of theological
poetry. Here Father Meyendorff could with other scholars of both
the East and West, the likes of Yves Congar and Paul Evdokimov,
suggest that there were ways in which the *Filioque* could be brought

back into authentic Trinitarian theology, and even more radically, that the Creed be restored to its original form from 381. It was until after his death that this latter step was taken by the Vatican, at least when Christians of the East were present. Other very troublesome issues that Father Meyendorff did not shy away from were the continuing obstacle of the Eastern Catholic churches, the so-called Uniates, and their often disruptive, provocative presence in parts of eastern Europe where the Orthodox were in the majority. Father Meyendorff, well before the now controversial and much attacked Balamand Statement, vigorously challenged Rome to accept that the "Uniate" situation was becoming an even greater impediment to unity than the doctrinal issues of previous centuries. But also before Balamand and other statements and gestures of both Patriarch Bartholomew I and Pope John Paul II, Father Meyendorff did not hesitate to understand and call the Orthodox and Catholics "sister churches."[47]

Christian Witness: The Mission of the Church and the Christian to the World

Do we always realize how much of our day-to-day existence is dominated by the power that Death still exercises in the world? Each one of us, from the very moment of birth, is menaced with sickness, suffering, sometimes hunger, and so many other anxieties. All these are only preliminaries of what is the inevitable fate of all mankind. And it is the conscious—or unconscious—awareness of each man and each woman that death is forthcoming which leads them to struggle for existence, most frequently against their neighbors. What is the real origin of all the conflicts, all the wars, all the social injustices, all the terrors and repressions which man wages against man, if not the desire of individuals or groups to gain—at the expense of their neighbors—a little more illusory security, a little delay in the inevitable end? The imminence of death generates this fear and this insecurity, while the latter lead to desperate self-defense, which excuses any action against one's fellow men. This is the situation of sinful and mortal mankind which Christ came to save through His resurrection from the dead. The Resurrection breaks the vicious circle of death and sin. It brings to man the hope of immortality, and makes his "struggle for existence" unnecessary.[48]

Thus Father Meyendorff addressed the readers of the national newspaper of the OCA at Pascha 1973, holding out what he called in another Easter editorial the "ethics of the resurrection," a freedom and end to fear coming only from the victory of the Lord over all forms of death in his own death and rising.

Human life is inevitably dominated by worries, preoccupations, fears or concerns connected with the one sure fact of the future for all of us: physical death. These concerns and worries are sometimes quite unconscious, but, nevertheless, omnipresent. There is no way in which we can avoid being concerned about our income, our insurance policies, our savings, as well as about the availability of such services which our society can offer us to provide us with a measure of security in our old age or when we are sick. But have we ever thought that all these preoccupations are basically connected with one reality: the ultimate inevitability of death, which we understandably want to postpone and make as harmless as possible? . . . Furthermore, is it not true that our mortality serves—quite unconsciously again—to justify our concern for ourselves, instead of our neighbors? . . . Moreover even the laws of this mortal world of ours are made in such a way that their main purpose is to preserve my rights and my property. They justify violence as a form of self-defense. And the history of human society is one of conflicts and wars in which individuals and nations struggle and kill others in the name of temporal benefits which will be destroyed by death anyway. But this is still considered as "justice." Such is, indeed, the inevitable logic of a world, which St. Paul describes as the "reign of death"(Rom. 5:14). On Easter Day, however, we celebrate the end of this reign. . . . The victory which our Church celebrates so brilliantly, so loudly, so triumphantly, is not simply a guarantee of "after life." Rather it changes the entire set of our ethical priorities even now. There is no need for self-preservation anymore because "our life is hidden with Christ in God" (Col. 3:3). . . . This is indeed total "foolishness" in the eyes of the world but it is the wisdom of God, revealed in the Resurrection of the Lord.[49]

It is all too easy to pigeonhole Father Meyendorff as an intellectual. Fluent in several languages, his mind would often be moving far more rapidly than his mouth, and thus, even in public lectures, one received the impression of an enormously well read, intelligent yet somehow good-natured, bumbling personality, the quintessential absent-minded professor. The impression even led some colleagues to believe that he lacked the focus and skills for administration, and thus that a parish, students, faculty, any organization in his responsibility would best be advised to seek order and direction elsewhere. Yet the appearance of scholarly preoccupation was only that, an appearance. Father Meyendorff was the first faculty member at St. Vladimir's to seriously begin preparing for its academic future, not only in adding buildings but especially in encouraging the very best students to pursue further graduate work and careers in research and teaching, either here or abroad. Perhaps surprisingly, given his academic stature and cosmopolitan good-natured way, he was much sought after as a confessor and spiritual father.

Yet it is not at all surprising, when one wanders through his prodigious writings, to consistently encounter not only a scholar but also a priest and at root a man of faith and of prayer. One essay in which all of these aspects of his identity converge is "Confessing Christ Today," originally presented in 1974 in an international theological consultation at the Romanian monastery of Cernica. It is closeness to Christ that has brought about the almost miraculous recovery of closeness among Christians historically divided, suspicious, and even hateful of each other.[50] Now Father Meyendorff had written substantial studies on Christology, but it is not another such investigation that we find here but a bold proclamation of what faith must look like in our world and in our time. Once again the imprint of his teachers is evident as the Church comes immediately front stage as the community in which we encounter Christ and are linked to each other. And the source of this unity, the very center of the Church's identity and structure, is the Eucharist. As Dimitri Obolensky noted in an obituary, Father Meyendorff cited Fathers Kern and Afanasiev as the principal shapers of his theology and spiritual life.

The witness and presence of the Orthodox churches in the twentieth century has unfortunately been hampered, he points out, by the practical absence of unity among them, despite their claims to oneness in faith and sacramental life. Here is a theme we have already seen as consistent in his thinking and one in which he was unafraid of making even harsh criticism of prevailing church practices such as competing jurisdictions, numerous bishops in the same city, refusal to work together as a church. He also echoed another of the stances so typical of his teaching and writing: the need for Christians to enunciate their criticism of dominant social, political, or even religious ideologies clearly and forcefully.

However, what is of greatest significance are the powerful Christian affirmations he offers as essential for our time. "Authentic human life presupposes not a secular 'unity of mankind' but communion with God," he argues.[51] Contrary to our modern understanding of man as autonomous in the universe, the Tradition of Christian faith rather sees man as made in the image and likeness of God, therefore called to communion with God, to "deification" and sanctification, to becoming more and more like the Holy One in whose image we already are fashioned. Thus our faith is not so much another weapon in the arsenal for making a better world but the "way" in which we as persons become the instruments of God's work in the world.

> Only a person can be baptized, not an institution, a social theory, or a philosophical ideology. Only a person can ultimately be "saved" and "redeemed," and salvation always implies an interplay between the divine all-powerful gift of grace and man's free response, and never the magical sanctification of a thing or an idea. Matter is indeed sanctified in the Eucharist, but as the "Bread of Heaven" which is offered to *man* so that he might partake of it. Only living and personal beings can be truly *thankful*, i.e. truly participate in the Eucharist. Similarly, the Church represents a unity in Christ of living free persons, gathered together by the power of the Holy Spirit. It is not an impersonal institution established *over* them.[52]

Christ alone in the Holy Spirit is the giver of authentic unity in the Church, and this, Father Meyendorff argues, must be said over against the then and still reigning view that doctrine divides and work unites. Whether the WCC or any church body, the true Christian witness in the world comes from faith, from unity in Christ that is given to us, not from our own versions of agreement. Rather than agreement what we find is more division, and this cannot be the source of our courage and energy for doing the work of God in the world. Quoting one of the true masters of the Russian emigration in Paris, the philosopher Nicolas Berdiaev, in another talk given in the WCC Faith and Order Commission in 1971, Father Meyendorff identifies the surrender to political, social, economic, or ethnic determinism as one that is "spiritually bourgeois." Berdiaev asserts, "The bourgeois spirit wins every time when, among Christians, the City of the earth is mistaken for the City of heaven, and when Christians stop feeling as pilgrims in this world," this from the very first number of the famous periodical *Put', The Way,* published by the émigrés in March–April 1926.

One is tempted to say, in contrast, that this scholar and teacher, himself from Russian aristocratic roots, was even more antibourgeois when it came to the realm of the spirit. Perhaps those who knew him in other ways, as a father confessor, as a priest, even in their reticence capture something of his largesse. At the conclusion of a journal issue devoted to his memory, a former student of his, Jean Colosimo, now theologian and faculty member at his alma mater, St. Sergius, recalled some of the characteristics of Father Meyendorff's being a "confessor" in more than the sacramental sense, although this was both the most hidden yet luminous aspect of his ministry. What is evoked is exactly what I myself have heard, both from a friend of many years and from another gifted former student of his: the immediate recognition of his deep generosity, patience, sense of humor, and love for life. Though by no means an intimate of his, I too experienced this in his lecturing, preaching, and conversation and in a more personal way. It was his instinct and perception that prompted him to give me the name of yet another former student of his, now a priest, to contact because he lived and worked close to where I lived. That connection, born I think of genuine insight on his part into both our personalities, led to a deep friendship and much common work as collaborators both in priestly ministry and scholarship.

Perhaps as a publication of St. Vladimir's Seminary suggested, Father Meyendorff was the last of his kind, the last of his generation, excepting Fr. Boris Bobrinskoy, and the last with a direct link to not only the St. Sergius Institute and its teachers but as well to the incomparable experience of the Russian emigration in the West. Though in personality he was quite different from his lifelong colleague and friend, Fr. Alexander Schmemann, he nevertheless shared many characteristics with him. Both were truly cosmopolitan, men "of the world," in the best Christian sense. They not only knew and understood their Russian heritage and the culture of France in which they grew up, but they also sank roots deeply into America's life. This was not without criticism, not without some awkwardness, born of Old World courtliness and civility. And yet these were men who loved the beauty of the creation of this world, a good novel, a fine meal and wine, travel, the company of family and colleagues. There was a "lightness of being" to both, as well as the deeper joy and freedom in Christ that was its source. In particular, they were able to speak frankly and forcefully, not only about the foibles of the times in which they lived, but also about the failings of their fellow Orthodox Christians. I believe that they in many ways put the Orthodox Church "on the map" of the United States as did no others. I should like to think that perhaps someday they will be depicted, in an icon, holding a small church building, offering it to Christ, much as other preachers of the gospel and planters of the Church before them: Peter and Paul, Cyril and Methodius, Nina and Vladimir and Olga, among others.

CHAPTER ELEVEN

Alexander Men

A Modern Martyr, Free in the Faith, Open to the World

Fire and Freedom

Christ calls people to bring the divine ideal to reality. Only short-sighted people imagine that Christianity has already happened, that it took place, say, in the thirteenth century, or the fourth, or some other time. I would say that it has only made the first hesitant steps in the history of the human race. Many words of Christ are incomprehensible to us even now, because we are still Neanderthals in spirit and morals; because the arrow of the Gospels is aimed at eternity; because the history of Christianity is only beginning. What has happened already, what we now call the history of Christianity, are the first half-clumsy, unsuccessful attempts to make it a reality.[1]

Not all of the connections among the figures profiled in this volume are direct ones. In some cases, such as the relationship of Fr. Alexander Men to others, it was one of reading and then citation and, most important, alignment with their perspectives. On May 5, 1998, according to local newspaper and television reports, the burning of books written by a number of significant contemporary Orthodox theologians took place with the approval and quite possibly in the presence of Bishop Nikon of Ekaterinburg (now resigned at the urging of the Russian synod of bishops). The books were burned, their reading by seminary students, clergy, and laity was banned, and a recently ordained priest, Fr. Oleg Vokhmianin, was suspended from priestly duties (an action since reversed, it appears, through the direct intervention of Patriarch Alexis of Moscow, primate of the Russian Orthodox Church). The books were committed to the flames be- o cause, though written by the Orthodox priest-theologians Nicolas Afanasiev, Alexander Schmemann, John Meyendorff, and Alexander Men, they were felt to contain "Western contaminated" ideas, even "heresy." A friend and follower of Father Men, George Kochtekov, formerly rector of Sts. Cosmas and Damian parish in Moscow and a leader in liturgical and catechetical renewal, was suspended on baseless charges and only reinstated, though not in a parish, in spring 2000.

Because these are individuals of some repute, the outcry and protest were considerable. There were letters to the patriarch of Moscow from Father Schmemann's widow and Pulitzer Prize–winning journalist son, Serge, letters from Metropolitan Theodosius, primate of the Orthodox Church in America and from other concerned clergy and laity here and abroad. An extremely critical assessment of the situation appeared in *Le Monde* on June 10 by the eminent French Orthodox lay theologian Olivier Clément: "Difficulties and Indispositions of the Russian Church." Likewise, Professor Nicolas Lossky of the University of Paris and son of theologian Vladimir Lossky, expressed sharp reaction in the summer number of *Service Orthodoxe du Presse.* In February Lossky himself was the target of harassment and charges of heresy from an audience of monastics and clergy while delivering a lecture at the Moscow Theological Academy along with the secretary of the WCC, Dr. Konrad Raiser, and other officials.

Across the Orthodox churches, there is a growing conflict between two perspectives and their adherents. Although some decry the use of such descriptions, it is not inaccurate to call one of these groups, as several in France have, *integristes,* traditionalists who oppose any development in liturgy or theology as "innovation" and who are against participation in ecumenical activity, particularly membership in the World Council of Churches. It is not clear what the other perspective should be labeled. Their opponents call them "liberals," "innovators," "Western contaminated," "Protestants," "ecumenists," and generally "heretics." These are Orthodox clergy and laity convinced of the enormous freedom within the Great Tradition of the Church, the Scriptures, the Fathers, the councils, the liturgical services, and the whole heritage of the faith in various places and times. These Orthodox are open to, even fraternally disposed to, other Christian confessions, committed to the goal of healing the schisms that divide Christianity. They point back to the undivided Church of the first millennium, to the great litany's petition for the "union of all," and even to more recent actions such as the embrace of Pope Paul VI and Ecumenical Patriarch Athenagoras I and the mutual lifting of anathemas as signs that then and now Christ and the Holy Spirit are "present everywhere, filling all things," as the liturgical prayer to the Spirit and the New Testament say. Clément notes that this cleavage is characteristic of many places, not only Russia. He also recognizes that these characterizations do not fully capture the complexity either of the circumstances or of the experiences of the Orthodox Christians in these locations. That believers often manifest extremes of both inclusivity and exclusivity is not so rare. Tendencies toward rigid conformity to tradition are often met with more moderate leanings toward adaptation and openness.

As we saw, Fr. John Meyendorff confronted this very issue throughout his life and in his writing. Consistently he argued that authentic tradition is living, always changing, while in its truth remaining the same. Father Men himself understood this tension, especially in the history of his own Russian Church, reflecting on it through the figures of the monks Ferapont and Zossima from Dostoyevsky's *Brothers Karamazov*. Both tendencies are present, and, Father Men argued that they are necessary checks or better, complements to each other. In many ways, this tension exists as a backdrop to virtually every one of the living icons.

Father Men, still dismissed today, a decade after his death, as too ecumenical, too liberal, not traditionally Orthodox enough, was in fact very much devoted to the Tradition of the Church, the Scriptures especially, the liturgy and the Eucharist in particular, but equally to the many smaller details of churchly piety. The primer he prepared on prayer and worship describes and explains the details of Orthodox liturgical practice: how to prepare for communion, how to observe Lent, how to follow a daily discipline of prayer, among many other things. Always the teacher, he explains the meaning and points out where a particular observance has been obscured or even undone in historical practice, as well as where and how it could be restored and renewed. The frequent reception of communion and the opening of the royal doors and praying aloud of various parts of the liturgy aloud would be examples of these. However, in his deep love for the Tradition of the Church, Father Men, much like his confreres, is driven by an equal love for the people who enact this tradition and make it living and for those who have yet to discover it. From faithfulness to Christianity comes a rich and fearless openness to the diversity of Christian churches, to other communities of faith, and to the culture of our complex modern world. Father Men embodies the renewed and creative spirituality of the Eastern Church I have traced in the other living icons. In his life and teaching and ministry we encounter a radical but faithful openness of Christ to the world. In him we see yet another example of holiness in our time, a living out of the gospel in very difficult circumstances in Soviet Russia. Tragically, we also see the conflict among Christians of the East colliding, perhaps even eventuating in his death. Yet we also come to recognize that Father Men's legacy is not only for those in the Church of the East but also for all Christians.

A Modern Martyr

Fathers Afanasiev, Schmemann, and Meyendorff were condemned, one might say, in absentia, after their deaths. The same was true for one more author, whose books were committed to the flames in the courtyard of the Ekaterinburg seminary. He was a priest and educator who through reading the books of the other three had not only been educated but spurred on to the renewal of the life of the Church in his country, Russia. For the last of those whose books were burned, however, the least known here in the West, condemnation took a more decisive form, the witness or *martyria* of death. In commenting on his roots in the faith and the Church in a letter, Father Men was able to pinpoint his sources:

Fr. Seraphim (Batiukov) was a disciple of the *startsy* [elders] of Optina. . . . He baptized my mother and me, and for many years

undertook the spiritual direction of the whole family. . . . [M]y
mother, who is now dead[,] . . . had a great deal to do with determining my spiritual life and orientation. She lived an ascetic and
prayerful life, completely free of hypocrisy, bigotry, and narrowness; traits often present in people in her state. She was always
filled with paschal joy, a deep dedication to the will of God, and
a feeling of closeness to the spiritual world, in a certain way, like
St. Seraphim or St. Francis of Assisi. . . . She had a trait similar to
the character of the *startsy* of Optina, a trait so dear to them: openness to people, to their problems, and to their searching; openness
to the world. It is precisely this quality that drew the best representatives of Russian culture to Optina. After a long rupture,
Optina did in fact renew the dialogue between the Church and
society. It was an undertaking of great, exceptional importance,
despite the lack of confidence and opposition of the authorities. . . .
This idea of dialogue with the world has stuck with me all my life;
it should never be interrupted. I have always felt I should participate in that conversation with whatever meager force I have.[2]

Alexander Men was born in the midst of the Stalinist era, on January 22, 1935, in Moscow. His mother, Elena Semenovna Zupersein,
was from Kharkov and was a Jew. She married Vladimir Grigorevich
Men, an engineer and also Jewish, in 1934, and they had two sons,
Alexander and Pavel, born in 1938. Through her sister, Vera Yakov-
levna Vasilevskaya, Elena came to know the underground, or "catacomb," church, networks of clergy and laity who went underground
not only because of the systematic persecution by the Bolshevik
regime but also because they refused to recognize the authority of
the bishop who presided over the Russian Church since the death of
Patriarch Tikhon in 1925, Metropolitan Sergius Stragodorsky. When
several diocesan bishops broke with him, after his public declaration
of loyalty to the Bolshevik government, the underground movement, which consisted of worshiping communities, clergy, and even
groups of secret monastics, began to form. It would not be until
Sergius' death in 1945 and the election of Patriarch Alexis I, accepted
as legitimate by them, that the underground church would surface
and at the insistence of several of its bishops and many of its priests
assimilate into the still embattled but public Church.

Especially important in the underground communities were gifted spiritual fathers such as Seraphim Batiukov, mentioned in the quote above. He had been pastor of one of the most active parishes in Moscow before the revolution, that of Sts. Kir and John, a gathering place for many young intellectuals who had returned to Christian faith and life. Himself a disciple and spiritual child of one of the last great elders of the Optina monastery, the monk now canonized Nektary. Father Batiukov was a gifted confessor and counselor and became the center of a catacomb web of monastics and laity, among whom was Vera, the aunt of Alexander Men, who had gotten to know him through a colleague. However, it was Elena Men and her first-born, "Alik," who were first baptized by Father Seraphim in September 1935, and Vera was baptizied a bit later. Father Seraphim lived in a small house in Zagorsk, not far from the famous Holy Trinity–St. Sergius monastery founded by the great Russian saint of the same name in the thirteenth century. Several nuns of the monastery founded by Saint Seraphim of Sarov himself, Diveyevo, lived with Father Batiukov, and after his death Mother Maria led the community on a regular basis.

It was the spirit of the elders of Optina and of the priests of Moscow parishes like that of Father Batiukov and the famous Maroseika Street St. Nicholas parish, with the father and son priests Sergius and Alexis Metchev, that became the atmosphere in which Alexander Men grew up. In the letter quoted above he cites the lack of hatred for others in the faith, something rare in those days, and a radical openness and compassion to people, to the world, that characterized their spirituality. The fathers of the monastery at Optina in the nineteenth century had made it a home for troubled and inquiring souls, in particular the intellectuals and professionals struggling to regain faith and to put Christ and the gospel into contact with modern life. Dostoyevsky was but one of the notables who went to Optina for counsel and prayer.

Alexander lived with his family in a cramped Moscow apartment, excelled in his schoolwork, and read voraciously at home. Encouraged in his study by Mother Maria of Zagork, former catacomb priest Boris Vasilev, and lay theologians Nicolas Pestov and Anatoly Vedernikov, director of the reopened theological school at the Holy Trinity–St. Sergius monastery, he read widely, not only in the

Scriptures, the Fathers, and Orthodox writers, but in Western Christianity as well. He began a lifelong attachment to the figures of the Russian religious renaissance of the twentieth century as well as their nineteenth-century predecessors such as Khomiakov, Soloviev, Bukharev, and Fedorov. Barred from university studies because of his Jewish background, in the mid-1950s he took an alternative path in biological science at the Fur Institute, first in Moscow and then in Irkutsk. There he became active in the cathedral parish in a number of capacities, involvement that later cost him his final exams and graduation from the institute. He and Natalya Grigorenko had married in 1956, and on leaving the institute his spiritual father, Nicolas Golubtsov, and Professor Vedernikov convinced one of the vicar bishops of the Moscow diocese, Makary, to ordain Alexander a deacon. This was on Pentecost, June 1, 1958, and he was attached to a parish in Odintsovo. He served there for two years in great poverty and with a most difficult rector. On September 1, 1960, he was ordained priest by Bishop Stepan, another vicar in the Moscow diocese, and assigned as assistant at the parish in Alabino. For a few years there he began a kind of ministry that would come into full bloom only years later, toward the end of his life, at Novaya Derevnya parish. He would not only restore the icon screen and wall paintings but also begin to preach and teach the faith at every opportunity. He ingeniously requested the renewal of the permit to hold a funeral service for a civil servant more than two hundred times, thus preaching at many cemetery memorial services on anniversaries of deaths as well as services in people's homes. He preached at every service in church, every celebration of a sacrament and of course the Sunday liturgy. He used some space in an attached church building to have regular hours for visiting by any who wished to talk. The parish had a car, a rare thing at the time, and he was able himself to visit parishioners who could not come to church. In short, he revived a form of pastoral ministry that had flourished before the revolution in such places as the Moscow parishes and Optina monastery, a ministry of openness to all and of teaching.

At Alabino, nicknamed "the abbey," Father Men's efforts resulted in the parish becoming a locus of renewed faith, not only among parishioners, but also among those who came from other places to listen, ask questions, and learn. There Father Men had his first encounters with the Soviet regime: his home and library were searched for books allegedly stolen from abroad, and he was interrogated for suspicious activities, namely, all the preaching and teaching so unusual for a priest of that era. Also during this time Father Men became part of a group of clergy who not only gathered for regular collegial conversation but eventually became notorious for their efforts at protest in renewal in the then still harassed and subservient Moscow Patriarchate. There was Fr. Dmitri Dudko, who boldly held question-and-answer sessions, not allowed under punitive Soviet religion laws at this time.[3] He was later arrested and imprisoned and eventually recanted his "errors" in a pathetic display of enforced loyalty. Also in the group were the two young priests Nicolas Eschlimann and Gleb Yakunin, whose open letter to the patriarch protesting the Church's passivity and the bishops' lack of leadership earned them only a reprimand, though it stimulated the beginning of more public criticism of the regime by intellectuals, a wave that would crest in the 1970s and 1980s and lead to the glasnost policies of Gorbachev in the 1990s. Others who came to know and rely on Father Men in the Brezhnev years included Anatoly Levitin, Alexander Solzhenitsyn, and other samizdat writers and dissidents. It is of interest to note that throughout these decades Father Men studiously avoided direct confrontation with either the Church or the regime. Not only did he begin to regularly publish articles in the *Journal of the Moscow Patriarchate,* with assistance from his old supporter Professor Vednerikov, he also began a kind of *tamizdat* (published over there; i.e., abroad) career of his own. From the late 1960s on to glasnost, through the instigation and connections of Assia Douroff, he published a series of his books with the Brussels Christian publishing house La-Vie avec Dieu. From his first book, *The Son of Man,* to his catechetical handbook on liturgy, the church year, and prayer, *Heaven on Earth,* to his series on the world's religious traditions and biblical studies, *In Search of the Way, the Truth and the Life*—all first appeared abroad under pseudonyms such as A. Bogolyubov (literally, Theophilus, "lover of God") and E. Svetlov ("light bearer") from the Brussels press.

Later in the 1960s Father Men was transferred to the parish of Taraskova, just north of Moscow, again as assistant priest, and finally in 1970 he was sent to the parish of Novaya Derevnya. He served as assistant there until 1989 and was the rector until his death in 1990. Throughout the last twenty years of his life, Father Men continued the pastoral ministry he had initiated in his earlier parishes. He very carefully sought to restore more frequent communion and to renew liturgical life along the lines Father Schmemann would urge in America. His ministry was marked especially by the same emphasis on preaching and teaching the faith to Christians and nonbelievers alike, for in the Soviet era any kind of learning about religious, even the most basic handbooks, was unavailable. While the growth of dissident protest grew and multiplied in the 1970s and 1980s, Father Men was for the most part not directly involved. He was close to many of the voices of dissent, because in these years intellectuals, young professionals, and persons seriously inquiring about Christianity began to flock to his parish, to the room he had for pastoral meetings. More and more in these years Father Men was called to people's homes for baptisms, conversations, blessings of civil marriages, and memorial services. In the summertime, people would take vacations in the region around Novaya Derevnya to attend liturgy and other services at the parish, to visit and be counseled by him. Gradually he encouraged the formation of small groups, especially throughout Moscow, who would gather each week over tea and cake for bible study, prayer, and discussions. Tape recordings, transcriptions, and translations of these "house conversations" were made, as were videotapes of baptisms and other liturgical celebrations at the parish. These now serve as both records and witnesses to the dynamic personality and warmth of Father Men.

Even against the backdrop of the ever-growing dissent movement, Father Men's highly unusual ministry could not help but evoke comment and criticism. He experienced regular KGB interrogations, house searches, and surveillance for the rest of his life. Some fellow clergy denounced his approach as "not Orthodox," his respect for other faith traditions, particularly his warmth for the Roman Catholic Church, vilified. In print as well as in anonymous letters, his Jewish background was reviled. That he was Jewish also became the explanation for his heretical innovations in church work. As recently as spring 1999, almost ten years after his death, the very same pastoral activities of Bible study, prayer, and discussion in people's homes were denounced by an archpriest in the diocese of Alama-

Alta and in spring 2000 several clergy who were accused of engaging in such "innovations" were removed from ministry, their pectoral crosses ripped from their necks. One of Father Men's followers, Father George Kochetkov, was suspended for more than two years and his efforts at catechetical work, liturgical renewal, and pastoral ministry in Father Men's footsteps likewise denounced.

However, with the ascendancy of Gorbachev, a thaw or opening began to appear, especially during the 1988 celebration of Russia's millennium of Christianization. Beginning in spring of that year, Father Men went public in an unprecedented way for a Russian priest. Church school was openly held, along with adult classes at his parish. Visits to hospitals, particularly the children's hospital in Moscow, started and then were banned. From spring 1988 until his death in September 1990, Father Men presented more than two hundred public talks, some on television, most in schools and other accessible locales. Many of these are available now in transcription and translation in the anthologies of his writings. He covered much of the material on which he had published abroad: the world religious traditions leading up to Christianity, liturgy, prayer, the creed and the teachings of the Fathers, the Bible and how to read it, and the religious and cultural heritage of Russia. Friends and parishioners alike often wondered whether he would give out under the amazing pace of parish services, counseling, meetings, and public lectures. He claimed to have more energy in his fifties than he had had in his twenties. Yet he also had some sense that time was rapidly passing for him. Some claim he even spoke with clairvoyance of imminent death. He was in good health, excellent spirits, never more joyful. This still is most apparent in the videotapes, not only his great sense of humor but something else, the same peace and light that others found in the faces of Father Bulgakov, Father Schmemann, Paul Evdokimov, and the others we have met here. There were no stereotypical elements that appear in hagiography; these are emerging a decade after his passing. What people remembered was the feeling that he was completely present for them, totally at home with the saints as well as with the one in front of him.

There are several accounts of Father Men's death, at best hypothetical reconstructions of what must have happened, as there were no eyewitnesses to the event. On his way to celebrate Sunday liturgy in his parish church early on the morning of September 9, 1990, he walked to the nearby commuter rail station to travel from Semkhoz, where he and his family lived, to Novaya Derevnya. On the path he most likely turned to someone who called him. From behind his head was torn open by a sharp instrument, probably an ax. He managed to crawl back to the gate of his house. Several people saw him stumble back home with great difficulty. His wife was the one who discovered him. Hearing groans, she saw a severely injured person by her gate, called the ambulance service, and only on their arrival and inability to save the man was able to recognize that it was indeed her husband, his appearance was so disfigured by the attack. Father Men's attackers have never been apprehended and brought to trial. Their identity and motivation remain matters of speculation. As with numerous other assassinations in the chaos of Yeltsin's Russia, the logic would point to the political-cultural and religious extreme right wing, partisans of the group *Pamiat* (Remembrance) and like traditionalist factions, for whom his writing and speaking was anathema, precisely the perspective of those who would eventually burn his books.[4]

In the last few years, Father Men's biography and a selection of his preaching, teaching, and writing have been translated and published. First came Yves Hamant's biographical study.[5] Then Oakwood issued a collection of his sermons from Lent through the Paschal season.[6] Continuum issued Elizabeth Roberts and Ann Shukman's excellent anthology of articles, selections from his books, interviews, and transcriptions of lectures.[7] Father Alexis Vinogradov has translated a selection of Father Men's "house conversations," transcriptions of his extemporaneous responses to questions at home gatherings.[8] And Oakwood has also published a translation of perhaps the best known of Father Men's books, *The Son of Man*, first published more than thirty years ago and revised before his death.[9]

Christian communities are only beginning to become acquainted with this charismatic man and his work, and the early reaction is telling.[10] An unsigned, negative review of his house conversations in one diocesan periodical summarily dismisses him within the first three paragraphs as one who "wandered from the Orthodox Church's teaching on several subjects."[11] Readers of this publication are informed that Father Men did not have the mind of the Fathers and was mistaken in his notion that the apostle Paul would recognize something of the early Church's dynamism in the contemporary liturgical assemblies of the non-Orthodox Christians. Father Men, it is claimed, succumbed to ecclesiological relativism, evidenced by his favorable mention of Savonarola, Hus, and Eckhardt among those "renewing the Church" and his criticism of ascetic exaggerations and Orthodox hostility toward those of other religious traditions, including other Christians.[12] Father Men is revealed to be guilty of being an "ecumenist" for his appreciation of certain constructive aspects of the papal office and also is castigated for alleged, though unprovable dismissal of monasticism as "outdated," "rooted in pagan cults," and nonevangelical in its renunciation of the world. Those who would be interested in the topics Father Men treats— Christ, the Bible, the liturgy, prayer, the Church, among others—are advised to turn rather to the numerous publications of the Orthodox seminary presses for the truth. This judgment would appear to have been made without inspection of the rather traditional "primer" on liturgy, faith, and prayer, *Orthodox Worship: Sacrament, Word, Image,* originally published in 1980. Another unfavorable review of the Men anthology, in an Orthodox periodical from the U.K., similarly perceives Father Men as lacking balance in the Tradition, too christological, and not Trinitarian enough, and veering too far in criticizing the ecclesial past and too close in encountering the culture and society of our time.[13]

Orthodoxy and Openness

It would be a fascinating endeavor to track those thinkers who have been and are becoming the targets of conservative criticism from within the Orthodox churches.[14] Father Men joins a select group, including Fathers Bulgakov, Afanasiev, Schmemann, and Meyendorff. To be thorough, those desiring to rid themselves of the "Western pollution" of Orthodox truth would have to add to their bonfire all of the figures profiled in this book and many others I have named, all of whom could be accused of one or another deficiency, exaggeration, or deviation. Father Men explicitly acknowledges Bulgakov, Schmemann, and Berdiaev, among others, as shapers of his thinking. Even before the recent book burning, yet after Father Men's death, there has been relatively little written or said positively about him by Orthodox scholars and clergy. One finds more critical commentary than anything else, although a summer 1999 conference on him and his work at Drew University in Madison, New Jersey, attracted over one hundred participants.[15] A group of translators continues to bring out Father Men's writings, and a documentary film is in progress. On the tenth anniversary of his death, a number of articles appeared, raising again the lack of closure in the investigation of his murder, the question of his ongoing legacy in Russia, and the very basic issue of his stature there.[16]

It is premature to attempt a thorough assessment of Father Men's work.[17] Though the publication of his writings continues, much is still not available. Thus we have but a partial version of his thought. It may also be the case that it is too soon to attempt a meticulous biographical study, with family, associates, and disciples located in the present ecclesiastical, social, and political turbulence in Russia. Efforts at examining him thus far better achieve an appreciation of the backdrop of the Church's struggle under the Soviet regime and the sources of his spiritual development than a dispassionate biographical and intellectual study.[18] Father Men's situation is further complicated by the context and genre of his work. He was not part of the Russian academic theological establishment, never having held an advanced degree or faculty appointment. Yet he was a teacher of the faith in direct and creative ways. It is said that he used every opportunity, every medium to teach and preach. Beyond the bibliography provided in the anthology, consisting of his world religion series, several short books on prayer, liturgy, iconography, and the Scriptures, it is not clear how much of his correspondence, notebooks, and journals survives and might be published. Neither do we know how many transcriptions there are of the numerous talks, lectures, and interviews of his last years. Even the transcriptions of his talks that we have are distinctive, in the spontaneous, "live" style of his delivery and his thinking. Some very basic bibliographic inventory and organization appears to be necessary, then editing, translating, and publication. Given the dismal economic conditions for such in Russia as well as the open hostility of much of the Russian clergy and hierarchy to his person and work, it is hard to say when this work will be accomplished.

Much of Father Men's writing, preaching, lecturing, and interviews were practical in motivation and in construction. He was attempting to provide what we in the West would consider elementary education in world religions, in the Scriptures, and finally in the basics of Orthodoxy. For most of his life as a priest he functioned in a Soviet atmosphere explicitly hostile to any religious education except antireligious propaganda. It was only in the last years of his life that he could publish under his own name, rather than pseudonymously or anonymously from abroad, and preach, lecture, and teach openly, all this in the wake of the Gorbachev "thaw."

What we have of his work spans several genres: transcribed lectures, interviews, discussions, and sermons, many in a conversational, extemporaneous style. There are the books and essays he published for a general readership, not academic specialists, efforts at basic religious education rather than original scholarship. This is not to say, though, that nothing fresh or original is to be found in his work. Father Men contributed, not only to the rebuilding of faith in his own Russia, but also to our deeper understanding of Christianity today. Finally, a decade after his death, some more objective and probing assessments of his life and work are beginning to appear.[19] He was fond of saying, in different ways, that Christianity, historically, both in Russia and worldwide, was still in its infancy, still just beginning to live. The editors of the anthology of his writings are not wrong in employing the title of his last lecture, delivered the night before his murder, as the title of the collection and a characterization of his thinking: "Christianity for the Twenty-first Century." Does this imply that Father Men was a theological futurist, intent on streamlining sacred tradition for modern, postmodern, and future consumption? Such a stereotype would grossly misinterpret his actual theological perspectives. Father Men's vision of the gospel and the Church is one of radical openness to the world, of an irenic but determined ecumenical outreach to the other Christian churches, one of commitment to the service of the poor and the suffering, and finally a way of life in which one's faith is constantly enacted in one's life. He explicitly credits this vision to a line of clergy and faithful who formed his own Christianity, a line stretching back to the remarkable monastery of Optina and the monks there, the *startsy* who since the nineteenth century had welcomed all sorts of people, especially those estranged from the Church and troubled in their hearts. Father Men thus holds out a dynamic model of holiness for our time, a pattern all the more striking for its crafting in the repressive last decades of the Soviet era.

The Church and the World

The leading feature of his theological writing, and, as it turned out, of his pastoral work, was the legacy of Optina, further embodied in the witness of the Russian renaissance, particularly in the emigration in the West. Much of this book has focused on leading figures of at least two generations of this emigration Theirs was a vision of the Church at once catholic and missionary, a confidence in the fullness of the tradition within Orthodoxy with an openness to other Christians and to those outside the Church. Such an ecclesial consciousness was expressed in the passionate desire to bring the Church and the world into dialogue, to foster the encounter between the Church of the East and those of the West. It would be correct to say that intense awareness of the Incarnation, the "humanity of God" (*Bogochelovetchestvo*) led these Orthodox thinkers to be committed to the meeting of God and humankind in every context. This is an aim strikingly evangelical and evangelistic. Yet it is by no means idiosyncratic for Father Men. The desire to establish dialogue between the East and the West, to bring theology and modern society together, to live out "the liturgy after the liturgy" can be found in the disparate and disagreeing thinkers comprising the Russian emigration. Both Fathers Bulgakov and Florovsky, an important Orthodox figure in the United States after World War II, were theoretically opposed, but both were integral to the beginning of the Russian Christian Students Association, in the foundation of the Fellowship of St. Alban and St. Sergius, and in the work of the Faith and Order Commission of the World Council of Churches.[20] Mother Maria Skobtsova was intent on a form of monastic life for our time, in the

world, for the service of the suffering.[21] Paul Evdokimov spent the
first half of his adult life directing ecumenically sponsored hostels
for refugees and immigrants.[22] Fr. Lev Gillet constantly moved across
ecclesial lines in a ministry of writing, preaching, teaching, and counseling. Fr. Nicolas Afanasiev and Fr. Kyprian Kern inspired the liturgical theology and renewal of the Eucharist in their student, Fr.
Alexander Schmemann.[23] Fr. Alexander Men stands in a formidable
and admirable procession of Orthodox whose return to the sources
opened them to other Christian communities and the world. Though
cut off from them in Soviet Russia, he came to share their larger
vision of the Church as sacrament in and to the world and their sense
of the "churching" of all of life, hardly innovations but treasures of
the tradition to share.

If we follow Father Men's thinking about the Church, we find a
dynamic vision, open and hopeful. This ecclesial view is catholic and
classical, rooted in the Scriptures and the Fathers, centered in the
Eucharist, framed by liturgical and personal prayer, fellowship, and
service to others. It also contains a perspective on holiness for our
times, but exactly like the view of Evdokimov the past is not frozen
but constantly appropriated to our world, without abandoning the
tradition.[24] From the renaissance of Russian religious thought, Father Men inherited an understanding of the Church that extended
beyond the religious realm to politics and history, to culture and
society. Overall, the strongest impression his writing leaves is that of
a challenging, I would say sacramental, dialogue: between Christianity and the world, between liturgy and life. The imprint of a long
line of Russian authors is clear, and the most basic sense is that so
powerfully expressed by the fourteenth-century Byzantine lay theologian Nicolas Cabasilas, echoed recently by another remarkable lay
theologian, Paul Evdokimov.[25] Both have a vision rooted in St. Paul:
God's love for creation, particularly for humanity, is so strong, so
relentless, yet so self-abasing as to be absurd, foolish (*erōs manikos*).
Such divine philanthropy is enacted in the Incarnation, ultimately in
the emptying and humiliation of the suffering, crucified Christ
(*kenōsis*). The image of a God of boundless love dramatically deter-
mines the rest of one's theological outlook. And this vision of the
great Lover of humankind, undeniably strong in the Fathers, also
shapes one's understanding of and response to the world.[26]

Throughout Father Men's work, I would argue, it is precisely this theology that impels his consistent effort to meet even the most difficult terrain of Soviet society with openness and compassion, without the judgment and harshness so understandable for a Church greatly oppressed. It is my opinion that such an attitude is precisely that most faithful to the tradition and most like the heart of God, called so often in the liturgy of the Eastern Church "the Lover of mankind" (*Philanthropos*). Such an attitude is also an enormous challenge to contemporary Orthodoxy, so easily tempted to accentuate differences, condemn contemporary excess in our culture, and pretend to have the perfect, complete way out. Over against such impulses, Father Men's way is full of the Kingdom's freedom and joy. Thus it is threatening and liable to continue to evoke criticism and rejection more from conservative Orthodox than from any other quarter.

"Churching"

Both from biographical details and his work, it is difficult to describe Father Men as anything but an "ecclesial being," in Evdokimov's words. Surely this is to be seen in the majority of his life, when being associated with the Church at all was costly. His attachment to the bishop and cathedral in Irkutsk, where he had studied at the Fur Institute, led to his being denied the final exams that would have allowed him certification and professional work. From his ordination as deacon through his early years as a priest, he was bounced from parish to parish, often subject to the whims of the parish's rector, usually in difficult financial situations overcome by his wife's full-time work as an accountant. In his first full post as pastor at Alabino, he displayed some of the traits that would characterize the rest of his ministry. He restored the church interior, began preaching and teaching the basics of the faith, the creed, the liturgy, the Scriptures. He also actively visited parishioners, continued adding to his library and writing, mostly articles for the journal of the Moscow Patriarchate. And as throughout the rest of his ministry, he was reported, interrogated by the KGB, and had his home searched.

Both the accounts of friends and parishioners and Father Men's own writings confirm his priestly ministry as singular in its rooting in essentials. Rather than merely go through the motions of the weekend and other services, he constantly catechized, urged full participation in the liturgical life, particularly frequent reception of Holy Communion, and actively reached out to his flock. Later such elements would draw numerous Moscow intellectuals to him for pastoral counsel, instruction, and baptism; his parish in Novaya Derevnya became a center of worship and gatherings for teaching. As with Father Dudko, who was also harassed and later detained, Father Men made preaching a standard part of each liturgical service, and the house conversations, his responses to questions by those at such gatherings, grew out of his passion for teaching and the hunger of so many deprived of even basic education concerning Christianity and other world religious traditions.[27] Over time, Father Men's ministry, while always anchored in the Divine Liturgy and other liturgical services at his parish, branched out to include many others: intellectuals unchurched and searching, dissidents, Christians of other confessions.[28]

Much of Father Men's writing and work can be characterized as what theologians of the Russian renaissance called churching. This is the cosmic plan of salvation history, begun in the Old Covenant and fulfilled by Christ in the New through the Incarnation, the Fathers' vision of all things being gathered and restored in Christ.[29] By extension, it came to also mean the building up and renewal of authentic ecclesial consciousness and existence, either among those who knew nothing of the faith or among those for whom it had become reduced to a few ritualistic observances. The vision was of all of life being incorporated in the ecclesial assembly and liturgically offered in the Eucharist. But it was not merely a theoretical view. "Churching," above all, meant the dynamic connection of ecclesial faith with one's existence, the enactment, in St. John Chrysostom's words, of a "liturgy after the liturgy," the living out of liturgy at work, at home. Evdokimov put it best: "It is not enough to *say* prayers, one must become, *be* prayer, prayer incarnate."[30] Father Men's widow, Natalya, has credited the Radio Liberty broadcasts by Father Schmemann and by Archbishop John (Shahavskoy) with giving her husband the courage to write and teach about the faith, despite the strictures and dangers in the USSR of the 1960s and 1970s.[31]

Like Father Schmemann, in returning to the sources, Father Men's ecclesial vision proved refreshing and threatening in its radical simplicity. While not denying the Orthodox preservation of the Church's Tradition, there is a clear rejection of triumphalism; in fact, the humility and freedom of being in the truth is constantly displayed. Thus Father Men can recognize sanctity after the schism, outside the ecclesiastical boundaries of the Orthodox Church. In a couple of sentences, he brings together a *sobor,* or assembly of saints, startling in ecumenical breadth, reminiscent of the assemblies noted in Fr. Lev Gillet's *Orthodox Spirituality* and those depicted by Sister Joanna in frescoes at Saint Basil's House chapel in London. Father Men brings together Ambrose of Milan and John Chrysostom, Pope Martin and Maximus the Confessor, the Byzantine defenders of the icons and the Russian monastic proponents of poverty, the "nonpossessors." He connects Fra Savonarola and Jan Hus with Maxim the Greek and Philip of Moscow. He sees the communion in the faith shared by Francis of Assisi, Sergius of Radonezh, and Andrew Rublev the iconographer, despite the schism.[32] Further, while recognizing the importance of traditional forms of piety—the lighting of candles, the sign of the cross, prayers for the dead, fasting—he also is quick to observe that these can become reductions of the faith, as Father Schmemann termed them, substitutes for living out love, almost superstitious practices divorced from the spirit and meaning intrinsic to them in actual Church Tradition.[33]

Paganism is a primitive religion. . . . [I]t is born of the human psyche—the human drive to establish a bond with prevalent mystical powers. Each one of us is a pagan. At difficult times we are always ready to have our fortunes told, to forecast. The pagan lives within us because in each one of us there are forty thousand years of paganism and only two thousand years of Christianity. Paganism is always easier for us. Primitive religion is always easiest. It is natural to people, and often what passes for Orthodoxy or another Christian confession is simply natural religiosity which, in its own right, is a kind of opium of the people. It functions as a sort of spiritual anesthetic, it helps a person adjust to his surrounding world, over which he can hang the slogan, "Blessed is the one who believes that it is cozy in the world." . . . This is all wrong! Even if I were a Muslim and came to you, having read your Christian books I would have to say to you: "Folks, it's not this way. Your religion does not consist in this at all. Your God is a consuming fire and not a warm hearth, and he is calling you to a place where all sorts of cold winds are blowing, so that what you imagine does not exist. You adapted and developed a completely different teaching to suit your own human needs. You transformed Christianity into a mediocre, popular religion."[34]

Father Men repeatedly summarizes the basic elements of Christian faith and life, lest one conclude from such statements that he is but another iconoclast deconstructor of Church Tradition. Daily prayer, reading of the Scriptures, common liturgical worship, particularly the Eucharist, fellowship, love and service of others—these have always been the crucial ingredients of the life of the Christian community, the Church, East and West, before and after the schisms. Still today they are the ways in which we "encounter" the Risen Christ.[35] All of these have but one goal, to bring to birth in us the freedom of the children of God, the openness to God and to all he has made. But "people crave a freedomless Christianity."[36]

It is both exhilarating and disturbing, to some, to hear Father Men speak of atheism as a gift, to acknowledge the diversity and development within Orthodoxy, the need for renewal, and those such as Saints Tikhon of Zadonsk and Seraphim of Sarov, later Alexander Bukharev, Soloviev, Berdiaev, and Bulgakov, among others, who recovered the vitality and the radical freedom of theology and of the life of the Church.[37] Father Men proceeded with this conviction, that openness to the world meant no abdication to secularism but rather a churching of culture and society, a discovery of all that is good in divine creation, in humanity, in all that is an icon of God.[38] Over against this is the sectarian fear of those who are different, the isolation within Tradition, the abhorrence of anything but the Fathers, a profound suspicion, even loathing, quite at odds with the Fathers, for marriage, children, literature, art, "secular" culture, in short, the world, all of which is God's creation.

"Two Understandings of Christianity"

In his lecture, "Two Understandings of Christianity," Father Men eloquently reflects on the seemingly opposing tendencies not only within Russian Orthodoxy, but beyond, within Christianity generally.[39] Drawing on Dostoyevsky's two figures from *Brothers Karamazov*, the luminous elder Father Zossima and his counterpart, the rigid, ascetic, and judgmental Father Ferapont, Men surprisingly does not condemn the latter's flight from the world and repulsion for it to celebrate the former's openness. The world-affirming and world-denying instincts were not always so opposed in either the history of Israel or the Church, as the Scriptures but also the sayings of the desert fathers and the writings of many other fathers attest. In time, however, the worst kinds of polarization have indeed developed out of both orientations. The Church has withdrawn from society to turn in upon itself in the quest for salvation through ascetic struggle and denial. In such a quest it is easy then for the world, and certainly all those who would appear to believe incorrectly, to be condemned. In more recent times exactly the opposite has occurred, with the Church embracing anything and everything around as holy and good. We are still grappling with the folly of this, particularly in the West. It is easiest to want to rejoice in the Optina elders' openness to the world and castigate the narrowness of conservatives, yet Father Men asserts, "[N]either of the two understandings . . . is wrong, but each as it were takes one side and wrongly develops it. Fullness of life lies in the synthesis of the two."[40]

It is not difficult to hear the echoes of Soloviev and Berdiaev in Father Men's respect for differences, even in his insistence that such differences cannot categorically be condemned since they may well lead to the truth. He boldly, like them, pushes this with regard to schism-torn Christianity. As a student of history, he knew that there had always been diversity in Christianity, different languages used in worship, preaching, and teaching, various forms of hymnody and iconography and ways of celebrating feasts. Without espousing any "branch" theory of the Church, he challenges the Orthodox with the continued role of a chief pastor in Roman Catholicism:

As concerns the question of Peter's preeminence among the Apostles, this problem belongs to the area of faith. If the Catholics believe God acts through the Vicar of Peter, then let it be. This is impossible to prove historically or scientifically. And if in our polemics against the Catholic structures we begin to posit the notion that previously such a power did not exist, then the Protestants can rebound with our own argument and say: "Previously there was no sacrament of marriage, there were no icons, there was none of this. So what does this mean? Let's get rid of them and much else!"[41]

Far from seeing the divided confessions of Christianity as just signs of decay and breakdown, Father Men preferred to understand them as signs of the unity that once was and again could be, even citing Patriarch Sergius (Stradogorsky) on the constant progression from pluralism to unity in the Church's history.[42] For him, the extreme conservatism of the Russian Orthodox Church, virtually isolationist and sectarian in some expressions, was not defensible. Such alleged means of survival under the Soviet regime did not serve the best interests of the faith and believers then or now, when one could speak and act freely. Father Men, along with Father Schmemann and others, suggests that there are ways in which the Church's tradition can be a creative source for outreach and mission to a complex, secularized modern world.[43]

A Credo

Perhaps the most representative, revealing, and, for some, problematic aspects of Father Men's ecclesial vision can be found in the selection titled, "Credo for Today's Christian," in the Roberts-Shukman anthology.[44] It should be noted that this collection was arranged from a number of his writings, interviews, and lectures and that he did not produce the integrated piece as such. In the Russian publication it was called "Basic Features of a Christian Worldview: According to the Teaching of the Bible and the Tradition of the Church." It constantly draws on the Scriptures for the very expression of faith. Hence Christianity is the "Good News," not abstract doctrine, ideology, or system of rituals, a "Way" of life oriented toward the future coming of Christ and the kingdom of heaven.

In about fifty points, Father Men both affirms the content of the faith and denies its distortions. One will look in vain for arguments against divinity in Christology, or about inclusive language for the Trinity, or about the oppression and full recognition of particular interest groups, or to whom should ordination be extended, or the imperial absolutism of Christian doctrine. I think it was not just because Father Men was a Russian priest writing for Russian believers that the incendiary theological issues of the West are not to be found in his work. Rather he is so profoundly and unselfconsciously ecclesial, in the Fathers' "mind," that these controversies, of which he was well aware, do not enter his theological horizon.

But other matters do. He refuses to accept as normative a literalist interpretation that would, for example, find the Scriptures' or the Fathers' statements about natural science valid for all time. Likewise he cautions against the desire for extraordinary happenings or miracles as the regular revelation and action of God. He sees no opposition between the God of the Old and New Covenants, no contradiction between the Bible as God's word and the ability to learn about its history, archaeology, and anthropology.

Christ is confessed to be present and active everywhere in the Church, especially in the sacraments but in the simplest and more ordinary places too. Liturgical forms, rules, canon law, along with iconography and hymnody—all of these ecclesial elements are necessary and important but always have been diverse, always have been changed, and thus are not unalterable and should not be uniform everywhere. The mystery of the Incarnation and the work of the Holy Spirit in history are pointed to as the foundations for such a view, in addition to the undeniable historical record of diversity and modification. As crucial as the sacraments and other rites and devotions are, these cannot be said to exhaust the life of the Church or of the individual Christian. Sanctification of the world, teaching, the loving service of the neighbor cannot be subordinated or neglected.

Despite the saving presence and power of God in the Church, there have always been sinful and inhuman excesses: authoritarianism, paternalism, fanaticism, mistreatment of those judged not to believe correctly, abusive mixing of political power seeking and maintenance with the sacred, misunderstanding of national character and culture for the faith. The Church and the Christian must constantly recognize these tendencies, confess and turn from them.

However, the overwhelming spirit of these commentaries is positive, constructive. All that is beautiful, creative, and good belongs to God and is part of the secret activity of Christ's grace. All of our life, all sectors of society, the economy, the government, work, our homes and families are places where the gospel can be lived. In sum, the "last times" have already begun, so too the judgment of God. The future does not blot out the present, for the Kingdom of God that is to come is also already within us, powerful and active.

Father Men and Christianity Today

In contrast to other traditions, Christianity is not simply based on a system of the views and legacies of its founder, but on the experience of a continuous living communion with him. . . . The cornerstone of the Church is faith, which is revealed in love. Without this foundation, "churchliness" (*tserkovnost'*) is dead and preserves only an outer shell, as once was the case with the teachers of the Law and the Pharisees. The Church is not only an organization or union of people of like belief; it is a miracle, a many-sided incarnation of the spirit of Christ in humankind.[45]

It would be a misunderstanding to write off Father Men as the captive of his own era, his own Russian context, even his own sources—the Optina elders and other Russian renaissance thinkers. As noted earlier, much of what he says, that which is simultaneously exhilarating to some and threatening to others, has been heard before. He is no mere recording, though, for he makes distinct contributions of his own. As we have seen, his teaching on the Church and on the Christian life is traditional but provocative, "radical" in the best sense. What he says about prayer in his Lenten-Paschal sermons, in the house conversations, and in his basic handbooks alone would be a rich subject for study.

Father Men's emergence in translation and publication at this time is providential, for his mind and voice have much to say not only to contemporary Orthodoxy but also to the entire Church. Inasmuch as he looks both at the core of the tradition and at the various understandings and forms that have developed, he is able to shed light on much of the turmoil and confusion within the churches today, in particular the conflicts between extreme perspectives appearing among Christians of both the East and the West. His meditation on the "two understandings of Christianity" is most relevant here. Insightful commentators have recognized the emergence of extremely conservative, even sectarian Orthodox tendencies in America and in Europe and the serious danger in these.[46] It is no longer issues such as the retention of Greek, Arabic, or Slavonic in the liturgy, not even just the "old" calendar versus the "new." Any contact with other "heterodox" Christians is being branded as the so-called heresy of ecumenism, based on their reading of several ancient canons. The Orthodox churches of Georgia and Bulgaria have dropped out of the WCC and a pan-Orthodox consultation in Thessalonika has advocated only limited Orthodox participation in further WCC activities, including the recent general assembly. Very noticeably and significantly, Orthodox participants are by this consultation not to attend any liturgical services at such gatherings. While particularly problematic services have marked recent WCC gatherings, this decision seems to echo the current conservative claim that to pray with any non-Orthodox Christians is to defy the canonical ban on praying with "heretics."

Sadly, the list goes on: the claim that outside Orthodoxy Christ and the Holy Spirit are not present, that there is no Church and no grace, thus no sacraments, thereby requiring the rebaptizing of all who enter Orthodoxy; the outright rejection of the Balamand Statement of the international Orthodox–Roman Catholic dialogue and of the ideas of "sister churches" or of the churches as "two lungs" of the Body as contemporary expressions of the despised "branch theory" of ecclesiology; refusal to take Ut Unum Sint of John Paul II as an authentic expression of a desire to heal the schism, and what

can only be characterized as hostility, not only toward non-Orthodox Christians, but especially toward Orthodox clergy and laity
who demonstrate openness and a desire to work for unity with them.
The burning of books in Ekaterinburg was a notorious public expression of these attitudes, as was the public abuse of Nicolas Lossky
and others in Moscow. Whether actions of "appeasement" or harassment, there have been others, those already described as well the
suspension of the best-known Russian iconographer Father Zinon
and the suppression of his monastery in Pskov, the persecution of Fr.
Ignaty Krekshin and his monastic community, both for having maintained fraternal relationships with Roman Catholics, the suspension,
reinstatement, and continued harassment of Fr. George Kochetkov
as mentioned earlier. In polemical attacks in print and on the Inter-
net, both the living—Ecumenical Patriarch Bartholomew, Metropolitan Philip of the Antiochan archdiocese, in America, retired
Archbishop Iakovos of the Greek archdiocese in America, Bishop
Kallistos in the U.K.—and the deceased—Archbishop Athenagoras
of Thayteira and Great Britain, Ecumenical Patriarchs Meletios,
Athenagoras, and Demetrius, and Moscow Patriarch Nikodim— are
accused of heresy and heretical actions.

However, the traditionalist Orthodox have no monoply on ex-
tremism. More recently the teaching document from the Sacred
Congregation for the Propagation of the Faith, *Dominus Iesus,* has
raised again the question of the position of all other churches with
respect to Rome. The claim of this document that the "one, holy
catholic and apostolic Church" inheres most fully, in fact perfectly,
in the Roman Catholic Church and everywhere else imperfectly, de-
fectively, if at all, this the pre–Vatican II ecclesiology of supremacy,
has raised much protest and debate. The conflict in the Orthodox
churches that I have described here and in other places in this book
does not exist in a vacuum, and my concern here is not just with
Christians of the Eastern Church. The lives and vision of Father Men
and the others stand over against the hardening once again of positions, the ease with which condemnations flow, no matter the source.

There are, however, other small signs of hope, of "springtime" as
Pope John XXIII called the Taizé community, of the kind of open-
ness that Father Men preached. In Russia, against formidable odds,
Karina and Andrei Chernyak, both spiritual children of Father

Men, lead the Hosanna community, an association primarily of
laypeople linked by promises of prayer and faithfulness, in a variety
of ministries, including work with young people. Yakov Krotov
observes that others closely associated with Father Men continue
in outreach work dear to his heart, the parish of Sts. Cosmas and
Damian under Father Borisov and the St. Filaret Institute under
Father Kochetkov, both deeply committed to liturgical renewal and
catechetical work, such as the Russian Children's Hospital fund.
Beyond these that are directly linked to Father Men are other communities close in spirit, some that he knew, others that have emerged,
such as the communities of Taizé and the Beatitudes in France, of San
Egidio in Italy, and monastic communities such as that at Bose in
Italy and New Skete in Cambridge, New York.

Father Men did not opt for some abstract synthesis, an overspiri-
tualized compromise of these perspectives, the one of openness and
freedom, the other of enclosure and rigor. With great discernment,
he said that each vision needs the other. There will always be a Father
Zossima and a Father Ferapont, each with something to give to the
Church. And this is precisely where his voice, itself silenced by ex-
tremism, still proves timely. His affirmation of culture and society
as God's creation and the arena for redemption and salvation ought
to be juxtaposed with the shrill condemnations of all that is weak,
sick, and sinful in our society. His unshakable faith in the Church
makes Christianity for him not closed and isolated but open, outgoing in mission to the world for the life of the world. His freedom
and openness are manifestations of the boundless capacity that Fr.
Michael Oleksa has described as Orthodoxy's gift for incarnationally and sacramentally embracing a culture, a people, and building
up, from what is already there, the gospel and Kingdom of God in
the life of the Church.[47]

CHAPTER TWELVE

Holiness in Our Time

The Church in Our Age: Stagnation, Conflicts, Recoveries

Nowadays, Christianity no longer is the active agent of history, but the spectator of events that escape its hold and run the risk of placing the Church at the margins of the world's destiny. Social and economic reforms and the liberation and emancipation of groups and classes are affected by factors of this world far removed from the church. . . . In a climate of indifference or open hostility, the Church, having lost her formal audience, can rely only on the faith of the people of God, freed from any compromise and conformity.[1]

This is how Paul Evdokimov described things at the start of the 1960s, echoing his "open letter" to the churches composed just after World War II's end.[2] The parade of events and people in the century just past is overwhelming. It was a century of wars, genocide, and revolutions. It was also a century in which walls of repression were torn down and oppressive regimes were toppled from within. Technology leaped forward, faster even than forecasters could expect. It was a century in which economies, both on the national and global scales, surged and fell, wrecking not only fortunes but also many lives.

The century was one of enormous challenge and change for the Christian faith and for the Church in the truly ecumenical sense. I mean the Church everywhere and all of the Church. The Roman Catholic Church experienced a springtime of renewal, the Second Vatican Council being the high point of a new opening attitude to the world, greatly encouraged by the pastoral activity of Popes John XXIII, Paul VI, and John Paul II.

The emergence of ecumenical consciousness, that is, a desire for unity and peace rather than division in the churches, was not one-sided. From their hostility toward Rome and suspicious distance from the East, the churches of the Reformation, particularly the Anglican, Lutheran, and Reformed, have entered official relationships with each other and with the Catholic and Orthodox churches for study, prayer, cooperative service work, and the healing of the schisms. This has developed within the arena of the WCC, now under much criticism and attack. Within the churches, by decisive actions of the bishops and theologians, there are now both international and domestic dialogues. Some of these meetings for study, prayer, and fellowship have produced closer relationships among clergy and laity of the churches. Some extraordinarily fine theological work has also been accomplished. There has been clarification of the understandings of salvation, *theōsis* or deification, justification, the sacramental nature of the Church, the creed, baptism, the Eucharist, and ordained ministry. For example, the impetus for the recent Finnish study of Luther's catholic theological roots came from years of amicable and productive dialogue between the Russian Orthodox and Finnish Lutherans.[3] Sadly, there have also been absolute rejections of any contact whatsoever with "heretics," namely, any Christians outside one's own ecclesial borders, canonical or not.[4]

In an atmosphere completely without support, in a time of religious decadence and rigid conservative opposition to any change, the Russian Orthodox Church began the process of reform and renewal in the very first decade of the twentieth century.[5] This tiny stream, accompanied by the amazingly creative thinking of those who returned from the intellectuals' alienation from the faith, those of the Russian religious renaissance, made authentic returns to the sources in a theological and church climate that could not envision the slightest change. This "springtime" culminated in the astonishing flood of ideas, some of which sparked virulent attack and rejection, others which have sedimented themselves into our self-identity as Christians in the modern era. Most of those whom we have met here were part of this renewal, either direct producers of it or profoundly shaped by it. An analogous stirring among Protestant and Catholic thinkers in the West, almost contemporaneous with that in Russia, again in locations not at all favorable to renewal, led to a thaw in the understanding of Church Tradition and practice.

It is not surprising that the return to the sources and to the Church first manifested itself liturgically, both in the East and in the West. Specifically, this was seen in the return to the Scriptures and the Fathers and in the restoration of the Eucharist as the center of Church life. There were many further developments, some common to both East and West, some specific to one or the other. One such so widespread as to be characterized as universal was the encouragement of more frequent, even weekly communion. In the renewal of service books there was also the return to the ancient *ordo* of the liturgy. In the West, the celebration was again facing the assembly. In the East, the icon screen was lowered or simplified and the doors and curtain of the same opened. The language of the people was restored instead of Latin, Greek, or Slavonic. Prayers formerly said inaudibly were now recited so that all could hear them. Much teaching and preaching accompanied this liturgical renewal. Along the way other liturgical actions in addition to the the Eucharist were affected. Baptism, marriage, and Christian burial returned from "private" forms of celebration and ways of thinking to more communal ones. Even the daily prayer of the Church, along with reading of the Scriptures, staples of not just monastic practice but universal Christian spiritual life, have made important returns.

While the Second Vatican Council of the Roman Catholic Church was not an "ecumenical" council, one for the whole of the Church, impossible because of the ongoing schisms, it nevertheless served not only also as a milestone of renewal for the Roman Catholic Church but also as a conduit for communication of this elsewhere. Despite attacks on it more recently, there can be no doubt that the World Council of Churches also served to bring Christians of the divided churches together and allowed the dissemination of their research and thinking. From the Eastern Church perspective, it is nothing short of miraculous that the work of theologians such as those we have met here was enthusiastically received by Catholics and Protestants.

The wonderful consequences of the thaw, the springtime of encounter among the churches, are varied and numerous. Just one concrete sign of the reemergence of an authentic *oikumene,* a truly catholic and universal and full Christianity is the presence now of icons in Roman Catholic basilicas, monastic chapels, and places of worship and prayer of the Reformation churches: Anglican, Lutheran, and Reformed. Another is the clear return to the ancient sacramental tradition of the Church in the *Baptism, Eucharist, Ministry* document prepared by the Faith and Order Commission of the WCC and presented at the plenary assembly in Lima in 1982. On closer view, the past several decades have witnessed many authentic gestures of renewed contact among Christians, besides the official ecumenical encounters. The less known, more quiet examples are not the healing of the schisms but nevertheless moments of reconciliation, acts of Christians behaving as if there were no division. Paul Evdokimov, who wrote much about the "mystery" of both division and union, was able to imagine, during mass at his friend Dom Celestine Charlier's chapel, the eucharistic fellowship of the undivided Church. He perceived the image of the restoration of unity in the work of the students in his hostel, Catholics, Protestants, Orthodox and others, building stone by stone, a chapel for their daily prayers. Vladimir Lossky, who wrote his dissertation on the thirteenth/ fourteenth-century Dominican preacher and mystic Meister Eckhart, regularly visited the tomb of St. Genevieve, patroness of Paris, in the church of St. Etienne-sur-Mont in his neighborhood. Thomas Merton's journals are punctuated with the names of Father Bulgakov, Evdokimov, Olivier Clément, and Vladimir Lossky and extensive notes on their writings. Father Lev preached in a Reformed congregation in London while their pastor was gone, not so different from the liturgies of the first French-speaking Orthodox parish in Paris, which met in the Lutheran Church of the Holy Trinity there. Fathers Schmemann and Meyendorff preached in the cavernous Episcopal cathedral of St. John the Divine in New York City and St. Paul's chapel at Columbia University among other Western Church locations. They frequently lectured for Protestant and Catholic groups. Both served on the faculties of schools such as Columbia, Fordham, and Union Theological Seminary.

Many are the Western Christian visitors to services in the Three Hierarchs chapel of their seminary, St. Vladimir's, in Crestwood, New York. The liturgical calendars of the Episcopal, Lutheran, Roman Catholic, and Orthodox churches in America cross-commemorate saints such as Augustine, Basil, John Chrysostom, the Gregorys, Sergius of Radonezh, Benedict of Nursia, Vladimir and Olga. It was Dorothy Day, a devout Roman Catholic, who introduced the writer Jim Forest to the beauty of liturgy in the Eastern Church. Pope Paul VI and Ecumenical Patriarch Athenagoras I embrace in the kiss of peace, pray together, exchange the gifts of the episcopal stole with each other. For almost three quarters of a century Anglicans and Orthodox meet each summer for prayer and study in the Fellowship of St. Alban and St. Sergius in the U.K. Despite no significant breakthrough and a number of difficult disagreements, Catholics and Orthodox representatives at the meeting of the international dialogue in summer 2000 prayed together and venerated the historic icon of the Mother of God of Sitka, Alaska, there since the earliest days of Russian missionary work.

As honest and sincere as these gestures are, they do not, in themselves, approach the healing of the great division. Yet they point through the centuries of separation and ignorance, toward where and how the unity of Christians will come about—in the acquisition of the Holy Spirit, in prayer that only he teaches, and in the universal vocation to service and holiness.

Rediscovering the Church and the Priesthood of the Baptized

Amid all this reform, renewal, and restoration, there is yet another rediscovery, that of the Church as the whole people of God. Integral to this, synonymous with it, is the recovery of the universal priesthood of all the baptized. Here is yet another fundamental return, to recognition of the calling of all Christians to life in Christ, to acquisition of the Holy Spirit, to holiness. Some decry this as a "Protestantizing" effect or a politicization of the Church. They condemn the appropriating of models from another part of Christianity, the churches of the Reformation, or from the larger culture and society and its political ideology. Thus any "democratizing" of the Church is perceived as a revolt against her essentially hierarchical nature or a capitulation to the dominant values of the modern age. Yet nothing could be farther from the truth. Sadly, despite the springtime and the recoveries, the Church both in the East and the West remains far from the pattern of the first centuries, most clearly a "conciliar" one, that which the Russian theologians using the Slavonic for "catholic" referred to as *sobornost'*, and what Afanasiev insisted on as a eucharistic ecclesiology and more recently others have termed *koinōnia*, or a communion ecclesiology.

Despite some critics' arguments that such a recovered understanding of the Church is too much taken up with one sacramental mode, namely, the Eucharist, and negligent of the deeper baptismal character of the community, that it unduly subordinates the position of bishops, or that in it too much emphasis is given to the local church and too little to the universal, I would suggest deeper consideration of Afanasiev's full view, that provided in the posthumously published *Church of the Holy Spirit*, still a cut-down version of the truly massive ecclesiological study he envisioned, incorporating not only New Testament and early patristic sources but also the canons and ecclesiastical history, a combination rarely brought to bear on the understanding of the Church.[6] Perhaps surprising to many, who would expect it in other theological approaches (especially those of the Lutheran heritage), the very eucharistic ecclesiology Afanasiev sought to recover from the New Testament and early Church is founded precisely on the baptismal priesthood of all the faithful. It is this fundamental, Trinitarian transformation that makes possible the very celebration of the Eucharist and preaching of the gospel, also the setting apart by laying of hands of bishops, priests, and deacons and the ministry of service to the world that is the consequence, even the fulfillment of the communion-community.

Father Afanasiev's contribution was noted in the proceedings of the Second Vatican Council and shaped the understanding of the Church and the liturgy in the two conciliar constitutions crafted there, *Lumen Gentium* and *Sacrosanctum Concilium*. Later, this eucharistic understanding of the Church would also feature importantly in the new *Catechism of the Catholic Church*. As we saw in the chapters on Fathers Schmemann and Meyendorff, both his students, Father Afanasiev's vision came to significantly shape their theological efforts. Through them, his vision achieved practical expression in the ecclesial and liturgical life of Orthodox and other Christian churches. The rediscovery of the Church as the people of God and the awareness of the universal vocation of all the baptized— these are themes that run through the writings and more so, the lives of the men and women profiled here. Another way of expressing these themes is to be found in their embodiment of the gospel. This is none other than the universal vocation to be "very similar to God," to be holy, to be saints.

Which God? The God of Love and Freedom

Already in the great Council of 1917–18 in Moscow and in a number of thinkers before, the conciliar understanding of the Church— as a community of love patterned on that of the Trinity—had emerged in the Russian context. Thinkers as widely varying as the nineteenth-century theologians Khomiakov, Bukharev, and Soloviev, and the twentieth-century figures Florensky, Berdiaev, Karsavin, and Bulgakov, to mention only several, recovered the "paradigm of love" that is the Holy Trinity, as Fr. Michael Meerson and Paul Valliere have so eloquently argued.[7] Nadia Gorodetsky and others followed these earlier figures in pointing to the "kenotic" God who empties himself for us in love, becoming our companion in suffering. To discover again what it means to be holy we must also discover again what the Church, our fundamental community, is. We must proceed further, to rediscover God himself, to see again who and what he is and does.

Some who are disturbed by the course of the Church's life through the century just past have seized on its rigidity, what Meyendorff called "dead" traditionalism. Still others have taken aim at more tragic acts of injustice committed by members of the Church. Pope John Paul II and the bishops concelebrating with him on the Sunday of Forgiveness in Lent of 2000 begged pardon for the evil and suffering inflicted on others by the sons and daughters of the Roman

Catholic Church over the centuries. Many others have indicted not only his communion but the rest of the Christian churches for inaction during the Holocaust, for allowing terrible enslavement and oppression of cultures in the name of mission and colonialism. The list of sins is extensive: racism, misogyny, alliance with the rich and powerful, favoring of the interests and outlook of the middle class, partisan feeling that has fomented hatred among ethnic groups and communities of faith, pride toward other Christian churches divided, not united, in witness to the gospel. The Catholic Church of the West has no monopoly on such a list. It will not do to insist that in her preserving of tradition, the Church of the East has avoided such sin. Neither can the churches of the Reformation, in all their zeal to renew in the gospel, escape such guilt.

Yet this hardly exhausts contemporary response. The other categorical attitude is almost an opposite view, namely, that things have become so terrible because confusion, looseness, permissive, weak, sentimental feelings have conquered in the Church. If anything, the error has been on the side of freedom and love. It not only is possible but it has in fact been the case that the Church—and here it is particular members of the clergy and laity—has allowed too much, overlooked too much, even forgiven too much, in the name of compassion. In canonical terms, *oikonōmia* has smothered *akribeia,* indulgence suffocated rigor. In Dostoyevsky's vision, Father Zossima has won and the demanding Father Ferapont is in eclipse.

The messy lives of Christians, the doctrinal, ethical, even liturgical diversity and confusion in which we exist all suffer from this excess of freedom and compassion. If continued rage and protest about the sins of the past are heard from the Left, from "radicals" and "liberals" (often given further epithetic labels), bitter indictments of the anarchy and looseness of the present Church issue from the Right, from "traditionalists," "conservatives," "integrists." There are also voices somewhere between these extremes of the spectrum, discerning minds and perceptive personalities who recognize the truth at the radical ends without its accompanying baggage of exaggeration, distortion, and plain falsity. While I regard the persons of faith we have encountered here as such, clearly others have had quite different readings. Otherwise why would their books be burned, in the case of Father Men, his life taken?

I have heard opinion voiced that in the end Father Schmemann erred on the side of freedom. I would contest the charge that such was "error." At his funeral, Father Schmemann's friend and colleague, Veselin Kesich summed him up as a man of freedom and joy. Perhaps this is the best summation of all those living icons we have reflected on here. They were filled with love for God and thus loved the world, in which they saw his imprint but which they also sought to transform into his Kingdom. All of the Christians of the Eastern Church we have examined here are similarly guilty of this characterization. If freedom and joy were their sins, then in St. Augustine's words, they sinned boldly, because of God's limitless love. In addition to the recent book burning, all paid for their freedom, their joyous creativity, their loving openness in ways large and small throughout their lives. Many were tagged with labels such as "heretic," "innovator," "apostate," "ecumenist," "Protestant," even "Catholic" (as if these were epithets), and such scorn came almost exclusively from within the Orthodox milieu, that is, from those with whom they were in communion. Though the treasures of the Eastern Church, one seldom hears of their names, their lives, or their work. Yet I am not aware of one who, in all of this, lost the joy, peace, and love that are the gifts of the Holy Spirit's presence and the "signs of the Kingdom." From Father Bulgakov at the beginning of the century down to Father Men toward the end, all had much to say and to give to our time.

As we have seen, these persons of faith contributed a great deal to liturgical renewal in the churches, to the struggle of the divided churches to understand and approach unity again in the ecumenical movement, to better understand the tradition of the Church: the Scriptures, the Fathers, the icons. Some were by training and position scholars and teachers in the church, advisers to synods of bishops and individual hierarchs. Through teaching in theological school they helped to shape suceeding generations of clergy and laity. They not only wrote articles for scholarly journals and books, but contributed regularly to publications read by a broad range of church members. They consistently accepted invitations to give talks in parishes and conduct conferences and retreats for all sorts of groups. However, this has not been a primer in academic Eastern Church theology or history. Still others among our persons of faith, such as

Father Gregory and Mother Maria, were not primarily educators or writers. All of these men and women, though, witnessed to the beauty of the Kingdom of God in their personalities, in their dealings with their neighbors, whether fellow Orthodox Christians or not. In different ways they urged us to put into practice what we confess in the creed and in every celebration of the Eucharist. They themselves did not write or lecture about but *lived out the gospel.*

Mother Maria expressed the gospel way most eloquently in her essays but even more powerfully in her love for the poor, the suffering, for all discarded by society. One could criticize the details of her person and life—her hats, the cast-off shoes and food-stained habit she wore, her continued love of Gauloises, smoking usually seen as incompatible with monastic asceticism, her unquenchable passion for debate and discussion with fellow intellectuals and artists. Some found her extremely passionate personality, often given to outbursts of indignation, frustration, and compassion, disturbing to their sense of civility and monastic propriety. Even her admirers were often embarrassed by her eccentricities. But her bishop, Metropolitan Evlogy, and her spiritual father, Sergius Bulgakov, and friends such as the literary scholar Mochulsky and the philosopher Berdiaev understood her and recognized the fire within her. For all her idiosyncrasies she was a living icon of the gospel, not just in the poetry and provocative essays she somehow wrote in a frantic life, but even more vividly in the bags of produce she hauled from the markets at Les Halles, in the pots of soup she made for the cafeteria of her hostel at Rue Lourmel, in her evening hours at bistros, listening over a glass of cheap wine to people's miseries. Her fire and her love were also stitched into the beautiful embroidered tapestries, vestments, and icons she made for her chapel. In all of these activities, she was her own person, an individual, from the cigarettes to the temper to the tears. Even today, more than a half century after her death, the mention of Mother Maria's name evokes strong reactions. Several I interviewed who knew her could not resist acidic comments despite their affection and admiration for her. Yet like the woman in the gospel story who though a sinner was bold enough to anoint and dry Christ's feet, drying them with her hair, kissing them—outrageous actions, a scandal—her glory was not her personal eccentricities or failings but her "great love" (Luke 7:47).

Father Lev Gillet, who regularly accompanied Mother Maria on the nighttime pastoral visits to the bistros, likewise preached and taught, conducted many retreats, and wrote exceedingly lucid meditations on the Bible. Yet his personal counsel, his compassion, even his own difficult personality traits and struggles shine more brightly as the path of one seeking the Kingdom and radiating it. He clung to Christ despite his sensitivity, his tendency to bitterness, depression, and self-pity. Like so many others we have met here, Father Lev was deeply hurt by many of his superiors, the leaders of the church. He was scandalized by the lethargy, the indifference, the terrible smallness of so many clergy to those genuinely searching for an ecclesial home. As he was able to overcome the handicaps of his own personality, he came to learn how to overlook the cruelty and failings of others, those who sought him out and even his fellow clerics. More than anything else he wrote, his "dialogues" with "limitless Love," with the Savior, reveal the directness of his own communion with God and how he grew and changed by relationship with the Lord. Here was the source of his openness and accessibility to so many different people all across Europe and the Near East.

Father Schmemann, who is remembered with great love for his wit and discernment, for his priestly work and not only for his theological scholarship and administration, described very powerfully the personal images he kept as precious souvenirs of Father Sergius Bulgakov. Although he saw little of use in the latter's theological "system" and obsession with the figure of Sophia, Father Schmemann nonetheless saw in Father Bulgakov a flame burning in a very dark time, full of love for God and for his neighbors. He vividly evokes Father Bulgakov's face, radiant with joy at the Holy Week services in the chapel of St. Sergius Institute, incandescent as he celebrated his regular early morning liturgies there in his last years. Father Bulgakov titled one of his early efforts to descibe his journey back to the faith *Unfading Light,* evoking the Vesper hymn in the Eastern Church, "O Gladsome Light." He saw Christ, the light of the world, even in the terrible grief of his little son's death, and later in the terrors of forced migration, separation from family, and the constant press of sickness and extreme poverty. Father Bulgakov saw Christ the light and received that light, became that light, radiated it at the altar, in confession, even on his deathbed. For all the thousands of pages he produced, still to be discovered and appreciated, it is more Father Bulgakov's light that endures—his luminous prayer, his priestly ministry, his gifts as counselor, his maintaining peace even with his most vociferous critics. It says much about Father Schmemann that toward the end of his life he had deepened in his appreciation of his teacher, Father Bulgakov. Though he expressed reservations about Father Bulgakov's writings many times in print, Father Schmemann confided to a colleague of mine that no one had transformed and shaped him more profoundly.

Everyday yet poignant are the images of many of these remarkable people, preserved by their friends. Elisabeth Behr-Sigel remembers Paul Evdokimov as the young father, bathing and feeding his small children, cooking and delighting in household chores while his wife taught school. Friends of Evdokimov recall how his work in restaurant kitchens many years earlier, as a poor, recent immigrant to Paris, made him a master chef, whose invitation to dinner was a singular treat. What a wonderful turn of things, a theologian who not only prays but cooks and delights in feeding people! Evdokimov touched the lives of dozens who lived in the hostels he administered. Thirty years later, reading the reminiscences and tributes of those who were his charges or his colleagues is moving, whether a noted Catholic theologian or a simple African pastor.

Father Schmemann is still remembered by a former student, his eyes twinkling as he sat down to a thick steak and a good bottle of wine, completely enjoying Saturday evening gatherings of family and friends for a drink and hors d'oeuvres after vespers in the summer colony at Labelle, Quebec. Now that selections from his journal have been published, a far more complex personality is revealed. One can read of his doubts about the institutional structures of the Church, his painful awareness of his own human weakness as well as that of others charged with the leadership of the people of God. Some will be offended by his discernment that the Eastern Church bears the peculiar weakness of obsession with its tradition and the beauty of worship, so much so that in the midst of these God, his love, and freedom are forgotten. Even in a limited selection of passages it is striking, the transformative journey of this soul in the last decade of his life.

The ebullient laughter of Father Men, his rich voice singing with his guitar accompaniment, are captured in video- and audiotapes. One can also watch his efforts at maintaining order in the baptism and chrismation of over a dozen adults in his parish church: "Hmm, did I anoint you yet?. . . Now, let's not forget to come back to church next Sunday, even though it's not a feast!" Listening to tapes of the house conversations Father Men conducted, one also hears, in addition to his lively presentations, babies crying, teaspoons tinkling against cups, plates crashing to the floor, Christ being preached amid sandwiches and tea. I myself recall how distracted Father Meyendorff could be in the midst of a lecture, when the words, in several languages he was using, would come faster to his head than to his mouth, the results often unintended comedy. I remember his decision, at the end of a long liturgy and blessing of the stream at St. Vladimir's Seminary on Epiphany, with seminarians' children restlessly bouncing on the chapel floor, to preach a sermon—of one sentence.

Father Gregory is remembered, in exquisite detail, by his monastic colleague, Father Barsanuphius, even to the mélange of odors that filled his skete with "une atmosphère spécifique," a most unusual atmosphere, given Father Gregory's use of garlic, vinegar, rancid linseed oil, ammonia, decomposed egg whites and greatly fermented casein, "cheese," as he called it, in the making of his icons. Elisabeth Osoline, herself a gifted iconographer, has fixed in her memory his round face, wreathed with his long hair, shining in a smile. Remembering him, more than forty years ago, her face too breaks spontaneously into a smile. Having stood before his icons in the Three Saints Church in Rue Petel in Paris, in the chapel of the Holy Spirit in the old Berdiaev house in Clamart, and in the church of St. Seraphim in Montgeron, I felt the strength of his presence and his theological and iconographic convictions. I could hear his arguments that the hands of Christ should be that big for the children to see, that the Mother of God be there in the Pentecost icon, his loud debate with Fr. Euthymius Wendt about how Divine Wisdom should be portrayed on the walls of the church the latter had designed in Moisenay. I have also seen how deeply the presence of such a living icon as Father Gregory can be felt by someone who, like me, never met him. I was visiting a priest friend in his small Orthodox church nearby

filled with the icons of Fr. Andrew Tregubov, who not only has preserved Father Gregory's icons in photography but written and lectured about them. Not surprisingly, Father Gregory's spirit and style
have shaped Father Tregubov's own gifted painting of icons over the
years. As these very "Krugian" icons were shown to me, I began to
tell the pastor of the church about the life of Father Gregory, much
as I have related it here—about his eccentric, often difficult personality, his nervous breakdown and hospitalization, his sharing of the
food his sister brought with his fellow inmates, helping them to
survive the near starvation imposed by the occupying Nazis, his
gradual recovery with the help of his spiritual father, his monastic
profession and quiet years of icon painting at his skete in Mesnil–
St. Denis. My friend, the pastor of the church, stopped me, choked
up and with tears in his eyes, feeling very intensely the presence of
this iconographer-monk he had never met. Not long before he had
visited the monastery and tomb of St. Nectarios of Aegina in Greece
and had very powerfully felt his presence among the sisters of that
convent and in an icon of him painted by one of his parishioners.
Looking at the icons of Father Tregubov and hearing about Fr. Gregory Krug, he felt again the same living presence of a holy person and
communion with him. This is what I wanted to re-create here in this
book, a true sense of communion, the communion of saints that we
are given in the Church.

Moreover, I wanted to convey precisely how the full, authentic
humanity of these men and women conveyed the God they loved
and served. Like the Virgin Mary, Theotokos, they "gave birth to
God the Word," not only spiritually, but in the very material reality
of their own words and actions. What these living icons (as I have
dared to call them), these persons of faith, reveal to us as images and
likenesses ("very similar") is the God they revered and with whom
they conversed, lived, and worked. Which God, we might ask, for
not only on the Areopagus, but in Paris, New York, Moscow, or
Montreal we could arguably detect many gods, not just simply the
pseudogods and idols of our culture. Years ago, J. B. Phillips wrote
a challenging essay, "Your God Is Too Small." Are these men and
women saying the same?

Their God is there, all through the Scriptures: the one who wants
to share his life and beauty in Paradise, the one who hears the groans

and sees the misery of his people in their captivity in Egypt. He is the inextinguishable "burning bush," of whom Father Lev was so fond, "Lord Love," "Limitless Love," who reaches out in every face, in all the corners of our days and nights. This God promises himself to his people in a marriage covenant several times: with Noah, with Abraham, on Sinai with Moses, in the Red Sea drowning Pharaoh. Like Hosea, he is the faithful spouse who pursues his faithless beloved, who takes her back, loves her always and again. He is the shepherd looking for the one lost sheep of the flock of a hundred, the Lover who mounts the cross as though it were the marriage bed, emptying himself in suffering for us, sharing our suffering, an absurdly foolish "Lover of humankind." (So the liturgy of the Eastern Church names him, repeatedly.) "And when I am lifted up from the earth, will draw all to myself" (John 12:32). The arms of Christ remain stretched out on the cross, open in love to all.

Those who have charted the threads of the Russian spiritual heritage, despite the different finds they unearth, agree on the centrality of the God who suffers, the kenotic Christ, and, following him, all sorts of holy people who embody this suffering love. Father Michel Evdokimov provides especially striking examples of the incarnation of holiness in his studies of Russian spirituality.[8] There are the innocents, Boris and Gleb, who accept assassination rather than plunge their people into deeper strife, thus becoming "passion bearers." There are "holy fools" who do not suffer violence but whose lives challenge and ridicule tsar and patriarch, monastic and merchant, dramatically making of themselves the gospel's inversion of all values and ways of living. Freaks, clairvoyants, homeless vagrants, village idiots, sometimes closer to quiet nobodies, they nevertheless are witnesses to another life, that of the Kingdom of God. Yet the parade of saints, known and unknown, is hardly restricted to Holy Russia. We find them everywhere the Spirit is. There are monastics and bishops, wives and widows, ordinary civil servants and professionals, parents and peasants. In our time they include the desert hermit Charles de Foucauld, the Yupik priest's wife and healer Olga Arsamquq Michael, the journalist and radical social activist Dorothy Day, the writer Flannery O'Connor, the author and monk Thomas Merton, and the lover of paradoxes Simone Weil, as well as an innumerable multitude whose names we do not know. Yet all of them are lights burning brightly, people who have, in St. Seraphim's words, acquired the Spirit and who transformed many around them.

The Lord Jesus, in the gospel, tells us that we all keep our treasures in our hearts. "What you live for," Martin Luther said, "that is your god." The men and women we have encountered here indeed show us their God. For some he will be too mushy and compassionate, too permissive and disorderly. Much like Christ before the Grand Inquisitor in Dostoyevsky, such a God is not good for religion. His "absurd love" is really the undoing of good ecclesiastical order. Freedom is always a threat to someone's sense of law and order, even God's freedom. How often it appears that we judge ourselves better than he in keeping his commandments, administering his justice, adhering to his rites and rules.

To be sure, there is a complex relationship in the economy of salvation, the most delicate of dialectics in the drama of God's creation, humankind's fall, God's seeking to save us. Those who push the limits of classical theology believe in the "restoration of all" in God, the *apokatastasis*.[9] God is just, but he is also infinite compassion. His deepest desire is that we be one with him again, "very similar" to him, holy. There can be, however, no eliminations here. Father Schmemann kept the elements together elegantly in his triad of creation, fall, and redemption. Discard or underemphasize the fall, the reality of evil and death having invaded and now inhabiting human nature and the world, and what is left is the empty "religion" ruthlessly rejected from Luther and Kierkegaard to Niehbuhr and Bonhoeffer. In such a vision, there is no need for the cross, for the suffering and death of the Son of God, for ultimately all is and remains good. Only forces external to us, institutionalized means are guilty of evil. Familiar, this overly optimistic view, so routine that of our culture of "niceness." However, it is as bad if not worse when evil so dominates the picture that the essential goodness of creation, its "likeness" to God, fades. How pervasive this vision is throughout the history of religious traditions, particularly that of Christianity. It remains powerful in our time, and no Christian community is immune. In the extreme, such a perspective demands flight from the world and the imputation of much that is human to the domination of evil. Creation being so profoundly fallen, the leading image of God must be that of both judge and executioner. The whole saving action of Christ, from Incarnation to the Ascension, becomes an effort in divine futility.

For all the "world rejection" in the Scriptures, the Fathers, the liturgy, and the spiritual literature of the Church, the heart of the gospel still remains. God's love is so relentless and unreasonable that, though rejected, he yet must suffer and die for the life of the world. "The Father is crucifying Love, the Son is crucified Love, the Holy Spirit is the invincible Love of the cross," so runs the often quoted doxology of the greatest Russian preacher of the nineteenth century, St. Filaret, metropolitan of Moscow. And there is the figure dear to Alexander Bukharev and Evdokimov, of the Lover-Christ, who stands at the door of our hearts, as a beggar: "Behold, I stand at the door and knock; if anyone hears my voice and opens the door, I will come in to him and eat with him, and he with me" (Rev. 3:20).[10] This suffering God wants to break and share the bread of our suffering. He is the Lamb being sacrificed from the beginning of the world, to save us. He is the God of the living, not the dead, who wants us to choose life, to turn from our own ways and live, to forgive as he does, seventy times seven—"limitless Love." In death, he lets a thief into paradise, as a priest friend of mine preaches, without baptism or conversion, without confession or fasting or any other religious actions, just the cry, "Lord, remember me in your kingdom." This is the Father who forgives and forgets all the waste, all the destruction of his prodigal child, who spares no expense in the feast of that wanderer's homecoming, thus incurring the hatred of his stay-at-home "good boy," the one who kept all the rules and rituals.

It is no wonder that in the realm of religiosity, such a God has enemies, the greatest being his special officials and most devoted, meticulous followers, who, like the "good boy" of the parable, require justice, yes, but only on their terms. The constant temptation for us is to want to draw the line that separates those on the Lord's right hand at the final judgment from those on his left, the sheep from the goats, the blessed from the damned. But, as Father Bulgakov perceptively observed, this line is really only in one place: right down the center of our hearts! Again, as we read the pages of the Gospels, as we look at the icons, we see not only the saints, the holy people before us. We also see there, reflected by them in fact, ourselves as saints in the making.

Hidden Holiness, for All

In his exquisite study of the vocation of marriage, Paul Evdokimov writes of the "new holiness" of our time.

> It appears that a new spirituality is dawning. It aspires not to leave the world to evil, but to let the spiritual element in the creature come forth. A person who loves and is totally detached, naked to the touch of the eternal, escapes the contrived conflict between the spiritual and the material. His love of God is humanized and becomes love for all creatures in God. "Everything is grace," Bernanos wrote, because God has descended into the human and carried it away to the abyss of the Trinity. The types of traditional holiness are characterized by the heroic style of the desert, the monastery. By taking a certain distance from the world, this holiness is stretched toward heaven, vertically, like the spire of a cathedral. Nowadays, the axis of holiness has moved, drawing nearer to the world. In all its appearances, its type is less striking, its achievement is hidden from the eyes of the world, but it is the result of a struggle that is no less real. Being faithful to the call of the Lord, in the conditions of this world, makes grace penetrate to its very root, where human life is lived.[11]

Despite what we may think in this age of popular "spirituality," the path of holiness leads not just from the individual to God but through the Church and the world of the brother and sister around us. If the figures we have come close to in this book converge in their understanding of a God who is love, in a faith best characterized by freedom, they also put these into practice with respect to the neighbor at hand and the life in which they find themselves. In his collection of selections translated from Father Bulgakov's writings, Rowan Williams makes a helpful point about the life of holiness in the world of our time. In his contribution to the important collection, *Vekhi*, Williams notes, Father Bulgakov chose to write about "heroism and the Spiritual Struggle," this after his own political service as a deputy in the Second Duma in 1907, an experience of the worst in political disorder. After his immersion in theoretical Marxism and a firsthand political encounter with the hardness of the human heart, Father

Bulgakov came to very practical terms with the heroism of great efforts, noble ideals, and soaring goals for society.

> It is as if Bulgakov is suggesting that the sober virtues of citizenship will always depend upon a kind of secret discipline of humility and self-abnegation as demanding as the obedience of the monk: the apparently dull surface of the good citizen or the good administrator conceals a spiritual drama no less intense than that of the radical hero, but one that is more authentic, since it is not performed for an audience and is directed not to self-fulfillment but to the inseparable goals of holiness and the social good. The "hero" of Bulgakov's critique of heroism is a figure intriguingly close to the Lutheran paradoxes of Kierkegaard or even Bonhoeffer on the hiddenness and anonymity of holiness in the modern context.[12]

Here we come to some of the most important conclusions of this book. It is not for us to try to emulate the people of faith we have encountered by wishing for their gifts and sufferings, their lives and places in the world. We learn from them and profoundly regret their absence, for their deaths and, moreover, the ignoring or rejection of their lives and teachings leaves a great void in the life of the Church. But we would have very much missed what they tried to convey to us if it ended there, with only regret or admiration, at a distance. Evdokimov perhaps says it best. He argues that the charisms or gifts of the spiritual life, so dramatically enacted by the martyrs and then by the fathers and mothers of the desert and the monastic tradition, are given to *all* Christians. There is no oligarchy even if there is a hierarchy in the Church. Each person who is baptized into the death and resurrection of the Lord and sealed with the anointing of the Spirit is "Christified." It is from this that we in English popularly refer to the sacramental initiation as "christening," recalling Tertullian's line, "A Christian is made, not born."

Every Christian receives the vocation of prophet, priest, and king. Whether archbishop or factory worker, elder or small child, scholar or uneducated peasant, each Christian is before all else a new being, transformed in Christ. St. Augustine admitted that when most threatened in his office as bishop, his membership in the holy people of

God gave him strength. Contrary to the popular notion, it is not just the clergy and monastics who have vocations.

> Each layperson participates in the unique priesthood of Christ by his sanctified being. . . . [E]very baptized person is sealed with the gifts, anointed by the Holy Spirit in his very essence [and] is the priest of his own existence, offering in sacrifice the whole of his life and existence. . . . This is the consecration of one's whole life to the ministry of the laity, a ministry that is essentially ecclesial, of the Church. . . . The eschatological emphasis of the prayer [of tonsure] reinforces this meaning: "May he/she give glory and have all the days of his/her life the vision of the joys of Jerusalem." Thus every instant of time is directed to the eschatological dimension. Every act and word is in the service of the King. In the rite of tonsure, every baptized person is a monk of interiorized monasticism, subject to all the requirements of the Gospel. . . . In addition to those commissioned as missionaries by the Church, every baptized and confirmed person is an "apostolic being," each in his or her own way. It is by my whole being and life, that I am called to give constant witness. . . . The laity forms an ecclesial dimension that is, at one and the same time, of the world and of the Church. . . . By the simple presence in the world of "sanctified beings," of "priests" in their very substance, of "dwelling places of the Trinity," the universal priesthood of the laity bears the power of the sacred in the world, celebrating the liturgy of the entire cosmos therein. Beyond the church walls, lay people continue the liturgy of the Church. By their active presence, they introduce into society and all human relationships the truth of the dogmas they live, thus dislodging the evil and profane elements of the world. . . . Here is a magnificent definition[,] . . . by one's whole being, by one's whole existence, to become a living theology— theophanic—the luminous place of the presence of the *Parousia,* God's coming again.[13]

Evdokimov concludes his powerful argument with the magnificent passage already quoted in the chapter on him. It is worth recalling here. Every Christian is a person freed by the faith from all the fears of our age and of all time. If we are freed from the ultimate fear, that of death, we are unshackled from every other fear, even those imposed by the rules and rituals of "religion." The faith of such a Christian, Evdokimov asserts, "is always a way of loving the world, a way of following the Lord even into hell." For all the good that God created in us and in the world, there is much that we have done to distort ourselves and it, in other words to make of what was paradise hell. Thus it is that for every age, the gospel, as it appears in the life of each Christian is "messianic, revolutionary, explosive."[14]

> In the domain of Caesar, we are ordered to seek and therefore to find what is not found there—the Kingdom of God. This command signifies that we must transform the world, change it into the icon of the Kingdom. To change the world means to pass from what the world does not yet possess—for this reason it is still this world—to that in which it is transfigured, thus becoming something else—the Kingdom.[15]

Evdokimov lays image upon image to create a fresco that is alive with the dynamic vision of God, burning, shining in the lives of his sons and daughters.[16] By their love, through them, he will change and save the world. One immediately may think here of great saints like Seraphim and Francis of Assisi, of the remarkable persons we have encountered, and of others. But Evdokimov, himself one of these, is not speaking of an elite but of us all. There are already enough persons of faith for me to easily fill another volume. I have not included here any persons of faith still living. Elisabeth Behr-Sigel at ninety-five is an extraordinary living link to many we have encountered here, a woman of great discernment and witness, still active as a theologian and great-grandmother. Metropolitan Anthony Bloom at eighty-six continues to regularly preach in London, his many lectures and books on prayer still valuable. Fr. Roman Braga, though retired, still resides at the Dormition monastery in Rives Junction, Michigan, a treasure trove of wisdom, much rooted in his personal experience of persecution in Romania. Also retired is Fr. Laurence Mancuso, founder of the New Skete communities, a remarkable renewer of liturgical and monastic life. Fr. Boris Bobrinskoy heads the St. Sergius Institute and a parish in Paris. Fr. Michel Evdokimov, emeritus professor of the university at Poitiers, continues to edit

Service Orthodoxe de Presse, to translate Russian theology, and to lecture on the Christian life in our time. Sophie Koloumzine, who died in fall 2000 at ninety-six, was also such a relatively "hidden" treasure. Very well known within Orthodox circles but not so well recognized beyond them, here was a woman whose life was full of accomplishments. She became early on a bridge between the Russian Orthodox émigré community and the West, even coming to study at the Union Theological Seminary in the late 1920s.[17] From the beginning she was involved with Mother Maria and many others profiled here in the growth of the Russian Christian Students Movement. She raised a family, somehow survived the Nazi occupation and World War II. She emigrated to the United States and became the "mother" of Christian education in the Orthodox Church; many of the materials she produced are still in use. She translated many books for use in Russia. But beyond all of these remarkable achievements, she made every person she encountered feel welcome, listened to, even loved. Sophie has that quality of radiating the Kingdom of God without having to say one thing theological or religious. The list of persons of faith, of remarkable witnesses, is daunting in its length.

A priest friend who has followed this book project has wisely observed that it would be good if such a collection of profiles could also include men and women whose lives were even more ordinary and hidden and less known. In fact, every one of them, to a greater or lesser extent, was a public person in the life of the church, even if relatively unknown to many Christians both of the West and of the East today. His suggestion is, of course, quite appropriate. Yet it is also very difficult to accomplish, for it would require another entire book to tell the stories of the hidden saints in our communities. And then the list would be virtually endless. We would have to include those whom I have known as well as the persons of faith known to every other reader of these pages.

However, the issue of holiness, even "hidden holiness," is not just about other people. There remains one last corner into which to look, and that is ourselves. Father Schmemann spoke of the "paradise of the moment," that portion of the Kingdom God gives to us all of the time, both as a gift to delight in and as a challenge to transform.

One of Osip Mandelshtam's poems, devoted to the eucharistic liturgy, the main service of Christian worship, includes this wonderful verse: "Take into your hands the whole world, as if it were a simple apple . . ." In an apple, and in everything within the world, faith sees, recognizes, and accepts God's gift, filled with love, beauty and wisdom. Faith hears the apple and the world speaking of that boundless love that created the world and life and gave them to us as our life. The world itself is the fruit of God's love for humanity, and only through the world can human beings recognize God and love him in return. . . . And only in truly loving his own life, can a person thereby accept the life of the world as God's gift. Our fall, our sin, is that we take everything for granted—and therefore everything, including ourselves, becomes routine, depressing, empty. The apple becomes just an apple. Bread is just bread. A human being is just a human being. We know their weight, their appearance, their activities, we know everything about them, but we no longer know them, because we do not see the light that shines through them. The eternal task of faith and of the Church is to overcome this sinful, monotonous habituation; to enable us to see once again what we have forgotten how to see; to feel what we no longer feel; to experience what we are no longer capable of experiencing. Thus, the priest blesses bread and wine, lifting them up to heaven, but faith sees the bread of life, it sees sacrifice and gift, it sees communion with life eternal.[18]

Father Schmemann wanted to emphasize the connection of liturgy to life and of the Kingdom of God to this world and our life in it. We are not directed to holiness through mystical visions, though perhaps a few enjoy these. We are not guided to sanctity principally through performance of intricate rituals, though it is both a most human and divine reality that we celebrate feasts in the church year. Despite the literature on saints of the past, there is no warrant for following extreme, unusual formulas of behavior—ascetic, miraculous, or otherwise—to attain to God. The bridge, the path to God is solely through *this* family, *these* friends and neighbors around me, through *this* education and work, through *this* parish and pastor, through *this* mix of body and mind and soul that I am.

This is not a recipe for apathy. Neither is it a condemnation of the status quo. There is a pathology peculiar to the Eastern Church, so richly blessed with the ancient forms of the Church's tradition, and that is to believe that "nothing can change," that what is, is the best. But enter the New Testament or the liturgy even briefly and it becomes clear that such is at best a half truth and at worst a grave distortion. All of our life in Christ is filled with the movement of the Holy Spirit. Our existence is pilgrimage, ever toward the Kingdom. This is the "eschatological maximalism" that Evdokimov saw in the first desert fathers and mothers, handed on down to the monastics and to all of us Christians. It is the luminous face of St. Seraphim that Motovilov saw, the radiance that Father Schmemann recognized in the face of Father Bulgakov during liturgy and Sister Joanna saw on his deathbed, that others saw in the faces of Paul Evdokimov, Father Lev, Mother Maria, and Father Men.

In the saints, and here we must also say, *in ourselves,* there is an urgency for the gospel's turning everything inside out and upside down: *metanoia.* The cry of all the Church is *"Maranatha.* Amen. Come, Lord Jesus." Christ came once. He will come again. But he is also coming to us at every moment. Mother Maria is quite correct in maintaining that we, the Church, are left on earth, but *with Christ,* to be the yeast that raises the dough, the salt that heals and preserves, the light that should not be hidden under a basket.

Yet our lives are "hidden with Christ, in God." Very few of us have any public significance. Celebrities are, by definition, rare among us. In Evdokimov's phrase, each of us is given an "interiorized monasticism," whether married or single, clergy or laity. Each of us is called to be an "apostolic person," an "ecclesial soul," a "liturgical being." Our life is equipped with the same basic tools and essentials, the Scriptures, the sacraments, prayer. But we are not just to recite prayers, attend services, and participate in Bible studies. We are to "become prayer, prayer incarnate."

There is no state in life, no occupation, no human activity that does not bear within numerous possibilities for holiness. All of the people we have examined here witness to this, some more explicitly than others. Sadly, we have become accustomed to thinking of religion in stereotypic terms: heroic humanitarian deeds, insightful theological productions, large and wealthy parishes, financially secure divisions within church bodies, successful effort in capital development for institutions operated by the churches. Yet in the radical view of the gospel even none of these is to be rejected as too crass or corporate or corrupted. The tax collectors and prostitutes take the Kingdom by force. There are innumerable points of contact with the Kingdom, many possibilities for acquiring the Holy Spirit, for doing the work of the gospel every day, no matter who we are, no matter our work, our class status, even our place in the Church. If anything, we have to learn that *all of our daily life is liturgy,* Mother Maria's "liturgy outside the church building," St. John Chrysostom's "liturgy after the liturgy." There is a sacrifice of praise and thanksgiving in all we say and do. There is a "paradise of the moment," quite contrary to our tendency to view ourselves as either "on" or "off" religious duty.

The desert fathers and mothers used to teach that if you wanted to see God, you only had to look in front of or next to yourself, at the neighbor, the brother or sister immediately there. "When you see your neighbor, you have seen your God." We know quite well that we cannot love the God we cannot see if we do not love the brother whom we can see (1 John 4:20). But turn the perspective around. Each of us is made to be an image and likeness of the Lord. Baptism, anointing, and especially the Eucharist fill us with Christ, the Spirit and the Father. Each of us then "becomes God" to others, God seeing, hearing, forgiving through our eyes, ears, and hearts. Again, Evdokimov puts it in a surprising way.

> The Gospel of John brings a saying of Christ that is perhaps the most serious one addressed to the Church: "He who receives anyone whom I send receives me and the one who receives me receives him who sent me" (John 13:20). If the world, mankind, the person in front of me, receives a member of the Church, one of us, he is already inside the gradual movement of communion, he is no longer outside the holy circle of the Trinity's communion, of the Father's blessing. The world's destiny depends on the Church's resourcefulness, on the Church's skill in making herself welcome. Hell does not depend on God's anger. It depends perhaps on the

cosmic love of the saints: "To see the Lord in one's brother," "to always feel oneself hanging on the cross," "not to cease adding fire to fire, until death."[19]

Like those we have met here, we too are called to be living icons of God in our lives. A contemporary prayer from the Western Church says it most eloquently:

Lord God, you have surrounded us with so great a cloud of witnesses. Grant that we, encouraged by the example of your servants may persevere in the course that is set before us, to be living signs of the Gospel and at last, with all the saints, to share in your eternal joy.[20]

AFTERWORD

Reaching the end of the final chapter, I laid down *Living Icons* with this as my dominant impression: How vivid and diverse are the personalities of the men and women described in this work! How wide-ranging the variety among the "persons of faith" within the twentieth-century Orthodox Church! It is not sanctity, I said to myself, but evil that is dull and repetitive. As Father Michael Plekon convincingly indicates, holiness does not have merely a single voice or an identical face.

The truth of this is all the more evident when we reflect that, as Fr. Michael Plekon himself observes, there are many others whom he could also have included. But, rather than turn his book into a catalogue of names and dates, he has wisely restricted himself to no more than ten representative figures. All except one of these were Russians; and apart from the first, St. Seraphim of Sarov, all of them were deeply influenced by the "Russian religious renaissance," as it is commonly termed, which animated the church in the early years of the last century.

Father Michael would, I am sure, be the first to acknowledge that he could easily have chosen an altogether different gallery of "living icons." He could, for example, have placed much greater emphasis upon the so-called Neopatristic tendency within the Russian emigration. The names of its leading spokesmen, Archpriest Georges Florovsky and the layman Vladimir Lossky, do indeed appear from time to time in this book, but each could have formed the subject of an entire chapter. More could also have been said about the contribution made to this Neopatristic current by two theologians who do figure in the book, Fr. Alexander Schmemann and Fr. John Meyendorff: the first with his research on the early liturgy, the second with his studies on patristic Christology and fourteenth-century Hesychasm.

It would likewise have been possible to include, among the "persons of faith" in twentieth-century Russian Orthodoxy, such representatives of the ascetic and monastic tradition as St. Silouan of Mount Athos and his disciple Archimandrite Sophrony (Sakharov). In this connection much might have been said about the influence of *The Philokalia* and the Jesus Prayer, not only within the Russian Church but throughout the Orthodox world and far beyond. This surely constitutes one of the most constructive elements in the witness of contemporary Orthodoxy. And, passing outside the Russian world, there are Archpriest Dumitru Staniloae and Elder Cleopas in Romania, Panagiotis Nellas and Protopresbyter John Romanides in Greece, and Philip Sherrard in the West (I limit myself, as Fr. Michael does, to those already dead).

All of this is said, not in criticism of Fr. Michael—far from it!—but simply to indicate that what he presents to us in this deeply impressive account is but a small part of the total picture.

A small part, yes, but also a crucially important part. The witness of these ten "persons of faith" is especially timely at this present moment, when there is a tendency in many circles to narrow and harden the meaning of Orthodoxy. These ten, in their different ways, were all opposed to harsh negativity and rigorism. All of them believed in the freedom of the Spirit. All of them upheld an Orthodoxy that is generous, kenotic, and compassionate. They saw the Eucharist not in defensive or exclusivist terms, but as a way of "churching" the universe. Loyal to tradition—although not afraid of controversy—at the same time they sought a dialogue with the world, with non-Orthodox Christians, with unbelievers, with the philosophy and culture of their time. Fr. Michael has placed us greatly in his debt by reminding us of their creative vision. Now, more than ever, we need their openness, their imaginative courage, their eagerness to explore.

Bishop Kallistos of Diokleia

NOTES

ONE.   Finding "Living Icons"

1. See Robert Royal, *Catholic Martyrs of the Twentieth Century* (New York: Crossroad, 2000); Susan Bergman, ed., *Martyrs* (Maryknoll, NY: Orbis, 1996).

2. Robert Ellsberg, *All Saints: Daily Reflections on Saints, Prophets and Witnesses for Our Time* (New York: Crossroad, 1997). Also see Elisabeth A. Johnson, *Friends of God* (New York: Crossroad, 1999).

3. For profiles of some of these, see George A. Gray and Jan V. Bear, *Profiles of American Saints*, (Los Angeles: OCA Diocese of the West, 1998); Mark Stokoe and Leonid Kishkovsky, *Orthodox Christians in North America, 1794–1994* (Wayne, NJ: Orthodox Christian Publications Center, 1995); and Constance Tarasar and John Erickson, eds., *Orthodox America, 1794–1976*, (Syosset, NY: OCA Department of History and Archives, 1975).

4. Elisabeth Behr-Sigel, "La création de la première paroisse Orthodoxe de langue française," *Service Orthodoxe de Presse [SOP]* supplément no. 237, April 1999, a presentation given at St. Sergius Theological Institute, February 28, 1999, 3.

5. Elisabeth Behr-Sigel, *The Place of the Heart: An Introduction to Orthodox Spirituality,* trans. Steven Bigham (Crestwood, NY: Oakwood/SVSP, 1992).

6. See Elisabeth Behr-Sigel, *Prière et sainteté dans l'église russe* (Bégrolles: Bellefontaine, 1982); and Paul Evdokimov, *Saint Seraphim of Sarov: An Icon of Orthodox Spirituality* (Minneapolis: Light and Life, 1988), *L'amour fou de Dieu* (Paris: Éditions du Seuil, 1973), and *Le Christ dans la pensée russe* (Paris: Cerf, 1986). Quite a few of the essays in *L'amour fou* are translated in the anthology *In the World, of the Church,* cited below.

7. Perhaps the best study is by Irina Gorainov, *Séraphin de Sarov* (Paris: Desclée de Brouwer, 1979). Also see Valentine Zander, *St. Seraphim of Sarov,* trans. Sister Gabriel Anne, SSC (Crestwood, NY: SVSP, 1975), and the chapter on him in the marvelous study by Donald Nicholl, *Triumphs of the Spirit in Russia* (London: Darton, Longman & Todd, 1997) 11–66, and

Little Russian Philokalia, vol. 1, *St. Seraphim* (Platina, CA: St. Herman Press, 1991). See Alexis Artsybouchev, *Mémoir du coeur: St. Seraphim de Sarov* (Paris: François-Xavier de Guibert, 2001).

8. While the literature interpreting the Eastern Church in the West continues to grow, a contemporary classic, exceptional for its clarity and comprehensiveness, is Timothy Ware (Bishop Kallistos), *The Orthodox Church,* new ed. (New York: Penguin, 1993). Written with a Western, predominantly Lutheran audience in mind is the succinct and very readable Archbishop Paul (of Finland), *The Faith We Hold* (Crestwood, NY: SVSP, 1981), and *The Feast of Faith* (Crestwood, NY: SVSP, 1982).

9. Collections of reproductions of icons abound, along with commentaries on the liturgical feasts and texts with which they are associated. Among the best, see Leonid Ouspensky and Vladimir Lossky, *The Meaning of Icons* (Crestwood, NY: SVSP, 1983); John Baggley, *Doors of Perception: Icons and Their Spiritual Significance* (Crestwood, NY: SVSP, 1988), and *Festival Icons for the Christian Year* (Crestwood, NY: SVSP, 2000); Michel Quenot, *The Icon: Window on the Kingdom* (Crestwood, NY: SVSP, 1991); Leonid Ouspensky, *Theology of the Icon,* 2 vols., trans. Anthony Gythiel and Elizabeth Meyendorff (Crestwood, NY: SVSP, 1992); Andrew Tregubov, *The Light of Christ: The Iconography of Gregory Kroug* (Crestwood, NY: SVSP, 1990); Konrad Onasch and Annemarie Schneider, *Icons: The Fascination and the Reality* (New York: Riverside, 1997); and Higoumène Barsanuphe, *Icônes et fresques du Père Grégoire* (Marcenat: Monastère Orthodoxe Znaménié, 1999).

10. Daniel Clendenin, *Eastern Orthodox Christianity: A Western Perspective* (Grand Rapids, MI: Baker Books, 1994). For two popular accounts from within the Orthodox Church by a Westerner, see Frederica Mathews-Green, *Facing East* (San Francisco: Harper, 1997), and *At the Corner of East and Now* (New York: J. B. Tarcher, 1999).

11. "Pro domo sua," in *L'orthodoxie,* new ed. (Paris: Desclée de Brouwer, 1979), 41–43.

12. Samuel P. Huntington, *The Clash of Civilizations and the Remaking of World Order* (New York: Touchstone, 1998).

13. Victoria Clark, *Why Angels Fall: A Portrait of Orthodox Europe from Byzantium to Kosovo* (London: Macmillan, 2000).

14. Nicolas Zernov, *The Russian Religious Renaissance of the Twentieth Century* (New York: Harper & Row, 1963).

15. For a recent expression of this traditionalist stance, see Patrick Barnes, *The Non Orthodox: The Orthodox Teaching on Christians Outside of the Church* (Salisbury, MA: Regina Orthodox Press, 1999).

16. Two important sources in these controversies about relationships with non-Orthodox Christians and the reception of the same into the Orthodox Church are Archbishop Peter L'Huillier, *The Church of the Ancient Councils* (Crestwood, NY: SVSP, 1996), and the article by Archimandrite Ambrose Pogodin, "On the Reception of Persons into the Orthodox Church, Coming to Her from Other Christian Churches," *Vestnik Russkago Kristianskogo Dvizheniya* 1, 173 (no. 1996) and 2, no. 174 (1997), trans. Fr. Alvian Smirensky, and available at www.holy-trinity.org.

17. For an attempt to counter, see John W. Morris, *Orthodox Fundamentalists: A Critical View* (Minneapolis: Light & Life, 1998).

18. Zernov, *Russian Religious Renaissance.*

19. The profiles of these people of faith are the culminations of a number of years of study, translation, and publication. Earlier articles on some include "Monasticism in the Marketplace, the Monastery, the World and Within: An Eastern Church Perspective," *Cistercian Studies Quarterly* 34, no. 3 (1999): 339–67; "Open in Faith, Open to the World: The Work and Witness of Alexander Men," *Eastern Churches Journal* 5, no. 2 (1998): 105–30; "'Always Everywhere and Always Together': The Eucharistic Ecclesiology of Nicolas Afanasiev's *The Lord's Supper* Revisited," *St. Vladimir's Theological Quarterly,* 41, nos. 2–3 (1997): 141–74; "Interiorized Monasticism: A Reconsideration of Paul Evdokimov on the Spiritual Life," *American Benedictine Review,* 48, no. 3 (1997): 227–53; "The Church, the Eucharist and the Kingdom: Towards an Assessment of Alexander Schmemann's Theological Legacy," *St. Vladimir's Theological Quarterly* 40, no. 3 (1996): 119–43; "Paul Evdokimov: A Theologian Within and Beyond the Church and the World," *Modern Theology* 12, no. 1 (1996): 85–107; "The Face of the Father in the Mother of God: Mary in Paul Evdokimov's Theological Writing," *Contacts* 172 (1996): 250–69; "The God Whose Power Is Weakness, Whose Love Is Foolish: Divine Philanthropy in the Theology of Paul Evdokimov," *Sourozh* 60 (1995): 15–26; "An Offering of Prayer: The Witness of Paul Evdokimov, 1900–1970," *Sobornost* 17, no. 2 (1995): 28–37; "Alexander Schmemann: Father and Teacher of the Church," *Pro Ecclesia* 3, no. 3 (1994): 275–88. There are also translations: Paul Evdokimov, *Ages of the Spiritual Life,* ed. and trans. Michael Plekon and Alexis Vinogradov (Crestwood, NY: SVSP, 1998); and *In the World, of the Church: A Paul Evdokimov Reader,* trans. Michael Plekon, ed. Alexis Vinogradov, and *Discerning the Signs of the Times: The Vision of Elisabeth Behr-Sigel,* ed. and trans. Michael Plekon and Sarah E. Hinlicky (Crestwood, NY: SVSP, 2001).

20. See Alexis Kniazeff, *L'Institut Saint-Serge* (Paris: Beauchesne, 1974).

21. Elisabeth Behr-Sigel chronicles many of these figures in her important biography, *Lev Gillet, a Monk of the Eastern Church,* trans. Helen Wright (Oxford: Fellowship of St. Alban and St. Sergius, 1999).

TWO.   St. Seraphim of Sarov

1. See his magisterial essay, "Holiness in the Tradition of the Orthodox Church," in *In the World, of the Church,* 95–154.
2. Zander, *St. Seraphim,* 83–94.

THREE.   Sergius Bulgakov

1. James Pain and Nicolas Zernov, eds., *A Bulgakov Anthology* (Philadelphia: Westminster Press, 1976), xvi–xvii.
2. "Trois Images," *Le Messager Orthodoxe* 1, no. 57 (1972): 17.
3. "Orthodox Dogma and Modern Thought in Bulgakov's Late Works," paper presented at the annual meeting of the AAASS, Philadelphia, November 20, 1994.
4. Paul Valliere, "Sophiology as the Dialogue of Orthodoxy with Modern Civilization," in *Russian Religious Thought,* ed. Judith Deutsch Kornblatt and Richard F. Gustafson (Madison: University of Wisconsin Press, 1996), 176–94.
5. Translator's preface to *The Holy Grail and the Eucharist,* trans. Boris Jakim (Hudson, NY: Lindisfarne Books, 1997), 9.
6. "Un destinéee exemplaire," *Le Messager Orthodoxe* 1, no. 57 (1971); 2, no. 98 (1985): 10.
7. Ibid., 10. Also see Andronikov's "La problématique sophianique," 45–56.
8. Rowan Williams, *Sergii Bulgakov: Towards a Russian Political Theology* (Edinburgh: T. & T. Clark, 1999), 172–81.
9. *A Bulgakov Anthology,* 3–4, 10.
10. Ibid., 7–8.
11. For the biographical material on Father Bulgakov I have used the anthology just noted as well as Williams, *Sergii Bulgakov; Russian Religious Thought,* particularly Paul Valliere's masterful essay, "Dialogue of Orthodoxy with Modern Civilization," 176–94; the special numbers of *Le Messager Orthodoxe* (no. 57 [1971], no. 98 [1985]), devoted to the centenary of Father Bulgakov's birth and to the papers of the June 1984 colloquy on him, particularly that of the editor, Nikita Struve, "Un destinée exemplaire,"

3–12; Constantin Andronikof's afterword in *The Holy Grail and the Eucharist;* and Sister Joanna Reitlinger's memoir, "The Final Days of Father Sergius Bulgakov," in Sergius Bulgakov, *Apocatastasis and Transfiguration,* trans. Boris Jakim (New Haven, CT: Variable Press, 1995).

12. Williams, Sergii Bulgakov, 4–6.

13. *A Bulgakov Anthology,* 10–11.

14. Ibid., 11.

15. Ibid., 11–12.

16. *La lumiére sans déclin,* trans. Constantin Andronikof (Lausanne: L'Age d'Homme, 1990), 28–30.

17. "Un destinée exemplaire," 4. Struve also notes the recent discovery of Father Bulgakov's never-published personal journal, where the record of his mystical experiences was left.

18. Williams, *Sergii Bulgakov,* 6–13.

19. Boris Jakim's translation of this seminal and original work published by Princeton University Press (1998).

20. Williams, *Sergii Bulgakov,* 55–112.

21. See Paul Evdokimov, *Gogol et Dostoievski: La descente aux enfers,* new edition, (Paris: Desclée de Brouwer, 1984), 289–98. Also his *Dostoievski et le problème du mal,* new edition (Paris: Desclée, 1978), and *Ages of the Spiritual Life,* 135–56.

22. The Hale Memorial Sermon he preached at Seabury-Northwestern is in Williams, *Sergii Bulgakov,* 273–86.

23. See "Dying before Death," in *A Bulgakov Anthology,* 22–27.

24. See some of the reminiscences in *Le Messager Orthodoxe* 1–2, no. 98 (1985): 131–39.

25. Paul Valliere, *Modern Russian Theology: Bukharev, Soloviev, Bulgakov* (Grand Rapids, MI: Eerdmans, 2000), 291–301.

26. "Trois Images," 2–20.

27. Ibid., 13–14.

28. *SOP,* supplément no. 196, March 1995.

29. Paul Evdokimov, *The Art of the Icon: A Theology of Beauty,* trans. Steven Bigham (Crestwood, NY: Oakwood/SVSP, 1990), 352.

30. Olivier Clément, *Orient-Occident, deux passeurs: Vladimir Lossky, Paul Evdokimov,* (Geneva: Labor et Fides, 1985), 22–83.

31. Foreword, vii–xvi.

32. Ibid., xii–xiii.

33. Thomas Hopko, "Receiving Fr. Bulgakov," *St. Vladimir's Theological Quarterly* 42, nos. 3–4 (1998): 373–83. Also see Myroslaw Tataryn, "Sergius Bulgakov (1871–1944): Time for a New Look," 315–38, in the same issue.

34. Valliere, *Modern Russian Theology*, 373–403.

35. A happy addition to this scholarship is the collection edited by Judith D. Kornblatt and Robert F. Gustafson, *Russian Religious Thought*, focused on Soloviev, Florensky, Bulgakov, and Frank. More recently there is Catherine Evtuhov's study of Bulgakov's early years, *The Cross and the Sickle: Sergei Bulgakov and the Fate of Russian Religious Philosophy* (Ithaca, NY: Cornell University Press, 1997). Michael Meerson's *The Trinity of Love in Modern Russian Theology* (Quincy, IL: Franciscan Press, 1998) examines the Trinitarian theme in Soloviev, Ivanov, Merezhkovsky, Berdiaev, Florensky, Karsavin, and Bulgakov. Valliere's important study, *Modern Russian Theology*, has finally been published. There are the indefatigable translators of Bulgakov, the recently deceased Constantine Andronikov, who brought most of his books into French, and Boris Jakim, who has been working on bringing essays and parts of the greater trilogy into English, to date mostly in very small presses. A major contribution to contemporary literature is Jakim's translation of what is perhaps Bulgakov's most important work, the last volume of his trilogy, *The Bride of the Lamb* (Grand Rapids, MI: Eerdmans, 2002). Abroad one must recognize the ongoing work of GRER-Groupe de Recherche sur L'Émigration Russe, based at the Sorbonne's Institut d'Études Slaves, and Nikita Struve's own scholarship over the years, especially his *Soixante-dix ans d'émigration russe* (Paris: Fayard, 1996). With the exception of this more encyclopedic effort, there has been no effort to grasp the sweep of the emigration's own creativity, much less their contribution to the West. The late Donald Nicholl's *Triumphs of the Spirit in Russia* (London: Darton, Longman & Todd, 1997) is insightful but unusual. The Dominican Aidan Nicols' studies, while perceptive, are somewhat slanted (*Theology in the Russian Diaspora: Church, Fathers and Eucharist in Nikolai Afanas'ev*, [Cambridge: Cambridge University Press, 1989]) and eccentric in selection and focus (*Light from the East: Authors and Themes in Orthodox Theology* [London: Sheed & Ward, 1995]). There still remains nothing comparable to Nicolas Zernov's magisterial study of almost forty years ago, *The Russian Religious Renaissance of the Twentieth Century*.

36. Himself an active participant in the Russian Christian Student Movement, the Fellowship and Ecumenical Conference, Nicolas Zernov, for many years the chief spokesman for Orthodoxy in the U.K. through his post as Spalding Lecturer at Oxford, chronicles the history of Orthodox participation in *The Russian Religious Renaissance*, 250–82.

37. It is a sad fact that with profound changes in the understanding of doctrine and worship in the WCC, even after the landmark publication of *Baptism, Eucharist, Ministry*, the "Lima Document" in 1982, in the last few years Orthodox participation and membership has decreased. Several

Orthodox leaders were instrumental in removing their churches from membership, several others effected a suspension of eucharistic celebrations at meetings, and a pan-Orthodox group has agreed to a period of reevaluation of the WCC's organization, goals, and self-understanding so that future Orthodox participation may in turn be reassessed.

38. *A Bulgakov Anthology,* 101.

39. Both passages from "By Jacob's Well," in *A Bulgakov Anthology,* 103.

40. *Russian Religious Renaissance,* 267–68.

41. Father Lev proposes "spiritual communion" in the September 1935 issue of the *Journal of the Fellowship of St. Alban and St. Sergius,* and Father Bulgakov responded positively in the same journal in December 1935.

42. *A Bulgakov Anthology,* 108.

43. Ibid., 111.

44. *Sergii Bulgakov: Towards a Russian Political Theology.*

45. Catherine Evtuhov, *The Cross and the Sickle;* Michael A. Meerson, *The Trinity of Love in Modern Russian Theology.*

46. Paul Valliere, *Modern Russian Theology.*

47. Antoine Arjakovsky, "La sophiologie du père Serge Bulgakov et la théologie occidentale contemporaine," presented at Bulgakov Conference, Dom Russkovo Zarubeye, March 5–8, 2001 and at the Philosophical Institute, Kiev, June 16, 2001. Also see his study, *La revue La Voie (1925–1940), revue de la pensée russe,* (Paris: EHESS, 2000).

48. Ibid., xix–xxv. See *Le Christ dans le pensée russe,* 179–94; *Le Messager Orthodoxe 98,* 130–39; *Russian Religious Renaissance,* 138–50.

49. The art historian Vladimir Weidlé. See *Russian Religious Renaissance,* 149–50.

50. "The Final Days of Father Sergius Bulgakov," in *Apocatastasis and Transfiguration,* 31–53.

51. The Russian text was first published in *Vestnik Khristianskogo Dvizheniia* 159 (1990): 51–79.

52. *A Bulgakov Anthology,* 19–20. Father Bulgakov frequently terminated his writings with this prayerful cry from the primitive church, "Amen. Come Lord Jesus," the exclamation closing the Book of Revelation 22:20.

FOUR.   Maria Skobtsova

1. The best biography of Mother Maria is Fr. Sergei Hackel's *Pearl of Great Price* (Crestwood, NY: SVSP, 1981). Also see the excellent spiritual biography by the daughter of Mother Maria's chaplain, Father Klepinin, Hélène Arjakovsky-Klépinine, "La joie du don," in *Le sacrement du frère*

(Paris/Pully: Le Sel de la Terre/Cerf, 1995) 13–69. This anthology of Mother Maria's writings is forthcoming in English in the Orbis Books series, Modern Spiritual Masters. Also see Laurence Varaut, *Mère Marie, 1891–1945, St. Petersbourg-Paris-Ravensbrück* (Paris: Éditions Perrin, 2000).

2. T. Stratton Smith, *Rebel Nun* (Springfield, IL: Templegate, 1965), 135.

3. *Le sacrement du frère*, 126.

4. Ibid., 121.

5. Ibid., 126.

6. Ibid., 127.

7. Ibid., 131.

8. Ibid., 141–46.

9. Ibid., 132.

10. Ibid., 133.

11. Ibid., 134.

12. "Types" was published in the Paris-based Russian journal *Vestnik* 176, nos. 2–3 (1997), and translated by Fr. Alvian Smirensky and published in *Sourozh* 74, 75, 76 (1998–99): 4–10, 13–27, 21–35.

13. *Sourozh* 75: 15.

14. Ibid., 16–17.

15. Ibid., 17.

16. Ibid., 21–22.

17. Ibid., 27; *Sourozh* 76: 20.

18. *Sourozh* 76: 24.

19. Ibid., 25.

20. Ibid., 26–27.

21. Ibid., 28.

22. Ibid., 31–32.

23. Both are reproduced in *Le sacrement du frère*, 64, 67. A collection of images of her iconography can be viewed at http://www.multimedia. com/kruger365.

24. *Sourozh* 76: 34.

25. Cited in Hackel, *Pearl of Great Price*, xi–xii.

26. Alexander Elchaninov, *The Diary of a Russian Priest*, trans. Helen Iswolsky (Crestwood, NY: SVSP, 1982), 53.

FIVE. Lev Gillet

1. *Orthodox Spirituality*, 2d ed. (Crestwood, NY: SVSP, 1978), x–xi. Much of what follows is indebted to Elisabeth Behr-Sigel's masterful and

extensive biography, *Lev Gillet: "Un moine de l'église d'Orient"* (Paris: Cerf, 1993), now in English: *Lev Gillet: "A Monk of the Eastern Church,"* trans. Helen Wright (Oxford: Fellowship of St. Alban and St. Sergius, 1999).

2. See Kari Kotkavaara, *Progeny of the Icon* (Åbo: Åboakadenis Förlag, 1999).

3. Reproductions of these are in the French edition of Behr-Sigel's biography, between 312 and 313 and in the illustration section of this book.

4. *In Thy Presence* (Crestwood, NY: SVSP, 1977), 71–72.

5. Helle Georgiadis, "The Witness of Father Gillet," *Chrysostom* 5, no. 8 (1980): 235–38. Also see Bishop Kallistos (Ware) response, *Chrysostom* (Spring 1981): 16–17.

6. See Georgiadis, "The Witness of Fr. Lev," 235–38; and Behr-Sigel, *Lev Gillet*, 9–12, 441–42.

7. See Zernov, *Russian Religious Renaissance*, 196.

8. Letter of March 9, 1928, in *Contacts* 49, no. 180 (1997): 309. This is one of a series of letters from Father Gillet to his bishop, Metropolitan Andrei Szeptycky, recently discovered in archives in Lviv and here excerpted and translated by Behr-Sigsel. Also see Cyril Korolevsky, *Metropolitan Andrew Sheptytsky,* ed. and trans. Serge Keleher (Fairfax, VA: Eastern Christian Publications, 1997).

9. See his preface, "Le père Lev Gillet: Grand théologien du Dieu souffrant et de l'Amour sans limites," in the anthology of Father Lev's writings, *Au cœur de la fournaise,* ed. Maxim Egger (Paris/Pully: Cerf–Le Sel de la Terre, 1998), 9–23.

10. See Elisabeth Behr-Sigel, *Alexandre Boukharev: Un théologien de l'Église orthodoxe russe en dialogue avec le monde moderne* (Paris: Beauchesne, 1977); Paul Evdokimov, *Le Christ dans la pensée russe, L'amour fou de Dieu* (Paris: Seuil, 1973); and my essay, "The God Whose Power Is Weakness, Whose Love Is Foolish: Divine Philanthropy in the Theology of Paul Evdokimov," *Sourozh* 60 (1995): 15–26.

11. *The Burning Bush* (Springfield IL: Templegate, 1976), 12–13.

12. Ibid., 17–18.

13. Ibid., 33–34.

14. Ibid., 48–49.

15. See Paul Evdokimov, *In the World, of the Church,* 11–36.

16. *The Burning Bush,* 51.

17. Ibid., 51.

18. Ibid., 52.

19. Sergius Bulgakov, *The Bride of the Lamb,* 349–526.

20. Such as *Jesus: Dialogue with the Savior* (New York: Desclée, 1963).

21. Peter L. Berger, *The Sacred Canopy: Elements of a Sociological Theory of Religion* (New York: Anchor Doubleday, 1967); and *A Rumor of Angels: Modern Society and the Rediscovery of the Supernatural*, 2d ed. (New York: Anchor/Doubleday, 1990), 59–85.

22. *In Thy Presence*, 37–38.

23. Ibid., 47–49, 54.

24. Ibid., 56, 66–70.

25. "My Monastic Life," *Cistercian Studies Quarterly* 8 (1973): 187–97.

26. Sergei Hackel, *Pearl of Great Price*, 20–27. See also the anthology of Mother Maria's writings, *Le sacrement du frère*.

27. Excerpts from these essays, mostly cited passages, are to be found in *Le sacrement du frère* and *Pearl of Great Price*.

28. See *Ages of the Spiritual Life*, 133–54, 227–39; and my essays, "Monasticism in the Marketplace, the Monastery, the World and Within: An Eastern Church Perspective," *Cistercian Studies Quarterly* 34, no. 3 (1999): 339–67, and "Interiorized Monasticism: A Reconsideration of Paul Evdokimov on the Spiritual Life," *American Benedictine Review* 48, no. 3 (1997): 227–53.

29. Thomas Merton, *A Search for Solitude: The Journals of Thomas Merton*, vol. 3, 1952–60, ed. Laurence S. Cunningham (San Francisco: Harper, 1996), entry for April 28, 1957, 87.

30. *Lev Gillet*, 129.

31. Quoted in M. Villain, *L'Abbé Paul Couturier, Apôtre de l'unité chrétienne* (Paris, 1957), as cited in A. M. Allchin, *The World Is a Wedding* (New York: Crossroad, 1982), 80.

SIX.   Paul Evdokimov

1. *The Sacrament of Love*, 61–63.

2. New editions by Desclée de Brouwer, Paris, are *Sacrement de l'amour*, 1977; *La femme et le salut du monde*, 1978; *L'orthodoxie*, 1979; *Gogol et Dostoïevski ou la descent aux Enfers*, 1961; *L'art de l'icône. La théologie de la beauté*, 1970; *Dostoïevski et le probléme du mal*, 1978; *Les âges de la vie spirituelle*, 1980; *La prière de l'Église d'Orient*, 1984; *La conaissance de Dieu selon la tradition orientale*, 1988.

3. These collections are *L'amour fou de Dieu* (Paris: Seuil, 1973); *La nouveauté de l'Esprit* (Paris: Bellefontaine, 1977); *Le buisson ardent* (Paris: P. Lethielleux, 1981). In addition to many articles, collected in a chrono-

logical bibliography by Peter C. Phan, *Culture and Eschatology: The Icono-graphical Vision of Paul Evdokimov* (New York: Peter Lang, 1985), 303–21, there are the important studies of the Holy Spirit and of the contributions of Russian theology: *L'Esprit Saint dans la tradition orthodoxe* and *Le Christ dans la pensée Russe* (Paris: Cerf, 1969, 1970). See also Plekon and Vinogradov, *In the World, of the Church.*

4. See *The Eucharist* (Crestwood, NY: SVSP, 1988), 149 ff.; *Church, World, Mission* (Crestwood, NY: SVSP, 1979); and "The Problems of Orthodoxy in America: I. The Canonical Problem, II. The Liturgical Prob-lem, III. The Spiritual Problem," *St. Vladimir's Theological Quarterly* 8, no. 2 (1964): 67–85; 8, no. 4 (1964): 164–85; 9, no. 4 (1965): 171–93. Also see my essay, "Alexander Schmemann: Father and Teacher of the Church," *Pro Ecclesia* 3, no. 2 (1994): 275–88.

5. *Waiting for God,* trans. Emma Craufurd (New York: Harper & Row, 1973).

6. *The Church Is One* (Seattle, WA: St. Nectarios Press, 1979), sec. 2.

7. See Aidan Nichols, O.P., *Theology in the Russian Diaspora: Church, Fathers and Eucharist in Nikolai Afanas'ev (1893–1966)* (New York: Cam-bridge University Press, 1989). Also see Andrew Blane, ed., *Georges Flo-rovsky: Russian Intellectual, Orthodox Churchman* (Crestwood, NY: SVSP, 1994).

8. On the Orthodox community in France, see *Lev Gillet,* 177 ff.

9. *The Orthodox Church* (Crestwood, NY: SVSP, 1988).

10. *L'orthodoxie,* 334–45; *La femme,* 218–19.

11. "Un ministère pétrinien dans l'Église peut-il avoir un sens?" *Con-cilium* 4, no. 7 (1971): 109–12.

12. *L'orthodoxie,* 334–46; *L'esprit saint,* 49–78; "Quelques jalons sur un chemin de vie," in *Le buisson ardent,* 26; *In the World, of the Church,* 37–48; "Communicatio in sacris: une possibilité?" *Le Messager Orthodoxe* 14, no. 25 (1963): 17–31.

13. The following is based on Olivier Clément's *Orient-Occident: Deux passeurs, Vladimir Lossky et Paul Evdokimov* (Geneva: Labor et Fides, 1985).

14. These themes wind throughout Evdokimov's writings, particularly in *The Sacrament of Love, Woman and the Salvation of the World,* and *Les âges.*

15. *Contacts* 73–74 (1971): 225–40, 261–67.

16. *In the World, of the Church,* 37–48. Also see *Orient-Occident,* 110–13, 142–49, 158–59.

17. Hackel, *Pearl of Great Price.*

18. *Lev Gillet,* 287–301; and Gillet's own *Amour sans limites* (Cheve-togne, 1971).

19. *The Life in Christ,* trans. C. J. de Catanzaro (Crestwood, NY: SVSP, 1974), 162–65.

20. *In the World, of the Church,* 175–94.

21. Perhaps the strongest statement of these affirmations is to be found in *Ages.*

22. *In the World, of the Church,* 155–74.

23. Robert W. Jenson, *Unbaptized God: The Basic Flaw in Ecumenical Theology* (Minneapolis: Fortress, 1992).

24. See *Le Christ* and the treatment of St. Seraphim in *In the World, of the Church,* 95–154.

25. *In the World, of the Church,* 49–60; "Vers le concile? Appel à l'Église," in *Orient-Occident,* 197–210; "Fondements de la spiritualité," "Ecclesia domestica," *La nouveauté,* 13–107, 218–36; *In the World, of the Church,* 175–230; *L'orthodoxie,* 301–46; *Ages,* 13–17; and *Woman and the Salvation of the World,* 9–28, 113–36, 177–88.

26. See *Le Christ* and *Ultimate Questions,* trans., Ashleigh E. Moorhouse, ed. Alexander Schmemann (Crestwood, NY: SVSP, 1977).

27. See *Le Christ* 179–94, 206–13; Clément, *Orient-Occident,* 90–98; and Nichols's *Theology in the Russian Diaspora* passim on Bulgakov and Afanasiev and their critics.

28. See *New Skete Communities* (1985) and *Monastic Typikon,* 2d rev. ed. (Cambridge, NY: New Skete, 1988).

29. "Problems of Orthodoxy in America, III," 177 ff.

30. *L'orthodoxie,* 7–44.

31. Elisabeth Behr-Sigel, *The Ministry of Women in the Church, the Place of the Heart* (Redondo Beach, CA: Oakwood, 1991).

32. *Woman and the Salvation of the Word,* 197–270; *In the World, of the Church,* 155–74. Also see my essay, "The Face of the Father in the Mother of God: Mary in Paul Evdokimov's Theology," *Contacts,* no. 172 (1995): 250–69.

33. *In the World, of the Church,* 49–60, 195–216, 217–30; "Vers le concile? Appel à l'église," in *Orient-Occident,* 197–210.

34. Kavanagh, *Elements of Rite, on Liturgical Theology* (New York: Pueblo, 1982); Senn, *The Witness of the Worshipping Community* (Mahwah, NJ: Paulist Press, 1993); Schmemann, *For the Life of the World, Of Water and the Spirit, The Eucharist, Liturgy and Tradition* (Crestwood, NY: SVSP, 1973, 1974, 1988, 1990).

35. See especially *The Sacrament of Love, Woman and the Salvation of the World,* and *Ages.*

36. See Behr-Sigel's study, *Lev Gillet, Un moine de l'Église d'Orient,* cited above and that of Bukharev below.

37. See Schmemann's *The Mission of Orthodoxy* (Mt. Hermon, CA: Conciliar Press, 1989), as well as his taped retreat talks on conversion, available from the Alexander Schmemann Bookstore, c/o The Sign of the Theotokos Orthodox Church, 4829 rue Resther, Montreal, QC H2J 2V6, Canada, and his *Celebration of Faith, Sermons*, 3 vols., *I Believe, The Church Year, The Mother of God*, trans. John A. Jillions (Crestwood, NY: SVSP, 1991, 1994, 1995). Also see Nadejda Gorodetzky, *Saint Tikhon of Zadonsk* (Crestwood, NY: SVSP, 1976); Behr-Sigel, *Alexandre Boukharev; Little Russian Philokalia*, vol. 1, *St. Seraphim of Sarov* (Platina, CA: St. Herman Press, 1991). Clément underlines the example of Alyosha in Dostoyevsky's *Brothers Karamazov* as an enactment of the same: *Orient-Occident*, 105 ff., 120–22, 152–54.

38. Rowan Williams, "Bread in the Wilderness: The Monastic Ideal in Thomas Merton and Paul Evdokimov," in *Monastic Tradition, East and West: One Yet Two*, ed. M. Basil Pennington (Spencer, MA: Cistercian Publications, 1976); Peter C. Phan, "Mariage, monachisme et eschatologie: Contribution de Paul Evdokimov à la spiritualité chrétienne," *Epheremerides Liturgicae* 98 (1979): 352–80; "Evdokimov and the Monk Within," *Sobornost* 3, no. 1 (1981): 53–61. See my article, "Interiorized Monasticism": A Reconsideration of Paul Evdokimov on the Spiritual Life," *American Benedictine Review* 48, no. 3 (1997): 227–53.

39. On Kierkegaard's theory of the Church's "disintegration" (*Udglidning*), see Berndt Gustafsson, *I den Natt. Studier till Søren Kierkegaards forfallsteori* (Stockholm: Diakonistyrelsens Bokforlag, 1962); Kresten Nordentoft, *"Hvad siger Brand-Majoren?" Kierkegaards opgør med sin samtid* (Copenhagen: Gad, 1973); Bruce H. Kirmmse, *Kierkegaard in Golden Age Denmark* (Bloomington: Indiana University Press, 1990); and my essay, "'Introducing Christianity into Christendom': Reinterpreting the Late Kierkegaard," *Anglican Theological Review* 64 (1982): 327–52.

40. *Ages of the Spiritual Life*, rev. trans. Michael Plekon and Alexis Vinogradov (Crestwood, NY: SVSP, 1998), 83–96.

41. Ibid., 71–76, 103–8. See Thomas Merton, *The Monastic Journey*, André Louf, *The Cistercian Way*, Charles Cummings, *Monastic Practices*, (Kalamazoo, MI: Cistercian Publications, 1992, 1989, 1990); *My Song Is Mercy: Writings of Matthew Kelty*, ed. Michael Downey, (Kansas City, MO: Sheed & Ward, 1994). Also see my essay, "Monasticism in the Marketplace, the Monastery, the World and Within: An Eastern Church Perspective," *Cistercian Studies Quarterly* 34, no. 3 (1999): 339–67.

42. *Ages*, 115–34.

43. *The Word in the Desert* (New York: Oxford University Press, 1993), 181–296.

44. *Ages*, 141–46.

45. Ibid., 146–55.

46. Ibid., 143–45.

47. Ibid., 193–209.

48. Ibid., 143–45.

49. Ibid., 223–24.

50. Ibid., 231–48.

51. *L'orthodoxie*, 123–66.

52. Ibid., 65–72, 121–26, 165–71.

53. *Lumières d'Orient* (Limoges: Droguet et Ardant, 1981); *Pèlerins russes et vagabonds mystiques* (Paris: Cerf, 1987); *La Prière des chrétiens russes* (Chambrey: CLD, 1988); *L'orthodoxie* (Paris, 1991); *Le Christ dans la tradition et la littérature russes* (Paris: Desclée, 1996); *Une voix chez les orthodoxes* (Paris: Cerf, 1998).

54. *Ages*, 231–48.

55. Ibid., 240–41.

56. Ibid., 241–43.

57. The principal works of both Frs. Kyprian Kern (*Evkharistia* [Paris, 1947]) and Nicolas Afanasiev (*Trapeza Gospodnia* [Paris, 1952]), Father Men's teachers, have not yet been translated from Russian and published, though much of their insight and Father Schmemann's own contributions are to be found in the latter's *The Eucharist*.

58. "Eucharistie, mystère de l'église," *Pensée Orthodoxe*, 14 (1968): 53–69; *In the World, of the Church*, 243–70.

59. *L'orthodoxie*, 346.

SEVEN. Gregory Krug

1. See Jean-Claude Marcadé and Valentine Marcadé, eds. and trans., *Moine Grégoire: Carnets d'un peintre d'icônes* (Paris: L'Age d'Homme, 1983). Father Gregory's sister, Olga Ivanovna Krug, painstakingly collected and transcribed these notes from the papers left after his death in 1969.

2. *The Light of Christ: Iconography of Gregory Krug* (Crestwood, NY: SVSP, 1990).

3. *Icônes et fresques du père Grégoire*, text by Father Barsanuphius (Marcenat: Monastery of Znaménié, 1999).

4. *Le Père Grégoire, moine iconographe du skit du Saint-Esprit, 1908–1969*), ed. Fr. Barsanuphius (Doumerac: Monastery of Korsun, 1999). Two other collections have recently been published: Bernard Pardo, Emilie Van Taack, and Anne Philippenko-Bogenhardt, *L'iconographie de l'église des*

Trois Saints Hiérarques et l'oeuvre de Léonide A. Ouspensky et moine Grég-oire Krug (Paris: Paroisse des Trois Saints Hiérarques, 2001); and Père Simon Doolan, *Le redécouverte d'l'icône: La vie et l'oeuvre de Léonide Ouspensky* (Paris: Cert, 2001). The June 1999 conference presentations have been published: Jean-Claude Marcadé, ed., *Un peintre d'icônes: Le père Grégoire Krug,* Cahiers de l'émigration russe no. 6 (Paris: Institut d'Études Slavs, 2001).

5. Ibid., 88–89.

6. Ibid., 76.

7. Father Nicolas Ozoline, a scholar of iconography and close to Leonid Ouspensky and later to Father Gregory, has documented the dates of much of Father Gregory's work for various church iconstases. Much of what follows here is from his essays. *Le Père Grégoire,* 37–40 for "L'evocation de la vie et de l'oeuvre du Père Grégoire" and "Le penouveau contemporain de l'icônographie orthodoxe et les débuts de l'École cite de Paris," *Collogue sur l'Orthodoxie en France* (Paris: Comité Orthodox des Amitiés Françaises, 1983).

8. Catherine Aslanoff, "Des ténèbres à la lumière," in *Le Père Grégoire Krug,* 35–41.

9. *Le Père Grégoire,* 63–66.

10. The above is based on the recollections of Father Barsanuphius in the collection he edited. Ibid., 19–26.

11. *Carnets,* 25.

12. Ibid., 32–33.

13. Ibid., 34.

14. *Carnets,* 90–92.

15. Ibid., 95–96.

16. See the collection of Vladimir Lossky's essays edited by John Erickson and Thomas E. Bird, *In the Image and Likeness of God* (Crestwood, NY: SVSP, 1985), 195–210.

17. Ibid., 169–94.

18. *Carnets,* 99.

19. Anne Bogenhardt, *Étude sur l'oeuvre et la vie du R. Père Grégoire Krug,* Memoire de Maîtrise (Paris: Université de Paris X, 1977).

20. *Carnets.*

21. *The Art of the Icon, a Theology of Beauty.*

22. According to Father Ozoline, the Montgeron icons were painted by Father Gregory between 1960 and 1962. *Le Père Grégoire,* 40.

23. Six of these seven roundel icons are magnificently reproduced in Father Tregubov's *The Light of Christ,* as are the large, principal icons of Christ, the Mother of God, and St. Seraphim: 13, 21, 23–31, 39. Also in the same volume are reproductions of the fresco of the Trinity and of the icon

of the burial of Christ, the shroud (*Epitaphion/Plashchenitsa*) carried in procession and venerated on Good Friday and Holy Saturday: 45, 49.

24. Reproductions of all these as lithograph icon prints are found in *Little Russian Philokalia,* vol. 2, *St. Seraphim.*

EIGHT.   Nicolas Afanasiev

1. The *Lord's Supper,* hereafter *LS* (*Trapeza Gospodnia* [Paris: YMCA Press, 1952], in Russian), trans. Michael J. Lewis (Crestwood, NY: St. Vladimir's Orthodox Theological Seminary, 1988), 1–2.

2. Nichols cites the explicit mentionings, particularly of the essay that summarizes much of Afanasiev's specific arguments, "The Church Which Presides in Love," in *The Primacy of Peter,* new ed., ed. John Meyendorff (London: Faith Press, 1963; Crestwood, NY: SVSP, 1992), in *Acta Synodalia Sacrosancti Concilii Oecumenici Vaticani Secundi* (Vatican City, 1971), vol. 1, pt. 4, 87; note 2; vol. 2, pt. 1, 251, note 27; vol. 3, pt. 1, 254, cited in *Theology in the Russian Diaspora: Church, Fathers, Eucharist in Nikolai Afanas'ev (1893–1966)* (Cambridge: Cambridge University Press, 1989), 253, 270.

3. Of the considerable literature, see J.-M.R. Tillard, *Church of Churches: The Ecclesiology of Communion* (Collegeville, MN: Glazier/Liturgical Press, 1992); Avery Dulles, *Models of the Church* (Garden City, NY: Doubleday, 1991); Walter Kasper, *Theology and Church* (New York: Crossroad, 1989); John Zizioulas, *Being and Communion* (Crestwood, NY: SVSP, 1988); Paul McPartlan, *The Eucharist Makes the Church: Henri de Lubac and John Zizioulas in Dialogue,* and *Sacrament of Salvation: An Introduction to Eucharistic Ecclesiology* (Edinburgh: T. & T. Clark, 1993, 1995); Hans Urs von Balthasar, "Who Is the Church?" in *Explorations in Theology,* vol. 2, *Spouse of the Word* (San Francisco: Ignatius Press, 1991), 143–91, cited and discussed in David L. Schindler, "At the Heart of the World, from the Center of the Church: Communio Ecclesiology and 'Worldly' Liberation," *Pro Ecclesia* 5, no. 3 (1996): 314–33; Leonardo Boff, *Church, Charism and Power* (New York: Orbis, 1985); Leonardo Boff, *Ecclesiogenesis* (New York: Orbis, 1986).

4. Nicholas Healy, "Communion Ecclesiology: A Cautionary Note," *Pro Ecclesia* 4, no. 4 (1995): 442–53.

5. "The Local Churches and Catholicity: An Orthodox Perspective," *The Jurist* 52 (1992): 490–508.

6. "The Estonian Crisis: A Salutary Warning," *Pro Ecclesia* 5, no. 4 (1996): 389–96.

7. See Bishop Kallistos "Communion and Intercommunion," *Sobornost* 7, no. 7 (1978): 550–67. The latter issue of eucharistic practice comes from Afanasiev's essay, "Una Sancta," discussed below.

8. Zizioulas, *Being as Communion*, 24–25, 132–69, 257–59; Nichols, *Theology in the Russian Diaspora*, 177–206.

9. See *Ecumenical Perspectives on Baptism, Eucharist and Ministry*, ed. Max Thurian (Geneva: WCC, 1983); *Churches Respond to Baptism, Eucharist and Ministry*, 6 vols., ed. Max Thurian (Geneva: WCC, 1986–88); *Orthodox Perspectives on Baptism, Eucharist and Ministry*, ed. G. Limouris and N. M. Vaporis (Brookline, MA: Holy Cross Orthodox Press, 1985).

10. *Unbaptized God* (Minneapolis: Augsburg Fortress, 1990), 1–13, esp. 90–103 on the Church.

11. Stanley Harakas, "The Local Church: An Eastern Orthodox Perspective," *Ecumenical Review* 29 (1977): 143; Peter Plank, *Die Eucharistieversammlung als Kirche* (Würzburg: Augustinus Verlag, 1980); John Meyendorff, "Review of Theology in the Russian Diaspora," *St. Vladimir's Theological Quarterly* 34, no. 4 (1990): 36–64.

12. *Tserkov' Dukha Sviatago* (Paris: YMCA Press, 1971); *L'Église du Saint-Esprit* (hereafter *EGS*), trans. Marianne Drobot (Paris: Cerf, 1977).

13. "The Church Which Presides in Love," 92–116.

14. This in both personal conversation and in a course on ecclesiology at St. Vladimir's Theological Seminary in 1998–99.

15. *On the Sacred Liturgy*, 2, 47–48; *On Priests*, 5–6; *Lumen Gentium*, 7, 11, 26, 28, 34, 50; *Catechism*, 1396, 1407; *Baptism, Eucharist and Ministry*, Faith and Order Paper no. 111 (Geneva: WCC, 1982), Eucharist, 1–33. The Eucharist-Church relationship permeates the entire section.

16. *L'Église du Saint-Esprit*, 19–22.

17. "Fr. Nicolas Afanasieff—In Memoriam," *St. Vladimir's Theological Quarterly*, 10, no. 4 (1966): 209.

18. "The Eucharist and the Doctrine of the Church: On the Book of the Rev. N. Afanasiev: The Banquet of the Lord," *St. Vladimir's Theological Quarterly* 2, no. 2 (1954): 7–12.

19. *The Eucharist: Sacrament of the Kingdom*, trans. Paul Kachur (Crestwood, NY: SVSP, 1988), 14. Afanasiev's imprint on his student, Schmemann, is also evident in the latter's first major work, *Introduction to Liturgical Theology*, trans. Ashleigh E. Moorhouse (London: Faith Press, 1966), as well as in perhaps his best known, *For the Life of the World: Sacraments and Orthodoxy*, originally published in 1963 by the National Student Christian Association and in later, expanded editions in 1965 and 1973.

20. Long out of print in the original Russian and only available in specialized library collections, it has not yet been published in a French

translation, to the best of my knowledge, and the cited M.Div. thesis by Fr. Michael Lewis is the only available English translation. Following Father Schmemann's urging more than forty years ago, it is hoped that a revised translation can soon be published by SVS Press.

21. See Zizioulas, *Being and Communion* (Crestwood, NY: SVSP, 1985), 24–25, 132–69, 257–59; also his *L'Eucharistie, l'Évêque et l'Église durant les trois premiers siècles,* trans. Jean-Louis Palierne (Paris: Desclée de Brouwer, 1994); Ware, *Communion and Intercommunion* (Minneapolis: Light and Life, 1980), and *Sobornost* 7, no. 7 (1978): 550–67; Nichols, *Theology in the Russian Diaspora,* 181–83.

22. See Marianne Afanasiev's discussion (*EGS,* 20–21) of the fate of *The Limits of the Church,* partial publications in the Russian version of *La Pensée Orthodoxe* in 1948, 1949, and 1954, and "L'Église de Dieu dans le Christ" in the French version of *La Pensée Orthodoxe* 13, no. 2 (1968).

23. *LS,* 116–18.

24. *Evharistiia* (Paris: YMCA Press, 1947). Not only is it desirable that *Trapeza Gospodnia* be published in translation, so too Kern's study, both significant milestones in contemporary liturgical and ecclesiological "returns to the sources" and themselves the inspiration for subsequent work, particularly that of Alexander Schmemann.

25. See Bulgakov's *The Orthodox Church,* rev. trans. Lydia Kesich (Crestwood, NY: SVSP, 1988); "Le dogme eucharistique," *La Pensée Orthodoxe* 4 (Lausanne: L'Age d'Homme, 1987), 40–90; and "By Jacob's Well," in *A Bulgakov Anthology,* 100–13; Evdokimov's *L'orthodoxie,* 2d ed. (Paris: Desclée de Brouwer, 1979), 239–99; *La prière de l'Église d'Orient,* 2d ed. (Paris: Desclée de Brouwer, 1985); "Eucharistie-Mystère de l'Église," *La Pensée Orthodoxe* 14 (1968): 53–69.

26. *L'Esprit-Saint dans la tradition orthodoxe* (Paris: Cerf, 1969), 88–110; *L'orthodoxie,* 262–68.

27. L'Église, 26, 32. The first three chapters, "The Royal Priesthood," "The Establishment of the Laity," and "The Ministry of the Laity," elaborate the charismatic nature of the Church, 35–122.

28. *EGS,* 2 ff., 349–50, 360–61.

29. Ibid., 51–64.

30. Ibid., 361–64.

31. *LS,* 2, 12.

32. Ibid., 112.

33. Ibid., 7.

34. Ibid., 41–43.

35. Ibid., 43–46.

36. Ibid., 48.

37. "The Church Which Presides in Love," 91–144; "Una Sancta," *Irénikon* 36 (1963): 436–75.

38. *LS,* 12 ff.

39. Ibid., 22–23.

40. See "The Church Which Presides in Love," 92–116; and Zizioulas, *Being and Communion,* 155–58, 200–1.

41. "The Church Which Presides in Love," 111–12.

42. *LS,* 32.

43. Ibid., 21 ff.; *EGS,* 360–61.

44. LS, 20–21.

45. *EGS,* 348–49, 367–72.

46. Ibid., chaps. 4–7: "L'oeuvre du ministère," "Les présidents dans le Seigneur," "Celui qui rend grâces," "L'évêque," 123–346.

47. Ibid., 35–122.

48. *LS,* 65, 69.

49. Ibid., 68–69.

50. *For the Life of the World,* 45–48; *Of Water and the Spirit: A Liturgical Study of Baptism* (Crestwood, NY: SVSP, 1974), 115–21; *The Eucharist,* 10–26.

51. Schmemann, "Problems of Orthodoxy in America, II. The Liturgical Problem," *St. Vladimir's Seminary Quarterly* 8, no. 4 (1964): 178; and *Church, World, Mission* (Crestwood, NY: SVSP, 1979), 147–57, 172 ff. Also see Alexis Kniazeff's article cited below.

52. Zernov, *The Russian Religious Renaissance;* Behr-Sigel, *Lev Gillet.* Also see Nikita Struve, *Soixante-dix ans d'émigration russe, 1919–1989* (Paris: Fayard, 1996).

53. For examples of the former, drastic efforts toward a "catholic iconoclasm," see Gordon Lathrop, *Holy Things* (Minneapolis: Fortress Press, 1993), 155 ff.; and for restraint and wisdom in renewal, see Kavanagh, *Elements of Rite.*

54. *LS,* 75–76.

55. It would be provocative to explore, descriptively, a Sunday morning, say, in 1950, in an Orthodox, Roman Catholic, Anglican, Lutheran, Methodist, Presbyterian, and Baptist setting, with an eye toward what did and did not occur eucharistically.

56. *LS,* 74.

57. Ibid., 79–92.

58. Ibid., 33–57.

59. Ibid., 35, 76–78.

60. *Theology in the Russian Diaspora,* 177, 181–88. Nichols has other problems (188–215) with Afanasiev's understanding of the de facto universal

ecclesial reality, the role of the councils and of primacy, yet he recognizes the value of the trenchant criticism Afanasiev provides.

61. *LS,* 84–85.

62. Ibid., 85.

63. Ibid., 94–95.

64. *Being and Communion,* 110–14, 123–42.

65. "The Local Churches," 504–8.

66. *LS,* 97–98.

67. *EGS,* 38–42, 244–49, 349.

68. *LS,* 100–2.

69. *Pravila Pravoslavnoi Tserkvi s Tolkovaniami* (St. Petersburg, 1911).

70. *LS,* 103–10.

71. Ibid., 111.

72. Symeon the New Theologian, *The Discourses,* trans. C. J. de Catanzaro, (Ramsey, NJ: Paulist Press, 1980), 86–87.

73. "Holy Things for the Holy," in *Great Lent: Journey to Pascha* (Crestwood, NY: SVSP, 1974), 107–33.

74. *The Sacred Canopy* (New York: Doubleday, 1969); *A Rumor of Angels* (New York: Doubleday, 1970); *The Heretical Imperative* (New York: Doubleday, 1979); *The Homeless Mind,* with Brigitte Berger and Hansfried Kellner (New York: Random House, 1973); and *A Far Glory* (New York: Free Press, 1992).

75. The image that comes to mind here is the closing of the royal doors on the Saturday in Easter/Bright Week, after they have been continuously open since the celebration of the Resurrection, a sad return to the "real world," while a powerful reminder of where the "real world" actually lies.

76. Schmemann, "World as Sacrament," in *Church, World Mission* (Crestwood, NY: SVSP, 1979), 217–27.

77. *LS,* 113–14.

78. Ibid., 118 ff.

79. "Problems of Orthodoxy in America, I. The Canonical Problem, II. The Liturgical Problem, III. The Spiritual Problem," *St. Vladimir's Theological Quarterly* 8, no. 2 (1964): 67–85; 8, no. 4 (1964): 164–85; 9, no. 4 (1965): 171–93; *The Eucharist,* 230, 242–44.

80. For another view, more specifically sociological, see Robert N. Bellah, Richard Madsen, William M. Sullivan, Ann Swidler, and Steven M. Tipton, *Habits of the Heart* (Berkeley: University of California Press, 1985); and *The Good Society* (New York: Knopf, 1991).

81. *LS,* 119–20.

82. Ibid., 123.

83. Ibid., 123–25.

84. Ibid., 123.

85. *Adv. Haer.* 3.24.1.

86. "L'ecclésialisation de la vie," *La Pensée Orthodoxe,* 4 (Lausanne: L'Age d'Homme, 1987), 108–35.

87. In addition to Nichols's fine treatment, see Nicolas Zernov's classic study (cited above) as well as Lewis Shaw's recent contribution, "John Meyendorff and the Heritage of the Russian Theological Tradition," in *New Perspectives on Historical Theology: Essays in Memory of John Meyendorff,* ed. Bradley Nassif (Grand Rapids, MI: Eerdmans, 1995), 10–44.

88. Meyendorff, "Review," 363.

89. Paul Evdokimov offers the best accounting of the Church's essential spiritual life, conserved within monasticism and capable of adaptation to any place and time: *Ages of the Spiritual Life,* rev. trans. Michael Plekon and Alexis Vinogradov (Crestwood, NY: SVSP, 1998).

90. See my essays, "Interiorized Monasticism: A Reconsideration of Paul Evdokimov on the Spiritual Life," *American Benedictine Review* 48, no. 3 (1997): 227–53, and "Monasticism in the Marketplace, the Monastery, the World and Within," *Cistercian Studies Quarterly* 34, no. 3 (1999): 339–67.

91. See his 1936 article, "The Canons of the Church: Changeable or Unchangeable?" *St. Vladimir's Theological Quarterly* 11, no. 2 (1969): 54–68.

92. *Hist. Eccl.* V, 24, 16; "Una Sancta," 459–65, 474–75.

93. "Una Sancta," 472–74; Bulgakov, "By Jacob's Well," 109–13.

94. *The Sacrament of Love,* trans. Anthony P. Gythiel and Victoria Steadman (Crestwood, NY: SVSP, 1985), 62.

95. *Woman and the Salvation of the World,* trans. Anthony P. Gythiel (Crestwood, NY: SVSP, 1994), 223. Also see his "Le Saint Esprit et la Mère de Dieu," in *La nouveauté de l'esprit* (Bègrolles: Abbaye de Bellefontaine, 1977), 253–78; Sergius Bulgakov, *The Orthodox Church,* 116–28; and *Le buisson ardent,* trans. Constantin Andronikov, (Lausanne: L'Age d'Homme, 1987); and my "Le visage du Père en la Mère de Dieu: Marie dans les écrits théologiques de Paul Evdokimov," *Contacts* 172 (1995): 250–69.

96. *The Eucharist,* 244; Irenaeus of Lyons, *Adv. Haer.* 3.24.1.

NINE.   Alexander Schmemann

1. Alexander Schmemann, "The Sanctification of Time," in *Liturgy and Life: Christian Development through Liturgical Experience* (Syosset, NY: Department of Religious Education, Orthodox Church in America, 1974), 88.

2. Something of the wealth of Father Schmemann's person and think-
ing is now accessible in the publication of selections from his journals,
The Journals of Father Alexander Schmemann, 1973–1983, ed. and trans.
Juliana Schmemann (Crestwood, NY: SVSP, 2000). For further biographi-
cal details, see Serge Schmemann, *Echoes of a Native Land* (New York:
Knopf, 1997).

3. For a collection of his most significant essays on these themes, see
Liturgy and Tradition: Theological Reflections of Alexander Schmemann,
ed. Thomas Fisch, (Crestwood, NY: SVSP, 1990).

4. Alexei Khomiakov, *The Church Is One* (Seattle, WA: St. Nectarios
Press, 1979); "On the Western Confessions of Faith," in *Ultimate Questions:
An Anthology of Modern Russian Religious Thought,* ed. Alexander Schme-
mann (Crestwood, NY: SVSP, 1977), 31–69. See the chapter on Fr. Nicolas
Afanasiev for citation of his principal works and for Father Schmemann's
explicit acknowledgment of his teacher's influence on him.

5. See, for example, his contributions in *Aleksandr Solzhenitsyn: Critical
Essays,* ed. John B. Dunlop, Richard Haugh, and Alexis Klinoff (New York:
Collier, 1979); "On Solzhenitsyn," 28–40, "A Lucid Love," 382–92; and
"Reflections on *The Gulag Archipelago,*" 515–26.

6. See *The Historical Road of Eastern Orthodoxy,* trans. Lydia Kesich
(Crestwood, NY: SVSP, 1966, rept. 1977). In addition to the Solzhenitsyn
essays and the *Ultimate Questions* collection already cited, other examples
are to be found in Paul Garrett's bibliography: *St. Vladimir's Theological
Quarterly* 28, no. 1 (1984): 11–26.

7. See "Problems of Orthodoxy in America: III. The Spiritual Problem," *St. Vladimir's Theological Quarterly* 9, no. 4 (1965): 11–22, 171–93;
"For the Life of the World" and "Worship in a Secular Age," in *For the
Life of the World: Sacraments and Orthodoxy* (Crestwood, NY: SVSP,
1973), 117–34; *Church, World, Mission* (Crestwood, NY: SVSP, 1979), 7–24,
193–208. Of Peter Berger's work, see, for example, *A Rumor of Angels,*
expanded ed. (New York: Anchor/Doubleday, 1990); *The Heretical Imperative* (New York: Anchor/Doubleday, 1979); *A Far Glory* (New York: Free
Press, 1992).

8. *Liturgy and Tradition,* 89–100.

9. Several tapes of conferences on the Cross, the Mother of God, conversion, and discernment are available from the Fr. Alexander Schmemann
Bookstore, c/o The Sign of theTheotokos Orthodox Church, 4829 rue Resther, Montreal, Quebec, Canada QC H2J 2V6.

10. *Liturgy and Life* and *The Celebration of Faith* , 3 vols., trans. John A.
Jillions (Crestwood, NY: SVSP, 1991, 1994, 1995).

11. Veselin Kesich, "Freedom and Joy," *St. Vladimir's Theological Quarterly* 28, no. 1 (1984): 41–42.

12. *Journals,* 16.

13. Ibid., 291–92; original emphasis.

14. Ibid., 310.

15. Ibid., 310, 320, 327–28, 144, 23–25.

16. "That East and West Yet May Meet," in *Against the World, for the World,* ed. Peter L. Berger and Richard John Neuhaus (New York: Seabury, 1976), 126–37, also published as "The Ecumenical Agony," in *Church, World, Mission,* 193–208.

17. "That East and West Yet May Meet," 136–37; original emphasis.

18. See Paul Garrett's already cited bibliography for these Russian language articles of 1947–53: *St. Vladimir's Theological Quarterly* 28, no. 1 (1984): 11–13.

19. "Pentecost, the Feast of the Church," *St. Vladimir's Theological Quarterly* 1, nos. 3–4 (1953), 38–42; "The Eucharist and the Doctrine of the Church," *St. Vladimir's Theological Quarterly* 2, no. 2 (1954): 7–12; "The Mystery of Easter," *SVTQ* 2, no. 3 (1954): 16–22; "The Sacrament of Baptism," *The Word* 1, no. 1 (1957): 36–40, 47; "Liturgical Theology: Its Task and Method," *St. Vladimir's Theological Quarterly* 1, no. 4 (1957): 16–27.

20. 2d ed., trans. Ashleigh E. Moorhouse (Crestwood, NY: SVSP, 1975).

21. *Introduction,* 27. Father Kern's study is *Evkharistia* (Paris: YMCA, 1947).

22. "The Canonical Problem," *St. Vladimir's Theological Quarterly* 8, no. 2 (1964): 67–85; "The Liturgical Problem," 8, no. 4 (1964): 164–85; "The Spiritual Problem," 9, no. 4 (1965): 171–93; and "The Underlying Question," in *Church, World, Mission,* 7–24.

23. *Vvedenie v liturgicheskoe bogoslovie* (Paris: YMCA Press, 1960), preface.

24. (Crestwood, NY: SVSP, 1974, 1988), the latter translated by Paul Kachur. Father Schmemann also summarized much of his liturgical teaching in the introductions he wrote for the paperback editions of feast day services still published by the OCA Department of Religious Education.

25. See Aidan Kavanagh, *On Liturgical Theology* (New York: Pueblo, 1984), who provides the citation from *Patrologia Latina,* 50, coll. 555.

26. *For the Life of the World,* 65.

27. See *Little Russian Philokalia,* vol. 1, *St. Seraphim of Sarov,* 3d ed. (Platina, CA: St. Herman Press, 1991); vol. 3, *St. Herman of Alaska;* Sergei Hackel, *Pearl of Great Price: The Life of Maria Skobtsova* (Crestwood, NY: SVSP, 1980).

28. See "The Time of Mission," in *For the Life of the World,* 17–66; "The Missionary Imperative," in *Church, World, Mission,* 209–16; "The Sacrament of the Faithful" and "The Sacrament of Remembrance," in *The Eucharist,* 81–100, 191–12. Also see *Liturgy and Life* throughout.

29. *The Witness of the Worshipping Community* (Mahwah, NJ: Paulist Press, 1993).

30. "Liturgy and Eschatology," in *Liturgy and Tradition,* 98–99.

31. "The World as Sacrament," in *Church, World, Mission,* 223, 225.

32. "The Missionary Imperative," in *Church, World, Mission,* 216.

33. See "Problems of Orthodoxy in America, II. The Liturgical Problem," 172–75, 183–85; "III. The Spiritual Problem," 173–74. Also see "The World in Orthodox Thought and Experience," in *Church, World, Mission,* 67–84.

34. "The Liturgical Problem," 164–69, 174–75; "The Spiritual Problem," 171–73, 177–86. Contemporary responses to these important essays by Frs. Robert Arrida, Alexis Vinogradov, and Archbishop Peter (L'Huillier) are in "The Blossoming of Orthodoxy in America," *Jacob's Well* (Fall 1999–Winter 2000): 3–8.

35. "The Spiritual Problem," 178.

36. "The Liturgical Problem," 178. Also see my essay, "*Sola Ecclesia:* For the 'Churching' of the Church," *Lutheran Forum* 24, no. 1 (1990): 14–17.

37. "The Liturgical Problem," 175–80; "The Spiritual Problem," 186–93.

38. "The Spiritual Problem," 179–80; original emphasis.

39. "Towards a Theology of Councils," in *Church, World, Mission,* 169–70. Also see John Zizioulas, *Being as Communion: Studies in Personhood and the Church* (Crestwood, NY: SVSP, 1985).

40. *Church, World, Mission,* 164, 170–78.

41. "Freedom in the Church," in *Church, World, Mission,* 182–85.

42. See "The Public Church," in *The Good Society* 179–219; on the Methodists and Lutherans, see Carl E. Braaten, "The Gospel—or What?"; Robert Benne, "Don't Quote Me: Off-the-Record Reflections on a Continuing Folly in the ELCA"; Paul R. Hinlicky, "Against the Quotas," all in *Lutheran Forum* 26, no. 4 (November 1992): 4–10, 58–60, 64–68.

43. "The Missionary Imperative," in *Church, World, Mission,* 209–16.

44. Ibid., 212.

45. Ibid., 213.

46. Ibid., 212.

47. Ibid., 213.

48. Ibid., 216; original emphasis.

49. *For the Life of the World,* 113; original emphasis.

TEN.   John Meyendorff

1. *Living Tradition* (Crestwood, NY: SVSP, 1978), 7–8; original emphasis.

2. Biographical details have come from Dimitri Obolensky's obituary essay on Father Meyendorff in *Sobornost* 15, no. 2 (1993): 44–51.

3. "Church and Ministry—For an Orthodox-Lutheran Dialogue," *dialog* 22, no. 2 (1983): 114–20.

4. *Défense des saints hésychastes,* 2d ed., 2 vols. (Louvain: Specilegium Sacrum Lovaniense, nos. 30–31, 1973); *Introduction à l'étude de Grégoire Palamas* (Paris: Éditions de Seuil, 1959).

5. *The Orthodox Church: Its Past and Its Role in the World Today,* 4th rev. ed. (Crestwood, NY: SVSP, 1996); *Orthodoxy and Catholicity* (New York: Sheed & Ward, 1966); *Christ in Eastern Christian Thought* (Crestwood, NY: SVSP, 1975); *Byzantine Theology,* 2d ed. (New York: Fordham University Press, 1973); *Byzantine Hesychasm* (London: Variorum, 1974); *Byzantium and the Rise of Russia* (Cambridge: Cambridge University Press, 1981); *The Byzantine Legacy in the Orthodox Church* (Crestwood, NY: SVSP, 1981); *Catholicity and the Church* (Crestwood, NY: SVSP, 1983); *Witness to the World* and *Vision of Unity* (Crestwood, NY: SVSP, 1987); John Breck, John Meyendorff, Elena Silk, eds., *The Legacy of St. Vladimir* (Crestwood, NY: SVSP, 1989); *Imperial Unity and Christian Divisions: The Church 450–680 A.D.* (Crestwood, NY: SVSP, 1989); *Rome, Constantinople, Moscow* (Crestwood, NY: SVSP, 1996).

6. *Marriage: An Orthodox Perspective* (Crestwood, NY: SVSP, 1975). See also Paul Evdokimov, *The Sacrament of Love.*

7. *New Perspectives on Historical Theology: Essays in Memory of John Meyendorff,* ed. Bradley Nassif (Grand Rapids, MI: Eerdmans, 1996); and the special issue of the journal of St. Sergius Institute in Father Meyendorff's memory, *La Pensée Orthodoxe,* no. 6 (1999).

8. *Witness,* 13–14.

9. Ibid., 17.

10. *Living Tradition,* 97.

11. "Catholic Consciousness," *St. Vladimir's Theological Quarterly* 14 (1970): 188–89.

12. *Vision,* 175–76; original emphasis.

13. Ibid., 177.

14. Ibid., 167.

15. Ibid., 175.

16. Ibid., 175–76.

17. Ibid., 177–78.
18. Ibid., 189–90.
19. *Living Tradition*, 136.
20. *Sources chrétiennes* (Paris: Cerf, 1964), 39–40.
21. Ibid., 137.
22. Ibid., 96–97.
23. *Vision*, 139–44.
24. Ibid., 139–40.
25. Ibid., 130–35.
26. Ibid., 89–91, 100–2, 128–29, 76–79, 108–10.
27. *Witness*, 22.
28. Ibid., 27–29, 32–34.
29. Ibid., 38–39.
30. Ibid., 176–77.
31. Ibid., 177.
32. Ibid., 42–43.
33. Ibid., 46.
34. Ibid., 50–58.
35. Ibid., 67.
36. Ibid., 74.
37. Ibid., 78–83.
38. Ibid., 88–144.
39. Ibid., 133.
40. Ibid., 143–44.
41. Ibid., 158–60.
42. Ibid., 211–13.
43. *Orthodoxy and Catholicity*, 124.
44. *dialog*, 22 (1983): 118–19.
45. *Witness*, 59–83.
46. See Afanasiev's important essay, "The Church Which Presides in Love," in *The Primacy of Peter*, 2d ed., ed. John Meyendorff (Crestwood, NY: SVSP, 1992), 91–143.
47. *Witness*, 82–83.
48. Ibid., 170.
49. Ibid., 172–73.
50. *Living Tradition*, 115.
51. Ibid., 122.
52. Ibid., 123–24; original emphasis.

ELEVEN. Alexander Men

1. *Christianity for the Twenty-first Century: The Prophetic Writings of Alexander Men,* ed. Elizabeth Roberts and Ann Shukman (New York: Continuum, 1996), 185.

2. Prot. A. Men, "Pismo k E.N." [letter to E.N.], in *Aequinox,* quoted in Yves Hamant, *Alexander Men: A Witness for Contemporary Russia, a Man for Our Times,* trans. Steven Bigham (Torrance, CA: Oakwood, 1995), 38–40.

3. A collection of these question-and-answer discussions conducted by Father Dudko and his parishioners both in church and in home meetings has been translated by Paul D. Garett: *Our Hope* (Crestwood, NY: SVSP, 1977).

4. Subsequently, several of Father Men's colleagues and disciples have come under fire from conservative groups within the Russian Church, most notably Frs. George Kochetkov and Alexander Borisov, who headed the Russian Bible Society and Sts. Cosmas and Damian parish in Moscow, for liturgical and catechetical "innovations," and for ecumenical openness, especially to the Roman Catholic Church. See *SOP,* January 1995. Also see Sue Talley, "Christianity and Russia," and David Toolan, "A Visit to Sts. Cosmas and Damian," *The First Hour* 9, Pentecost (1994): 4–9.

5. *Alexander Men.*

6. *Awake to Life! Sermons from the Paschal Cycle,* trans. Marite Sapiets (Torrance, CA: Oakwood, 1996).

7. *Christianity for the Twenty-first Century.*

8. *About Christ and the Church,* trans. Alexis Vinogradov (Torrance, CA: Oakwood, 1996).

9. More recently, his primer for basic religious education, *Orthodox Worship: Sacrament, Word and Image* and *Seven Talks on the Creed,* both translated by Colin Masica, with assistance from Olga Trubetskoy, and released by Oakwood in 1999. There have been several collections of Father Men's writings translated into French: *Le christianisme ne fait que commencer,* trans. Françoise Lhæst and Hélène Arjakovsky-Klépinine (Paris: Cerf, 1996), and *Manuel pratique de prière,* trans. Michel Evdokimov (Paris: Cerf, 1998).

10. Father Men's death was covered by television news reports on the major networks, by articles in the *New York Times,* and even by Lawrence Elliot, "Murder of a Russian Priest," *Reader's Digest,* July 1991.

11. *The Orthodox Vision* 1, no. 1, (1996): 7.

12. Ibid., 8.

13. Anastasia Heath, review of *Christianity for the Twenty-first Century*, in *Forerunner*, 17–20.

14. Likewise, though beyond the scope here, would be a look at those in ascendancy among the same, such as the late Fr. Seraphim Rose, Frs. Patrick Reardon, Alexy Young and Frank Schaeffer, perhaps the chief spokesman, and their targets. See, as a particularly contentious example of this perspective, Schaeffer's *Letters to Father Aristotle: A Journey through Contemporary Orthodoxy* (Salisbury, MA: Regina Orthodox Press, 1995).

15. Though stopping just short of denouncing him as a heretic, a recent critique in Russian is very severe in its assessment: Feliks Karelin, Sergei Antiminsov, and Andrei Kuraev, *On the Theology of Archpriest Alexander Men* (Zhitomir: Nika, 1999), charging him with Nestorian, Pelagian, and Arian positions, doubting his interest in parapsychological research, studies in comparative religion, forms of alternative medicine, one writer concluding that at best he was a subversive Eastern Rite Catholic.

16. Yakov Krotov, "Alexander Men and His Imitators," *Sevodnia*, September 9, 2000; Alexei Lavrukhin, "Ten Years without Alexander Men," *Nezavismaia Gazeta*, September 9, 2000; Mikhail Gorkhman, "Is the Investigation Complete?" *Isvestiia*, September 9, 2000.

17. While there are several collections of memoirs and some efforts at assessment in Russian, listed in the bibliography of the Roberts-Shukman anthology, there is still little in English. However, see Michael Meerson, "The Life and Work of Father Aleksandr Men," in *Seeking God: The Recovery of Religious Identity in Orthodox Russia, Ukraine and Georgia,* ed. Stephen K. Batalden (DeKalb: Northern Illinois University Press, 1993).

18. Without shortchanging his effort, Hamant's study tells us much about Father Men and his work but not enough to give us a full, deep understanding of him as an individual. Yet Hamant provides a rich and invaluable panorama of the historical backdrop of the Orthodox Church in Russia in this century. Also see Trevor Beeson, *Discretion and Valour,* 2d ed. (London: Fount, 1982); Dimitri Pospielovsky, *The Russian Church under the Soviet Regime, 1917–82* (Crestwood, NY: SVSP, 1984); Michael Bourdeaux, *Patriarchs and Prophets: Persecution of the Russian Orthodox Church Today* (London: Mowbray, 1975); *May One Believe—in Russia?* (London: Darton, Longman & Todd, 1980); *Risen Indeed: Lesson in Faith from the USSR* (Crestwood, NY: SVSP, 1983); Pierre Pascal, *The Religion of the Russian People* (Crestwood, NY: SVSP, 1976); and Nikita Struve, *Christians in Contemporary Russia* (London: Collins, 1967).

19. See Janet M. Wehrle, "'The Life of Aleksandr Men': Hagiography in the Making," *Religion in Eastern Europe* 19, no. 3 (June, 1999).

20. See *Le Messager Orthodoxe,* special issue, I–II, Colloque P. Serge Boulgakov, 1985. Also see the literature on Florovsky, Bulgakov, and Gillet cited above.

21. See the anthology of her writings, *Le sacrement du frère.*

22. See Clément, *Orient-Occident.*

23. See Afanasiev's *L'Église du Saint-Esprit;* "The Church Which Presides in Love; "Una Sancta"; and Cyprian Kern, *Evharistiia* (Paris: YMCA Press, 1947).

24. Paul Evdokimov, *Les âges de la vie spirituelle,* 3d ed. (Paris: Desclée de Brouwer, 1995), revised translation by myself and Alexis Vinogradov, *Ages of the Spiritual Life* (Crestwood, NY: SVSP, 1998).

25. See my essay, "The God Whose Power Is Weakness."

26. See Evdokimov, *Le Christ dans la pensée russe;* and Michel Evdokimov, *Le Christ dans la tradition et la littérature russe* (Paris: Cerf, 1996).

27. Notorious in the later years of the Soviet era and responsible for his harassment and detention were Father Dudko's talks, *Our Hope,* trans. Paul D. Garrett, (Crestwood, NY: SVSP, 1977).

28. Hamant documents this far-reaching ministry in both text and images, including Father Men's connections with dissidents such as Sakharov, Solzhenitsyn, and Frs. Gleb Yakunin, Nikolai Eshliman, and Dimitri Dudko.

29. For one version, see parts 2 and 3 of Sergius Bulgakov, *Apocatastasis and Transfiguration,* trans. Boris Jakim (New Haven, CT: Variable Press, 1995).

30. On this concept's implementation in the Russian emigration, see Alexis Kniazeff, "L'ecclésialisation de la vie," *La Pensée Orthodoxe,* vol. 4 (Lausanne: L'Age d'Homme, 1987), 108–35 On its application to Orthodoxy in America, see Alexander Schmemann, "Problems of Orthodoxy in America, I. The Canonical Problem, II. The Liturgical Problem, III. The Spiritual Problem," *St. Vladimir's Theological Quarterly,* 8, nos. 2–4, (1964): 67–85, 164–85; 9, no. 4 (1965): 171–93; Paul Evdokimov, *The Sacrament of Love,* trans. Anthony P. Gythiel and Victoria Steadman (Crestwood, NY: SVSP, 1985), 62.

31. Personal communication from a visit to her by Sue Talley. A collection of Father Schmemann's Radio Liberty broadcasts has been published: *Celebration of Faith,* 3 vols., *I Believe, The Church Year, The Virgin Mary,* trans. John Jillions (Crestwood, NY: SVSP, 1991, 1994, 1995).

32. *Christianity for the Twenty-first Century,* 122, 142.

33. *Awake,* 12–13, 33, 47, 50; *About Christ,* 38, 50–54; *Christianity,* 161. The above-cited manual or primer by Father Men, *Orthodox Worship,* provides detailed information on such practices as when to make the sign of the

cross, when to bow and how profoundly, fasting, and other specifics of traditional churchly piety, expressly for so many in Russia deprived of both instruction and models to imitate. Father Men was no mere critic of traditional practice. He does, however, explain why something is done, sometimes how it could be done more faithfully to original intention, but he is always careful not to scandalize or denigrate authority in the Church.

34. *About Christ,* 52–53.

35. Ibid., 23, 37–40, 54, 105–10.

36. Ibid., 36.

37. Ibid., 33. See Elisabeth Behr-Sigel's study, *Alexandre Boukharev, un théologien de l'Église orthodoxe russe en dialogue avec le monde moderne* (Paris: Beauchesne, 1977).

38. See Alexander Schmemann, "III. The Liturgical Problem," 178; also *Church, World, Mission* (Crestwood, NY: SVSP, 1979), 147–57, 172 ff.; and *For the Life of the World* (Crestwood, NY: SVSP, 1973).

39. *Christianity,* 151–63.

40. Ibid., 162–63.

41. *About Christ,* 82–83.

42. Ibid., 83.

43. See Alexander Schmemann, "The Mission of Orthodoxy," *Concern* 3, no. 4 (1968), reprinted by Conciliar Press, 1989; and Michael Oleksa, "Orthodox Missiological Education for the 21st Century," *St. Vladimir's Theological Quarterly,* 37, no. 4 (1993): 353–62.

44. *Christianity,* 68–74.

45. Archpriest Alexander Men, *Orthodox Worship: Sacrament, Word and Image,* trans. Colin Masica (Crestwood, NY: Oakwood/SVSP, 1999), 3.

46. Thomas Hopko, "The Narrow Way of Orthodoxy: A Message from Orthodoxy in America to Eastern Europe," *Christian Century* 112, no. 9 (March 15, 1995): 296–99. Clément's observations came in the November 1996 issue of *SOP.* Also see Kallistos (Ware), "The Estonian Crisis: A Salutary Warning," *Pro Ecclesia* 5, no. 4 (1996): 389–96.

47. See his edited collection, *Alaskan Missionary Spirituality* (New York and Mahwah: Paulist Press, 1987); and his study, *Orthodox Alaska: A Theology of Mission* (Crestwood, NY: SVSP, 1992).

TWELVE.   Holiness in Our Time

1. *The Sacrament of Love,* 93–94.

2. This open letter, or "Message to the churches," appears in the anthology, *In the World, of the Church.*

3. *Dialogue between Neighbors: The Theological Conversations between the Evangelical Lutheran Church of Finland and the Russian Orthodox Church, 1970–1986*, ed. Hannu T. Kamppuri (Helsinki: Luther-Agrikola Society, 1986), and its effects in *Union with Christ: The New Finnish Interpretation of Luther*, ed. Carl E. Braaten and Robert W. Jenson (Grand Rapids, MI: Eerdmans, 1998).

4. See the volume produced by the U.S. Lutheran-Orthodox Dialogue, *Salvation in Christ*, ed. John Meyendorff and Robert Tobias (Minneapolis: Augsburg, 1992). Many fine papers from this dialogue, begun in 1965, enough to fill several volumes, regrettably remain unpublished. Likewise, the appropriation of Orthodox theology in the West is becoming increasingly widespread. See, for example, in liturgy, Jean Corbon, *The Wellspring of Worship*, trans. Matthew J. O'Connell (Mahwah, NJ: Paulist Press, 1988); in ecclesiology, J.-M. R. Tillard, *Church of Churches: The Ecclesiology of Communion*, trans. R. C. De Peaux (Collegeville, MN: Liturgical Press, 1992), and the *Catechism of the Catholic Church* (New York: Image/Doubleday, 1995), passim, especially in part 2, "The Celebration of the Christian Mystery."

5. See a classic but not unbiased account, *Ways of Russian Theology*, trans. Robert L. Nichols, vols. 5 and 6 of *The Collected Works of Georges Florovsky*, ed. Richard S. Haugh and Paul Kachur (Belmont, MA: Nordland, 1979, 1987), as well as Paul Valliere's fine studies, "Theological Liberalism and Church Reform in Imperial Russia," in *Church, Nation and State in Russian and Ukraine*, ed. Geoffrey A. Hosking (London: Macmillan, 1991), 108–30; "The Liberal Tradition in Russian Orthodox Theology," in *The Legacy of St. Vladimir*, ed. John Breck, John Meyendorff, and Elena Silk (Crestwood, NY: SVSP, 1990), 93–106; "Sophiology as the Dialogue of Orthodoxy with Modern Civilization, in Kornblatt and Gustafson, *Russian Religious Thought*, 176–92, and his forthcoming book from T. & T. Clark. Also see James W. Cunningham, *Vanquished Hope* (Crestwood, NY: SVSP, 1981).

6. An English translation of this most important work is in preparation by Alexis Vinogradov and is forthcoming from SVSP.

7. *The Trinity of Love in Modern Russian Theology* (Quincy, IL: Franciscan Press, 1998); and *Modern Russian Theology*.

8. See his studies *Pèlerins, russes et vagabonds mystiques* (Paris: Cerf, 1987); *La prière des chrétiens de Russie* (Tours: CLD, 1988); *Le Christ dans la tradition et la littérature russe; Une voix chez les orthodoxes* (Paris: Cerf, 1998).

9. See Sergius Bulgakov, *Apocatastasis and Transfiguration*, trans. Boris Jakim (New Haven, CT: The Variable Press, 1995), from his great trilogy,

vol. 3, *Nevesta Agnetsa* (Paris: YMCA Press, 1945), *The Bride of the Lamb*, 349–76. Also see Paul Evdokimov's adaptation of Bulgakov, "Eschatology," in the collection *In the World, of the Church*, 11–36.

10. Alexander Bukharev, the gifted monk-priest who was harassed and silenced by ecclesiastical officials and who returned to lay status was regarded by many, including Florensky, Bulgakov, and Berdiaev, as the first Orthodox theologian in the modern era to seek to open a dialogue between the Church and the modern world. See Elisabeth Behr-Sigel, *Alexandre Boukharev: Un théologien de l'église orthodoxe russe en dialogue avec le monde moderne* (Paris: Beauchesne, 1974); and Paul Evdokimov, *Le Christ dans la pensée russe* (Paris: Cerf, 1986). A summary article on him by Behr-Sigel appears in the collection, *Interpreting the Signs of the Times*, 55–80.

11. *The Sacrament of Love*, 92.

12. *Sergii Bulgakov*, 68.

13. *Ages*, 232, 234–35, 238, 239.

14. Ibid., 242.

15. Ibid., 242.

16. I am reminded here again of Sister Joanna Reitlinger's frescoes in St. Basil's House, created in memory of Father Bulgakov, her spiritual father, where Father Lev served as chaplain for many years. See the illustration section.

17. See her remarkable autobiography, *Many Worlds: A Russian Life* (Crestwood, NY: SVSP, 1980).

18. *Celebration of Faith*, 2:160–61.

19. *The Sacrament of Love*, 93.

20. *The Lutheran Book of Worship* (Minneapolis: Augsburg, 1978), 36.

INDEX

Abraham, 2, 3, 275
Acts
  2:44, 159
  10:15, 89–90
  28:1–10, 93
Adam and Eve, 2
Afanasiev, Nicolas, 103, 115, 128,
  149–77, 214, 227
  on the *antidoron*, 168, 169
  on baptism, 151, 158–59, 168, 169, 173,
    266
  on the clergy, 151, 152, 154, 158–59,
    162–66, 173
  on communal nature of the Church,
    175
  criticisms of, 107, 149–52, 156, 160,
    163, 164, 165, 168, 172, 173, 174,
    227, 235, 266
  death of, 154–55
  early life of, 152–53
  and ecumenism, 149–50, 152, 154, 156,
    161–62, 166, 175
  on the Eucharist, 13, 17–18, 52, 116,
    125, 149–52, 154, 156–64, 165,
    167–69, 170–72, 174–75, 176, 177,
    180, 191, 207, 208, 213, 249, 266
  on the Holy Spirit, 158, 159, 161–62,
    168, 173
  on individualization of worship,
    157–58, 171–73, 174–75
  influence of, 16, 17–18, 149–50, 151,
    152, 154, 155, 156, 158, 173, 179, 180,
    187, 205, 210, 231, 249, 266–67,
    300n.57, 303n.19
  on John XXIII, 175
  on local churches, 150, 151, 160–61,
    164–66, 266
  personality of, 155–56
  on prayer, 169

  relationship with Bulgakov, 17, 52,
    106, 153, 158
  relationship with Evdokimov, 106,
    158, 173
  relationship with Men, 300n.57
  relationship with Meyendorff, 17–18,
    152, 205, 210, 231
  relationship with Schmemann, 17, 18,
    151, 152, 155, 179, 180, 191, 249,
    267, 300n.57, 303n.19
  during Russian Revolution, 153
  on secularization, 169–71, 174
  at St. Sergius Theological Institute,
    153–54, 156
  on unity of the Church, 86, 160–61,
    175–76, 208
Afanasiev, Nicolas, writings of, 300n.57
  burning of, 235, 237
  The Church of the Holy Spirit, 17, 117,
    151, 154, 156, 158, 160, 162, 165, 168,
    173, 175, 266
  "The Church Which Presides in
    Love," 160–61
  The Limits of the Church, 156
  The Lord's Supper (*Trapeza
    Gospodnia*), 17, 149, 154, 155,
    156–62, 165, 167–73, 304n.24
  "Una Sancta," 160, 175–76
Les âges de la vie spirituelle, 103, 112
Alexandra, Tsarina, 20
Alexis I, 238
Alexis II, 235
Alexis, St., 81
Ambrose of Milan, St., 252
American Catholic Bishops, 3–4
Amsterdam, 1939 ecumenical
  conference in, 48
Andronikov, Constantine, 30–31, 115,
  292n.35